Praise for *The Business of History*

'Libraries are crowded with books attempting to define the attributes of a successful business, capable of enduring decades, let alone centuries. This book has done something refreshingly different. Levitt offers lessons and analysis from the past and warnings for the future, a "warts and all" account of the titans of business spanning some 200 years. The companies that will be written about in another century, I believe, will be the ones that embrace their purpose, giving back more than they take, rejecting "business as usual". Those that don't will be consigned to the graveyard of dinosaurs. CEOs would be wise to reflect upon the lessons in this book.'

Paul Polman, former CEO of Unilever

'What stands out for me in Tom Levitt's fascinating new book is how great Victorian companies, a few of which have survived to this day, saw themselves and acted more or less as 'social' enterprises. And that was long before governance, environment and corporate social responsibility obligations had to be introduced to tame the behaviour that excessive adherence to the late-twentieth-century concept of 'shareholder value' had encouraged.'

Professor Vicky Pryce, former joint head of the
UK Government Economic Service

'This enjoyable journey through the history of some prominent British businesses – some still household names, many no longer in independent existence – is full of both drama and insight. There are lessons here for the future of today's companies in an era of technological transformation and climate change.'

Dame Diane Coyle, Bennett Professor of Public Policy at the
University of Cambridge

'It is far too simplistic to label all businesses as destroyers of nature or engines of social injustice, ignoring the positive contribution from enlightened, innovative and responsible businesses. This book revisits the history of UK business, providing a new baseline with which to evaluate today's business world environment, drawing out fascinating insights while providing recommendations to inspire and shape a better world.'

Professor Ian Thomson, Chair in Accounting and Sustainability,
School of Business, University of Dundee

'As a business school academic, one theme in this fascinating book made for very uncomfortable reading. Levitt suggests that the main impact of UK business schools on firms has been to help institutionalize neo-classical economic thought and its derived management practices. Some of the fateful outcomes of that process are well illustrated in the book. It should prompt my colleagues in business schools to reflect on what we've been part of, what our purpose is, and how we need to change business schools to reflect this.'

Professor Martin Kitchener, FCIPD FLSW FAcSS,
Cardiff Business School

'Climate, the economy, human rights, supplies of natural resources, ... There appears no end to the challenges confronting businesses and their supply chains today. In this evocative work we can sense that many of those problems arose accidentally, despite the best of intentions. Levitt assures us that whilst in its recent history business may have caused or exacerbated these issues, companies also have many of the necessary solutions within their grasp.'

Dr Suresh Gamlath, Pro-Vice Chancellor (Business Development) at
University of West London and former dean of
Claude Littner Business School

THE BUSINESS OF HISTORY

THE BUSINESS OF HISTORY

Tales and Lessons from Two Centuries
of British Commerce

Tom Levitt

LONDON PUBLISHING PARTNERSHIP

Copyright © 2025 Tom Levitt

Published by London Publishing Partnership
www.londonpublishingpartnership.co.uk

All Rights Reserved

ISBN: 978-1-916749-36-8 (hbk)
ISBN: 978-1-916749-37-5 (iPDF)
ISBN: 978-1-916749-38-2 (ePUB)

A catalogue record for this book is
available from the British Library

This book has been composed in
Adobe Garamond Pro

Copy-edited and typeset by
T&T Productions Ltd, London
www.tandtproductions.com

Cover picture: 'Bubbles' painted
by Sir John Everett Millais, 1886,
in interior Lady Lever Gallery
in Port Sunlight/Alamy

Printed and bound by
CPI Group (UK) Ltd,
Croydon, CR0 4YY

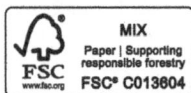

Contents

Introduction

One hundred years ago a man with an intense curiosity for and fascination with business committed to paper a collection of informed reflections on thirty-two of Britain's top companies of the day. He read about them, met key people working for them and visited some of their premises. The result was *Romance of Great Businesses*, published in 1926. William Henry Beable's respect for these industrial titans of their time oozes from every page.

For us to understand all aspects of what business means today we must understand its history. Where did today's business practices come from? How and why did they emerge? Unfortunately, whilst Beable's stories are evocative, detailed and perceptive, they lack insight, comparisons and conclusions. What they give us, however, is a baseline upon which to construct that analysis – a convenient yardstick against which to measure progress.

It goes without saying that his world of 1925 is very different from that of today. The businesses he described were successful (history is, after all, the story of winners), driven by inspiration, passion and dedication. We will attempt to answer questions that Beable left unasked. Why, for example, did the era of family ownership end? Exactly who were these dynamic entrepreneurs? We will track how social and environmental issues came to be regarded as intrinsic to the world of business – something that was not the case in 1925. The research resources deployed in *Romance* were meagre compared with today's electronic media; so, in using today's research methods, we gain some surprising conclusions and insights. To maximize the value of Beable's work, we extend his study's scope from 1925 to 2025.

What Beable did not know, could not know, was that his era, that period following World War I, was pivotal in British company history; post-war economies and the world of business were evolving rapidly. His thirty-two choices, however he decided them, proved serendipitous.

We know little about our source. William Henry Beable was born around 1861 in Plymouth and by 1921 was living in a modern, semi-detached home on Kirkstall Road, Streatham Hill, London, with his wife Elizabeth (b. 1860). A decade earlier, his children Gladys May (b. 1886) and Joseph Mackenzie

(b. 1892) had also lived there. How exactly William made his living and when he died are mysteries, though he had spent time in America (Joseph was born in New Jersey). Where did his interest in business come from? Had he worked in commerce, perhaps, or publishing? His first book came out when he was almost 50, and he was 65 when *Romance* emerged – there must have been some productive work between 1880 and 1910!

Figure 1. In 1921 Beable was living in Streatham, South West London.

Beable wrote an eclectic set of works. As a member of the Aldwych Club Lodge, his guide to Freemasonry, *On the Square* (1923), was frank. His amusing *Epitaphs: Graveyard Humour and Eulogy* (1925) ran to three editions, revealing an eye for tradition. However, many other titles are so mundane as to discourage exploration: he is described as the author of *On the Road, After Dinner Stories, Behind the Counter, Ancient and Modern Oratory* and an ominous 'etc.'.

His *Russian Gazetteer and Guide* (1910) and *Commercial Russia* (1918) were innovative and informed by tours, possibly as a commercial traveller, pre revolution.[1] A contemporary, Boston academic Harry R. Tosdall, described *Commercial Russia* as 'the most comprehensive [work] on Russian commercial methods which has yet been published'.[2]

But Tosdall is not entirely complimentary, opining that other sources are 'more readable and more authoritative' and querying some omissions. Maybe Beable was unaware, for example, that in 1909 Tsar Nicholas II himself had visited the Isle of Wight to re-energize Anglo-Russian trade following the 1904 Dogger Bank incident. (Russian naval ships had fired both at some Hull trawlers and at each other, a case of mistaken marine identity that resulted in several casualties and a prolonged diplomatic impasse.)

Beable knew some of the characters in his 'romances' personally, including the recently but controversially ennobled Lord Waring (of Waring & Gillow) and a Lyons co-founder, Montague Gluckstein. (Gluckstein had died in 1922, indicating that *Romance* was years in the making.) He also knew Lord Riddell – then managing director of Newnes publishers – well enough to commission from him a foreword to *Romance*. George Riddell, a rich lawyer and former editor of the *News of the World*, had been awarded a hereditary peerage despite being divorced. In his succinct contribution, barely 150 words, Riddell quotes Napoleon ('Britain is a nation of shopkeepers') and rightly describes *Romance* as 'an entertainment, an example and an inspiration'.

He also wonders whether a book on business failures might have been as entertaining and, perhaps, more valuable.

In his own introduction, almost as compact, the author acknowledges his subjects' cooperation whilst declaring that he remains untainted by 'mercenary or other unworthy motive'. He contrasts his work with a yet unwritten sequel on 'industry' (steel, shipbuilding etc.) and postulates that 'equally good stories' might be sourced in other countries. He also speculates about a volume 2 of *Romance*, but none of these ideas reached fruition.

THE 'ROMANCES'

My battered copy of *Romance of Great Businesses* once graced a public library shelf. The original 320 rough-hewn pages plus ninety illustrations, likely a vanity publication, contain photographs of production lines, sketches of factories, austere portraits of Victorian and Edwardian gentlemen with profuse facial hair. The book's title is possibly an homage to shopkeeper Harry Gordon Selfridge's 1918 publication *The Romance of Commerce*.

Whilst Beable's pen-portraits were a subjective and partial record, they do indicate what British companies were doing not just 100 years ago but since their inception up to 150 years before that, at the dawn of the industrial revolution.

Table 1 is our cast list.

Table 1. The thirty-two companies.

Retail	Boots (chemist[a])	Gamages (general)
	Martins (tobacco)	Waring (furniture[a])
	Whiteleys (general)	WHSmith (stationers)
Manufacturing	Bass (beer)	Boots (chemist[a])
	Bryant & May (matches)	Cadburys (chocolate)
	Colman's (mustard)	Dunlop (tyres)
	Glaxo (infant formula)	Hartleys (jam)
	Horrockses (cotton/textiles)	Hovis (bread)
	Huntley & Palmers (biscuits)	Lever Bros (soap)
	Lyons (food[a])	Mackintosh (toffee)
	Pears (soap)	Prices (candles)
	Schweppes (soft drinks)	Skippers (fish)
	Swift (cars)	Waring (furniture[a])
	Wedgwood (pottery)	
Service	Cassells (publishing)	Kelly's (data)
	Lyons (catering[a])	Mudies (libraries)
	Newnes (publishing)	Odhams (publishing)
	Pearsons (publishing)	Waring (construction[a])
Primary	British Petroleum (oil)	

[a] Listed in more than one category.

Beable's unbounded enthusiasm verges on the overconfident. Two companies had lost their independence by 1925 and others were in trouble: had he noticed? He flags up no threats, his SWOT analysis would identify only Strengths and Opportunities. 'If they could survive the Great War ...', he maybe mused.

Beable omitted some icons of his time. He overlooked banking, railways, shipbuilding and most primary industry (agriculture, mining, quarrying, steel) yet chose four publishers, possibly hinting at his own background. He describes six retailers and several popular consumer brands. His chosen businesses would have been known to the general public of 1925, when one in three Britons worked in manufacturing and half in services, with one in three of those in retail. Only 5% of employees were 'professionals' (teachers, doctors, lawyers, accountants), whilst one in seven worked in a primary industry. For comparison, today more than four in five jobs are in services.

Just four of the initial thirty-two companies survive intact today, all hugely expanded: Unilever (then Lever Bros), WHSmith, GSK (then Glaxo) and British Petroleum. Boots appears intact, but under the bonnet it has changed significantly. Eight are lost without trace. Brands and companies were one and the same in 1925, but for twenty of the thirty-two today the brand survives but the entity has long gone – almost unthinkable pre World War I. We summarize 'Brand survival' in table 8.

Our study is divided into two parts, the first addressing three analytical themes.

'Governance', the first chapter of part I, looks at how the companies have changed from inception to 1925 and since then. The concept of governance covers ownership models, employee relations, regulation, taxation, legislation and ethics. We ask what aspiring business leaders were being taught – if anything – over the years.

Chapter 2, 'Social', examines the businesses as social players, including their approach to communities and key issues such as slavery. Although Beable would not recognize the word, we ask how the companies engaged with 'stakeholders'. Whereas governance is of universal and eternal application, social issues were of merely accidental interest to companies in Beable's day. There was no strategic planning to balance the interests of stakeholders; the treatment of female employees, for example, was governed by pragmatism, not principle.

The subject of chapter 3, 'Environment', was even lower down the business agenda in 1925. Many of today's key ecological issues were simply not evident then, let alone regarded as the responsibility of business. Man-made climate change was already happening – it had been postulated as early as 1896 – but the first evidence that it was real came in 1938, when the finding was largely ignored. That it posed an existential threat both to business and beyond was not apparent until the second half of the twentieth century.

The above chapters correlate with the modern concept of business risk known as ESG (environmental, social and governance).

Part II rewrites Beable's original stories, casting aside his rose-tinted spectacles. We make extensive use of the internet, well beyond Wikipedia, referring not least to JSTOR, ChatGPT and *The Oxford Dictionary of National Biography*, as well as works by both Beable's contemporaries and modern authors. We present more complete versions of his stories, extended forward to the present day. It transpires that Beable often failed to tell us everything: he overlooked major frauds, significant examples of industrial strife and even a murder. Such omissions – including the 'Splendid Bankrupt', the Match Girls' strike, the Preston Lock-Out and that fatal shooting – are rectified. Beable's trepidation in the face of 'big finance' (see Horrockses) is also explored.

The Latin derivation of 'company' is 'those who break bread together'. That this phrase also describes a family was not lost on Victorian companies, which were mostly family-owned. Success is not defined by Beable, although growth is one obvious candidate, longevity another. Most of the stories introduce charismatic entrepreneurs (Beable used neither the adjective nor the noun) and their inheritors. Nowhere in *Romance* will the reader find 'total share-holder return', 'EBITDA' or 'bottom line', and there is only one table! Today's balance sheets, stock market valuations, social value assessments and sustain-ability reports each give us only a partial definition of success, and none is a 'unit of romance' for comparative purposes. Electronic spreadsheets did not exist until 1979. For all these reasons we adopt narrative reporting.

Beable's accounts overflow with superlatives: 'the world's biggest', 'Britain's largest', 'the first ever'. His heroes generally led 'rags to riches' lives, with just one company (William Knox D'Arcy's BP) emerging as a plaything of the rich. Not one founder had the benefit of post-primary education, but each had a spark of inspiration: Stoney Smith's Hovis hunch about wheat germ, William Hartley's unreliable jam-maker, George Newnes's response to the 1870 Education Act, John Cadbury's retail temperance, and many more.

THE BACKGROUND TO THE COMPANIES

These are very English stories. It goes without saying that Britain's unique role in the world – in empire, warfare and the global economy – changed signifi-cantly during Beable's lifetime and continues to evolve to this day.

The reader will not be surprised that for the first 200 years of capitalism Britain's workforce was predominantly white, led by white, exclusively male owners and managers, nor that there was a marked difference in lifestyle between employers and employees. However, the religious and political pro-files of the families leading businesses absolutely do not reflect those of the British establishment of that era – we will explore how this came about.

There is no starting date to Beable's histories; each company trod its own path. Most are of nineteenth-century origin, although five – Wedgwood (1759), Bass (1777), Horrockses (1791), Schweppes (1792) and WHSmith (1792) – predate that era. Only two – the Anglo-Persian Oil Company (1901), later BP, and Skippers (1903), the trading name of William Lever's protégé Angus Watson – started in the twentieth (table 2). In 1925 most of the com-panies will have been familiar to the person on the Clapham omnibus, that touchstone of reasonability coined in the Court of Appeal in 1903.

Our stories portray innocence pre 1925 but increasing complexity post 1925, bordering on chaos (especially in the 1960s to 1990s). Beable did not know in 1925 that an unprecedented General Strike was just months away.

Table 2. Age of companies in 1925.

Age in 1925	Companies
0–25 years	Skippers (22), British Petroleum (24)
25–50 years	Lyons, Lever Bros, Mackintosh, Dunlop, Pearsons, Gamages, Newnes, Hovis, Martins
50–75 years	Swift, Hartleys, Glaxo, Whiteleys, Odhams
75–100 years	Waring, Mudies, Bryant & May, Boots, Cassells, Prices, Kelly's
100–25 years	Colman's, Cadburys, Pears, Huntley & Palmers
125–50 years	WHSmith, Horrockses, Bass, Schweppes
150–75 years	Wedgwood

The challenges of managing a Victorian startup were not wholly different from those of today: how to obtain finance and access to the market, manage costs, procure at a good price, get the best out of and retain staff. Risk had to be identified, managed and mitigated; success appeared to follow, though no one wrote the histories of those who failed. Prior to the onset of modern taxation it appears to be almost an occupational hazard for owners to become excessively rich. Wealth was often accompanied by a sense of responsibility, and the acquired abundance could not be guaranteed in perpetuity.

The motives of Beable's entrepreneurs were, initially, to do or make something useful; profit made the enterprise (and the often large family behind it) financially viable. Today some enterprises, including Unilever, prefer the term 'purpose-led' to 'profit-led', defining success in terms other than simply the bottom line and instead measuring the creation of positive change. But being 'profit-led' does not exclude being 'purpose-led', which Beable's chosen companies were, especially in their early decades. 'Maximizing profit' is championed in none of their prospectuses, though 'avoiding ruin' and 'safeguarding the future' are universally implicit.

The list of stakeholders in Victorian times was short: customer, owner, supplier, employee, community. Today 'owner' has become plural, often with thousands of shareholders having a claim to the name, and to this list are added regulators, policymakers, investors, creditors, media, unions, lobbyists, several supply chain tiers and more diverse communities, some of which operate on a global scale. In recent years we have extended this register of accountability still further to include resources, habitats, other species, landscapes, the air we breathe – even the planet itself.

Prior to 1925 companies were structured much as they had been for many decades: they were informal, family-owned, unaccountable but (by and large) responsible in a twenty-first-century sense, as they benefited from a long-term outlook. Businesses were not governed by comprehensive rules or even taxed independently of their owners. Compliance with the company law that began to emerge in the mid 1800s – limited liability status, involvement of shareholders – was initially optional. Well into the twentieth century, where shares were issued they were likely to be either non-voting (merely fundraisers) or largely, even wholly, retained by the owner or their close family.

Almost all British businesses in 1925 were small and privately owned; even today, fewer than 1,800 of the UK's 5 million companies are owned by shareholders and listed on the stock exchange. Most of our studies are of relatively large companies within a business community where, pre 1900, large takeovers and mergers were rare, hostile takeovers especially so. Owners and founders were people, not corporations or financial institutions. Where it existed, shareholding was unregulated: how different from today! How companies coped with the rise of shareholder power – and the frauds that followed in its wake – makes a fascinating thread.

There is a heavy geographical bias in our companies' origins, reflecting London's economic dominance and, possibly, Beable's South London horizons (table 3).

Table 3. Geographical origins.

London (14)	WHSmith, Pears, Lyons, Mudies, Schweppes, Bryant & May, Glaxo, Prices, Whiteleys, Odhams, Cassells, Pearsons, Gamages, Kelly's
North West (6)	Waring, Horrockses, Hartleys, Newnes (later London), Hovis, Lever Bros
West Midlands (5)	Cadburys, Wedgwood, Swift, Bass, Dunlop (via Ireland)
Elsewhere (7)	Skippers (North East), Mackintosh (Yorkshire), Colman's (East Anglia), Boots (East Midlands), Huntley & Palmers (South East), Martins (Channel Islands), British Petroleum (Persia/Iran)

Although we are identifying entrepreneurs with specific regions, there was mobility. Note that in the nineteenth century Britain included the whole of the island of Ireland, home to the families of John Boyd Dunlop (born a Scot) and Harvey du Cros (also of Dunlop). D'Arcy (BP) also came from Ireland, via Australia; Sam Waring's ancestors came from Northern Ireland. William Wilson of Prices had Scottish roots, and Glaxo had a New Zealand phase. The Swiss-German Johann Jacob Schweppe first found fizz abroad but developed his business in London. Within England, George Palmer came from Somerset to Reading to assist Joseph Huntley, whilst Newnes moved his business from Manchester to London. Others arrived in London seeking opportunity:

Odhams (from Dorset), Starley of Swift Motors (Sussex), Bryant (Plymouth), Pearson (Somerset), Gamage (Herefordshire), Whiteley (Wakefield), Cassell (Manchester) and Pears (Cornwall).

Whilst London was a magnet, some later moved (or extended) their activity to other regions, principally to the port city of Liverpool (Lever Bros, Prices, Huntley & Palmers, Schweppes, Waring, Hartleys, Bryant & May). Some non-London companies also operated in London (Hartleys, Huntley & Palmers, Hovis, Wedgwood), and Dunlop moved from Dublin to Birmingham.

All but the retailers Gamages and Whiteleys had a national profile in 1925, when the average age of our companies was 75 years (see table 2). Arie de Geus describes an unpublished report commissioned by Shell in the 1980s that examined the criteria associated with company longevity, defined as being over 60 years old.[3] The report was never published because the number of companies involved, thirty, was deemed too small for statistical validity. Our own sample, similar in size, reinforces the conclusion that long-lived companies share some common qualities.

- *Sensitive to their environment:* they were in harmony with the world around them and aware of social change, whether deliberately driven or not.
- *Cohesive, with a strong sense of identity:* valued employees shared the established company purpose (possibly for reasons of self-interest).
- *Tolerant:* they were open to change, innovation and succession. 'Dogmatic tolerance' is not incompatible with the autocratic leadership style that some of our companies experienced.
- *Conservatively financed:* they employed low-risk financial strategies with good assessment and management of risk.

Diversification of function (i.e. developing contrasting operations) is also a feature of long life, said the report, but that is a twentieth-century phenomenon. Only Sam Waring demonstrates it in our pre-1925 stories, briefly adding construction (Waring-White, 1904–10) to his furniture and fitting-out business. Later, after soap-maker Lever Bros became Unilever (1929) it extended its range considerably, initially with margarine, whilst Lyons moved from catering into manufacture and jam-maker Hartleys added canned goods, then jellies, to its line. In the 1930s Glaxo switched from infant formula to pharma, whilst later still Bass, once the world's biggest brewer, ceased brewing its own beer in favour of managing hotels. By 1930 one in five British businesses was multifunctional.[4]

Prior to 1925 the positive influence of 'abroad' was limited to supply chains, occasional offshore production and a French chemist. Only five of our companies existed in 1807, when slave trading was made illegal in Britain, but opposition to slavery prior to its complete banning in the country, in 1834, was universal amongst our business leaders whose opinions are on the record. Other than sugar importers, Gillows (later merged into Waring & Gillow) had perhaps the strongest link to the slave trade, which at that time formed part of the mahogany supply chain. Nevertheless, issues around African slavery would impact two of our companies – Lever Bros and Cadburys – even into the twentieth century, whilst Dunlop's early Malaysian rubber plantations may also be suspect (see the 'Slavery' case study in chapter 2).

Beable's subjects were not great, artificial, global corporations such as the East India Company, created to conduct international trade during the seventeenth century, and continuing into the nineteenth, but nor were they isolationist. Some were already manufacturing abroad in 1925 (Prices, Mackintosh, Anglo-Persian Oil Company (later BP), Colman's, Pears, Lever Bros) and most of the manufacturers were exporting. British India was a common destination, receiving finished goods made by Horrockses from Indian cotton, and Bass's India Pale Ale and Schweppes Indian Tonic Water got their names for a reason.

As our dwindling band traversed the twentieth and then twenty-first centuries, they generally took external developments in their stride, the most potent threats coming from changes to competition and ownership. No company suffered from globalization and the offshoring of British jobs and brands more than Wedgwood (today owned in Finland and manufacturing exclusively in Indonesia). The South African descendant of Prices is today both more successful than and very different from the now Italian-owned British candle-maker. The very English Pears soap is made exclusively in India.

The European Union appears explicitly in our companies' stories only twice: Lyons's ill-advised and unfortunately timed dash for growth (c. 1972), and Nestlé's tactical takeover of Rowntree (which had absorbed Mackintosh). Brexit (2020) has brought its own frustrations, adaptations and disappointments.

In Beable's world, trade with pre-revolutionary Russia was normal (see Bass, Prices, Beable's own career and Horace Rayner in the Whiteleys story). Germany, Japan and America existed only as competitors, and latecomers at that. France, with whom memories of conflict did not inspire confidence, was largely infra dig.

British businesses had diverse international suppliers from the start, generally preferring cheapness of supply over loyalty to the empire, where, other than India, trade was largely limited to Australia, New Zealand and South Africa. Outside the empire, South America saw nineteenth-century operations by companies including Colman's and Prices, following the eighteenth-century South Sea Company itself. The British Empire barely raises its head in Beable's accounts, despite occupying its maximum footprint in 1920 and its highest level of complacency:

Ultimately those making decisions about where to pursue profit in the 19th century did so on the basis of value and reliability of delivery and quality of product. Patriotism and imperial sentiment were not important factors, not even in the 1890s when Kipling and Chamberlain were exhorting [us] to believe the empire could be the answer to Britain's declining share of the world's economy.[5]

Imports such as cotton (Horrockses), rubber (Dunlop), chocolate (Cadburys, Mackintosh), sugar (Cadburys, Hartleys, Mackintosh, Huntley & Palmers, Bass, Hovis, Lyons), oil (BP, Prices), coconut and palm oil (Prices, Lever Bros) and chemicals (Boots, importing them from Germany) were sourced from wherever they were available.

EXTERNAL INFLUENCES

Britain is the world's sixth-largest economy, composed largely of services. In the globalized economy, UK manufacturing – the role of twenty-one of our thirty-two pre-1925 companies – has largely had its day. Below are some of the major events impacting British businesses over the last 250 years.

18th century	Most non-farming businesses are 'cottage industries'. Britain enjoys global trading power and naval dominance.
1780–1830	The industrial revolution: steam power.
1803–15	Napoleonic Wars disrupt trade. Income tax briefly introduced.
1807	British transportation of slaves made illegal.
1811–16	Luddite response to cotton mechanization.
1825	First steam-powered railway, financed by Quakers.
1832	Reform Act, rationalization of the electoral system (also 1867, 1884).
1833	Owning and trading of slaves made illegal.
1837	Victorian age: pace of industrialization and urbanization increases.
1838	5% of industrial power from steam engines.
1840s	Chartists call for democratic and other changes.
1842	Income tax introduced in third attempt.
1844	Joint Stock Companies Act.
1846	Peak railway construction. Repeal of Corn Laws.
1847	'The Panic', an economic and banking crisis prompted by Ireland's famine, the upcoming end of the railway boom and a tight money supply. Many companies fail.
1851	The Great Exhibition celebrates trade and business.

1853	Preston Lock-Out in the textile industry (see Horrockses).
1855	Limited Liabilities Act.
1857–8	First global recession starts in US.
1858	Britain terminates East India Company's mandate. 'The Great Stink' prompts construction of London sewers.
1859	Oil exploited in US.
1860	80% of industrial power from steam engines.
1861–5	Lancashire Cotton Famine.
1862	Companies Act extends limited liability.
1867–9	Global recession following American Civil War.
1868	Trade Union Congress formed.
1869	Suez Canal enhances global trade.
1870	Elementary Education Act: growth of primary education and literacy.
1870–1910	Era of mass industrialization.
1874	East India Company dissolved.
1888	Match Girls' strike (see Bryant & May).
1894	First four-wheeled petrol-driven car on a British road.
1899–1902	Second Boer War prompts political realignment.
1901	D'Arcy obtains Iranian oil concession (see BP). Queen Victoria dies.
1913	UK coal production peaks: 292 million tonnes.
1914–18	World War I: businesses help war effort.
1916	Federation of British Industries (later CBI) is first 'voice of business'.
1917	Whitley report on industrial relations.
1918	Some women vote in national elections for first time.
1919–26	Post-war depression: deflation exceeds 10% in 1920–1.
1920	Steel production reaches today's level (see 1970).
1922	British Empire peaks at a quarter of the earth's land, 450 million people. Ireland gains independence as a 'Free State'.
1925	UK car ownership exceeds 500,000.
1926	Nine-day General Strike supported by 1.5 million workers; prompted by pay cuts, over-strong pound, weak exports. Australia, New Zealand, Canada, South Africa become dominions within the empire.
1928	Women achieve same right to vote as men.
1929–39	Great Depression affects US economy, then the world.
1939–45	World War II.
1944	Bretton Woods conference establishes global structures of monetary management (e.g. World Bank), common measures such as GDP.

1945	United Nations Charter.
1946–51	Nationalization of some primary British industries.
1948	NHS founded. *Windrush* brings West Indians to UK to help economic recovery, launching Britain towards a multiracial, multicultural society. Indian independence marks beginning of the end of empire.
1949	British Commonwealth created.
1950	Services constitute half of UK economy, manufacturing 42%, agriculture 5%, construction 3% (compare with 2016).
1950s	IT revolution starts. Average shareholding period is eight years.
1951	Festival of Britain evokes 1851.
1956	Recession (two or more consecutive quarters of negative GDP growth). Also 1961, 1973–4, 1980–1, 1990–1, 2008–9, 2020, 2023.
1970	Equal Pay Act. UK steel production peaks at three times 1920 level.
1972	Britain joins (what will become) European Union.
1973–4	Oil price hikes (Middle East war). Miners' strike ('three-day week').
1979	'Winter of Discontent', public sector unrest.
1981	Public limited company (plc) designation introduced.
1984–5	Miners' strike.
1990	Motor vehicle production peaks.
1997	British Empire ends: Hong Kong under Chinese rule.
1998	First statutory UK national minimum wage.
2002	Britain becomes net importer of coal.
2008	Global banking crisis, financial crash. Climate Change Act commits UK to reducing production of greenhouse gases.
2015	United Nations aims its 17 Sustainable Development Goals at business.
2016	The economy: services 80%, manufacturing 16%, construction 5%, agriculture 1% (see 1950). Coal imports peak. Britain votes for Brexit.
2019	Coal production at pre-industrial levels. Britain commits to 'net zero carbon by 2050'.
2020	Steel production falls to 1920 levels. Covid-19 pandemic. Britain leaves European Union. Average shareholding period is five months (see 1950s).
2024	Britain's last producer of virgin steel and last coal-fired power station close – on same day. Britain commits to 'net zero carbon by 2035'.

Britain's geography had been perfect for spawning the industrial revolution.[6] In 1754 Sir John Dalrymple observed that in Britain 'the coal beds, the iron ore and limestone … the three raw materials of iron manufacture, were frequently found together and moreover in close proximity to the sea'. Two hundred years later, in 1948, Schweppes chairman Sir Eric Hooper wrote: 'The half century from the 1860s to 1914 saw ... sail replaced at sea by steam; first wood then iron replaced by steel; the world's railways built; whole continents virtually opened up; populations pyramiding ... productive power increased enormously.'[7] Hooper was a pioneer business consultant; fifty years earlier Britain had seen no management consultants, no business schools, no erudite business manuals and little business experience conveniently available to share.

It was perhaps inevitable that, once humanity had tamed iron, manufacture would become the dominant force in the global economy. In a recent book, Daniel Susskind ponders why the industrial revolution happened when and where it did.[8] His answer is surprisingly complex, going beyond the facts of mere geography.

For many hundreds of years, graphs show Britain had a 'steady state' economy, which began to blossom and boom exponentially over a relatively brief period starting 200 years ago. GDP, income per head, carbon emissions, life expectancy and educational qualifications, to name but a few, all took off in mathematically similar ways, over relatively short and overlapping periods, variously demonstrating correlation, causation or coincidence. This was not simply an economic function; indeed, national 'growth' was something few early economists cared to study. The trigger involved technology and – after centuries of separate, parallel existence – a critical mass of scientific knowledge spilling out of its silos and finding application in 'ordinary' life. James Watt's invention was a seismic contributory factor, but the key to growth, as Adam Smith predicted in *The Wealth of Nations*, was increased productivity, which many of Beable's companies experienced (without him ever using the word). Susskind calls this inflection point in the growth curve a moment of 'Industrial Enlightenment'.

In the National Portrait Gallery there is a remarkable 1856 engraving of *Men of Science Living in 1807–08*, by Sir John Gilbert. It includes Boulton and Watt (the steam engine), Allen and Howard (pharma; see Glaxo), Sir Joseph Banks (Captain Cook's botanist, founder of Kew Gardens), Sir Humphrey Davy (the safety lamp), Brunel and Telford (civil engineers), philosopher Jeremy Bentham, vaccine pioneer Edward Jenner, cotton technologists Crompton and Cartwright, and many more. The ubiquitous polymath Sir Joseph Priestley is absent, having very recently died. Whilst the depicted gathering was probably fictional – the Victorian equivalent of being 'photoshopped' – it could have happened; they were all fellows of the Royal Society at that time.

The Royal Society for Improving Natural Knowledge was founded by Sir Christopher Wren in 1660; in today's parlance it pursued the cause of science in a co-ordinated and cooperative manner. It initiated peer reviewing of scientific papers – a fundamental element of the modern scientific method – in 1832. From 1847 it took a special interest in the industrial application of science, supporting pioneering research into meteorology, astronomy, physics, disease, even Babbage's calculating machine (which owed its existence to Jacquard weaving looms). Universities started to take interest in science; amateur scientists formed organizations such as Birmingham's Lunar Society (1765–1813), which included intellectual luminaries such as Priestley and Erasmus Darwin and the industrialists Wedgwood, Watt and Boulton. British science was allowed to progress without having external ideologies imposed upon it, and nowhere else had that freedom and momentum.

Figure 2. *Men of Science Living in 1807–08,* by Sir John Gilbert. (*Source:* National Portrait Gallery.)

The progress of independent science in France, for example, was set back by the closure of universities in 1793 following the 1789 revolution, when many French scientists from the nobility (including Lavoisier) suffered the guillotine.[9] Universities were replaced by institutions designed to deliver narrow curriculums rather than explore new ideas. The following rigid regimes of Catholic, conservative and doctrinaire governments severely restrained any remaining French scientists. There were notable exceptions, such as the organic chemist Chevreul (see Prices), who worked in isolation, doing much of his best work in a Paris museum and then in industry. In the 1830s the reputation of science within education was briefly restored, but it waned with the more liberal regimes of the mid-century. This allowed Britain, where competition between scientists within universities and independent institutions was a creative force, to surge ahead of France in the science stakes.

In our stories we see how science and technology suddenly became available. John Dunlop is famed for his pneumatic tyre, but he utilized the primary inventions of others – not least Charles Macintosh, whose bonded cloth and dissolved rubber made a waterproof material that was also, accidentally, airtight. George Wilson of Prices candles became a brilliant all-round scientist yet never graced a university; neither did William Lever or Andrew Pears, who both experimented with soap recipes to find the best. Schweppe, too, was a genuine but amateur scientist who rose to a challenge that had long puzzled more eminent minds: the stabilization of water infused with gas. Palmer applied engineering principles, learned as an apprentice, to the mass production of biscuits, whilst fringe members of the Wedgwood family dabbled to great effect in applied science; Josiah* himself was both a sponsor of scientific application and an experimenter in his own right, not least in high-temperature chemistry.

Beable himself wondered, in the story of Swift Motors, why the modern bicycle emerged in the later nineteenth century and not a hundred years previously. There was no obvious reason why the necessary technology could not have been utilized: the (wooden) wheel was known, as was the axle; direct pedal power and iron wheel rims were not beyond imagination at that earlier time. Yes, it could have happened: but the economics may not have worked, the market opportunity did not exist, and thus the stars were not fully aligned. But once the floodgates opened ... remember that Neil Armstrong stepped on the moon only one lifetime after the Wright brothers, in 1903, flew the first aircraft.

Innovation post 1925 has been less primary, less scientific and more financially oriented. There were new financial structures and products, new markets and marketing techniques, a generally wider marketplace. Science never went away: both the Boot family's creation and Harry Jephcott's Glaxo pharmacy reached new heights of social value in the twentieth century.†

The growth of cities illustrates Britain's nineteenth-century dynamism. London's population grew from 1 million in 1800 to 7 million in 1900 (10 million today). In 1800 only London, Dublin and Manchester exceeded 100,000, with just seven more cities over 50,000. Just twenty years later five cities topped 100,000 and fifteen exceeded 50,000.

Dublin, in rural Ireland (population 170,000), grew by only 10% between 1800 and 1820, failing to industrialize to the same extent as the mainland.

---

*In several featured families first names are repeated in successive generations. We use the convention Josiah 2, Josiah 3 etc. to distinguish between generations after the first.

†'Social value' is a measure of the social (and environmental) impact of activity, including economic activity, at the level of company, community or nation.

Meanwhile, British ports and manufacturing centres – Manchester, Glasgow, Edinburgh, Liverpool, Birmingham, Bristol, Halifax and Leeds – all expanded by 50%.[10] The industrial revolution increased factory size, driving the demand for labour to migrate from the countryside and thus creating the economically convenient but socially challenging environment of nineteenth century cities, as witnessed by Dickens and Mayhew.[11]

Global foreign trade tripled between 1870 and 1914, mostly between industrialized countries. Although at the start of this period Britain was unquestionably 'top dog', by 1913 that dominance was lost: Britain, the US and Germany each had exports worth around $2.4 billion. Today China ($3.4 trillion), the US ($2 trillion) and Germany ($1.7 trillion) dominate, whilst the Netherlands, Japan and the UK cruise at under $1 trillion.[12]

In 1851 Britain produced two thirds of the world's coal and half of the world's iron and cloth. Exports grew fivefold, from £38 million in 1825 to £190 million in 1869, much of the increase coming from trade with countries outside the empire, such as the Americas.

In 1880 23% of world trade involved Britain, falling to 17% by 1910. Although discussion around tariffs to protect British trade was a live topic from the turn of the century, in 1925 none were in place. The first formal international trade agreement was between Britain and France (1860); the first global one was the General Agreement on Tariffs and Trade (1947). This was replaced by the rules of the 164-member World Trade Organization in 1994. In the twentieth century, globalization saw trade blocs emerge, such as the European Coal and Steel Community (1952), precursor to the European Economic Community (1958), which Britain joined in 1972 and which became the European Union in 1993. Today more than 300 multinational trade agreements exist, guaranteeing preferential access and treatment to their signatories but raising barriers to others. Britain recently left the world's largest free trade area, the European Union, bizarrely in favour of membership of the relatively tiny Comprehensive and Progressive Agreement for Trans-Pacific Partnership (2018).

Britain's imports in the nineteenth century were mainly of food, raw materials and finished goods. In 1880 Britain consumed half of the world's exports of tea, coffee and wheat, and almost half of all traded meat, with India replacing China as our main source of tea after the Suez Canal opened. Today (in terms of value) cars top the import league, with oil and gas, engineering products, electrical goods, and pharma filling the top ten. They are followed by clothing and plant material (we import almost half our food today).

In 1880 half of the world's merchant shipping was registered in Britain, and in 1890 four of every five such vessels were built in a British shipyard. These figures were declining in 1925.

If Britain's omnipotence in world trade was under challenge, finance was going in the other direction. By 1913 half of the world's capital investments originated in London, with the City's foreign investment doubling in the pre-war decade (from £2 billion to £4 billion), yet spectacular returns were rare and many investments failed.

Demand for coal was falling in Britain after World War I as the nation struggled to recover its pre-war competitive advantage, but eventually it did recover and demand for electricity grew from 1920 until 2000. Prior to the twenty-first century almost all electricity was generated by coal.

Also in 1920 came the biggest-ever decline in a single year of people employed in Britain (from 72.2% to 62.4%), ten years before the Great Depression, though the long-term trend remained upwards. No industry suffered more in this post-World War I period than cotton – which never recovered.

The impact of World War II on Beable's businesses was similar to that of World War I: military mobilization reduced staff availability, processes and facilities were commissioned for 'war work', key commodities were rationed, and supply chains were disrupted. Industrial infrastructure was targeted by enemy forces, whilst military technology powered business innovation. Post World War II, women were more accepted in the workplace. The returning heroes of 1945 voted for change, ushering in an era of social reform and forty years of public ownership of primary industries.

Finance became genuinely global and the internet made the world smaller, but only in the twenty-first century did the planet start to respond to the need for global solutions to global threats such as climate change. As company tax-ation and regulation evolved there was pressure to liberalize. A financial crisis in the US subprime housing market, exacerbated by a laissez-faire approach to regulation and an unprecedented degree of interdependence between major banks, triggered a global financial crisis in 2008, from which the UK economy has never really recovered (see figure 6). The influence of bankers and private equity on business and the broader economy was revealed to be profound.

In the century between Beable's opus and today the world has changed as much as in the first phase of the industrial revolution. Business regulation has grown, international finance has extended its influence ever further and the mood music has changed significantly. We have seen the adoption of gross domestic product (GDP) as a supposed measure of 'progress', the profession-alization of business, and the emergence of a new agenda of environmental and social concerns that can no longer be overlooked. It feels as though new technology has established a ubiquitous presence in the last half century, but there is much more impact to come from the next industrial revolution, that of AI. 'New technology' to Beable was the motor car, the electric light bulb and the automated production line.

PART I

THE LESSONS

Governance

The multifarious risks posed by poor corporate governance are well understood today. To Beable, board diversity meant an 18-year-old white English male sitting alongside his 80-year-old grandfather, whereas today the most forward-looking companies want the best people, irrespective of gender, race, age, orientation or disability. Often mocked as 'wokery', DEI (diversity, equality and inclusion) is a valuable tool when used constructively. In 2021 the Financial Reporting Council declared that company boards with gender diversity were financially more successful than those that were 'male, pale and stale'.[1]

Typical governance arrangements of the Victorian era would be unworkable today; they lacked accountability, diversity, reporting lines and systems of delegation. Personal progress up the greasy pole of management depended then on genes, today on track record. In 1925 eighteen of the twenty-nine independent companies on our list still had a member of the founding (or dominant) family in a leadership role; not one does today.*

Until 1925 the company chairman combined the roles of CEO, managing director and board chair. The chairman either owned the company or was the head of the family that did – in Lyons's case, a dozen members of the extended family chaired the organization over eighty-seven years. The chairman was all-powerful and, for tax purposes, was the same legal entity as his company. Succession planning was automatic; at a suitable age the chairman's heir (his oldest son) joined the company, then the board, eventually inheriting the top role. The board would include other family members, close associates and perhaps one or more significant funders. The chairman would rarely deem it necessary to have more than the minimum practical number of board members, and he usually had his way. Only Lyons, Boots and Hartleys of our thirty-two had had a female family member serve on its board by 1925 – all in the twentieth century and all only briefly.

---

*Pears and Prices had both been absorbed by Lever Bros by 1925, and Horrockses by the ACMT.

If a 'professional director' is one who is experienced, qualified and educated, whether in an executive or a non-executive position, then such individuals were unheard of back then. Similarly the portfolio director, with multiple directorships, was unusual pre World War I; we find them at Schweppes after the war, but their presence at the Amalgamated Cotton Mills Trust (ACMT) shocked Beable (see 'Case study: cotton' for the ACMT's relationship to Horrockses). Yet in the twentieth century both professional and portfolio roles proliferated, becoming subject to regulation only from the 1980s. These changing attitudes to corporate governance found expression in the 1992 Cadbury Report for the London Stock Exchange, authored by a former leader of one of our companies, known for its values-led heritage. The report followed multiple public failures of corporate governance, such as the Guinness takeover of Distillers (1987), the Maxwell pension funds (1991) and Polly Peck (1991).

Prior to 1925 company growth had been organic, careful and strategic, earned through increasing sales of quality goods. Later, in parts of the corporate world, 'growth for the hell of it' led to disproportionate wealth for a relative few.

Our companies underwent a more diverse range of experiences in the twentieth century than previously. Not only did they start from different places in their development, but there were changes in the expectations around business, both within the world of business itself and across society, including a tendency towards a view that 'anything goes'. Over time the rules of the game – law, regulation, international trade agreements – built frameworks and defined relationships and activities more rigidly. Nevertheless, twentieth-century business sometimes adopted policies of frantic acquisition, extracting rather than recycling profit, and ultimately normalizing both failure and then the concept of 'too big to fail'.

Today butterfly wings flutter in distant markets, continually changing the prices of stocks and commodities; back then businesses' attention could justifiably remain focused closer to home. From the 1960s future executives flocked to business schools, whilst their companies morphed to meet the changing demands of measurement, purpose and performance.

As the last century progressed, the Wind of Change blew through boardrooms, exchange floors, marketplaces and workplaces. Harold Macmillan's own 'Wind of Change' (his historic speech of 1960) marked the looming end of empire and the acceptance of colonial independence. For business there was also perhaps a retreat from order, an element of anarchy and self-determination, together with the downgrading of the missions and values that many of our companies had implicitly observed (and delivered) pre 1925.

In many ways the central third of the hundred years following 1925, roughly 1958 to 1992, would prove the most active and interesting period – and the most unstable.

FOUNDERS AND INNOVATORS

All thirty-two founders were male, white and – with the exception of Arthur Pearson, who lost his sight in adulthood – not restricted by disability; neither Josiah Wedgwood's dysfunctional leg nor William Hartley's mental health issues proved a handicap. Nor was youth a barrier to innovation: two founders (Hartley and Martin) were teenagers when they set up their business; seven were under 25 (table 4). Most were born into lower economic orders, although some, like Hartley, inherited a degree of comfort. William Knox D'Arcy alone got rich before creating his legacy (BP). Most came from families of multiple children, and none stayed in education beyond 14 years old – some left school at 10.[2] All joined their family concern willingly, though several set aside ambition – lawyer, vet, chemist, architect – along the way. One in six had been apprentice haberdashers or drapers (Cadbury, Whiteley, Gamage, Martin, Newnes), reflecting that trade's ubiquity. Hartley came from a line of grocers, Wedgwood a family of potters, but only a third had a background that would have granted insight into their initiatives. Our subjects were brave innovators.

Table 4. Founder's age on launch.

Founder's age	Founder
Teenage (2)	Hartley (16),[a] Martin (17)
Twenties (10)	Mackintosh (22), Cadbury (23),[a] Cassell (23), Gamage (23), Horrocks (23), Lever (25),[a] Pearson (25), Mudie (26),[a] Watson (Skippers) (29), Wedgwood (29)[a]
Thirties (9)	Newnes (30), Whiteley (33), Boot (34),[a] Kelly (35, est.),[a] Waring (35),[a] Colman (37), Nathan (Glaxo) (38), Pears (39),[a] Starley (Swift) (39)[a]
Forties (4)	Lyons (42),[b] Bryant and May (both 46), Huntley and Palmer (both 47), Dunlop (49)
50 and above (7)	Smith (Hovis) (50),[a] Schweppe (52), Smith (WHSmith) (54), Odhams (56),[a] D'Arcy (British Petroleum) (58), Wilson (Prices) (58), Bass (60)

[a] Family provided a relevant background.

[b] Average age of Lyons's four founders.

Whilst attaining ongoing family security was, no doubt, a strong motivator, broader motives were also evident (some founders fall into multiple categories). Wedgwood, Pearson and Julius Elias at Odhams wanted to do more and better in the craft in which they grew up, whilst the founders of WHSmith, Bass, Waring, Horrockses, Kelly's, Lever Bros, Hartleys and Lyons exploited a competitive edge over rivals. Walter Martin made the most of a legal loophole. The scientific dedication exhibited by Jacob Schweppe, the Starleys (see Swift's innovations in bicycles) and George Wilson (at Prices) was profound: each worked on establishing a 'unique selling point' (a yet-to-be-coined term) early. Dunlop, Glaxo, Boots, BP, Hovis and Bryant & May also benefitted from scientific or technological innovation, whereas Colman's, Whiteleys and Huntley & Palmers took advantage of hyper-local conditions. Niche markets were identified by Lyons (exhibition catering), Skippers (Norway's surplus fish), and Mudies and Newnes (both exploiting a growing market for accessible reading), as well as Pears, Mackintosh and Gamages. Other businesses were motivated by strong religious callings: John Cadbury and John Cassell were temperance activists, William Hartley was committed to comprehensive Methodist philanthropy, and Jesse Boot took a Wesleyan approach to health.

Where the initiative was in manufacturing, the company's initial product range was narrow: four simple biscuits (Huntley), matches (Bryant & May), chocolate drinks (Cadburys) or dried herbs (Boots). Hartleys jams were limited by the availability of seasonal fruits. Lever Bros learned from others that going too broad, too soon, was a mistake, taking advantage of over-committed, failing competitors.

In every case product quality was of prime importance. Lever Bros took soap-making in-house to ensure consistency; Pears pandered to the needs of the most sensitive (wealthy) skins; Boots, Skippers and Hartleys talked up their 'natural', unadulterated products. Novelty was also a vital selling point: witness Huntley & Palmers tins, Hovis's production and marketing techniques, Lever Bros' branded soap packets, Pears's adverts, and Dunlop's inflatable tyre, which had to combine performance with safety.

Breaking from family tradition does not imply rebellion. Breaks reduced inter-sibling rivalry in families with multiple offspring, especially in the early days. John 2 Horrocks was one of eighteen children, Walter Gamage seventeen, Josiah Wedgwood thirteen, whilst William Wilson (Prices) and Joseph Nathan (Glaxo) both had thirteen of their own, and Sam Waring twelve. William Lever had eight sisters and a brother. Lena (Gluckstein) Salmon, wife of a Lyons founder, was one of twelve siblings and mother to fifteen, six of whom died before the age of 5.

Once the company became established, promise of growth created opportunities for trusted and committed relatives whilst keeping wealth within the family (very explicitly so, in Lyons's Family Fund). Twelve Wedgwoods held senior management roles over 202 years, thirteen Glucksteins and Salmons over 87 years at Lyons, and twelve Huntleys and Palmers (mostly Palmers) over a century. However, inherited wealth also gave subsequent generations a financial springboard from which to depart the fold. Michael 2 Bass vetoed his unsuitable second son's involvement in the family firm, and third-generation Tom Pears suffered a similar fate in 1909. In the Wedgwoods we see both the easing out of an uncommitted son early on and the empowerment of wealthy descendants to branch out into horticulture, photography, politics ... and carbon paper. If indeed Susskind's 'Industrial Enlightenment' stemmed from the coming together of rudimentary commerce with a critical mass of science, then this is a positive feedback loop: business created 'spare capacity' of educated and financially independent men who went on to develop and grow the body of science still further. The patriarch Josiah Wedgwood, a scientist in his own right, used his wealth to actively sponsor other scientists (other members of his family supported poets such as Coleridge).

Brian Lawson Salmon, the last generation of Lyons's family leaders, concluded in the 1970s that in recent years family management (not necessarily ownership) had held the company back. By then his was one of only two remaining family-owned companies in our sample.

As with many small or medium-sized enterprises today, the founder ruled the roost. With few employees in the early days, he needed to discharge every leadership and management role: HR, marketing, procurement, product development, inward investment and more. The concentration of such power in one person was a difficult habit to shed as the company grew. It also meant that growth inevitably led to accumulation of personal wealth – how could it not?

That the character of the founder influences the initial development of the company is a universal truth. 'Founder syndrome' describes the leader who remains in place too long and, unwilling or unable to change, becomes a drag on progress. Tensions between founder and son, the perhaps impatient heir, were inevitable, but not fatally so in these successful companies. We do not know exactly why Jesse Boot sold out to the Americans instead of passing Boots to his son, or why the Odhams boys found it difficult to work with their father. Although it was common for the second generation of family owners to succeed their innovative fathers, it became rarer for later ones. There are several reasons why.

- Four generations is a century: market, economic and social conditions change.
- The children of later generations were more affluent, better educated and open to wider career choices.
- Larger businesses needed a broader range of skills and more management capacity than a single family might provide.
- Fewer children were born to later generations, so there may have been no suitable surviving sons.
- From early in the twentieth century the maturing system of shareholding created competition for ownership from external private finance, broadening the stakeholder base.

Stoney Smith, Hovis's creator, joined the board of Fitton but never pretended to be its leader. William D'Arcy likewise never ran the Anglo-Persian Oil Company (later BP), preferring to remain an investor and explorer. Nor did John Dunlop run the company that bore his name; his heart was never in the rubber business and he possibly felt out of his depth, leaving the company after only six years. Joe Lyons was but a titular head. Our founders hung around for an average of twenty-eight years, the longest tenures being the sixty of William Hartley and fifty-six of George Palmer. Most founder-leaders with a tenure of under fifteen years died in the post. The shortest that ended voluntarily was that of Schweppe, who established his London company in his fifties, selling it and retiring to Switzerland after just seven years, aged 60, with no male heir.

At 28 years old an organization is no longer a startup. Manufacturing was more labour-intensive than today, so in 1925 many of our companies had to govern hundreds, often thousands, of staff and managers in many diverse roles.

Dunlop sold his shares rather than pass on his interest to his family, whilst Waring, Schweppe, Angus Watson, John Boot and possibly Walter Martin had no surviving male heir. The ailing Pearson sold his company rather than leave it to his under-age son.

Ten companies were owned by a single family for more than a century (table 5). (Allen & Hanbury, taken over by Glaxo, had 158 years under family ownership.) At Colman's, Cadburys, Bass, WHSmith, Pears, Boots and perhaps others, family members remained on the board for some years after their period of outright ownership had ended.

The late Tony Benn, once a hereditary peer, condemned the hereditary principle in government on the grounds that were he an airline passenger he would not be reassured to know that the pilot's father knew how to fly a plane. That is a fair point, but it does not apply to Victorian business. In the

Table 5. Family ownership of 100 years or more.

Company	Years owned by family	Company	Years owned by family
Wedgwood	202	Colman's	124
WHSmith	180	Schweppes[a]	110
Cadburys	165	Boots[b]	107
Huntley & Palmers	141	Waring	105
Bass	131	Pears	102

[a] Kemp-Welch family, 1834–1944.

[b] Includes a thirteen-year hiatus.

nineteenth century there existed no manual on how to run a company, no training school and few precedents for operating on the scale that some of these businesses achieved; they were all 'flying blind'. Family memory, identity, purpose and ethos helped many of them to survive.

Figure 3 ranks the thirty-two companies according to length of family ownership, showing the proportion of that time for which the founder was leader.

Family-owned larger companies were dominant for less than 100 years, and our snapshot comes from just after their peak. The era began shortly after the start of the industrial revolution, but by World War I the trend was receding as quickly as it had arrived.

Figure 4 starkly shows the rise and fall of the family company. In the 1780s only three of our companies existed: Wedgwood, Bass and WHSmith. By the 1850s half of the thirty-two were in business, and the one that had left family ownership (Schweppes) was back, albeit under a different family. In the 1890s – the tipping point – no fewer than twenty-seven of the thirty existing companies were family-owned. Those that had ceased being family companies nevertheless continued largely along a similar course, maintaining independence, mission and identity. The exceptions were Horrockses, absorbed into the ACMT; Pearsons, which became part of Newnes; and Pears and Prices, both acquired by Lever Bros before 1925.

How could leaders have learned, other than from experience? In 1850 there were just four universities in England and four in Scotland, but as none of our leaders attended university, let alone business school, their existence is academic. By 1920 one British company in five was led by a graduate (none of ours were). This is half the rate of the US or Japan at the time, perhaps a factor in the rise of those countries' economies.

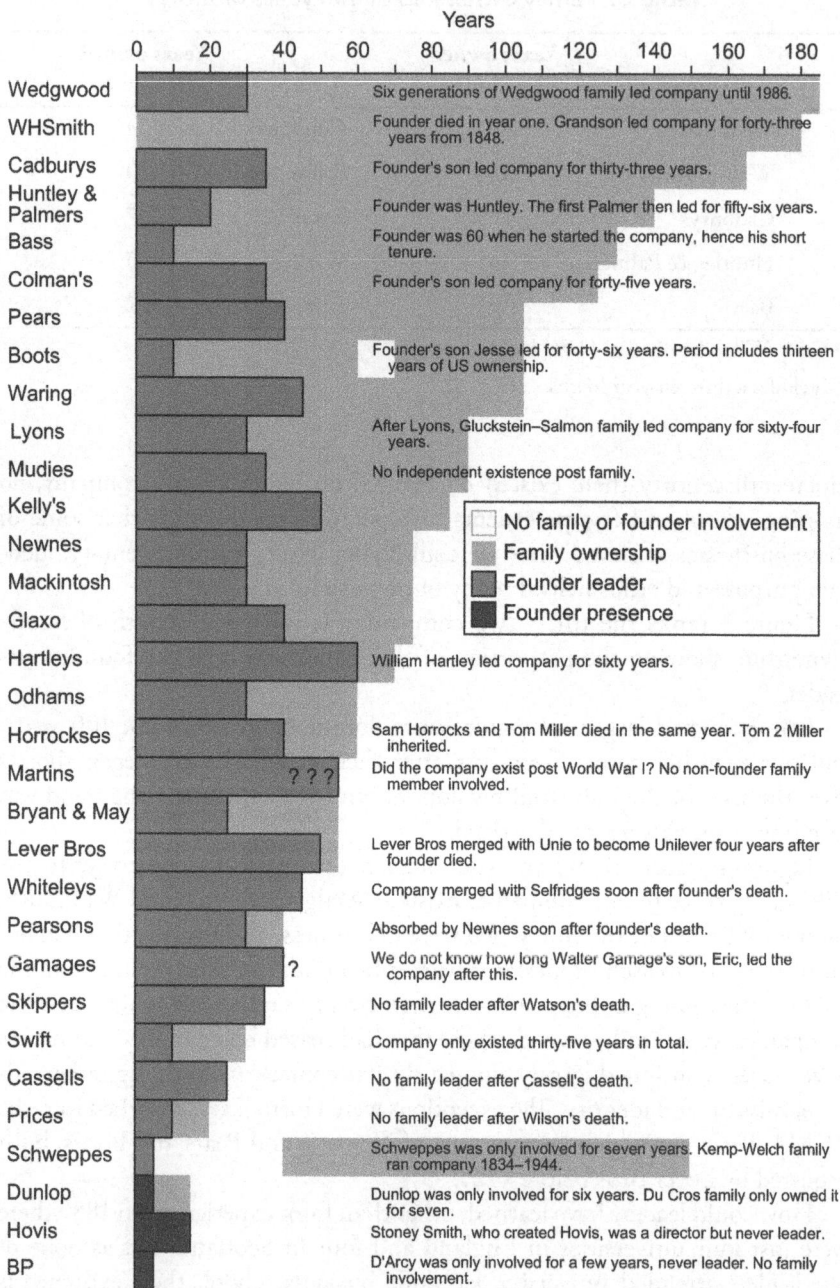

Figure 3. Duration of founder and family involvement.

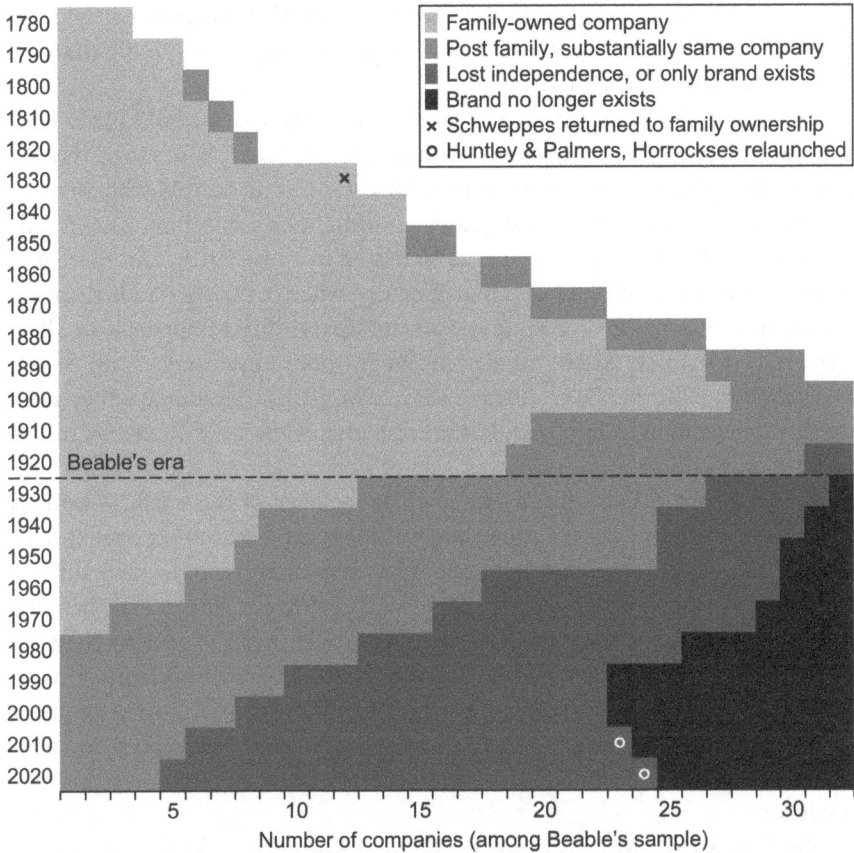

Figure 4. Changes in company ownership.

No son who inherited the leadership was a stranger to the company. The inheritor usually stepped up from a board or management position, having joined the company as young as 14 in a menial capacity, experiencing the business 'warts and all'. Many joined the board before the age of 20 (six teenage du Cros sons had leadership roles at Dunlop). Inheritors thus lived and breathed the business throughout childhood, learning about management over every breakfast, maybe with time out for military service (as with the Boot, Mackintosh and Palmer families) but otherwise knowing no other way of life. George Cadbury and George Palmer both served valuable apprenticeships away from the fold, bringing new and appropriate skills with them when they returned, still young. People only had one shot at a career, and if professional progression was laid out on a plate they took it. After all, in 1871 the life expectancy of English males was, on average, just 41 years: the security of the family firm came close to guaranteeing that their children would defy fate! Our founders died, on average, aged 66 with five of them passing 80 years old. It was not until the 1890s that life expectancy rose significantly.

Second- or third-generation leaders of family businesses would likely have had no expense spared on their education in fee-charging schools, though John Kelly appears to be the only founder's son in our sample who went to Eton (or its equivalent, as several grandsons did). State schooling was compulsory from 1880 but only to the age of 10 (rising to 14 by 1918), and there was little free provision for older children. Equally, where a sibling had little or no interest in the company – despite the advantages, this did happen – an alternative career path could be found. The Wedgwood, Lever and (WH) Smith families all saw brothers or sons take alternative paths. If necessary they were eased out, even bought out, with less rancour than viewers of *Succession* might have anticipated.

Longevity should also bring vision. If, at the back of the business leader's mind, there is always the nagging thought 'How can I leave this company to my son in a better state than I inherited it?', then it is natural, inevitable, to acquire a long-term business perspective. In that slow-moving era the benefits of long-term vision would not have been as explicit as in hindsight they are today, but some decisions could be based only on long-term horizons. Investing in plants or premises, relocating whole factories, or building a company village – common features of our stories – could never have been justified without long-term planning. 'Family memory' became a major repository of wisdom.

The twentieth century's failure to recognize existential risks such as climate change can be attributed to the loss of that long-term vision.

As Beable's businesses grew in the nineteenth and early twentieth centuries they were powerful players in their local economies. They employed hundreds in labour-intensive jobs, often providing work for whole communities. However poorly they were paid, life as an employee was preferable to worklessness before the advent of unemployment and other benefits; the Poor Laws were unreliable, insufficient and poorly focused compared with later support systems. Companies boosted local economies by procuring supplies nearby wherever possible, for common-sense reasons of cost and convenience.

The family ownership of relatively large companies also produced a cadre of responsible, even altruistic people willing and available to be involved in local and national politics. In the absence of government-funded public services in the Victorian era, business-owning families became a significant source of charitable funding.

FINANCING DEVELOPMENT

The founder needed to invest in the company to get it off the ground. The cash came from an existing venture (Hartley, Bass, D'Arcy/BP, Wilson/ Prices, Waring, Mudie, Schweppe), inheritance (Cassell, Joseph Rank in the Hovis story), savings (Whiteley, Gamage), marriage (Wedgwood) or local connections (Bass, Dunlop). Swift's James Starley was fortunate in acquiring a wealthy American sponsor. Several (including Mackintosh and Horrocks) started from scratch. Walter Gamage and William Hartley raised funds by public subscription, offering interest to savers, a practice common in Lancashire cotton mills. Prior to 1925 only one of our companies worked with multiple financial investors: Horrockses, in 1919, a story that did not end happily.

Sometimes the financier tried to wrest control from the entrepreneur, a fate narrowly avoided by Hartley and Pears, but most investors in our sample were amateurs and freelancers, benign and even aloof. Several companies innocently allowed fraudsters to get the better of them, one of them twice (see 'Fraud' later in this chapter). However traumatic the experience, they all survived.

Taking on debt was best avoided, but local banks were another source of funding from the mid nineteenth century. Although the banks regarded lending for investment as part of their role, they were nonetheless small, risk-averse, unsophisticated. Lending capacity was determined by customer deposits, and banking grew through mergers and failures (table 6).

Table 6. Banking capacity, 1875–1918.

	1875	1900	1913	1918*
Percentage of deposits held by the ten (*five) biggest banks, by value	28	41	61	80

The big five banks of 1918 were Barclays, Lloyds, Midland, Westminster and National Provincial. Older companies, making little distinction between capital and revenue, were financially self-sufficient; in 1914 half of all company investment was funded not by debt but by accrued profit. With no legal distinction between the company's money and the owner's, few companies paying shareholder dividends, very little tax to pay on net incomes, and none of today's accounting rules, owners could spend or accumulate resources exactly as they wished.

Post World War II the nature and practice of banking changed: from the 1960s, after decades of stasis, the main beneficiaries of investment shifted from investees to investors. Greater opportunities for investors and bankers were enabled by international trade and financial deregulation, as detailed below.

- In the 1960s there were sixteen UK clearing banks, but incorporation reduced this to just four by 1970: Barclays, Lloyds, NatWest and Midland.[3]
- In 1962 UK banks' sterling assets were ten times the value of their foreign currency assets; by 1979 their foreign currency assets were 20% higher than their sterling assets.
- In 1990 UK clearing banks had virtually no involvement in over-the-counter interest rate swaps, exchange-traded derivatives or euro bonds. Twenty years later this market was worth over £400 trillion.
- Between 1960 and 1990 half of all money held by UK defined-benefit pension funds was invested in equities, falling to under 2% by 2020 (mainly because the investment market was insufficiently diverse to manage this risk well; in the 1990s half of all equities were in just ten FTSE companies).
- Almost entirely British-owned in the early 1990s, today half of the shares on the UK stock market are foreign-owned.[4]

One way to grow was to boost sales through advertising. So much Victorian copy looks naive and dull to us today, but Thomas Barratt at Pears led a revolution in the 1870s – his audacious use of *Bubbles* (a painting by Millais) and celebrity endorsement were inspired, his willingness to spend unprecedented. Hovis also showed marketing élan, and Skippers and Colman's demonstrated originality, whilst Boots, Lever Bros and others acknowledged American influences. Though Gamages and Martins exploited mail order to boost sales, Wedgwood had developed the practice a century earlier. New media were rigorously and imaginatively exploited, whether mass-circulation papers (which saw full-page adverts for Mackintosh), cinemas (a venue for Lever Bros) or television (where Hovis and Cadburys would excel).

Only one story involved significant government investment – or, rather, rescue: Swift's descendant, British Leyland, absorbed £2.9 billion in subsidy in 1979–88, before being sold for a fraction of that sum. Such support was unavailable, unconscionable, in 1925.

THE PROFESSIONAL INVESTOR

> Where does he come from? Shares. Where is he going to? Shares. What are his tastes? Shares.
>
> —Charles Dickens, *Our Mutual Friend*

Dickens reveals that the professional investor existed in Victorian times (indeed, we witness their involvement in the stories of Bass, Hartleys, Prices, Dunlop and Horrockses). The twenty-first century entrepreneur James Dyson knows who is responsible for today's low standing of manufacturing in the

UK economy; he bestows upon the novelist almighty powers: 'I always blame people like Charles Dickens. Entrepreneurs in Dickens weren't middle class ... the middle class and aristocracy never aspired to manufacturing.'[5]

Dickens wrote what he saw, which included networks of investors at a time when the 'middle class' had few members. Those networkers were not professional investors, though some aspired to be; they were mostly successful middle-class merchants, bankers, lawyers and accountants. Some were members of several networks, and each network invested members' assets according to the collective view; how slow and difficult communication between them must have been![6] Individual investors also existed, their portfolios suggesting that assets were rarely chosen in a rational or focused manner, and that they were usually held for the long term – often for life.[7]

Prior to 1925 modern concepts of 'responsible' or 'ethical' investment were rare outside Methodist and Quaker circles, which withheld investment from companies involved in alcohol, tobacco and gambling as early as the eighteenth century. American Quakers added slavery and weaponry to the list of 'sin stocks'. In 1928 the first public investment instrument with such principles, the Pioneer Fund (today part of Amundi), was launched.[8] An investment of $1,000 in Pioneer then would have yielded $44 million today, four times the return on a random selection of 'mainstream' S&P 500 shares; the caring investor had a concept of risk that judged externalities better.

From 2004 a series of UN reports titled 'Who cares, wins' presented evidence that better assessment of the newly-coined ESG risk factors in investment decisions would produce more stable and predictable markets. In 2005 came the first mention of 'impact investing' – investing to prioritize positive social or environmental outcomes. This was not new, but what was new was the demand for investments that could meet these priorities without compromising 'traditional' returns. A range of investment vehicles were developed in response, not least to attract long-term investors such as pension funds. In 2006 the United Nations launched its 'Principles of responsible investment' (UNPRI), a register of 'responsible' (climate-sensitive) investors that soon reached $4 trillion in assets under management. This grew to $120 trillion in 2023, managed by 731 asset owners and supported by almost 5,300 signatories.[9] Of our thirty-two companies only BP will have suffered at the hands of investors diverting their money away from 'sin stocks', as fossil fuel production rightly joined the 'naughty list'.

Those who oppose 'responsible' investment, who favour the old ways of uncertainty and risk, long odds on high returns, do so only from a perspective of short-term self-interest.

A comprehensive system of regulating the pensions industry, to ensure high ethical and other standards, was introduced in 1995 in response to the rise of private equity, to which we will return.

Today the fundamental change we have seen is the recalculation of risk. The laws of cause and effect have not changed but the willingness to gamble certainly has. When Victorians bought shares many held them for life; today there are parts of the economy in which computers programmed for high-frequency dealing process thousands of share transactions each second, removing from some business operations the human element that *Romance* so celebrated.

COMPANY GROWTH

Although all thirty-two companies saw growth as an important focus for their company, their aim even in 1925 was not 'growth at all costs'. Company stability is like riding a bicycle: it is difficult to maintain a constant 3 mph without wobbling and falling off. At 30 mph there is a momentum that helps maintain forward motion, but the risk of disaster or losing direction following a tumble is high. To stay on the bike all day, a 10 mph tortoise will often beat the 'growth at all costs' hare.

Early in their lives most of our companies recognized that, to be financially sustainable, growth had to be organic, based on increasing sales, which was best achieved by selling good products at the optimum price. Acquisition was difficult, as before the existence of shares it could only be done by agreement; a healthy company suffering a predatory takeover was all but impossible. Mergers required consent. Finding companies working together in partnership based on 'gentlemen's agreements', combining complementary assets, was not uncommon either prior to or instead of merger or acquisition.

Pre 1925 WHSmith did not make a single major acquisition in 130 years of existence (and no game-changing one afterwards); several companies were over 100 years old before their first major acquisition or merger, Wedgwood over 200. Mackintosh made one significant acquisition in its first seventy years and then one a year for five years after the last family leader died.

Not one first acquisition (see table 7 and figure 5) represents a major change in purpose, direction or identity.

Only thirteen had carried out a significant acquisition of, or merger with, another company by 1925. With the exception of Lever Bros in 1885, all were mature (at least 18 years old) when they made that first acquisition. The takeovers usually had the effect of removing a rival from the marketplace, adding capacity in an existing market, or consolidating supply chains or market share. In 1925 the average age of our thirty-two companies was 75 years; the average age at which they had made their first major acquisition before 1925 was 52 (i.e. twenty-three years previously, within the twentieth century), but

Table 7. Company age at first significant acquisition or merger. (*Continued on next page.*)

Year	Company	Age	First acquisition	Note
1848	Prices	18	Night light manufacturer	Adds range, capacity
1871	Mudies	27	Hookhams' Library	Removes rival (Mudies only ever made two acquisitions)
1884	Bryant & May	34	Pace & Sons	Removes rival, adds capacity
1885	Lever Bros	9	(Unknown soap-boiler)	First of many
1885	Horrockses	96	Hollins (merger)	Mutual benefit
1892	Kelly's	57	Slater's Directory	Removes rival
1897	Waring	62	Gillows (merger)	Mutual benefit
1903	Colman's	89	Keen, Robinson, Belville	Adds capacity (and barley water)
1908	Gamages	30	Benetfink & Co., retail	Adds depot capacity
1918	Lyons	24	Horniman, tea	Adds range, guarantee of supply
1920	Cadburys	96	Fry's, chocolate	Removes rival, adds capacity
1921	Hovis	35	Marriage Neave, millers	Adds capacity, efficiency
1921	Huntley & Palmers	99	Peak Freans (merger)	Adds capacity and range
1924	Bass	177	Many small breweries (bought and closed)	Gretton's growth strategy was based on acquiring breweries
1929	Newnes	68	Pearsons, publishing	After eight years of co-working
1930	Mackintosh	40	Caley's	Adds chocolate capacity
1938	Colman's	124	Reckitt (merger)	After twenty-five years of co-working
1958	Glaxo	85	Allen & Hanbury (240 years old)	First of several mergers
1959	Odhams	50	Newnes/Pearsons	Several came together as the IPC in 1963

Table 7. *Continued.*

Year	Company	Age	First acquisition	Note
1961	Skippers	58	John West (merger)	Three partners came together
1968	Wedgwood	209	Six UK potteries	Waterford merger (1969) was bigger
1968	Boots	117	Timothy Whites	Followed by many more
1969	Schweppes	177	Cadburys, to form Cadbury Schweppes	Previously only minor acquisitions
1978	WHSmith	180	Do It All	Previously only minor acquisitions
1998	British Petroleum	89	Amoco (merger)	State-owned until 1978

after 1925 the average age of first acquisition more than doubled, to 115. This suggests that acquisition was a twentieth-century phenomenon, boosted by share markets.

When is a merger not a merger? When it is a takeover and the acquired party loses agency but not the brand, which may have been the target of the takeover. Not one of our companies was taken over prior to 1919, and only three (Pears and Prices, both by Lever Bros, and Horrockses by the ACMT) had been acquired by 1925.

Below are some of the major comings together for our companies since 1925.

- Among the **successful mergers** aimed at enhancing the company's mission, Lever Bros' with Dutch Unie (1929) was the big one. The few mergers that Glaxo undertook, later in life, were also large, strategic and positive.
- Boots's takeovers of Timothy Whites (1968) and Dollond & Aitcheson (2008) were **overt acquisitions** with multiple benefits. Both taken-over brands disappeared.
- Cadbury Schweppes (1969) **posed as a merger,** but Schweppes was the acquiring party. They separated after forty years. When their relationship broke down, each brand became the property of others.
- Waring with Gillows (1897), Huntley & Palmers with Peek Freans (forming Associated Biscuits, 1921), Colman's with Reckitt (1938) and Rowntree with Mackintosh (1982) all started as **arm's-length partnerships** over

several years before a merger. The partnership of Dunlop and Pirelli (1971), sharing a mission, was a **mismatch** that ended not in a merger but in tears. None of these partnerships survive today.

- Schweppes's acquisition of Hartleys (1959) sparked a **descent into inconsequentiality** for the jam-maker. A takeover by Allied Breweries in 1978 signalled the ignominious end of Lyons, and we explore the experience of Horrockses with the ACMT (1919) in 'Case study: cotton' towards the end of this chapter.
- Bryant & May, Hovis, Prices and some of the publishers all underwent repeated takeovers by **private equity** in the twenty-first century; Unilever famously resisted one. Boots's recent story is dominated by private equity.
- Bass's repeated takeovers of others, apparently reckless, with growing scale and pace in the twentieth century, led to **loss of identity** and mission.
- Newnes's purchase of Pearsons was a **mercy acquisition**. Wedgwood was saved twice, by Waterford and Fiskars.
- Lyons took a **varied approach** to growth: an acquisition in 1944 and a few occasional, small acquisitions thereafter, supplemented by innovation and taking on franchises.
- Kelly's acquired other directories to **reduce competition**.
- Mudies, Swift, Martins, Gamages, Colman's, Prices and Pears did not have an independent life long enough for game-changing acquisitions or takeovers of their own (some undertook small ones).

Once acquisition was tasted, companies came back for more: Lever Bros set about a strategic, rational, measured programme of expansion by acquiring small fry even prior to the formation of Unilever in 1929; Glaxo's acquisitions were steady and measured (1958, 1995, 2000, 2023), working with bigger fish. Various other companies or their successors underwent feeding frenzies in the later twentieth century, often as victims: Hartleys (from 1959), Huntley & Palmers (1960s–80s), the four publishers (1960–), WHSmith (1970s–80s, followed by a new period of stability), Bryant & May (1970s–80s), Cadburys and Schweppes (1970s–2008), Dunlop (1980s–), Waring (1980s–90s), Wedgwood (1980s–90s), Boots (1980s) and Prices (UK) (1990s–). These all happened in that 'middle third' of the hundred years following Beable. The Rowntree Mackintosh merger lasted eighteen years before the Mackintosh brand disappeared. The merger of Skippers with others to form John West lasted forty-five years, but only the Skippers name survived the subsequent takeover by MW Brands/Thai Union. Such acquisitive behaviour emerged as Friedmanism dominated business education and the business world was actively encouraged to ignore GDP's 'externalities'.

The period 1959–70 was a bloodbath: in eleven years ten of our companies – Hartleys, Newnes, Skippers, Bass, Odhams, Mackintosh, Huntley & Palmers, Gamages, Schweppes and Cadburys – lost their independence. Only ten of the subjects, either directly (four) or as a brand asset belonging to a bigger company (six), are owned by shareholders on the UK stock exchange today.

By the 1960s the traditional (executive) chairman's role had largely been split into two roles: chairman of the board and managing director or CEO.

PRIVATE EQUITY

Hovis had a particularly chequered career: subject to mergers in 1957 and 1962, sold to private equity (PE) in 1992, floated as independent in 2005, acquired by Premier in 2007, part of a joint venture with PE in 2009, and back to PE in 2020. Price UK, the successor to Prices, had several years in the ownership of PE, and Boots has been owned by PE for a decade.

PE is a category of finance used to buy and sell companies, often prioritizing short-term gain over longer-term consequences. Within the past century it has generated its own lexicon: venture capital, corporate raiders, barbarians (at the gate), activist investors, junk bonds, leveraged buyouts and more. This largely secret and unaccountable world sees company ownership as a means of achieving profit, irrespective of the consequences for the organizations bought and sold. At its worst it is a world of high-risk, high-stakes short-termism that both thrives on and helps create instability. In a 'leveraged buyout' the predator takes on debt to acquire the prey. Such investments were known in 1925 but were small in number – and mostly in America. Since the 1940s, however, they have grown in influence; the UK is the world's second largest PE base behind the US, with half of Europe's top ten PE firms based here. PE accounts for almost 2% of UK GDP.[10]

PE existed in the nineteenth century, and J. P. Morgan's purchase of Carnegie Steel in 1901, the biggest PE purchase of its time, was a watershed. Today's PE landscape emerged fifty years ago in 1978 and included a $380 million leveraged buyout of Houdaille by Kohlberg Kravis Roberts (KKR), who borrowed 97.4% of the necessary funds.[11] A 'boom and bust' cycle followed, with a surge in junk bonds and leveraged buyouts. The second cycle (1992–2002) included not only a recession, a savings and loans crisis, and exposure of insider trading and asset stripping, but also the dotcom bubble (1999–2000). Criticism and scepticism about PE grew. The third wave, from 2003, saw leveraged buyouts reach new heights and PE companies become institutionalized, almost respectable. Since the 2008 crash, buyouts have slowed. Some PE firms, ever more powerful, are now publicly traded (and thus less secret), and in recent years the boom–bust cycle has been tempered. The PE company

Inflexion, celebrating twenty-five years of activity, today has a commitment to ESG to rival the best, whilst even KKR has belatedly become a champion of shared ownership (a democratic phenomenon long recognized as a route to reliable profit) and green energy.

In 2021 the global market in private finance was around $7 trillion, of which $4.7 trillion was PE and $1 trillion managed by KKR alone: since Houdaille, the company had been involved in the record 1989 Nabisco buyout (see Huntley & Palmers), as well as the purchase of Alliance Boots and then Walgreens in 2007.

It has been argued that companies whose goal is maximum short-term profit are unsuitable as owners in fields such as long-term social care, where the PE company Southern Cross is often cited as an example (2011).[12] Mark Goyder of Tomorrow's Company argued that many such set-ups would fail a 'trust test' that measured the compatibility of values between a service and its owner.* Nevertheless, the influence of PE, which owns one in every eight social care beds in Britain, continues to be significant.[13] A similar situation exists today in the world of children's care homes (highly profitable, some-times with questionable delivery and value for public money).[14]

In 2017 Unilever, which had an attractive bottom line as a result of its commitment to long-term environmental and social sustainability, not despite it, fought hard against an exceedingly generous takeover bid led by a Brazilian PE company, 3G. Unilever argued that PE values were incompatible with those which had brought it success. 3G's goal was short-term profit maximization, which a conventional Unilever could certainly have delivered, but 'success' in Unilever's terms was measured both conventionally (outperforming compet-itors Mondelez, Nestlé and Danone) and in terms of improved ESG perfor-mance on many fronts. The bid was resisted and rejected by shareholders.

It is difficult to avoid the conclusion that a strategy based on acquisition as a short cut to or proxy for growth does not guarantee success for the long term. Of our four most successful companies, two took a conservative approach (Unilever and GSK), one was mostly nationalized during its lifetime (BP) and one, WHSmith, did get the 'acquisition bug' but returned to the measured approach from 2010. Some of 1925's successful companies have spent the last sixty years only as gambling chips, brand pawns, the victims of predators.

Perhaps the 'quick win' ethos of PE is changing, and the era is over? It has been estimated that returns to PE investors in 2024 were half what was predicted, yielding $400 billion less than expected over three years compared with the historical average.[15]

---

*Goyder's 'trust test' became BS95009 (2019): https://knowledge.bsigroup.com/products/
public-sector-procurement-generic-requirements-for-organizations-providing-products
-and-services.

BRAND SURVIVAL

Romance of Great Businesses describes thirty-two companies in 1925, of which four survive intact and eight have disappeared. Prior to 1925 each company was its brand; the brand described a single category of product, whether soap, candles, tyres, infant formula or jam. Four of the remaining twenty had little brand value as publishers (Pearsons, Odhams, Newnes, Cassells). In traditional publishing it is more common to buy and sell titles than whole companies or the publisher's imprint; by the 1960s all four heritages were encapsulated in a single entity, the IPC.

Name any remaining brand – Cadburys, Dunlop, Wedgwood, Hartleys, Hovis, Bass – and the distinctive mental image is one of quality, history, substance and reliability, positive values. It is no wonder that successive owners of the brands have sought to utilize, preserve and maintain these valued reputations. Not one of the products associated with these brands is made by an independent company sharing that brand name today.

Brand survival depends on adaptation to new circumstances through appropriate innovation plus a strategy of customer identification and retention, centred around a strong identity. In recent years that adaptation has involved meeting the digital marketing challenge, and more recently brand identity has increasingly been allied to a company's reputation around sustainability and responsibility issues. In the course of its ten-year Sustainable Living Plan (2010–20), for example, Unilever delivered a 300% return to investors, indicating close alignment between a brand and a strong, responsible and profitable message.

Building brand identity involves successful storytelling, creating an emotional connection with customers. Thus brands themselves acquire value and become commodities that can be bought and sold independently of the company that created or owns them. In recent years we have seen brands purchased by private equity for their intrinsic value without the encumbrance of a company attached to them (see table 8 and figure 5). In some cases this has happened more than once: the Hovis story suggests that a degree of cynicism was involved in passing the brand from one owner to another repeatedly over a relatively short time.

The Colman's story is brand evolution personified. The mustard's characteristic taste and proprietary recipe were developed 200 years ago, when the company was formed. Its distinctive brand colour and packaging was added soon after and has been retained ever since. The original brand also included other milled products, but the brand name irrevocably says 'mustard'. From 1926 the company worked in partnership with Reckitt, who shared a common interest in the American mustard market. The companies merged in 1948, ending Colman's independent existence, and by 1995 mustard's presence in what had become a household products conglomerate had become inappropriate. That year a food giant, the former soaper Unilever, bought the brand. This allowed it to use the mustard brand recipe, inherit the brand identity and expand the brand. Today the Colman's brand encapsulates ready meals, seasonings and recipe mixes for the first time – though the name still evokes the yellow blob on the side of our plate.

Table 8. Brand survival.

Description today	Brand (owner)
Acquired brand status in new role, owner of many brands, direct lineage to heritage company/brand	Unilever, formerly Lever Bros pre 1929; GSK, formerly Glaxo pre 1995
Strong brand, still owned by heritage company of the same name	WHSmith; British Petroleum, formerly APOC/AIOC pre 1954
Strong brand, major part of current owner's portfolio	Boots (Walgreens Boots Alliance), Hovis (Endless PE)
Strong brand, minor part of current owner's portfolio, brand identity sold (often repeatedly)	Colman's (Unilever), Cadburys (Mondelez), Schweppes (various), Pears (Unilever), Dunlop (various)
Weak brand (compared with previously), minor part of current owner's portfolio	Skippers (Thai Union); Hartleys (Hain); Prices (SER); Lyons (Pernod Ricard); Cassells (Octopus); Newnes, Odhams, Pearsons (all RELX); Wedgwood (Fiskars)
Brand exists only as a franchise	Bass (InterContinental Hotels)
Brand died, recently resurrected on a small scale	Huntley & Palmers (Freeman), Bryant & May (RTI)
Unclear whether brand still exists	Horrockses (Asos?)
Brand no longer exists	Martins, since c. 1930? Swift, 1931;[a] Mudies, 1937; Gamages, 1972; Kelly's, 1980; Whiteleys, 1981;[b] Mackintosh, 1987; Waring, 1988

[a] Plus Rover since 2008 (Land Rover excepted).

[b] Reopened as an up-market hotel and retail facility, 2025.

COMPANY FORMS AND REGULATION

In the late sixteenth century the Crown recognized that 'corporations' were distinct from 'real' people yet capable of perpetuating themselves. In the seventeenth century royal charters were granted to trading giants such as the East India, South Sea and Hudson Bay companies, and the king granted parliament the power to issue such charters. However, corporate charters were not appropriate – and too expensive – for smaller companies, for whom a simple contract of association conferred sufficient legality. Such contracts could not limit the degree of liability that a company's 'members' might endure, but back then sharing that liability between shareholders in an unregulated manner was potentially chaotic, a disincentive to invest.

In return for a loan of £7 million to finance the 1720 war with France, plus a hefty bit of debt underwriting, parliament issued a charter granting the South Sea Company a monopoly on South American trade. This caused the company's stocks to rapidly inflate on the immature stock exchange: 'money for nothing' was an attractive prospect! There was an explosion in the formation of new companies, many illegal or imaginary, whose only aim was to cash in on the wave of rising share prices. This ill-supported bubble inevitably burst and stocks collapsed, crashing many fortunes overnight. To prevent a repeat of the 'South Sea Bubble', the government legislated to ban most non-chartered companies. This unhelpful Act, born in a panic, was repealed in 1825.

The Joint Stock Companies Registration and Regulation Act of 1844 allowed any company with more than twenty-five shareholders in England, Wales and Ireland to become incorporated, and it established a register of those with shares nominally available to the general public. This did not limit the liability of their members, but the Limited Liability Act of 1855 did.

Following the period of the founder's ownership, the next stage for our companies was to take on limited liability (Ltd) status. This was neither required nor essential – some resisted for many years – but it had its uses: a limited liability company has its own legal assets, corporate identity, duties and responsibilities. The personal liability of individual owners and shareholders ('members') was limited to whatever they put into the company (if anything).[16]

The first of our companies to take on Ltd status was Bryant & May, though many were significantly older. There was a clear reluctance amongst founders (especially) to acquire the protection that limited liability brought, presumably because they believed they did not need it. However, several companies notably sought Ltd status shortly after their founder stepped down or died (see table 9 and figure 5), which may further indicate founder resistance. In Cassell's case, he obtained Ltd status in 1858 when he resumed ownership after standing down for four years.

Table 9. Year of acquiring limited liability status.

Year	No.	Companies assuming limited liability status
Pre 1860	2	Bryant & May, 1855; Cassells, 1858
1860–70	1	Mudies, 1864
1870–80	2	Schweppes, 1877; Boots, 1880
1880–90	4	Horrockses, 1885; Bass, 1888; Dunlop, 1889; Lever Bros, 1890
1890–1900	16	Newnes, 1891; Pears, 1892; Glaxo, 1893; Kelly's, Colman's, both 1896; Huntley & Palmers, Pearsons, Gamages, Waring, Swift, all 1897; Hovis, Lyons, Odhams, all 1898; Whiteleys, Cadburys, both 1899; Wedgwood, 1900
1900–10	2	British Petroleum (as APOC/AIOC), 1909;[a] Skippers, 1910[a]
After 1910	5	Martins, 1914; Hartleys, 1919; Mackintosh, 1920; Prices, 1922; WHSmith, 1929

[a] Both were formed in that decade.

By 1885, 9,344 companies had assumed limited liability, about 10% of the private sector economy. Demand for investment capital had been slow throughout the 1870s, but as the economy picked up in the 1880s interest in the protection afforded by limited liability grew. By 1914, 80% of all UK companies were 'limited'; in 2024 it was 93%, the remainder being mostly private companies or partnerships. (One in 500 today has 'unlimited liability', where owners forfeit the protection of limited liability in return for their finances remaining secret.)

If Beable thought that the companies he described in 1925 were set in stone, he was wrong. He witnessed stability, long-term relationships, caution and, in many cases, a broad sense of responsibility – many of those values have gone, but there was no single moment, no one tipping point, that wrought these changes (see figure 5).

By the end of 1925 just three of our founders were still alive: Watson, Gamage and Martin, none of them titans. Figure 5 shows us the following major changes since 1925.

- Twenty names today exist only as brands – ephemera, bought and sold like any other commodity, often frequently, owned by neither their original nor their 1925 owner.
- Eight no longer exist in any form.
- Just four survive as recognizably the same companies, the giants Unilever, WHSmith, Glaxo and BP, whilst Boots appears to have done.

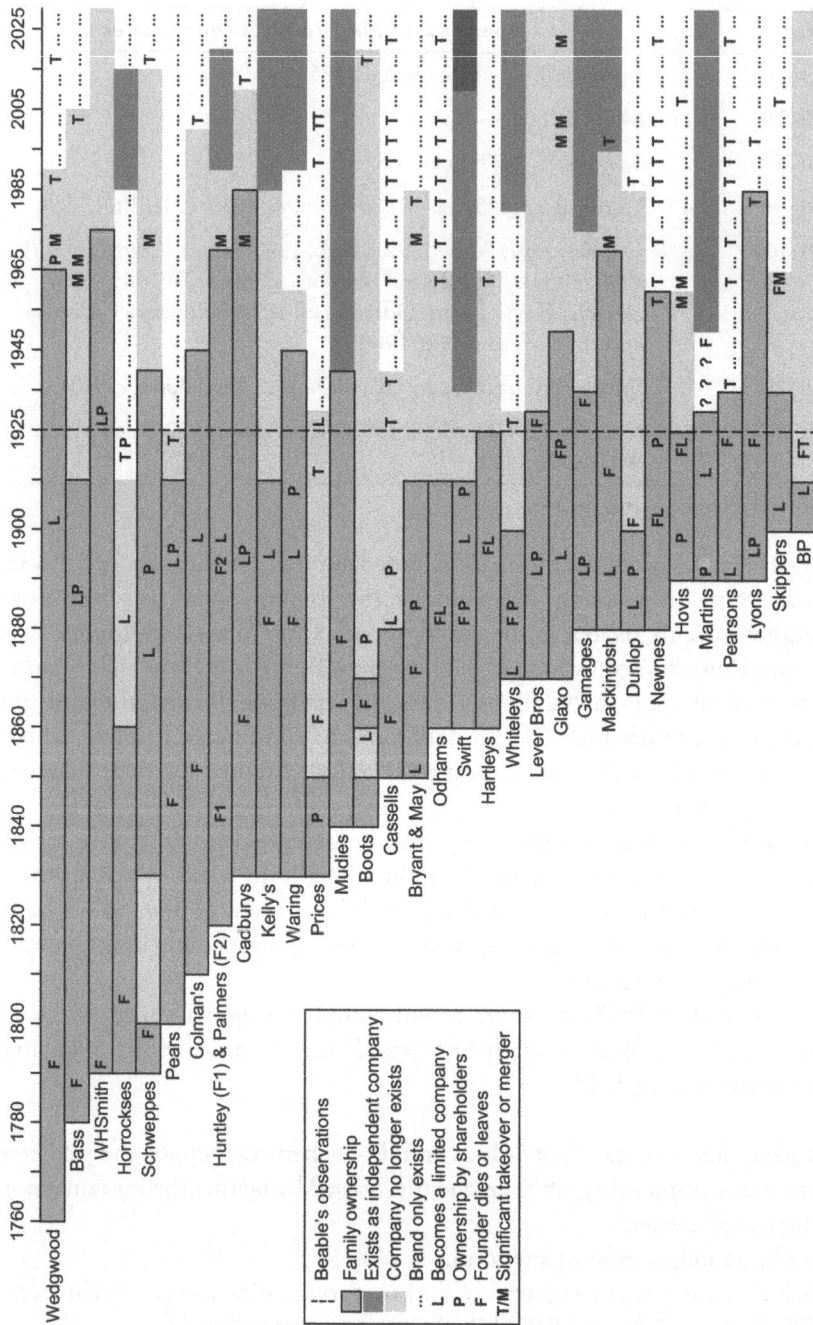

Figure 5. Company histories compared.

- Seventeen companies were family-owned in 1925. Post World War II there were seven, now none.
- Only WHSmith was not 'limited' in 1925; by 1929 it was.
- Wedgwood waited until family ownership ended (1965) before selling shares. All the others, except state-owned BP, were selling them by 1930.
- Publishers' imprints (Newnes, Pearsons, Cassells, Odhams) were bought, sold, transferred and cannibalized more frequently than brands in other fields.
- The years 1955–75 saw a concentration of mergers (only Glaxo merged at scale after this period, doing so three times).

It would be wrong to conclude that there is no place in the twenty-first century for family ownership of large (or largeish) companies, though there are now many alternative governance models. The construction company Wates, founded in 1897, remains family-owned to this day. It has a standard professional board, of a form recognizable in most modern companies of their size, but also a senior, family-dominated board with a long-term brief. Its website states: 'Our owners, the Wates Family, are committed to handing over to the next generation an even stronger, more sustainable business. This approach drives all our investment decisions.' Commitments include embedding social value, promoting inclusion and diversity, achieving net zero carbon emissions by 2045 and being net positive on biodiversity. Wates's values, of environmental sustainability and community engagement, are consistent with those of family-run firms of the past.

When banks were small, so were their investment ambitions, so bigger businesses needed an alternative source of finance. This had consequences for patterns of ownership.

In the mid nineteenth century, railways required unprecedented levels of capital investment, far beyond what individual banks had available. The first steam railway, the 200-mile Stockton and Darlington route, was financed by a consortium of rich Quakers in the 1820s, the Furness railway (1850s) by the uber-rich Duke of Devonshire, to take his iron ore to port, but most railway businesses had neither a sugar daddy nor access to public investment. Nevertheless, by 1840 Britain had constructed 2,390 kilometres of railway track, and 14,603 kilometres by 1860 (half its 1920 maximum). Larger railway companies were by necessity innovators; never being owned by families, they recruited professional executives from the start, and their size dwarfed other privately owned companies. But where would this huge investment in track and rolling stock come from? The new, multi-source finance needed to achieve that scale was share ownership.

Up to 1840 the then 70-year-old London Stock Exchange had little influ-ence, but that changed with 'railway mania'. An unsophisticated market in railway shares boomed, attracting 'ordinary' investors, speculators and con-men, and prompting banks to issue competing bonds. The market had a rocky few years, but from the 1860s it stabilized, helping to normalize both share ownership and the concept of investing for the longer term. Investment of surplus funds had even attracted the landowning aristocracy, who had their own banks, such as Rothschilds (1769), Barings (1762) and Coutts (1692).

Having limited liability did not oblige companies to create shares, and even today a company can be either 'limited by guarantee' or 'limited by shares'. Family firms of the mid to late nineteenth century were privately owned, with no share ownership, at least from the start. Even when shares were issued there was no obligation to sell them to the public, and they were regularly retained by family, or family and friends. Hartleys issued non-voting public shares in 1884 simply to raise funds. Between 1870 and 1936 most of our companies started to offer shares to the public in an initial public offering (IPO). Wedgwood only did so in the 1960s after abandoning its traditional family-ownership model, and BP in the 1980s when the government sold its dominant holding (table 10).

Table 10. Year of first share issue.

Decade	No.	Companies issuing shares
Pre 1880	1	Cassells, 1878
1880–90	3	Bryant & May, 1884; Swift, 1888; Bass, 1888
1890–1900	11	Schweppes, 1890; Boots, 1890; Lyons, 1894; Lever Bros, 1894; Dunlop, 1896; Pears, 1897; Newnes, 1897; Gamages, 1897; Mackintosh, 1898; Cadburys, 1899; Whiteleys, 1899
1900–10	1	Waring, 1910
1910–20[a]	3	Martins, 1919; Glaxo, 1919; Horrockses, via the ACMT, 1919
1920–30	2	Odhams, 1925; WHSmith, 1929
1930–40	2	Hovis, 1933; Hartleys, 1936
After 1940	2	Wedgwood, 1967; British Petroleum, 1982
Never	7	Colman's, Skippers, Mudies, Huntley & Palmers, Prices, Pearsons, Kelly's

[a] IPOs were restricted during World War I.

The rapid expansion of share ownership replaced family ownership, though the purposes and missions of our companies did not immediately change.

Founding families often retained a seat on the board, even in successor companies (in Colman's case for more than fifty years).

Nevertheless, Beable's only references to shareholders in 1925 are in the Horrockses drama and his mention of 'sleeping capitalists' in the story of Prices. External investors then were passive sources of money, receiving dividends when available but making few, if any, demands on management.

Prior to 1773, stock exchanges (plural) were informal gatherings of those who bought and sold shares in business ownership, typically centred around London coffee-houses. By the early nineteenth century self-governing rules were emerging and evolving. Activity in London gravitated towards the Royal Exchange, rebuilt after a fire, whilst other cities, notably the railway hubs of Manchester, Leeds and Liverpool, had exchanges of their own. By 1900 the London Stock Exchange was boasting the latest communications technology (telephone, telegraph, ticker tape) and dominating the trade of listed shares. The exchange closed in 1914, concerned that the war would damage the economy as stockbrokers failed to recover German debts, though it would reopen only five months later to halt the unregulated 'street' trading of shares that had broken out.

In 1907, 569 companies were registered on the London Stock Exchange, and 1,712 by 1939. Only 88 companies had more than £1 million of share capital in 1884, rising to 940 by 1935.[17] There were 3,200 of these in 2007, falling steadily, almost by half, by 2024.[18] This fall, more marked than in other countries, is due to factors ranging from consolidation and growing company size to Brexit uncertainty and the growth of private equity.

FRAUD

Share ownership opened the door to fraud on a significant scale. Even in those innocent early days, brokers were often intense, money-oriented, inward-looking characters with one-track minds, with little time for dealing with the human beings who wanted to buy or sell shares. A new profession, 'promoters', emerged to act as go-betweens, bringing share sellers and purchasers together. Promoters learned to parasitize the market, often gaining the most from their deals.

The silver-tongued Nottinghamshire Baptist Ernest Terah Hooley (1859–1947) was a freelance promoter (see Dunlop, Schweppes and Swift) who borrowed money to buy shares that he sold at vastly inflated prices, whilst Horatio Bottomley, MP (1860–1933; see Odhams) was a smaller player. Unlike these two, James White (1877–1927; see Dunlop, Whiteleys and 'Case study: cotton') never went to prison, but the most prolific, Clarence Hatry (1888–1965), did. Hatry worked on occasion with both White and Bottomley. Once a

director of fifteen corporations simultaneously, each of his several bankrupt-
cies left him richer than the last.

In 1905 Bottomley, who experienced extremes of wealth and poverty over
his lifetime, sold shares in the Basingstoke Canal without revealing that it was
loss-making, structurally unreliable and had never paid a dividend. He had no
authority to sell the shares; his adviser was Ernest Hooley. The Canal affair led
to a second Bottomley bankruptcy, obliging his dismissal from parliament in
1912. His next company, offering investment advice, was clearly a scam, but
the courts failed to prove this.

Rochdale-born London resident James White, once a child worker in a cotton mill, lived in luxury. He sponsored circuses, theatres and boxing matches,
including the first black-versus-white bout at Earl's Court, in 1911 (which was
banned for fear of disorder). White had enjoyed some success in land, though
neither his racehorses nor his American oil interests thrived. Financial transactions were restricted during war time so upon Sir Joseph Beecham's death in 1916
White inadvertently became head of the Beecham's Trust's investment portfolio,
with neither the experience nor temperament for the role. Sir Joseph's son, the
conductor Sir Thomas, recalled that White was prone to panic, behaving 'like
a comet across the sky'. White purchased West End property on behalf of the
Trust, including, ineptly, Covent Garden market (1924).

When cotton giant the ACMT (see 'Case study: cotton' and Horrockses)
issued 1.3 million ordinary £1 shares in 1919, White bought many with Beecham Trust money for £3 each – setting a trend followed by other investors.[19]
This threatened to create a bubble, but before the exponential growth phase
could kick in the value of the shares plummeted. The main difference between
White and Hooley was that Hooley understood what he was doing.

As a friend of the newly knighted Sir Arthur du Cros (Dunlop), White
also arranged for the Beecham Trust to invest in Dunlop and Austin Motors.
He blended naivety, ignorance and lust and should never have had charge of
other people's money; his 'recklessness blighted the lives of many', one of those
being Harry Gordon Selfridge (see Whiteleys).[20] In 1927 White killed himself
by drinking prussic acid, leaving his second wife and family penniless.

In one sense White was a pioneer: he had advocated selling bundles of
shares as 'units', owned by trusts, an American practice new to Britain. When
the stock exchange refused to allow trade in 'unit trusts' his scheme naturally
failed, but it was introduced from 1931 to aid post-Depression recovery.

Amongst Hatry's possessions were Britain's largest private yacht and the
only full-size domestic swimming pool in Mayfair. On 24 September 1929
he took lunch at Claridge's after confessing to multiple frauds. The stock
exchange suspended trading in his massive £24 million share fortune, and
he submitted himself for arrest that same day, possibly helping to trigger the

Wall Street Crash of a month later. Hatry served nine years of a fourteen-year stretch and later owned booksellers Hatchards. When he died his estate was worth a mere £828.[21]

But Hooley was a law unto himself. He made £2 million from Dunlop, his biggest win. In each of sixteen cases he borrowed cash to buy the private company (a 'leveraged buyout') and then used exaggerated claims to float it to prospective shareholders. Dunlop was his first victim, but he did the same for Bovril, buying a company worth £1.5 million for £2 million and selling it to shareholders for £2.5 million; Bovril's success was as a temperance drink, so teetotaller Hooley was a credible salesman. His scalps included Schweppes (he made £1.2 million), Starley's Swift (£375,000) and Dunlop France (£650,000), plus seven more bicycle and automobile manufacturers. In every case the new shareholders watched the inflated value of their newly acquired stock plummet, allowing Hooley to extract over £6 million in total. The 'Splendid Bankrupt' was Vanity Fair's featured 'Man of the Day' in December 1896.[22]

Angus Watson relates that Hooley visited William Lever at Thornton Manor, offering to buy Lever Bros using Bovril as leverage. After their lunch 'the Chief' went for a nap, returned and declined Hooley's offer. During his 'nap' Lever had discreetly authorized the purchase of Bovril shares, which Hooley later bought at an inflated price. When challenged by Watson, Lever smiled, refusing to confirm or deny the story.[23]

Hooley operated scams in China, Siberia (with the unfortunate Harry Lawson; see Swift) and Canada. After his death a red gown with ermine trim was found amongst his possessions; his anticipated elevation was credible, as Hooley had endeared himself to royalty.[24] In 1896 he had bought the 2,000-acre Anmer Hall estate, adjacent to Royal Sandringham, at a rock-bottom price. He then sold it to the then Prince of Wales* at no profit at the behest of the royal lover, Alice Keppell.[25] Europe's richest man of the era was described by the future Edward VII as 'my particular friend', and by a judge as 'the best Chancellor we never had'.

Briefly the Conservative parliamentary candidate for Ilkeston (1897), Hooley withdrew due to an impending bankruptcy. No one knew Hooley better than the courts: in 1911 he went to prison for twelve months for fraud plus a month for contempt. As an estate agent he served three years at His Majesty's pleasure in 1921. In 1939 the rich man with a lavish lifestyle went bankrupt a fourth time, prompted by the ongoing cotton crash, owing the Inland Revenue £700.

On a positive note, Hooley created Trafford Park, Britain's first industrial estate, in 1896.

---

*Anmer Hall is still the residence of the Prince of Wales today.

BUSINESS SCHOOLS

Businesses of 1925 valued a professional approach, though neither formal qualifications nor the routine transfer of expertise between companies was commonplace. Britain had just ten universities by 1910. The Fabian Society, inspired by George Bernard Shaw and Sidney and Beatrice Webb, had established the London School of Economics in 1895, not a business school despite its name; it would join London University five years later. The American Harvard University had run a summer school for business in London in 1905, and Edinburgh opened Britain's first proper business school in 1918, when barely one company in five was led by any kind of graduate. In the 1960s it became fashionable for British universities to cater for business skills as Ashridge, London, Manchester, Durham, Birmingham, Cranfield, Lancaster, Bradford and Warwick all opened their doors. Others followed, with Oxford and Cambridge launching their Saïd and Judge business schools only in the 1990s.

The first US business school was Wharton (1888); there were thirty by 1914. There were 400 US business consultancies in 1930. Boyce and Ville conclude that benefits from either source were unproven.[26]

In the first half of the twentieth century mainstream European thinkers such as Keynes were interventionist. They had been influenced by the Great Depression (accelerated by the Wall Street Crash of October 1929), one of the first economic events on a grand scale, outside war or revolution, to attract contemporary study from economists. Their ideas had seduced US President Franklin D. Roosevelt and would play a role after the next major economic upheaval, World War II, when governments came together to lay down common economic guidelines and structures at the Bretton Woods conference of 1944.

But a different approach dominated the second-oldest American business school: Chicago, dating from 1898. By the 1960s its neoclassical and monetarist economics had become associated with the academic Milton Friedman (1912–2006). The Chicago School's credo was that the 'free market' would operate most effectively if unencumbered, as far as possible, by legislation or regulation. The title of Friedman's famous 1970 essay for the *New York Times*, taken from his 1962 book, says it all: 'The social responsibility of business is to increase its profits'. Often paraphrased as 'the business of business is business', his philosophy was that maximizing shareholder return should be the first and only priority of any company.

By the mid-century many companies still did not have active shareholders; as late as 1960 a quarter of our thirty-two subjects were still family-owned (figure 5). As British businesses caught up with the Americans in marketing and other techniques, graduates were sought in leadership roles – and these graduates had to be getting their ideas from somewhere. Chicago was winning that ideological battle in business schools globally, by pushing at an open door. The new British business schools, in need of a credo, found one served up to them on a plate.

Two American reports – one by Robert A. Gordon and James E. Howell, the other by Frank C. Pierson – had called as early as 1959 for business degrees to be regarded as professional qualifications. They envisaged this happening through greater emphasis on research, the teaching of principles as well as techniques, and the infusion of values around a sense of responsibility. Both reports feared that the third pillar was not being treated as a priority, and they were right.[27]

'Shareholder primacy' had a profound effect on the teaching of business ethics in academic institutions across the world. This simple idea played to an undergraduate sense of ambition, entitlement and self-worth at a time when graduates – the educated elite – were less than 2% of the population. In this era shareholders were groups of disconnected individuals, not institutions (private equity took off in the 1960s and pension fund investment in the 1970s). The idea of getting rich by doing very little, of letting one's money 'do the talking', that money begets money, was attractive. Doing so with the minimum of rules and regulations was such a popular idea that 'government *interference*' (my emphasis) was frequently identified on business school curriculums. It has been suggested that, at the height of the Cold War, Friedman may have deliberately overstated the exciting appeal of profit in America's 'land of opportunity' in contrast to drab, Soviet conformity.

The philosophical basis for Friedmanism was 'rational choice theory', the idea that individuals, companies and markets, left to their own devices, act each in their own self-interest. Adam Smith did not go this far! Britain's first economist acknowledged that sometimes the best way of pursuing self-interest is to seek common or mutual self-interest, tempered by a degree of sensible regulation. Raw Friedmanism rejected this: the profit-focused approach excluded sentimentality. The beauty of adopting an approach based on the bottom line meant that everything could be reduced to spreadsheets. Bretton Woods' adoption of GDP as a lodestar appeared to endorse this approach (see 'GDP's externalities' in the 'Environment' chapter).

Politics lagged behind business thinking. Britain's post-war Conservative governments of the 1950s and 1960s, with their inclusive, paternalistic 'One Nation' approach, had more in common with the landowning agricultural Whigs of the past than with the 1980s monetarism of Margaret Thatcher. Her Friedmanite advisers included Sir Alan Walters and Sir Keith Joseph, a distant member of the Gluckstein family (founders of Lyons). Friedman himself served as adviser to Thatcher's economic soulmate, US President Ronald Reagan, whilst Chilean dictator General Augusto Pinochet was another fan.

Minimizing the regulation of business is in line with the 'small government' religion of Brexit, a twenty-first-century approach adopted by many on the right of British politics. This philosophy takes the view that taxes are an intrusion into personal liberty, that wealth (including inheritance) should be inviolate, and that public spending should be kept to an absolute minimum in order to keep those taxes down. And that internationally regulated markets governed through shared sovereignty are completely beyond the pale.

By the 1970s business schools across the world were teaching generations of future business leaders not only that they had been granted unique opportunities to create wealth but that they should resent any intervention that might impede them. Ultimately, only the future of the company and its power to generate profit mattered, which is why we saw acquisition being used as a tool not only to grow empires (no longer simply businesses) but to undermine and destroy rivals, too.

Once a business was making surplus profit, those with the power to extract cash from the system raked it in. Following the 2008 crash, British productivity, real wages, business investment and industrial output all flatlined (and have never recovered), whilst directors' pay, total shareholder return and wealth inequality have rocketed. Rare before 2000, the value of share buybacks – where companies create windfalls for shareholders by repurchasing their own shares – quadrupled in the US between 2012 and 2022, to $1.2 trillion, and doubled in China in a single year (2023–4). A leading fund manager, his bonuses no doubt linked to quarterly share prices, revealed his priorities: 'The dividend is just the dividend: grandma benefits, the long-term holder [benefits]. Buybacks benefit traders, hedge funds, senior executives [and] near-term share prices.'[28] These people believed not only that it was possible to drive profit at all costs, de-risk it, and remove the money it represented from the companies, communities and workforce that created it, but that doing so was their right.

Business schools make great play of teaching 'ethics', but 'ethics' is not values-neutral; it must imply a rules-based economy, with society and the corporate sector in harmony. Friedman's 'ethics' led to businesses actively disengaging from wider societal or environmental concerns, rejecting any meaningful long-term interpretation of 'corporate social responsibility'.

Thankfully today's British business schools – following the lead set by some major businesses – have moved on from that agenda, believing that they do indeed have a responsibility to serve the 'public good' and that the time has come to express it.[29]

Back in the 1960s Friedman's was not the only business philosophy available.

Frederic (Eric) Hooper (1882–1963) graduated in botany on the eve of World War I and spent three post-war years in banking. The often argumentative manager was then recruited by a Liverpool department store committed to employing graduates. He remained there twenty years before founding a Conservative-leaning research centre, from where he failed to secure a parliamentary seat. After World War II, Hooper, then a management consultant, told Schweppes they needed a new leader – so they appointed him! An advocate of profit-sharing, his modest salary with profit-linked bonuses made him one of the best-paid business leaders of his day.

In the 1960 Hooper Report on armed services recruitment, written as Britain was ending conscription into National Service, the World War I veteran emphasized the importance of both using modern advertising techniques to attract recruits and supporting a managed transition back into civilian life when their service ended. He identified the army, in particular, as carrying the 'stigma of providing a career only for those unable to find fruitful employment in civilian life'. Hooper was a supporter of both the army and trade unions, whilst amongst his dislikes were tax dodgers and … yes, fizzy drinks. He advocated a scientific approach of 'hypothesis, test, revise' in his successful time leading Schweppes (1948–62), arguing that industrial strife was usually caused by poor management.[30] Hooper credited the factory of Matthew Boulton and James Watt, the fathers of the steam-powered industrial revolution, with helping forge these views, and he built on the work of the American productivity guru F. W. Taylor (1856–1915). Cadburys cite the Quaker Taylor – a management consultancy pioneer who influenced Ford and, later, McDonald's – as a guide, despite Taylorism's later reputation for dehumanizing employment. Perhaps this contributed to the mutual attraction that led to the formation of Cadbury Schweppes in 1969?

Taylor's principles can be summarized as follows.

- Replace 'what works' with operating methods based on science.
- Systematically select, train and develop each employee.
- Give each worker clear instruction and supervision.
- Divide work equitably so that managers plan work scientifically and workers perform tasks effectively.
- Gain productivity by improving employee pay whilst reducing employee numbers.

A century before Taylor such division of labour was advocated by Adam Smith and practised by Josiah Wedgwood.

Hooper acknowledged that 90% of the workforce of Taylor's time were employed in manual labour, whereas post World War II this ratio was rapidly reversing, yet he claimed the same principles applied. The scientist Hooper talked also of the 'art of management', pointing out that any industrial conflict has only three possible solutions: imposed (either by management or the workforce), compromised or co-created. Imposition and compromise both embed disagreement and resentment, he argued, whilst co-creation credits both sides with ownership. Reaching that 'third way' is, indisputably, an art consistent with Hooper's view that employers should share 'power with' their workforce, not exert 'power over' them.

'The manager is not the employer, the customer is,' was another Hooper aphorism, as was: 'Dignity requires that work must have meaning.' Hooper would argue – as do twenty-first-century academics such as Colin Mayer of Oxford's Saïd Business School – that profit is not the same as purpose; profit can help achieve purpose (by keeping the purposeful company solvent) and be produced as a by-product. Mayer argues, wisely, that business should produce profitable solutions to the problems of people and planet, not profit from creating those problems.[31] This is sensible, positive, essential in a world that is still changing, radically and quickly, and it will remain so whether or not we successfully address major existential issues such as climate change.

'Purpose' is linked to goals – desirable social, economic and environmental outcomes that give meaning and motivation to employment. Hooper and Mayer represent a much more open, inclusive, appropriate and workable way forward for the twenty-first century than does the mainstream model that dominated business schools in the twentieth.

TAXATION OF BUSINESS

There was no direct taxation of business or personal income in Britain for most of the eighteenth century. There were taxes on land (the biggest source of government revenue), imports and windows (initially to finance the 1696 war against France), but not of humans. Duties covered more than 1,200 commodities by 1842, both basic items and luxuries: salt, candles, leather, beer, soap, wallpaper, starch, wine, silk, gold and silver thread, silver plate, coaches, hired horses, perfume, gloves, hats, and more. Tobacco has always been highly taxed, not that this initially bothered cigar merchant Walter Martin. In each case it was the manufacturer or trader who paid the tax, and duties rose regularly. At the start of the nineteenth century sugar was taxed at £30 per ton, beer at 10s (50p in today's money) per barrel, with more on hops and malt; there were levies on imported timber, glass, iron bars, hemp and cotton. Some tariffs protected British trade; others just punished French imports.

The Tory William Pitt the Younger, disciple of Adam Smith, introduced the first levies on wealth in 1783, albeit by proxy. Taxing the possession of servants, homes, horses and other areas hit the richest, the Whig landowners, the most. It is odd, from our perspective, that it was Tories who advocated taxing the rich! If the Tories were neither the party of the wealthy landowners nor the representatives of aspiring leaders of big businesses, who were they? They were the party not so much of small business but of the small-business mentality: of men who had something to protect or conserve but not enough to consider disposing of in an altruistic or paternalistic manner. As the voting population grew throughout the nineteenth century, it was these voters – think archetypal Rotarians, chambers of trade, Freemasons – who marched behind the Conservative banner of Peel and Disraeli.

Government income in 1792 was accordingly, at £18 million, 50% higher than ten years previously. By 1799 another war with France required even more money, so the first true income tax was introduced, with a top rate of 10% on incomes over £200 per year. Addington abolished it in 1802, but when peace proved fleeting it was reimposed at 5% (1803–16). It was reintroduced by Peel in 1842 (switching taxation from indirect to direct by halving the number of duties), initially temporarily. It was collected by the Inland Revenue from 1849, an arrangement that is still reconfirmed by parliament each year.[32]

Tax on personal income included taxing the income of companies owned by individuals, as companies were not taxed separately on their own incomes. This had consequences, not least as shareholders' investments started to be influential. Any necessary differentiation was maintained through conventions and bookkeeping practices rather than rules, regulations or laws, though Sir Arthur du Cros (Dunlop) and Lord Waring both got into hot water in the 1920s for treating company money as their own.

Pitt's rationalization of the piecemeal system of death duties in 1796 was also designed to 'sting' the wealthy. Several chancellors left their fingerprints here as each sought a 'fairer' system of taxing inheritance than their predecessor's. When W. H. 2 Smith died, in 1891, Pitt's system was essentially still in use; the cost of Smith's death duties was borne by the company. From 1894 the estates tax gradually got more progressive. The Smith experience was reprised in 1948 when his grandson, the third Viscount Hambleden, passed away, shortly before more reforms (1949 and 1959). The sums involved were so great that WHSmith had to be restructured and refinanced to manage the cost on both occasions. Corporation tax, which taxes companies separately from their owners, was only introduced in 1965, but it was not until 1976 that inheritance tax unequivocally protected companies from this particular anachronism.

War debts prompted reforms of indirect taxation after both world wars, with a focus on 'luxuries'. The purchase tax (1940) was replaced by the

European-harmonized value-added tax (VAT) in 1973. Locally collected business rates date back to the Poor Law of 1601, without having suffered radical change. Whilst there is unity over the belief that these rates are not fit for purpose, a viable and (heaven forbid) popular alternative still evades politicians.

We are accustomed to indirect taxes raising revenue from the purchase or use of things, such as VAT and duty on petrol, tobacco and alcohol. Such taxes are deemed 'regressive' as they are not based on affordability, but in modern times they are defended when they promote social good or penalize behaviour that damages individual or collective health or the environment. In days gone by, with governments both reluctant to tax people and lacking the wherewithal to do so effectively and fairly, indirect taxation was preferred. We will see how publishers benefitted from the abolition of several paper-related duties that, leading up to the 1870 Education Act, prompted a growth in literacy, publishing and reading, whilst Prices was pleased to see the end of the candle tax (1831).

Josiah Wedgwood exploited changes to the tax on tea. The Staffordshire man was at the peak of his career when parliament passed the 1784 Commutation Act, reducing the tea tax from 119% to just 12.5%. This move frustrated smugglers, increased tax revenues (as much more tea was imported legally), generated trade for the East India Company and improved relations with China by undermining the trade of Indian opium for Chinese tea.

Between 1761 and 1834 legal tea imports increased sixfold, overtaking adulterated or smuggled stock and generating demand for Wedgwood's teapots, cups and saucers. As tap water was often unsanitary, the main source of safe drink for the masses was (weak) beer, which was hardly perfect (though Bass was not complaining). Mortality figures were highest where people lived closest together, in the growing cities created by the industrial revolution. Yet in that same period Britain's death rate fell from twenty-eight per thousand to twenty-three, accounted for almost entirely by a reduction in waterborne disease. How? As the brew's strong flavour depends on it being made with boiling water, tea drinkers who knew nothing of microbes were, unwittingly, making their new drink sterile and safe.[33]

CASE STUDY: COTTON

In the watershed story of the Amalgamated Cotton Mills Trust (ACMT), the Trust stands out as innovative, disruptive and unpopular (see the consequences for Horrockses in that company's own chapter).

Cotton industrialists dominated Lancashire's economy in the nineteenth century, wielding unprecedented local power. In 1860 they owned 2,650 mills in the county, employing 440,000 and producing half of the world's cotton textiles.[34] The 1885 merger between Horrockses and Hollins Bros, two thriving Preston giants, was regarded as sensible, as was the later merger of the enlarged company with another local rival, Crewdson, Crosses & Co., forming Horrockses, Crewdson. After World War I, however, an awakening juggernaut arrived in Lancashire's cotton market.

Landowning aristocrats both in parliament and outside still wielded significant political power: W. H. 2 Smith was blackballed at the Liberal Reform Club – and then mocked when he became a cabinet minister – for the sin of being a tradesman. The country's elite had no place for those who were not 'natural' inheritors of money or land, so tradesmen rarely sat at the top table – nor did this emerging breed of professional capitalist.

To date, the 'money-men' had operated on a small scale, benign in impact and supportive of entrepreneurs. Beable was convinced that the sole beneficiaries of cotton's money-men were the capitalists themselves. They were hunting in packs, wanting both profit and control. Hostile takeovers were rare pre 1925, as acquisition of boardroom power without the owner's consent was almost impossible before shareholding with voting rights was commonplace. Companies regarded shareholding as a way to access finance whilst avoiding dependence on a single investor, thus sharing risk and diluting investor influence. What happened here was new: acquisition by stealth.

In 1918 the ACMT was born 200 miles south of Preston amongst a breed of London businessmen who used money to make money.

The Lancashire cotton mills had previously received substantial investment from banks and had opened themselves to public subscription by local individuals, introducing public saving schemes as early as the 1860s. These accounts paid a higher rate of interest than banks and made funding available to the companies without them ceding control to investors. But cotton was in trouble; such investments were not yielding the efficiencies that the changing global economy demanded. Something new was needed: but what?

Immediately after World War I international trade was more competitive than before the war, whilst demand in the UK economy was weak, rendering Britain vulnerable to both cheap imports and a competitive export market. John Maynard Keynes would later identify the Lancashire cotton mills as a case in point: the value of cotton exports in the 1920s was 60% below that of 1913, yarn 80%; producers were losing money. The export of finished goods to India alone was down by a quarter, largely due to Japanese competition. Between 1914 and 1932 Japan's share of India's imported cotton goods rose, incredibly, from 0.1% to 45%. The whole Lancashire cotton industry had become unsustainable.[35]

By 1918 the unco-ordinated actions of individual companies could no longer address the industry's existential problems. Simply reducing prices to increase competitiveness (slashing any remaining profits) was suicidal. It was clearly necessary to manage excess capacity across the entire industry but the sequence of choices presented was stark. They could

(1) reduce capacity and costs through a combination of job losses, pay cuts and reduced hours;
(2) share that burden across the industry, which would probably involve factory closures (there were plenty of obvious candidates but no volunteers);
(3) take the above action jointly (individually had not worked) and voluntarily; or
(4) have a solution imposed, by either bankers or this new breed of capitalists, or following a collective appeal for government intervention – which would be unprecedented.

Britain was also falling behind America and Europe in technology. The nature of British textiles manufacture had barely changed over fifty years, nor was it planning to in the next fifty. High levels of debt – supported by the Micawberish hope that 'something will turn up' – tempted some firms to remain in a market they should have left. No new cotton enterprises were emerging, and mill-owners were being denied the luxury of choice.

If more tumult was needed, 1918 provided it. The burgeoning money markets of London, growing in confidence, intervened. Within a year the money-men had purchased fifteen formerly family-owned Lancashire textile companies under the banner of Amalgamated Cotton Mills Ltd, owned by the ACMT. The Trust was then floated as a massive public company in 1919. As one of the larger cotton companies, Horrockses, Crewdson was not initially targeted, but its time soon came.

Horrockses, Crewdson had £1.2 million in capital, twenty mills, 10,000 looms and 1.25 million active spindles. The ACMT offered the board £5 million, and eventually more than sixty of the eighty shareholders assented. Most of the Horrockses, Crewdson board stayed in place, with two ACMT directors added.[36] In many respects it was business as usual, but both the company's purpose and its lines of accountability had been completely changed.

Until this point directors of companies were monogamous, focused on their trade and knowledgeable of their businesses, being family members or having risen through the ranks. But the ACMT directors attracted local and press scepticism because they were not textile folk; with their feet under several board tables, where did their loyalties lie? With maximizing the returns from all their investments.

However, in this uncertain post-war economy, amalgamation, rationalization and the eradication of excess capacity did at least constitute a plan, as Keynes would later argue.

Throughout its twenty-year existence the ACMT paid no dividends to its investors. Another group of investors, purchasers of cheaper, 'preference' shares, with no voting rights, received similar treatment from the shady Sperling Finance company.

So the demise of the Lancashire cotton industry was not caused by the intervention of capitalists per se; it was desperate for recapitalization and improved productivity! But the process was led by people like James White (see 'Fraud', above) with little knowledge of textiles, no desire to do anything other than make money and neither a strategy to save the industry nor the power to implement one – short-term thinking incarnate. The injection of cash did create a brief boom for the ACMT, keeping its companies afloat and helping to preserve jobs, but did nothing for the industry's long-term prospects.

Ultimately that lack of strategy and deliberate overpricing of shares condemned the recapitalization to fail. Additionally, the companies within the ACMT shared a relatively small pool of directors, some sitting on up to eighteen boards at once, militating strongly against them reducing excess capacity by allowing individual companies to go to the wall.

Much of the industry was on short time from 1921, a temporary and then permanent measure, yet plans to compensate companies for closing could not be agreed. Precious few volunteered, not least because the available compensation would not cover their debts.

The popular assertion locally that the financiers all came from London is not entirely true. White did, so too the regularly bankrupt Horatio Bottomley, but many local investors were drawn in, including jam magnate William Hartley and his son-in-law John Higham.

Beable was concerned that the ACMT's venture reduced local autonomy, denying agency to the entrepreneurs – but he did not know what was coming next. When the ACMT failed to save the industry, the Lancashire Cotton Corporation (LCC), backed by the Bank of England, was created. In 1928 the Bank judged that retail banks' involvement in the industry posed an existential threat to the financial system itself, so the LCC pledged to take 200 cotton businesses under its wing. Keynes again backed the idea, hoping that most of the thousands of 'useless' directors of cotton companies would be dispatched.

In 1929 the LCC invested almost £1 million of Bank of England money to purchase ninety-six firms, half their goal, in order to reduce the need for further price-cutting. In 1930 many of the LCC's directors resigned after their constituent companies protested that they were losing autonomy. The

LCC limped on, with fifty-three companies under its wing by 1950, a third of Britain's textile economy. The LCC was purchased by Courtaulds in 1964 following yet another attempt to impose a solution, the 1959 Cotton Industry Act. The decline continued, worsened by cheap imports of finished goods.

People were right to be concerned about confusion and ineffective solutions in the textile industry. The pre-World War I automotive business was similar; Starley's Swift, which ceased trading in 1931, was one of dozens of car companies that failed. From 1924 Bass would also demonstrate that acquisition alone was no guarantee of success.

Social

EMPLOYEES

Victorian laws on social issues evolved but slowly, with social progress assisted by the altruism, long-sightedness or business acumen of generations of business owners. No doubt most early-nineteenth-century industrial bosses regarded their men much as their forebears regarded agricultural employees: it was in the employer's interest to put bread (if little else) on the worker's table. An early employment law, the 1823 Master and Servant Act, made disobedience by a worker a criminal offence and banned workers from 'combining' in unions.* An 1867 law reduced that Act's scope and its harshest penalties, whilst an 1871 Act legalized trade unions.

Between 1833 and 1891, laws restricted child labour and capped the hours women could work. The employment of children under 14 was banned in 1932. Some safety measures were introduced, especially in mining. Even by 1925 such legislation either did not apply to our thirty-two businesses or required such low thresholds that they readily complied.

The Liberal governments of the early twentieth century brought in a swath of social reforms, but few had a significant impact on our companies. A 1905 job-creation scheme compensated businesses for hiring the unemployed. Non-contributory pensions arrived for a select few (but not the poorest) in 1908, replaced by a contributory scheme from 1925. From 1911 the National Insurance levy compensated wage-earners for some medical costs and provided a small unemployment benefit. When he created Britain's first legally enforceable minimum wage, in 1909, the then Liberal Winston Churchill told the House of Commons:

> It is a serious national evil that any class of His Majesty's subjects should receive less than a living wage in return for their utmost exertions ... But where you have what we call sweated trades you have no organisation, no parity of bargaining, the good employer is undercut by the bad and the bad undercut by the worst.

---

*In 1864 more than 10,000 men were imprisoned under this Act.

Through his Trade Boards Act employers had to observe a minimum hourly wage – but only in specified industries. The list of low-paid jobs covered was small but was later extended, first in 1912 to include mining and some unskilled work, and again in 1919, when boards were established to set minimum pay levels by industrial sector. An agricultural wages board was restored in 1948 after a 1920 attempt proved unenforceable, and it was the last such board to be abolished (2013). Britain was one of the last industrialized countries to create a legally enforceable national minimum wage (1998).

In the nineteenth century many companies looked after their workers well, by the standards of the day. WHSmith, Colman's and Boots were early providers of pensions, following the railway companies' lead, with Lever Bros, Hartleys, Prices, Cadburys and Skippers coming next, some with non-contributory schemes. Several provided on-site access to a nurse, a dispensary and even a doctor (Colman's, Whiteleys, Boots, Mackintosh). Some indulged in profit-sharing (Cadburys, Mackintosh, Prices, Colman's, Lever Bros, Skippers and Hartleys). William Hartley acknowledged the precedent of a long-established French profit-sharing scheme, which he praised for creating 'common cause' between employer and employee. However, of 299 known profit-sharing schemes in Britain in 1912, 169 soon collapsed. A third were never viable, whilst others failed due to insufficient profit (a basic requirement!) or underwent a policy change, often associated with a takeover.[1] The values of profit-sharing were highlighted in the growth of the cooperative movement from the 1840s, notably in Lancashire. It was seen as a collective 'third way' between individualistic capitalism and state control.

The height of paternalistic concern for employee welfare is the 'model village'. Bournville and Port Sunlight are well known, but Cadburys and Lever Bros, in the absence of public agencies, were not the first to believe that employees deserved decent homes. There is an undeniable benefit to the employer from having a grateful, healthy, well-motivated, some might say 'captive' workforce, literally on their doorstep.

A typical model village has well-built, sanitary properties, innovative designs (often of Arts and Crafts movement origin), gardens, open spaces, and community and sports facilities. Some have a pub, though those with Quaker roots were 'dry'. The quality of design and architecture suggests caring values. There are at least forty model villages of industrial origin in the UK, including Bromborough Pool ('Price's Village', 1853), Bournville (Cadburys, 1879), Hartley's Village in Aintree (1886), Lever Bros' Port Sunlight (1888) and Whiteley Village for pensioners (1908). Whiteley Village near Weybridge today is bold, busy and beautiful, with many more trees than its 264 houses, open vistas and a full complement of facilities for its elderly residents. It is effectively an almshouse development, like the smaller-scale Mackintosh homes in Halifax and those of Hartleys in Colne. Whiteleys also provided dormitory accommodation for 600 London staff.

Beable also mentions Wilsontown, Lanarkshire (1808), the largest of all, sponsored by the family behind Prices candles. The last of the Wilsons' homes for 2,000 iron-workers and their families was demolished in the 1930s; the site is now a historic monument. Other well-known settlements include nearby New Lanark (1786, the earliest), Saltaire (Bradford, 1851) and New Earswick (Rowntree's Quaker village, York, 1904). As late as 1940 Wedgwood built 100 homes for employees in Barlaston, whilst Colman's bought property and added homes and facilities piecemeal to a pre-existing village at Trowse, near Norwich.

George Cadbury famously did not want his workers to live 'where a rose cannot grow', but he actually developed the company's Bournville site *after* the City of Birmingham had addressed the very situation that had inspired him to act. Joseph Chamberlain (1836–1914) became Birmingham's Liberal mayor in 1873. The electoral reformer would fly Radical, Liberal and Unionist flags over his political lifetime and sire both a Nobel Prize winner and a prime minister. His slum clearance plan and support for universal free, secular education earned him the title of 'Father of Municipal Socialism'. In Birmingham's slums, well water was polluted and piped water only sparsely available. Mayor Chamberlain improved supply and ran the water company on a break-even basis, creating affordable homes on fifty acres around Corporation Street. Between 1873 and 1880 central Birmingham's death rate fell from fifty-three per thousand to just twenty-one, such was the environmental improvement.

The jewel in the crown of industrial villages is undoubtedly Port Sunlight. Even today its wide, green spaces, aesthetic grandeur, art gallery and calming environment impress all comers; its thousands of roses are beautifully tended. It celebrates its heritage proudly, and many of its original facilities remain vibrant, 150 years on. Unilever retains its registered office there in a splendidly modest building where a huge floor mosaic of the UK's heraldic arms welcomes visitors, although inexplicably omitting any reference to nearby Wales.

At no point does *Romance* consider organized labour. The miner-led General Strike of 1926, which raised the profile of trade unions, was on the horizon, although the broader union movement was still years from its most muscular. Trade union membership in Britain was 1.5 million in 1892, rising to 8 million in 1920 but halving after the Great Depression (1934). It rallied, reaching 13 million by 1990, but has fallen steadily since, from a third of the workforce to under a quarter, stabilizing around 6.7 million today.[2] Explanations are manifold: the number seems to most clearly reflect the switch from manual to white-collar work and the rise of public sector employment. The recent decline coincides with an era of low numbers of strike days lost in Britain. The 1970s was the most militant decade, peaking at 11.7 million working days lost (September 1979), more than at any point in the 'Winter of Discontent' of 1978/9. This was partly a response to 'unfinished business' in the public sector and a weak economy, but also opposition to the incoming Thatcher government's stated determination to curb union power. Only once since 1990 (in August 2011, when the issue was public sector pensions in the austerity era) has that figure approached anywhere near a million.[3]

Perhaps Beable was complacent, believing that such organizations were not required, and choosing to highlight companies with evidence of employer altruism and a desire to share (some of) the benefits of common labour. However, such benevolence was not universal; he ignores such profound injustices as those culminating in the Match Girls' Strike and the Preston Lock-Out. The unions were strongest in the primary industries – mining, transport, shipbuilding – which he also overlooked.

The 1853 Preston Lock-Out was one of the most significant events of its type (see Horrockses). The 'masters' had cut pay across the textile town by 10%, with a hollow promise to restore it when they could. A weak market had reduced demand for clothing, affecting every Preston mill. The dispute – the longest in Lancashire's cotton history – harked back to 1847 (with precedents in 1818, 1821 and 1826, as well as intermittent strikes in Preston and elsewhere from 1849). Whilst demand and output rose in 1853 the long-promised pay restoration did not, and when Stockport workers walked out (June to August) they had Preston workers' fervent support. The Preston Masters' Association, under Thomas 2 Miller, then owner of Horrockses, mounted a common front against the workers, demanding punishment for Preston men collecting money to support the Stockport strikers, or even for those voicing support for them. Some were arrested, which enabled Miller, as a magistrate, to determine their punishments.

Eighteen thousand Preston textile workers called for their wages to be restored and for union recognition. Whilst the Stockport bosses conceded, the Preston Masters' response to industrial unrest was to crush it, triggering the lockout of October 1853 with an empty threat to employ 'scab' labour. Tensions spread: 47,000 workers were barred from 183 Lancashire mills by the month's end. In February 1854 Preston's mills reopened without settlement; the lockout became a strike and skirmishes were common but, when Miller had eleven strike leaders charged with conspiracy, resistance dwindled. The strikers returned to work in April 1854, their demands unmet.

Following the 1871 Act legalizing unions, the Trade Disputes Act of 1906 gave them substantial immunity from prosecution for damages caused by legitimate industrial action. As industrialization progressed, especially in cities, local pockets of protest against exploitation and unacceptable risk grew, became co-ordinated and made the news. The Match Girls' strike in 1888 is a case in point (see Bryant & May). Were the Bryant brothers genuinely ignorant of workers' concerns about conditions, despite three earlier strikes? Did they deliberately ignore the dangers of hazardous material? Ignorance might be bliss, but it is no excuse. Did management and workers 'reach a comprehensive settlement acknowledging legitimate grievances'? Did bosses 'capitulate to workers' demands'? Or did Wilberforce Bryant, an active Liberal, concede for party-political reasons? Whichever explanation is correct, the Match Girls brought women and trade unions together on the social agenda for the first time.

During World War I parliament convened a committee under Halifax MP John Whitley (1866–1935), the Liberal Deputy Speaker of the Commons, to examine industrial relations. This was in response to a shop stewards' initiative to organize across industries, following Churchill's minimum pay rules, but was also intended to counter any demands for workers' control prompted by the Russian Revolution. One aim of Whitley's 1917 report was to reduce the risk of strife in war time, when a common front was most desirable. A 'Whitley Council' for each industrial sector was created in 1919 to identify potential conflicts, subject them to negotiation between management and workers, and avoid industrial action. Local Whitley Councils followed.

Although some trade unionists claimed that the councils usurped their roles, there was a strong appetite for them to succeed. In 1917 the dock workers' national organizer, Ernest Bevin (1881–1951), asked to meet chocolate manufacturers to discuss industrial democracy. (Five years later Bevin, associate of Julius Elias of Odhams, would found and lead the Transport and General Workers' Union.) A Baptist, Bevin admired the Quaker approach to management and found willing partners in George Cadbury's sons Edward (1873–1948) and George 2 (1878–1954). As pacifists, the Quakers believed that unnecessary conflict should be avoided, even in the workplace. Their respectful approach, concerns about employee welfare and recent conversion to profit-sharing made them enthusiastic supporters of Whitley. The company actively encouraged its workers to join a union, a rare stance.

Cadburys was one of the first to establish company-level Whitley Councils, separately for men and women. The process got off to a good start, with managers and workers continuing the local tradition of using first names. George 2 sat on the men's council and Edward and Dorothy (1892–1987) on the women's. (Dorothy, Edward's cousin and the first woman on their board, went on to have a distinguished career in industrial relations.) However, in 1926 almost half the male and one in six of the female workers at Cadburys joined the General Strike, when 1.7 million workers took at least some part in the nine-day action called by the Trade Union Congress in support of coal miners. The Cadburys were disappointed that action had been taken against them, as they saw it, when there was no question – the workers agreed – of management being at fault. Fortunately the disruption was brief, but the councils were subsequently less influential.

Edward Cadbury was concerned that if management was too supportive, too paternalistic or caring, then dependence might grow and efficiency become compromised. He did not want to dilute principles of dignity and mutual respect, and he was keen on managers excelling, but he knew that delivering the company ethos involved walking a challenging tightrope.

The apolitical Lord Waring held informal conventions at his Kent home, Foots Cray Place, in the 1920s to encourage management and labour to debate matters of common interest. There is no record of any lasting positive change resulting, but such leadership initiatives in that era are rare. Eric Hooper, chairman of Schweppes (1948–63), showed his colours when he wrote in his review of military recruitment techniques (1960): 'Before [World War II], employers relied on the threat of the sack as their main inspiration in getting men to work; today no business can thrive unless there is mutual trust between employers and the people they employ.'

Outside the workplace, life for many employees was grim, but not as grim as for those without work. 'Poor Laws' had existed since the fourteenth century, providing a 'safety net' to preserve life in the face of extreme poverty. An 1834 Act created workhouses for those unable to find paid employment, but they were deliberately uninviting; residents were obliged to toil in return for food and lodging. Workhouses were funded by local taxes, overseen by justices of the peace.[4] 'Relief' provided outside the workhouse was made illegal, but with massive loopholes. The cost of providing workhouses landed disproportionately on the poorest areas, where demand was highest, so their quality varied considerably. By the turn of the twentieth century attitudes towards the sick, elderly and destitute were more supportive. 'Poor Law hospitals' were provided from 1885 and more comfortable local-authority accommodation for the elderly from 1900, but services remained patchy. The growth of trade unions, charities and friendly societies (forerunners of building societies) moved self-provision forward.[5]

Workhouses were used as hospitals in World War I. Despite National Insurance from 1911, the number receiving support peaked only after 1918, with 'National Assistance' being introduced in 1921. The legal concept of 'pauper' was abolished in 1929, along with workhouses, but the poor had to wait until implementation of Beveridge's 1942 report (1945 on) for the modern welfare state.

WOMEN

Every founder of our thirty-two companies, their immediate successors, and every leader up to World War II and beyond was male. Of those companies where the original brand is still dominant, only two have had an established female leader: Glaxo/GSK (since 2017) and Walgreens Boots Alliance (2020–3). In 2022 GSK's Emma Walmsley was Britain's highest-paid female CEO at £8.45 million, the only woman in the UK's top ten earners. She was paid about half what the male CEO of GSK's rival, AstraZeneca, gets, though her 50% rise in 2023 went some way to remedy this.[6]

Child mortality was falling by the mid nineteenth century, but still one child in four would not reach five years old. One in seven died in childhood even in 1925. Victorian parents, denied sophisticated twentieth-century fertility management, brought many more children into the world than grew to maturity. This made motherhood a full-time occupation – at least until family wealth permitted the outsourcing of care. Our stories contain several examples of ten or more children born to founding families who did not (yet) have the protection of affluence.

Higher education was closed to women: just nine entered the University of London in 1868, the first to allow them, but their degrees were only validated ten years later. Oxford and Cambridge did not recognize female students until 1920 and 1948 respectively. Eighteen-year old Elizabeth Taylor, later George Cadbury's second wife, passed the Cambridge entrance exam in 1876 but did not take up her place, for obvious reasons, though she received an honorary MA from Birmingham University in 1919. (In our sample, no founder went to university, and only one second-generation leader did – Festus Kelly's son, John.)

Due to the burdens of motherhood, unspoken and overt prejudice, and lack of education, few women had the opportunity to contribute meaningfully to their family business. But some did engage and influence.

Florence Boot's sense of responsible commerce earned her a board position from 1917, and Glaxo appointed a female board member in 1946. The first female member of a FTSE board appears to be Mary Baker at Barclays, 1983. Pre 1925, Christiana Hartley served as a board member, even briefly as chair following her father's death in 1922, and Lena Salmon, the financial brains at Lyons, occasionally sat on the board too, as did Dorothy Cadbury, post 1925. Outside the board Caroline Colman's attention to workers' physical and spiritual health stands out, as does the political activism of Elizabeth Cadbury, Ethel Colman and Christiana Hartley, all Liberals. Anna Smith stepped up after her husband died within months of establishing his newsagents (1792), keeping the small business going until her newborn son, the first W. H. Smith, was old enough to take charge. Mary Boot did the same from 1860 to 1874. Anna's grandson's wife, Emily, widowed when W. H. 2 Smith died in 1891, was made a viscountess in respect of *his* achievements. She held the title for life, in trust for her son, but with no right to sit in the House of Lords. John Mackintosh gave up his job to support Violet's toffee initiative, but none of the above changed the path of the male dynasties.

In some cases (Boots, Lever Bros, Colman's, Mackintosh, Hartleys, Cadburys) these women initiated social support for workers, including events and 'play'. Providing chaperones for single female workers at jamborees and picnics was standard, though the practice barely survived post World War I. The Whiteleys story, possibly involving the sexual exploitation of female subordinates, was probably the tip of an iceberg.

The tales of Pears, Hartleys and Horrockses show how some men (Thomas Barratt, John Higham and Thomas Miller, respectively) boosted their careers by marrying into business-owning families.

Female workers, being poorly educated, had lower-skilled, lower-paid, often part-time jobs. By 1919 the target industries of Churchill's minimum wage legislation employed more women than men, but careers were generally unavailable to those whose first duty was expected to be to family and children. Even in 1925 women usually left the workplace upon marriage (see nurse Philippa Flowerday at Colman's), and married women were not expected to seek regular employment, even with otherwise enlightened employers such as Cadburys. Women's income was not taken into account by the administrators of Lyons's Family Fund.

Legislation obliged employers to pay women the same as men for performing work of the same value only from 1970, and only once does Beable stumble across the issue of women's pay. William Hartley protested that he paid women workers (most of his staff) more than other local employers did, though this fell short of guaranteeing women the same pay as men for the same job. Hartley knew what he was saying: he had to attract labour, especially when fruit was in season. It was always cheaper to employ women (and children) than able-bodied men, who were better suited to heavy manual labour.

Women had no vote in national elections until 1918 and were denied the right to vote on the same basis as men until 1928. Most nineteenth-century men could not vote in general elections either, because of property rules, though some local-election franchises did allow more men, even some women, to take part. Even so, major campaigns for 'universal suffrage', such as that of the Chartists (1836–48), actually demanded 'universal *male* suffrage'. The Cadburys, John Cassell, George Palmer and Angus Watson, even Josiah Wedgwood a century earlier, actively supported women's equal voting rights.

Although both the more peaceful suffragists and the strident suffragettes had been campaigning for the vote for fifty years, the 1918 milestone was achieved almost accidentally. The twentieth century began with women's voices at a crescendo, but at the start of World War I they suspended their campaigns in order to support the war effort. As the war progressed Lloyd George realized that thousands of (male) heroes returning from the war were disenfranchised because they had not been resident in Britain over the previous twelve months! Believing that parliament was not yet ready to permit equal votes at 21, he introduced urgent legislation to right the absentees' anomaly, whilst incidentally giving the vote to 8.4 million women who were 30 or over and owned, or were married to an owner of, a qualifying property.

Labour shortages brought new work and career opportunities for women during both world wars. This changed the workforce permanently, irreversibly, leading to (amongst other changes) the Sex Discrimination Act of 1975 and subsequent Equality Acts.

FAITH

In the 1851 census 49% of England and Wales identified as Anglican, 42% as members of other Protestant faiths – dissenters, primitives and nonconformists – and 3.5% as Roman Catholics. The remaining 5% were Jews, professed nonbelievers, and tiny numbers of Hindus, Muslims and Chinese in some cities.

The Church of England was the domain of the landowning and aristocratic gentry, to which parliament and the courts were constitutionally behoven. Benjamin Disraeli once described it as the 'Tory Party at prayer' (1872); the Jew turned Anglican would have known. The aristocracy, parliament and monarch constituted the Anglican establishment.

However, the religious convictions of our companies' founders show a very different pattern (table 11). Even given the unscientific nature of our sample, over three quarters are non-Anglican Protestants, a massive predominance. How can we explain this discrepancy?

Power in Britain in the eighteenth century lay with the monarch and parliament, dominated by Tory and Whig landowners. The monarch told the landowners what he wanted them to do and appointed men to parliament's upper house, the Lords, to do it. The monarch, as 'Defender of the Faith', led the Church of England as defined by Henry VIII. To be a lord or a member of parliament one had to be 'of the faith' and make a public declaration to that effect. The atheist Charles Bradlaugh was elected MP in 1880 but prevented from sitting for refusing to make an 'Oath to God'. He was expelled from parliament four times for this failure but returned in the ensuing by-election each time. He was finally allowed to remain in 1886, persuading parliament to allow subsequent members to choose a non-religious affirmation of loyalty to the monarch, an option chosen by a record 40% of MPs in 2024.[7] Lionel Rothschild, a Liberal MP, was elected in 1847 and 1852. A Jew who declined to take the Oath, Rothschild was also denied his Commons seat but was allowed to serve on committees rather than be expelled. Jews were explicitly admitted to parliament from 1858. There were also a handful of hereditary Catholic peerages, dating from the days of Catholic monarchs.

Table 11. Religious convictions of early company leaders.

Religion		Company founders/leaders
Nonconformist Protestant	Methodist	Smith at WHSmith, Hartley, Mackintosh, Boot, Cassell, Rank at Hovis
	Quaker	Cadbury, both Huntley and Palmer, both Bryant and May, the Allen line at Glaxo, Horrocks, Gretton at Bass
	Other non-conformist	Colman (Baptist); Wedgwood (Unitarian); Starley at Swift (Salvation Army); Watson at Skippers, Lever, Newnes (all Congregationalist); Mudie (undefined)
	Other non-Anglican	Wilson at Prices, Dunlop (both Scots); Waring (unknown, Northern Irish); Schweppe (unknown, Swiss/German)
Anglican		The Bass family
Catholic		Gillow at Waring & Gillow
Jewish		The Lyons extended family, the Nathan line at Glaxo, Elias at Odhams (Elias was non-practising)

In the family of a landowning aristocrat, rich from inheritance, from wealth collected either from tenant farmers or from the commerce of agriculture, mining or slavery, the head of the household was usually a peer of the realm. Peers' families were thus usually of Anglican stock. The first son of such a family, destined to inherit the peerage, therefore had to be Anglican. He would manage the family estates. The second son might try the Commons (encountering the Oath hurdle) or go up to university. Only from 1871 did the Universities Tests Act remove formal barriers to non-Anglicans attending universities, but change was slow: the first Jew was admitted twelve years later.

Beyond a career in the Commons or academia, the second and subsequent sons of landowners might become doctors or lawyers (the university Anglican issue did not go away), become an Anglican vicar or enter the army as an officer. Military service was no option for pacifists such as Quakers.

The only career options remaining for religious nonconformists were thus agriculture, trade and manufacturing. Some temperance campaigners turned faith into an opportunity, making a career from replacing the demon alcohol with chocolate drinks (Quakers Cadbury, Rowntree and Fry) or publishing religious texts (Cassell). The last resort had become their first option.

From the mid nineteenth century there was increasing public and legal acceptance of religious diversity, but this did not stop pressure on minorities to conform. John Gretton at Bass was not the only Quaker to engage in brewing or even military service, a route also taken by later members of the Palmer and Cadbury families. The about-turn on safety standards of Quaker Wilberforce Bryant also suggests that eighteenth-century values waned over the generations.

CHARITY AND COMMUNITY

In the absence of a health service, state schools, a welfare state or significant income tax, the eighteenth and early nineteenth centuries provided no state support for communities.

Before 1800 acts of philanthropy were random and disorganized outside religious institutions and hospitals (a word that literally means 'places of hospitality'), usually run by monks or nuns. There were few calls for state intervention or secular community initiatives. Censuses, from 1801, provided data on poverty, mortality and deprivation that enabled strategic action to be taken, especially in cities. The question was, by whom?

The progressing industrial revolution made available a new source of philanthropic funding: industrialists. Many nineteenth-century benefactors with 'new money' invested not only in their workforce but also in the communities from which they drew labour. Whereas churches, local officials and early charities fretted over the need to discriminate between 'deserving' and 'non-deserving' poor, our industrial philanthropists, by and large, got on with it.

The Coutts banking family, Andrew Carnegie (see Mudies) and George Peabody (an American banker who built social housing in London from 1864) were profuse personal philanthropists who distributed wealth derived from business. The concept of a corporate business setting up a charitable foundation to distribute funds is a twentieth-century one: examples include the Joseph Rowntree Trust (1904), the Barrow Cadbury Trust (1920), the Wellcome Trust (1936; see Glaxo) and Boots Charitable Trust (1970).

Our companies were essentially local. Even where, in the twentieth century, additional operating sites were added, they were small in number, and owners' charitable behaviour remained focused on the immediate environs of each plant.

William Hartley exceeded threefold his pledge to give 10% of his lifetime income to good causes, though from 1885 a major part of those millions went to the fabric and operation of Methodist church buildings nationwide. The idea of a 'charitable cause' defined in law stems from the Statute of Mortmain of 1736, which deemed that gifts of land, or money to buy land, were illegal unless they had a 'charitable purpose' attached to them. This was to stop clergy getting personally rich from bequests and gifts made to the church in the name of some ill-defined notion of charity.[8] One way some rich people voluntarily helped the poor was direct funding, the giving of alms, typified today by the monarch's annual tradition of distributing 'Maundy money'. In the Poor Law era such practices were actively discouraged, but they were back in vogue by the early twentieth century through the medium of charities.

Prior to 1870 there was no state provision of education, leisure facilities, social services or housing. Only from 1880 were children obliged to remain at school until they were 10; schools provided by churches or Christian charities were insufficient and overcrowded. Some employers funded schools: Colman's, Lever Bros, Huntley & Palmers, Prices, Boots and Horrockses, initially for young employees but in some cases broadening their reach. W. H. 2 Smith and Mudie served on local school boards after 1870, whilst Jesse Boot, George Palmer and Elizabeth Cadbury all had schools named after them. W. H. 2 Smith, Charles Mudie and George Cadbury taught literacy personally, over decades. Some companies contributed sports facilities (Hartleys, Prices, Boots, Hovis, Colman's, Cadburys, Huntley & Palmers). 'University colleges' were eased towards full university status thanks to funding from our philanthropists at Nottingham (Boots) and Reading (Huntley & Palmers). William Lever (in his will), the Colmans and Christiana Hartley sponsored existing universities.

Lever Bros, Bass, Huntley & Palmers and Prices donated public parks. Wedgwood, Colman's and Huntley & Palmers endowed museums, Lever Bros a splendid art gallery, and Bass a suite of public buildings. WHSmith and Hartleys supported hospitals, as did Huntley & Palmers, which also sponsored a works library, then a public one. Watson gave Newcastle a war memorial (and student lodgings), whilst Whitehall's Cenotaph owes its existence to Lord Waring. Colman's even provided employees with coffins when needed.

The late nineteenth century, when many of our biggest and most effective charities were created, was a boom time for charitable funding. Charities provided ways of delivering 'public good' that were funded collectively, prioritized and organized. But how charitable were the businesses? Mackintosh's parties and cash handouts, the Hartleys profit-sharing jamborees, and Boots's, Bryant & May's, Colman's and others' holiday outings and days out – which sound like good fun – were designed to reinforce employee loyalty, usually in lieu of better pay. Inequality between employer and employee was huge, and being a benefactor looked good; employees who were weak, ill or impoverished were unproductive, as were new, casual or demotivated workers. Beneficence could address all of these issues! A cadre of able-bodied, experienced workers was worth paying for, which meant paying rates that were competitive in the local economy. The idea that the employer owed his employees or their community relief from poverty as a right was not even discussed.

POLITICS

As the industrial revolution took hold, England's minor gentry and small-business owners were, by and large, deferential Tories who believed parliament should oppose change unless the king willed otherwise. Their opponents, the paternalistic, landowning Whigs, were marginally more aspirational, believing in having a jolly good talk with the king before enacting his (hopefully compromised) wishes.

Prior to the 1832 Reform Act parliamentary constituencies bore no resemblance to those of today, and some vast populations with low levels of literacy, such as Manchester, had no representation at all. In Westminster itself, a densely populated inner city, only one in twenty adults had a vote. Even after the 1832 Act, only one in six men (8% of the population) were enfranchised. General elections took place over several days, voters having to attend a single polling station in each seat. Impersonation and bribery were rife – when elections happened – but votes were often avoided by powerful landowning families 'divvying up' multi-member seats in local areas. Many seats were 'rotten boroughs', where the number of electors was minimal (famously seven in Old Sarum in Wiltshire, 1831, which returned two MPs) and votes might literally be bought – after other forms of persuasion had failed.

The 1830 election saw Tory ranks split by disputes over Ireland and Catholic emancipation, allowing the Whigs a famous victory; electoral reform, the end of slavery and a generation of sanitary initiatives followed. Robert Peel became the first prime minister representing the newly reformed Conservative Party in 1841, and the first PM from an industrial background (textiles), as the Tories turned into something more like the twentieth-century Conservative Party. This redrawing of party lines, complicated by splits over Corn Law repeal, prompted Whig realignment too: the first government led by Liberals, their successors, was elected in 1859. Reform Acts in 1867 and 1884 brought more changes to the electoral system as half of all men were enfranchised.

The early twentieth century saw great political uncertainty. As World War I started, Britain was led by a minority Liberal government, followed by a Liberal-led coalition and a year under two different Conservative prime ministers, then a Conservative minority government, and finally the first Labour government, a minority administration led by Ramsay Macdonald (1924), which lasted ten months. All this happened in just ten years, over four general elections.

The 1918 Act that gave some women the vote also lifted the ban on voting by men in receipt of poor relief. Beable could vote, assuming he qualified, from 1881; he saw the franchise expand before his eyes.

For sixty years from 1858 power in the House of Commons was shared between Conservatives and Liberals. However, this balance is not reflected in the leadership of our thirty-two businesses. Of the eighteen families where political affiliation is known, thirteen contained declared Liberals, totalling twenty-one individuals between them, to the Conservatives' nine activists across six families (Palmers had both). The Liberal families sent eleven elected representatives to parliament, compared with eight Conservatives. The terms of eight of those MPs (five Liberals, three Conservatives) coincided in the 1906–10 parliament (see table 12).

The Parliamentary Labour Party was formed in 1906, when the party had twenty-nine MPs. Just two of our characters became Labour politicians: elected as a Liberal in 1906, Josiah 4 Wedgwood defected to Labour in 1919, serving parliament until 1943, and Odhams's Elias was a Labour peer, 1937–46. Although the first Wedgwood was elected to parliament in 1832 the patriarch was politically active long before that. When Josiah died in 1790 he had campaigned against slavery and for the French revolution, electoral reform, decent roads, and the rights of women and working people. Few MPs of any party espoused such a variety of causes, though publisher John Cassell in the 1850s was a similarly passionate advocate for educating the working classes, as was also the initially Radical Michael 2 Bass. The Radical group's independent existence dates from Henry 'Orator' Hunt and the 1819 Peterloo Massacre, but by the time of John Higham's (Hartleys) political engagement, almost a century later, they were a reformist faction within the Liberal Party.

Sir William Hartley, a progressive Liberal, declared himself solidly opposed to socialism, though both he and his daughter, Christiana, worked with Labour Party initiatives in Lancashire. His biographer explains that it was state socialism, as practised in Russia from 1917, that Hartley despised. George Cadbury had similar views, often undertaking joint initiatives with Labour in Birmingham in the early twentieth century. The views of Elizabeth Cadbury, an active Liberal post World War I, have been described as 'Christian socialist'. Angus Watson of Skippers is even more explicit. Pledging himself to equality of opportunity, he states in his 1937 autobiography: 'I am still an unashamed Liberal in politics and will remain so until Labour has finally repudiated its doctrinaire State Socialist left wing, when I may be able to throw in my lot with its uncertain future.'[9] Watson went further in his analysis. In an earlier collection of essays and speeches, *The Faith of the Businessman*, he wrote (p. 91):

> The first [task of industry] … is to provide the largest possible profits [and] return steadily increasing dividends to his investors; the other … primary obligation is to give service to the community in which both Capital and Labour are entitled to equal consideration … I venture to think that few industrialists are concerned with other than the first consideration.[10]

He went on to blame financiers for inflating wealth rather than creating it, an interesting analysis for its time.

Public honours were either won by election to parliament or conferred by the sovereign. Member, Order and Commander of the British Empire, introduced in 1917 to recognize civilian service in war time, were the first honours available to women as well as men, although female recipients were initially rare. A hundred years ago the most common public honour was 'sir', denoting either a non-hereditary knighthood or a hereditary baronetcy. The new female equivalent, 'dame', was awarded to Elizabeth Cadbury (OBE, 1918) in 1934. Pre-1958 elevations to the peerage, with a seat in the House of Lords for males, were all hereditary barons and viscounts. 'Earl' is informally reserved for some former prime ministers, the most recent being Harold Macmillan (Earl Stockton), whose peerage dates from 1984. 'Marquess' has fallen into disuse, and 'duke' describes certain royals. Life peerages all but replaced hereditary peerages in 1958, and lifetime honours were equally available (in theory) to women as they were to men. Of the only six hereditary titles created since 1965, four involved royalty and two are already extinct.

Historically such honours represent a deal between recipient and monarch, a reward for service past or promised, even a result of money changing hands. In the twentieth century such arrangements would have been less transactional, though both the Waring and du Cros (Dunlop) honours raise eyebrows. The first appointed Labour peer (John Burns, 1911) declined the honour. Several of the peers in our stories were elevated so late in life as to spend little time, if any, legislating. Some titles, with royal permission, are allowed to pass down the female line (minus parliamentary privileges) where there is no male heir.

Table 12 lists family members engaged with our companies who became politicians, knights or peers during or following their careers there. Surviving hereditary peerages are 'extant'; others are extinct through lack of an heir.

Table 12. Political honours and activism amongst company leaders.
(Continued on next four pages.)

Name	Party	Status
Bass, Michael 2 T.	Radical/Liberal	MP, Derby, 1848–83
Bass, Michael 3 A.	Liberal	MP, Stafford, 1865–8; Staffordshire Eastern, 1868–85; Burton, 1885–6
	—	Baronet, 1882–6
	—	House of Lords: Baron Burton of Rangemore and Burton-on-Trent, 1886–d.1909, extinct 1909; Baron Burton of Rangemore and Burton-on-Trent, 1897–d.1909, extinct 2013[a]
Bass, Hamar	Liberal	MP, Tamworth, 1878–85; West Staffordshire, 1885–98
Bass, Nellie (daughter of Michael 3)	—	2nd Baron Burton (via 1897 peerage), 1909–62, extinct[b]
[Bass] Gretton, John	Conservative	MP, Derbyshire South, 1895–1906; Rutlandshire, 1907–18; Burton, 1918–43
Boot, Jesse	Liberal	Baronet, 1909–29
		House of Lords: 1st Baron Trent, 1929–d.31
Boot, John Campbell	—	House of Lords: 2nd Baron Trent, 1931–d.56, extinct
[Boots] Blyth, Sir James	Conservative	House of Lords: Baron Rowington, 1995–2018, life peer[c]
[BP] Cargill, John	—	Baronet, 1920–d.54
[BP] Greenway, Charles	—	Baronet, 1919–27
		House of Lords: 1st Baron Greenway, 1927–d.34, extant
[BP] Fraser, William	—	House of Lords: 1st Baron Strathalmond, 1936–d.70, extant
[BP] Cadman, John	Conservative	House of Lords: 1st Baron Silverdale, 1937–d.41, extant
[BP] Peter Walters	—	Knighthood, 1984
[BP] Browne, John	—	Knighthood, 1998–2001
	Cross-bench	House of Lords: Baron Madingley, 2001–, life peer[d]

Table 12. *Continued.*

Name	Party	Status
Cadbury, George	Liberal	Councillor, Birmingham, 1870s
Cadbury, Elizabeth	Liberal	Councillor, Birmingham, 1919–24
		Parliamentary candidate, 1923
		Dame, 1934–d.51
Cadbury, Adrian	—	Knighthood, 1977–d.2015
Cadbury, Dominic	—	Knighthood, 1997–
Colman, John Jeremiah	Liberal	Councillor, Norwich, 1859–71
		MP, Norwich, 1871–d.95
Colman, Ethel (daughter of John Jeremiah)	Liberal	Lord Mayor of Norwich, 1923–4
		Deputy Mayor of Norwich, 1926–7
Colman, Jeremiah	—	Baronet, 1907–d.42
[Dunlop] du Cros, Harvey	Conservative	MP, Hastings, 1906–d.8
[Dunlop] du Cros, Arthur	Conservative	MP, Hastings, 1908–13
	Unionist	MP, Clapham, 1918–22
	—	Baronet, 1916–d.55
[Glaxo] Nathan, Alec	Liberal/Labour	Always voted Liberal or (later) Labour, d.1954
[Glaxo] Jephcott, Harry	—	Knighthood, 1946
[Glaxo] Girolami, Paul	—	Knighthood, 1988
[Glaxo] Sykes, Richard	—	Knighthood, 1994
[Glaxo] Witty, Andrew	—	Knighthood, 2012
Hartley, William	Liberal	Councillor, Liverpool, 1895–8
	—	Knighthood, 1908–d.22
Hartley, Christiana	Liberal	Councillor, Southport, 1920–32
		Mayor of Southport, 1921
[Hartleys] Higham, John	Liberal/Radical	MP, Sowerby, 1904–18

Table 12. *Continued.*

Name	Party	Status
Horrocks, John 2	Tory	Councillor, Preston, 1796–1802
		MP, Preston, 1802–d.4
Horrocks, Sam	Tory	MP, Preston, 1804–12
[Horrockses] Hermon, Edward	Conservative	MP, Preston, 1868–d.81
[Horrockses] Hollins, Frank	—	Baronet, 1907–d.24, extinct 1963
[Hovis] Rank, J. Arthur	—	House of Lords: 1st Baron Rank, 1957–d.72, extinct
Kelly, John	Conservative	MP, Camberwell, 1886–92
Lever, William	Liberal	MP, the Wirral, 1906–9
		Baronet, 1911–17
		House of Lords: 1st Baron Leverhulme, 1917–d.25, extinct
		Viscount Leverhulme, 1922–5, extinct
Lyons, Joseph	—	Baronet, 1911–d.17
[Lyons] Salmon, Isidore	—	Knighthood, 1933–d.41
	Conservative	Councillor, London County Council, 1907–25
		MP, Harrow, 1924–41
[Lyons] Salmon, Samuel I.	Conservative	Councillor, London County Council, 1949–65; Greater London Council, 1965–d.7
Mackintosh, John	Liberal	Councillor, Halifax, 1913–d.20
Mackintosh, Harold	—	Knighthood, 1922–35
		Baronet, 1935–48
	Independent/ Liberal	House of Lords: 1st Baron Mackintosh, 1948–57
		1st Viscount Mackintosh, 1957–d.64, extant
Newnes, George	Liberal	MP, Newmarket, 1885–95; Swansea, 1900–d.10
	—	Baronet, 1895–d.1910
Newnes, Frank	Liberal	MP, Bassetlaw, 1906–10

Table 12. *Continued.*

Name	Party	Status
[Odhams] Elias, Julius	Labour	House of Lords: 1st Baron Southwood, 1937–44; 1st Viscount Southwood, 1944–d.6; extinct
Palmer, George	—	Councillor, Reading, 1850–?
	—	Mayor of Reading, 1857–8
	Liberal	MP, Reading, 1878–85
Palmer, George 2 W.	Liberal	MP, Reading, 1892–5, 1898–1904
Palmer, Walter	Conservative	MP, Salisbury, 1900–6
	—	Baronet, 1904–d.10
Pears, Andrew 2	Liberal	Activist
[Pears] Dewar, Sir Thomas	—	House of Lords: 1st Baron Dewar, 1919–d.30, extinct[e]
Pearson, Arthur	Liberal	Baronet, 1916–d.21
[Schweppes] Hooper, Eric	—	Knighthood, 1956–62
		House of Lords: 1st Baron Hooper, 1962–d.3, extinct[f]
[Skippers] Watson, Angus	Liberal	Baronet, 1945–d.61[g]
		Councillor, Newcastle-upon-Tyne, 1930s
Smith, William Henry 2	Conservative	MP, Westminster, 1868–85 (Minister, 1874–80); Strand, 1885–d.91 (Minister, 1886–d.91)
Smith, Emily (widow of W. H. 2)	—	1st Viscountess Hambleden, 1891–d.1913[b]
Smith, Frederick	Conservative	MP, the Strand, 1891–1910
		House of Lords: 2nd Viscount Hambleden, 1913–d.28, extinct
[Swift] Starley, John K.	Liberal	Councillor, Coventry, 1890–6
Waring, Sam 2	—	Baronet, 1919–22
		House of Lords: 1st Baron Waring, 1922–d.40, extinct[h]

Table 12. *Continued.*

Name	Party	Status
Wedgwood, Josiah 2	Reform (Liberal)	MP, Stoke-on-Trent, 1832–5
Wedgwood, Cecil	Liberal?	Mayor, Stoke-on-Trent, 1910–11
Wedgwood, Josiah 4	Liberal	MP, Newcastle-under-Lyme, 1906–19
	Labour	MP, Newcastle-under-Lyme, 1919–42
		Cabinet: Chancellor of Duchy of Lancaster, 1924
		Mayor, Newcastle-under-Lyme, 1930–2
		House of Lords: 1st Baron Wedgwood, 1942–d.3, extant
[Wedgwood] Bryan, Arthur	—	Knighthood, 1976–d.2011

[a] The Bass baronetcy passed to Michael 3's nephew (Hamar's son) William Bass, who died before inheriting the 1886 peerage. Michael 3 was given a second peerage in 1897, which allowed the title to be passed to his daughter before reverting to the male line.

[b] See note a. Women were not permitted to sit in the Lords.

[c] The knighthood of James Blyth (Boots) predated his time at the company. He retired from the Lords in 2018.

[d] Lord Browne was a 'People's Peer', appointed for life following public nomination. Designated in 1974, 'cross-bench' peers are independent of party.

[e] Tommy Dewar was a Conservative MP (1900–6), knighted 1902, before joining Pears.

[f] Eric Hooper died before he could join the Lords.

[g] Watson's honour was for war service, not industry.

[h] Waring's appointment was embroiled in Lloyd George's 'cash for honours' scandal.

The propensity of MPs to change seats is marked; sometimes boundary changes prompted this, but geographical fealty was not considered essential. The Newnes family, for example, had no known prior connection with Swansea, Newmarket or Bassetlaw, nor did the du Cros family with their seats: the idea that voters might expect to see their Member occasionally dates from later in the twentieth century!

A hundred years ago there was a clear link between business careers and openings to political life – almost an obligation – but in the century since 1925 we are not comparing like with like. The companies are at a later stage of development, the family heritage was already disappearing by 1925, and we are confined not just to the same (already small) sample but to one that is more elderly and getting ever smaller.

In contrast to back then, politicians with a business-management background today tend to be Conservatives, not Liberals. As Labour MPs grew in
numbers they initially came from working-class backgrounds, later coming
from families with working-class parents; today they come disproportionately
from the public sector.[11]

Life peers appointed from a senior business background directly into min-
isterial office are not unknown. Recent examples include

- David Sainsbury, Sainsbury's, trade minister, 1998–2006 (Labour, retired
  2021);
- Digby Jones, CBI, trade minister, 2007–08 (Labour, then cross-bench,
  retired 2020);
- Paul Myners, Marks & Spencer/Bank of England, City minister, 2008–10
  (Labour, then cross-bench, d. 2022);
- Ian Livingston, BT, trade minister, 2013–15 (Conservative);
- James Timpson, Timpson's, prisons minister, 2024– (Labour).

In 2019 one peer in five had advisory, consultancy or director's roles with one
or more businesses, half of which were connected to finance. Around twenty-
five worked with energy companies, and the same number with defence
industries.[12]

Archie Norman is the only person ever to chair a FTSE 100 company
(Asda) whilst serving in the Commons. The Conservative MP (1997–2005)
subsequently chaired ITV (2010–16) and Marks & Spencer (2017–).

Royal warrants are issued for five years at a time, and the 686 issued by
Elizabeth II have been technically void since her death in 2023, although
companies can reapply for warrants from King Charles. Warrants are currently
held by Boots, Schweppes and Price's Candles. Jaguar Land Rover, of Swift
heritage, also has the honour. In 2024 Unilever and Cadburys were amongst
100 previously recognized companies dropped from the new king's list.

CASE STUDY: SLAVERY

Britannia ruled the waves in the eighteenth century, both in trade and in
naval support of her empire. She was thus, unsurprisingly, engaged in the
most lucrative high-volume trade the world had hitherto known: shipping
slaves from West Africa to the Americas.

Slavery includes both human trafficking and bonded labour, historically
providing a cheap workforce for, amongst others, plantations, mines and
domestic service. British people made money from trading slaves and using slave
labour itself, driving the Atlantic cycle of the eighteenth century. This 'trade
triangle' included moving the products of slavery from America to Britain and

a variety of goods (guns from Birmingham, candles, clothing) from Britain to African colonies. Other European countries had similar arrangements, and there were also slave routes from East Africa to Persia and India. Some African leaders colluded with traders, selling convicts into the system.

Slave labour was used in British and other colonies of the West Indies and America to produce sugar, molasses, cotton, tobacco, cocoa, rice, timber, construction materials, mahogany, rum and precious metals. Slaves were commodities to be bought or sold – for life. Many died young, not least in the unsanitary conditions of slave ships. Over 300 years perhaps 12 million slaves were sent across the Atlantic, of which over a million died before they got to the Americas. British ships transported a quarter of the total; only Portuguese vessels carried more.

At least six of our companies used sugar as a raw material; it served baking, brewing, chocolate and the rise in tea consumption, as well as the 'coffee shop culture' of financial wheeler-dealing. Three quarters of all plantation sugar came to Britain. Sugar was first imported to Britain from the Caribbean in the early seventeenth century, with trade formalized in 1660 by the formation of the Royal African Company.

Britain was the world's biggest consumer of sugar, which the government, of course, taxed. The duty was scrapped in 1874 as it was less effective at raising revenue once the slave trade had ended. This reduction in market price was dressed up as helping poorer people access a high-energy 'super-food'! Impressive accounts of the damage that dietary sugar could do, especially to children, were published as early as 1633 (Dr Hart) and 1769 (Dr Buchan).[13] Sugar also started to be available from other sources: the first factory to process British-grown sugar beet, in Norfolk, opened as late as 1910.

Every liberal with a conscience could support the abolition of slavery, but the trade was maintained by the greed of slavers and others, backed by political inertia. As industrialists grew more powerful they became increasingly outspoken opponents, in line with their non-establishment political and religious affiliations (see above).

The British slave trade peaked in the 1750s, when one ship in every four leaving Liverpool was somehow involved, as witnessed by city resident Thomas Bentley, Wedgwood's friend and collaborator. Slavery was already declining when British ships were banned from carrying slaves in 1807, and it was made illegal for Britons and the empire to be involved at all from 1833. Other European countries followed suit. The ban obliged the Bank of England to spend £20 million compensating companies and families for their loss of 'property' (800,000 slaves).[14] Despite this huge cost, this was victory for the abolitionists.

But commercial efficiency did not favour empty ships, so in the 1840s the British government encouraged people such as George Wilson (Prices) to make use of a cheap and ready supply of West African palm oil. Lever would later exploit the same commodity.

Palm oil created clean, slow-burning, odourless, solid candles – plus a waste product (olein) that proved a valuable lubricant. Prices advertising subliminally associated its new palm oil candles with the popular ending of slavery. Today palm oil is used in many foods, as well as soaps, shampoos and cosmetics, and as a biofuel. Wilson could not have realized that, 200 years later, irresponsible large-scale cultivation of palm oil would cause widespread deforestation and biodiversity loss, contribute significantly to climate change, and be associated with human rights abuses.

In 1901 the head of procurement at Cadburys, George's nephew William Cadbury (1867–1957), was told that some farms on São Tomé and Princípe – Portuguese-controlled West African islands from which the company obtained half its raw cocoa – still used slaves. The rumour proved true: a plantation's selling price of £3,555 was found to include 200 labourers. Although Portugal had abolished slavery in 1875, William found that slaves were still being traded between the islands and Angola, a Portuguese colony. Together with a missionary who had witnessed the trade, William – a director of the Anti-Slavery Society – went to Portugal in 1903 to confront the authorities and plantation owners. He was told that legislation to both ban the trade and return former slaves to Angola was 'in hand', but William was unconvinced. The Portuguese also reminded him that much of the aggressive colonialism in Africa associated with slavery was linked to British expansionism, led by the likes of Cecil Rhodes, who had died in 1902. William shared his concerns with fellow Quaker chocolatier, Joseph Fry.

Meanwhile a journalist picked up the story. Henry Nevinson of *Harper's Magazine* travelled to the islands and found conclusive evidence of 30,000 slaves on São Tomé and 3,000 on Princípe, 'volunteers' transported from Angola. His report was published in 1905, and in 1906 an independent investigator appointed by Cadburys, James Burtt – who had postponed his trip by nine months in order to learn Portuguese – confirmed the figures. Only 5% of São Tomé's cocoa came to Britain, rendering any potential unilateral boycott ineffective. William and George 2 took their concerns to Britain's foreign secretary, Sir Edward Grey, but he was busy negotiating a gold deal with a Portuguese government in political turmoil, so would not engage. The trio of Cadburys, Rowntree and Fry's agreed to give the government more time, but this delay had consequences.[15]

In 1908 the *Evening Standard* accused the Quakers of hypocrisy: profiting from slavery whilst dragging their feet on boycotting the islands. Cadburys sued for libel in Birmingham's courts, where the former solicitor general, Sir Edward (later Baron) Carson, defended the *Standard* whilst his regular

sparring partner, the Jewish Liberal MP Rufus Isaacs, led the Cadburys side.*
The *Standard*, owned by the Liberal Arthur Pearson (see Pearsons in 'The Four
Publishers'), had previously praised the company's practices, and Isaacs called
the Liberal foreign secretary as a pro-Cadburys witness. It was December
1909, and Liberals on both sides chose their courtroom words diplomatically,
aware that a general election which jeopardized their political majority was
due the following month. Cadburys won their case (plus substantial costs),
after seven days of trial. However, following barely an hour of deliberation the
jury awarded damages of just one farthing (a quarter of a penny), indicating
that they had not been fully convinced that the delay in acting against slavery
was unavoidable.

In early 1909 British importers had organized a collective boycott of São
Tomé and Princípe, though as American and German companies declined to
join them, little changed. But the publicity from the Cadburys libel case may
have helped: later that year Portugal did finally ban the trade. Concerns about
slavery in Angola continued to be raised until independence from Portugal
in 1975.

Modern slavery has thrived in the globally sourced world of 'fast fashion'.
Horrockses did not survive as a company far into the twenty-first century, but
had it done so, today's world of trafficking and sweatshops could have been
an issue for its supply chain. The profile of modern slavery was raised in 2013
when a defective eight-floor building, Rana Plaza in Dhakka, Bangladesh,
collapsed, killing more than 1,200 and injuring double that number. 'We
don't use sweatshops,' yelled British fashion houses and high street vendors as
one, before having to explain how their garment labels came to be found in
the rubble.

The short list for 'Theresa May's finest hour' is not a long one, but the
Modern Slavery Act of 2015, a world first, must be high up on it. She implemented the Act as home secretary and continued to champion the cause as
prime minister and since.[16] The Act boosted supply-chain transparency and
reporting to a unprecedented level, obliging larger companies to make an
annual statement of active compliance. Although the Act focuses on employment, it also impacts prostitution and domestic service. It is supported by an
independent commission, and – averaged over five years to 2023 – action has
resulted in roughly one prosecution per day in Britain. London has seen a
12% rise in modern slavery over three years since 2021, a trend not confined

---

*Carson successfully prosecuted Oscar Wilde (1895) and won Lever Bros' libel case
against Lord Northcliffe (1907).

to abuse of foreign nationals, according to an independent report endorsed by the UK's Anti-Slavery Commissioner.[17]

What has been exposed is the darkness around supply chains. Companies can always identify their tier-one suppliers, but mystery used to surround lower-tier providers, where child and bonded labour, excessive hours, poverty pay, inhuman working conditions, and trafficking could all be found. Such appalling conditions sound 'third world', but sweatshops were found even in cities such as modern Leicester.

Asos currently owns the dormant Horrockses brand. Its comprehensive approach to exposing and tackling modern slavery has included a partnership with the campaigning charity Anti-Slavery International.[18]

CASE STUDY: THE WRITTEN WORD

Publishing illustrates well how personal mission, the 'public good' and legislation can combine, with both positive and unintended consequences. Beable chose to highlight four publishers, a librarian and a bookshop following a period when the public appetite for the written word had surged.

Although newspapers, tracts (religious and political) and contracts had existed for many years, not all could read them. Stage plays were popular, as audiences did not need to be able to read to enjoy them, and Charles Dickens started his career not publishing books but giving public readings of his work.[19] In 1851 two thirds of males were literate, to a degree, but barely half of females. The 1870 Education Act boosted literacy so that by 1901 both men and women enjoyed basic literacy rates of 97%. This opened up publishing to new audiences, increasing demand for reading for pleasure, betterment, information and news – a publisher's dream!

Advertising duty was abolished in 1853, newspaper stamp duty in 1855 and paper duty in 1861, smoothing the way for public access to the 'mass media'. The first manual typewriter went on sale in 1868; Edison invented an electric one just four years later.

Before radio and television, 'the media' meant newspapers and magazines. Britain's favourite novelists, essayists and humourists passed through the offices of Odhams, Newnes and Pearsons.

This surge in literacy also fuelled the success of Mudies, making reading not only useful and enjoyable but fashionable too. From his father's experience as a bookseller Charles Mudie knew that demand for the written word was such that lending books would not work commercially without considerable scale. Both Boots and WHSmith followed him into the lending business, and with neither rival financially dependent upon the trade, their libraries persisted for many decades. When Mudie died in 1890 his business was at its peak: the beneficiaries of the 1870 Act were reaching adulthood.

But if legislation accidentally created opportunities for Mudies, at a time when public libraries were scarce, it also undermined it. Although a law of 1850 allowed local authorities to raise money to build and staff libraries (though not to stock their shelves), 'allowing' is not 'requiring'. By 1885 just a quarter of Britain's population had free access to publicly funded libraries.[20] Between 1882 and 1929 Andrew Carnegie's philanthropic library-building programme empowered the competition to Mudies by funding 660 new buildings across Britain. Carnegie, a Scot who had made his fortune in American steel, funded libraries only where others undertook to operate them without his further subsidy. Some on both sides of the Atlantic resented his intervention, claiming that he had gained his surplus fortune from paying his workers so little. Furthermore, he had used thugs to shoot protesting workers in the 1892 Homestead strike in Pittsburgh. Both charges were undeniable.

Mudie simply could not compete with free access to the written word.

The core technology of printing changed little in the nineteenth century, other than in scale: automation and steam power allowed previously unimagined quantities of printed material to flow from the presses. In the last half century many aspects of publishing have been rendered unrecognizable. This combination of legislation, literacy and technology – which started with improvements in domestic lighting – led to a boom in reading. Where would train passengers have been without WHSmith?

CASE STUDY: THE GREAT EXHIBITION

Fourteen of our companies were trading at the time of the 1851 'Great Exhibition of the Works of Industry of All Nations'. That the Hyde Park jamboree appears in so many of Beable's stories is no surprise, as a third of the British population visited the fair. It was undoubtedly a major showcase of the achievements of the industrial revolution, an international celebration (featuring Britain, its colonies and forty-four other nations) and a robust response to a French version of a few years earlier. The exhibition was organized by a committee under Prince Albert, the glass and steel 'Crystal Palace' was designed by Sir Joseph Paxton, the main business sponsor was Schweppes, and Cassells printed the official programme.

Just four years earlier Britain had experienced a banking crisis, a blow to economic confidence caused by a combination of events: the Irish famine, causing a big rise in government borrowing; the subsiding of the railway boom; and a rash of failures of non-bank lenders. The 1851 exhibition was part of the recovery plan.

The five-month festival of technology, manufacturing, engineering and science, initiated by the (later 'Royal') Society for the Arts, was a commercial success and a bold economic stimulus. It promoted the study of 'science, arts and commerce', involving writers, artisans, business people and busy diplomats. Its legacy includes countless international expos, an era of diplomacy and cultural understanding, and, in 'Albertopolis' on London's nearby Exhibition Road, three proud and distinguished national museums built from its profits, not to mention a centenary event, the 1951 Festival of Britain. The exhibition was a museum in itself: industrial processes working before the visitor's eyes, an opportunity to see artefacts from around the globe (such as Māori carvings) and a grand day out in the company of celebrity visitors. The whole building was a massive educational aid with a 138-by-500-metre footprint.

Trains ran special services with discounted tickets, and Thomas Cook's travel agents had a field day as peak daily attendance topped 100,000. People could peer down a microscope, witness voting machines of the future, even 'spend a penny' to enjoy a moment of privacy, obtained by putting a coin in a slot.

Bryant & May discovered here the power of red phosphorus, Pears won the top award for soap, and Huntley & Palmers got a bronze award for its biscuits. From tourist William Whiteley's visit came the inspiration for the first department store. Later, Lyons's original purpose was to cater for those who emulated the exhibition.

No other planned event in the Victorian era inspired so many across so many fronts. It was a beacon raising the profile of culture, technology and science and generating commercial ideas for decades to come.

And yet ... many criticisms were justified. It was extravagant and excessive, some argued, when those tackling social problems needed the money more. It was exclusive, with cheap trains not compensating for relatively expensive tickets, and it promoted tasteless tat. It glorified colonies, empire and power in an uncritical, even insensitive manner, superficially presenting colonial artefacts for ogling with little context or explanation. Whilst it provided a showcase for British manufacturing, it featured foreign businesses too, promoting 'unnecessary' competition. Many of the commercial benefits it brought proved short-lived.

Five months after it opened, the Crystal Palace was relocated in all its glory to an area of South London to which it gave its name. It stood there, proudly, for almost a century before burning down in 1936. Brunel's two water towers, which powered its spectacular fountains, were demolished in 1941 to prevent enemy bombers using them as navigational aids to locate strategic targets in London.

Environment

U nlike comparable economies the UK never recovered from the 2008
crash. Growth (as measured by GDP per head), productivity and
business investment have been stagnant since then (no doubt these
are connected), whilst real wages are barely back to their pre-Covid, let alone
pre-crash level. Shareholders, executives and financiers have suffered no such
indignities.

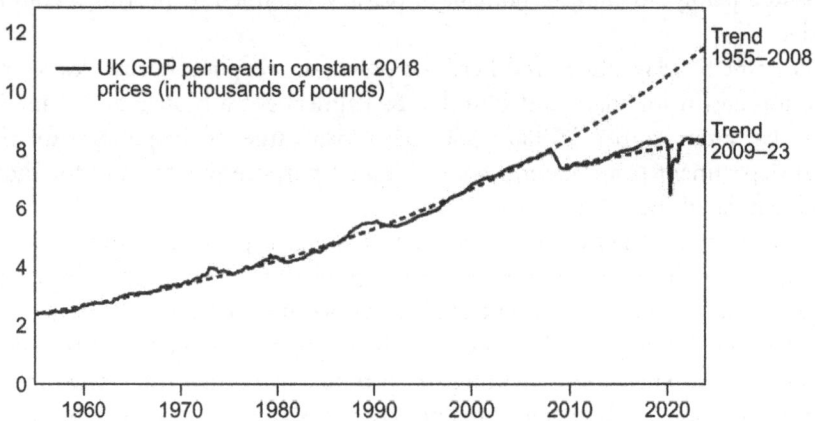

Figure 6. Trends in UK living standards. (*Source: Financial Times.*)

Looking at GDP per head reveals how the manna of GDP is distributed
amongst us. Figure 6 shows that recent living standards, by this measure, are
running well below the prior trend (the 2020–1 'blip' is Covid).[1]

But why does GDP feature in our 'Environment' chapter?

GDP'S 'EXTERNALITIES'

Simon Kusnetz (1901–1985), a Jewish Russian émigré, arrived in the US in
1922 and received his master's degree in economics shortly after *Romance* was
published. His influence was profound. Intrigued by how national income

changed and how it related to the woolly concepts of 'welfare' and 'progress', he created GNP – gross national product (today gross national income, GNI) – and the related GDP (gross domestic product).* GDP is a superficially simple but actually highly complex instrument often criticized for its subjectivity. Nevertheless it is widely used by countries to measure and compare economic performance. Technically,

$$GDP = C + I + G + (X - M)$$

or consumption + investment + government spending + (exports – imports). Every element is subject to error, rounding, incomplete assessment, baseline adjustment, time lags, estimation, multiple weightings etc.[2] The International Monetary Fund says that GDP 'measures the monetary value of final goods and services – that are bought by the final user – produced in a country in a given period'.

The 'given period' is usually a quarter or a year, and GDP outcomes are routinely re-evaluated retrospectively. Critics argue that GDP's selectivity, focusing only on monetary value, omits real welfare criteria. Surely, they argue, you should not be omitting cultural or educational activity. Why does 'final goods and services' include the manufacture of guns but not performing live music or providing nursery care? Wars and hurricanes are good for GDP as they generate economic growth! Kusnetz himself wrote, in 1934: 'The welfare of a nation can scarcely be inferred from a measure of national income.'

GDP was adopted by America in 1937 to monitor the nation's recovery from economic depression, and in 1944 at the Bretton Woods conference it was proclaimed the world's standard tool for measuring economic progress.[3] Governments can focus either on total GDP or on the often less flattering but slightly more realistic 'GDP per capita'.

In 1972 Bhutan went to the other extreme, espousing 'Gross National Happiness', but there are challenges there too. In 2016 Ireland announced that it was abandoning GDP as its principal measure of 'progress'. Alternative mechanisms, such as Michael Porter's Social Progress Index, appear to better measure how well a state and its people are faring. Porter shows that national wealth and social progress *do* grow hand in hand, but only where GDP per capita is under $10,000; in richer countries (those most wedded to GDP) increasing wealth bears no correlation to social advance.[4]

The biggest concern about GDP is its 'externalities'. These are the (allegedly non-economic) consequences of economic activity that are deemed 'external'

---

*GNP is GDP plus residents' earnings from abroad and foreigners' earnings within the country.

to the economy. Traditionally, the environmental and social aspects of ESG would both have been so classified.

The powerhouse of any western economy is its companies, generating the inherent 'goods' of economic growth – jobs, rising living standards and consumer choice – but economic activity produces 'bads', too. These include pollution (of air, water and land), net ecological damage (to biodiversity, habitats, landscape and food chains), human rights issues (including modern slavery, forced or child labour, and freedom of association), resource depletion, climate change, economic inequality and migration born of desperation. None of these externalities were routinely measured or quantified, maybe not even noticed, in the past. Today each could justifiably be termed a 'crisis'.

In the 200 years following the industrial revolution there was no tradition of asking companies who take from or damage the environment to restore, or compensate for restoring, the status quo ante, so such 'liabilities' went uncosted. 'Externality' came to mean 'can be disregarded' or 'not our problem'. Uncosted items do not appear on balance sheets and are thus (conveniently) of no concern to Friedmanites; uncosted damage went unmitigated. The default position was that where a remediation cost existed it was borne by the public purse. When economists did study this they found such costs either fiendishly difficult to calculate or financially unsustainable, necessitating higher taxes and more public spending. The necessary supporting mechanism – some internalization of externalities, the routine calculation of externality costs at source – never happened, yet GDP continues to be the touchstone of national economic (and therefore business) success. Meanwhile externalities such as greenhouse gas emissions remain poorly handled by mainstream economists.

The 1950s to 1970s was a hectic time for business, as we have seen. Mergers and acquisitions, the dash for growth, and the rise of profit maximization were all peaking, and the western economy was in overdrive. It is no coincidence that this was when the planet abandoned its homoeostatic approach to global temperature and rose – no, soared – towards 400 parts per million of carbon dioxide (CO_2) in the atmosphere for the very first time, principally due to the excessive burning of coal and oil. This had consequences for global warming, as the carbon crisis was delicately called for decades, a crisis that shows no signs of abating, let alone reversing. There is more on climate change later, not least in figure 7.

Carbon pricing (charging for CO_2 emissions) has been a belated response to the need to control one externality, but the price needs to be high, unavoidable and globally consistent if it is to change behaviour. Carbon trading (whereby excessive emitters buy unused emission permissions from low emitters) is a step in the right direction – but only a step. In 2022 barely twenty countries outside Europe either taxed carbon emissions or had an emissions trading scheme (almost all European countries do). Europe generally levies the highest cost (in excess of $60 per metric ton of CO_2 equivalent), though Uruguay's is the very highest at $167. Most non-European systems charge under $20, which is no deterrent to high emissions. Ultimately the only way to reduce carbon emissions and control climate change is to emit (a lot) less carbon.

Recent alternative models deal with externalities in a business-like fashion, including Dame Ellen Macarthur's circular economy (2010)[5] and Kate Rowarth's 'Doughnut Economy' (2017).[6] Both encourage us to regard the planet's resources as finite, because they are. The former sees waste as a resource; the latter defines 'floors' (minimum levels of consumption) to underscore the dignity of life and 'ceilings' (maximums) to reflect resource availability. The former is finding traction amongst major companies keen to avoid running out of resources, including our top survivors WHSmith, GSK, Unilever and Boots. The Doughnut theory is informing local economic planning in a growing number of communities across the globe.

Externalities threaten civilization, nature and the very planet. Addressing them must be an urgent priority both for business (for which there is a business case) and society.

CSR AND ESG

It is easy to dismiss much of the activity today branded 'CSR' as paid time off for happy employees sporting corporate T-shirts. Folk enjoy cleaning, painting, 'doing good for the community' and charitable fundraising (too often wearing unflattering lycra), despite it having little if any long-term, measurable impact: nothing really changes as a result.

Unfortunately, for much of the last half century what passes for CSR has been variations upon this superficial theme. In contrast, as Beable makes sure to highlight, his entrepreneurs used their (considerable) wealth to concretely improve the communities in which their employees lived; they had good, practical reasons for such engagement.

The term 'corporate social responsibility' was coined by the American Keynesian economist Howard Bowen in 1953, forty years after the first business-based charity was established and fifty since Carnegie, Burdett-Coutts and Rockefeller had demonstrated corporate philanthropy at scale. Bowen's CSR had three equal elements.

- *Generating jobs and economic growth.* This is the de minimis role of business in society. Like patriotism, when championed alone this clause represents the 'last refuge of a scoundrel'. Friedmanism decries further extension of CSR as divorced from the maximization of profit.

- *Behaving ethically* in respect of what we now call stakeholders; an appreciation that owners are not the only ones with a 'stake' in business success, and that 'success' has both quantitative and qualitative aspects. Today this is the 'G' (governance) of ESG.
- *Helping to improve the conditions of the society ('S') and environment ('E')* in which the company operates.

Note that Bowen used the word 'improve' in 1953, which goes beyond today's definition of sustainability![7] He is right: the planet needs to be repaired before we can risk behaving in ways that are merely 'sustainable'. As the pendulum swung towards Friedmanism these radical views cost Bowen his job at the University of Illinois.

Legitimate doubts about the practice of CSR (not specifically about Bowen's theory) started to emerge in the 1970s.

- It is difficult to measure the outcomes of CSR and therefore cost it or demonstrate its efficiency. Companies bidding for UK public sector contracts today can be asked to demonstrate their 'social value', their positive impact on the world, in a quantifiable format. The 2012 Public Services (Social Value) Act allowed such behaviour but did not mandate it; 2020 procurement guidance was more robust and was consolidated by the 2023 Procurement Act. Such practices have been particularly well developed in the construction industry (as with Wates, above).
- Companies usually record CSR in terms of input, not outcomes. Hours of employee volunteering and the quantity of money raised for charity are the tools of change, not change itself.
- CSR activity (such as team volunteering) is often used as something else: team-building, skill-building or a (paid) time-off reward, with Bowen's third purpose deprioritized. Used constructively, it can be a major contribution to employee skill development and even skills exchange between employees and the community, creating a positive and lasting impact.
- CSR activity is often unrelated to the company mission. It tends to be voluntary (thus not inclusive), superficial and temporary. A business–charity partnership where the partners have no element of common mission or longer-term commitment is a missed opportunity.

The key validating question should be: 'What positive, long-term difference did it make?' The relationships between GSK and Save the Children and between Boots and Macmillan Cancer Care led to clear, positive, long-term social impacts (and mutual gains). In the first instance the needs of vulnerable children in low-vaccine communities in Africa are met more fully, and in the second, personalized cancer care is delivered faster and more thoroughly than otherwise. Such tangible outcomes can be highly motivating for the staff involved.

For these reasons, many commentators believe that 'old CSR' – superficial, voluntary, transient action, even if positive in principle – is rightly on the way out. The business case for 'good CSR' remains strong, but CSR's brand is tarnished. An employee of a major bank summed it up: 'CSR is like the office fax machine; everyone knows what it does but no one knows why it's still there.'[8] In today's business world, motivating words such as 'mission' and 'purpose' have rightly entered the vocabulary. Extracurricular activity can create a sense of common purpose and even generate good PR, although unduly highlighting, isolating or exaggerating that final element is rightly excoriated as 'greenwashing'. In recent years the amount of cash that major businesses give directly to charities has fallen, indicating perhaps that companies' direct engagement with communities – cutting out the 'middle man', the charity – works.[9]

No company demonstrates mission and purpose better than Unilever, formerly Lever Bros, whose ten-year 'Sustainable Living Plan' (2010–20) proved not only environmentally and socially effective but highly motivating to its employees too. Workers are much more likely to move between jobs, even careers, than they were in 1925, so a personal sense of 'making a positive difference' can drive an employee to be better motivated and loyal, and thus more productive and long-lasting (making them cheaper to employ compared with constant rehiring).

When Bowen was invited to debate the achievements of CSR in 1978 he expressed profound disappointment: 'I have detected few gains in the quality of business stewardship,' he said, speculating that greater regulation may be necessary if a 'free society of plenty and justice' was to be attained.[10]

ESG is not CSR, although it is often lazily portrayed as CSR 2.0. This misapprehension explains much of the ESG-scepticism rife amongst those who believe that a company that adopts environmental and social goals and is being prissy about governance is being denied its absolute right to pursue profit – the Friedmanites again, especially in the US. Whereas it could once be argued that an organization had to choose between doing good and making a profit, today the two can – rather, must – go together. Why manufacture household goods that people cannot afford, as poverty rises? Or use up rare metals in cell phones to the point where no affordable virgin or low-risk source remains, rather than recycle them? Can your company survive a reputation of destroying precious habitats? Crucially, can your company resist, mitigate or adapt to the impact of a changing climate on your supply chains and marketplace? Can you be part of creating a stable planet where resources, habitats and the climate are more reliable in future than they are today?

That every skill needed to run a business is about anticipating, managing and mitigating risk is as true now as 100 years ago. In the old days 'risk' happened in marketplaces, workplaces, the wider economy. Since 2004 ESG has been a risk-based approach towards the non-financial aspects of running a business. Failing to take those risks into account – risks that will impact the financial – is a dereliction of business duty. ESG was developed in the early twenty-first century from within the world of high finance, where, to a professional investor, risk is everything. It arose, ironically, from a realization that maximized profit was itself at risk in the long term unless environmental and, perhaps less intuitively, social issues, those pesky externalities, were considered and addressed.

SUSTAINABILITY

In 2000 the United Nations published eight Millennium Development Goals, issues that the world needed to address for civilization to survive. They were archetypal 'charity' issues, traditionally the concern of the public and third sectors – poverty, health, education, women's and girls' rights – not normally regarded then as the responsibility of business. Following the world's failure to meet any of these goals in full, however, the seventeen Sustainable Development Goals of 2015 (the SDGs) most certainly were pitched at business.

UN Secretary-General Ban Ki Moon invited Paul Polman, Unilever's then CEO, to be one of the SDGs' authors; the outcome was deliberately phrased to involve and motivate companies.[11] However much governments might like to endorse or urge 'Decent work and economic growth' (goal 8), 'Responsible consumption and production' (12) or 'Affordable and clean energy' (7), these goals and others can only be secured if the private sector – business – puts its shoulder to the wheel and facilitates their achievement through behaviour change (whilst making reasonable profits on the way).

Only the four intact survivors of our thirty-two produce independent, comprehensive sustainability reports. Our other twenty remaining brands contribute towards the corporate performance of their parent companies in ways that we cannot readily extricate. Some may now be so operationally small that they would not be required to report were they still independent.

WHSmith's 2024 Sustainability Report is an impressive gathering of goals, achievements and aspirations, supported by an equally distinctive shelf of third-party accreditations such as a consistent 'A' rating from the Carbon Disclosure Project.[12] That year their scope 1 (fuel) and scope 2 (electricity) greenhouse gas emissions were down 80% on the Covid-affected base year of 2020, and on course for net zero by 2050. This is an approved 'science-based target' in line with guidance from the Taskforce for Climate-Related Financial

Disclosure. The company (whose diet is traditionally paper) is on course to reach net zero deforestation before their target year of 2050, whilst 2024 saw less than 1% of their waste sent to landfill (compared with 12% as recently as 2020). Of the company's board members, half were female, as were 9% of managers, 4% of whom were from ethnic minorities. The company's median gender pay gap amongst full-time employees stood at −0.32% (i.e. marginally in favour of women), and although its audit had identified a small number of human rights concerns in its 2023 supply chain, none were outstanding in 2024. This is a good report.

After ten years of Unilever's Sustainable Living Plan,[13]

- health and hygiene programmes had reached 1.3 billion consumers;
- zero industrial waste was going to landfill, and waste from consumer usage had been reduced by a third;
- greenhouse gas emissions from manufacturing were down by two thirds, and renewable electricity was used across all sites;
- sugar in sweetened beverages had been reduced by a quarter, and half of the company's food portfolio met the highest nutrition standards;
- more than 2 million women had benefited from measures to promote safety, skills and opportunities;
- half of the company's worldwide management was female.

Whilst Boots's report (as a subsidiary of the American WBA) is not so focused, its website has a dedicated page featuring suppliers with B Corp status, largely private sector companies that have voluntarily reached a high accredited level of sustainable and responsible policies on environmental and social issues. Until recently nine Unilever subsidiaries were registered B Corps, although Pukka Herbs has recently been sold (voiding its accreditation), whilst Ben & Jerry's may yet leave the Unilever family.

The US-based B Corp movement has brought together thousands of companies in 100 countries over twenty years – businesses that share a common commitment to delivering high levels of sustainability. Most are small (under 250 employees) and 'for profit'. Performance is measured across five operational fields, and a registered B Corp has to achieve at least 80 points out of an available 200, a test repeated every two years. There are concerns that the process is bureaucratic and onerous (hence few very large companies are certified), that the process can be 'gamed' (get 80 points and stop – why go further?), and that numbers may be exaggerated (maybe companies are not removed when a reapplication deadline is missed). Nevertheless, the movement's motivation is positive, the UK is one of its stronger regions, and its processes are under review. 'B Corp' is one of a growing number of accreditations available to companies aspiring to demonstrate their sustainability record. B Corps demonstrate that strength in sustainability is more than compatible with commercial success, that companies working with nature and society have an advantage over those that regard them as mere externalities.

Despite Brexit, most UK companies trading in Europe are bound by the EU Corporate Sustainability Reporting Directive, as of annual reports published in 2025.[14] This helps investors and others understand company performance on a rational, comparable basis.

Companies have different ecological footprints, and not every SDG is material to every business. GSK (formerly Glaxo) identifies eleven of the seventeen SDGs as pertinent.[15] BP champions the circular-economy aspect of its work and its role in developing alternative fuels such as hydrogen. Whilst the company's operational statistics are impressive, and it talks the talk better than most oil companies, its role in purveying climate-damaging hydrocarbon fuels can never be ignored.[16] But there is a role for oil in the future: heavy-duty, non-disposable plastic will increasingly be used in construction and manufacture. We just do not need to burn so much or dump shredded plastic into the environment, which includes babbling streams, Gulf Streams and bloodstreams.

Bowen's idea of businesses leaving the world better than they found it is consistent with the modern idea that 'sustainability' is not enough. Remaining 'sustainably' on the edge of a climate-shaped precipice is better than stepping off it; what is needed, however, is reform, regrouping and repair.[17]

Businesses, the operational agents of the economy, the historical burners of fuel, removers of rainforests, depleters of Earth's resources, need to lead the way in replenishing, restoring and renewing the planet – and they have the power to deliver. It is in their interest, which is our interest; the risks posed by the alternative are simply unthinkable.

CLIMATE CHANGE

Beyond any doubt, mankind's burning of hydrocarbons (coal, oil, gas) has added CO_2 (carbon dioxide) to our atmosphere at a level unprecedented in the span of recorded time, most significantly since the industrial revolution.[18]

The sun's heat reaches earth but is inhibited from being reflected back into space by CO_2 (and other gases with similar properties) in our atmosphere – a greenhouse effect. This gas has protected us from the absolute zero of space for millions of years, most recently at a Goldilocks-style optimum temperature that allowed life to develop and thrive, but over the last 200 years stability has been lost: excessive production of CO_2 (400 parts per million in our atmosphere compared with a historical 300 ppm for the last 800,000 years) has generated 'global warming'. This is not a great description: more accurately, we are creating 'climate chaos'. Figure 7 shows that since the last ice age (which reached 5 °C below average and ended 11,000 years ago) earth's temperature has been stable (plus or minus just half a degree) throughout human history, until relatively recently. However, since the start of the industrial revolution, 200 years ago, average planetary temperatures have risen without precedent.

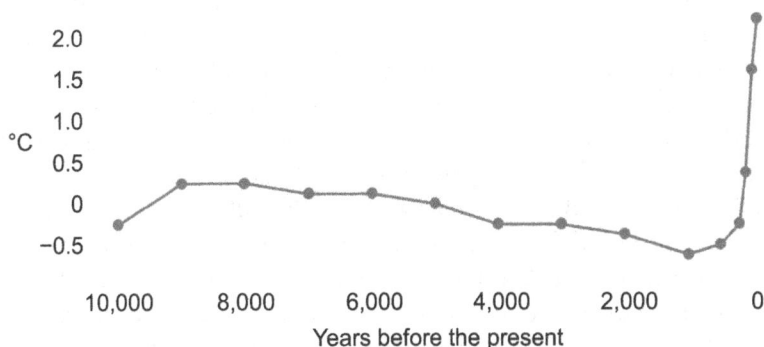

Figure 7. Global atmospheric temperature variation over human history (°C relative to the average for the period, projected to 2050). (*Source:* https://en.wikipedia.org/wiki/ Temperature_record_of_the_last_2,000_years.)

Earth's CO_2 levels over a million years again reveal a generally stable 'tail' with exactly the same recent exponential spike. It is no coincidence that over those last 300 years GDP exhibits an identical, exponential pattern. Our irresponsible way of measuring progress has actually been measuring the driving force behind climate change.

That additional heat (above the 'normal' 0.5 °C fluctuation) results in

- air moving faster, more extreme weather, physical danger and social disruption;
- warmer oceans, rising sea levels, reduced dissolved oxygen in the sea and broken marine food chains;
- glaciers and polar icecaps melting;
- desiccation and destruction of habitats and crops, leading to mass human migration.

Green plants remove CO_2 from the air through photosynthesis, the basis of every food chain, keeping the atmosphere in balance. Recklessly, we have slashed the plant world's ability to protect us by felling mature forests and not replacing them in a timely or effective manner.

Deforestation is not new: mankind has always sought to harvest wood, both for construction and to release land for agriculture. In the eighteenth century Britain's navy dominated the world, waging wars, protecting trade and defending the nation. Equipping that navy required massive deforestation; constructing a typical 110-gun warship required 4,000 oaks, or forty hectares of ancient woodland. The navy maintained 300 such ships, each of which saw, on average, only twelve years' service. Nelson's proud flagship, *Victory*, was made from 6,000 oaks plus many pines for its fixtures and fittings. That is 1.2 million mature oak trees, almost forty square miles of forest, for each generation of ships, not to mention the wood used to build houses, carts, boxes and furniture, and as fuel for heating, cooking and producing iron or pottery. These other uses consumed four times as much wood as the navy at its peak.[19]

The Amazon rainforest today bestrides nine South American countries but two thirds of it is in Brazil. Almost a fifth of it (300,000 square miles) has already been destroyed. The culprits are legal and illegal logging and burning, but most destruction (80%) is for large-scale agriculture, principally beef and soy. Much of the soy is sent to feed beef cattle elsewhere, whilst clearance also allows coffee, sugar and cocoa plantations. No amount of planting trees will make up for this in the short term (trees need twenty years to reach peak efficiency) but we should plant them anyway – if we want a long term. Businesses are starting to realize that they have the power to decide whether this damage will continue or not, whether remediation will happen or not. In Brazil, at least, a new government has reversed the previous destructive trend – only 1.14 million hectares was lost in 2023, compared with 1.77 million in 2022. The positive trend continued in 2024, although drought-related wildfires grew in impact. The country has ambitiously targeted zero deforestation by 2030. Meanwhile, since 2021 the Amazon basin has been releasing more CO_2 than it absorbs, which is ominous.

Alongside our war on forests we have devastated peat resources and denatured our soil through inconsiderate agricultural practices, fatally damaging two more valuable stores (or 'sinks') of sequestered, harmless or 'locked up' CO_2.

Today we are scrambling to find technological responses to climate change such as the unproven 'carbon capture and storage', when ultimately the only way to reduce the impact of raised atmospheric CO_2 is to produce less, a lot less, CO_2. That can only be achieved sustainably by vastly reducing the burning of coal and oil.

Because of its scale and nature, burning fossil fuels generates more climate change than any other manageable activity. As the timeline further below will show, people were not aware of the potential impact on our climate when wood or coal was first burned at scale (thousands of years ago), or gas (Victorian times) or even oil (150 years ago). It is only in the last fifty years that carbon emissions have started to even be noticed. The exploitation of hydrocarbons has accompanied industrialization, deforestation and the absence of mitigation, combined with increasing affluence and growing populations, especially in Asia.

A case in point: the electric air conditioner (A/C) was invented in 1902 but was not commercially significant until the late twentieth century. By 2018 1.6 billion units were in place, projected to rise to 5 billion by 2050. A/C uses a fifth of all American electricity, and in China the proportion of homes with A/C went from 8% to 70% between 1995 and 2004. Rising temperatures increase the demand for A/C, which increases the demand for electricity, which (globally) still mostly comes from carbon sources. This is a positive feedback loop: activity aimed at addressing a minor warming problem makes a major overheating problem worse. The story of climate change is full of positive feedback loops. Here is another: melting permafrost releases trapped methane into the atmosphere. As a greenhouse gas, methane is twenty-eight times more potent than CO_2, so melting permafrost creates more warming, more melting and more methane …

There is ample evidence that scientists were aware of climate change more than fifty years ago, and that oil companies – Exxon Mobil in particular (as disclosed in US court cases) – knew that it was caused by their products.[20] The US Center for Climate Integrity makes similar claims today that 'Big Oil' has hidden data since 1989 in order to promote virgin plastic made from oil and limit its recycling.[21] These echo allegations made about the tobacco industry sixty years ago: that evidence of massive public harm was deliberately hidden from view. More oil meant more climate chaos but also more short-term profit, in quantities of which oil executives could previously only dream. This put the oil industry up there with finance itself as exemplars of the Friedman principle – profit is king, devil take the hindmost, sod the externalities.

Although until recently BP has been one of the more enlightened oil companies, it is a low bar. It has been open on the subject of climate change and shown a willingness to adapt, even to the extent of briefly redefining 'BP' as 'Beyond Petroleum'; yet only a fraction of its investment, $1 in every $25, goes to renewable energy.

Let us consider a timeline of energy and climate change.

c. 1000 BCE   Coal mines, China.

c. 700 CE   Windmills, Persia.

1300s   Coal used for domestic heating in Britain.

1810   First use of coal gas (London's street lighting).

1859   Commercial exploitation of oil, Pennsylvania.

1896   Sweden's Sven Arrhenius predicts that accumulating atmospheric CO_2 will cause the planet to warm.

1901   Another Swede, Ekholm, agrees, coining the term 'greenhouse effect'.

1906   Canadian George Cove patents a thermocouple to convert solar energy to electricity. Fending off bribes and a kidnap attempt aimed at stopping his work, he maintains that solar energy has a future.[22]

1938   Amateur scientist Guy Callendar (1898–1964) tests Arrhenius's theory, analysing data from 147 weather stations worldwide. He concludes that earth is 0.3 °C warmer than fifty years ago, later proved correct. Arguing that this is caused by human-generated CO_2, he is widely ignored. He believes that the warming protects us against another ice age.

1940s   Callendar's work survives official scepticism, stimulates more research on anthropogenic CO_2.

1954   Aiming to sell more telephones in rural areas, Bell launches a selenium cell that converts solar energy into electricity at 0.5% efficiency. It demonstrates a silicon cell with 6% efficiency.

1958   Using five years of data, Charles Keeling shows that atmospheric CO_2 has risen, which he attributes to burning fossil fuels.

1962   *Silent Spring* by Rachel Carson documents the destructive impact of DDT, an insecticide, on the natural environment. Although narrow in scope, the book raises general awareness of humanity's negative impact on the planet.

1967   The first computer model of our atmosphere predicts that doubling CO_2 levels will raise atmospheric temperature by 2 °C. Anthropogenic CO_2 levels have already doubled since 1880, with average global temperatures rising by over 1 °C.

1968   Data predicts polar ice caps melting.

1969   Global temperature data available from satellites.

1972   The UN Conference on the Human Environment highlights problems in humanity's relationship with nature.

1985   Lithium-ion battery invented. Antarctic core drilling gives data on atmospheric CO_2 over 150,000 years, consistent with predictions. A hole in the ozone layer over the Arctic caused by chloro-fluorocarbon gases (CFCs, used in refrigeration and aerosols) allows dangerous levels of carcinogenic, mutagenic, ultraviolet radiation to reach us.

1987   The UN's Bruntland Commission report, 'Our common future', defines sustainable development as 'development that meets the needs of the present without compromising the ability of future generations to meet their own needs'.[23] The Montreal Protocol addresses the ozone hole, banning production and use of CFCs and proving that rapid, concerted action from governments and industry can work.

1994   UN Framework Convention on Climate Change: first international treaty to limit greenhouse gases, ratified by 197 countries.

1995   Rechargeable lithium-ion battery invented. Kyoto international protocol on climate change agreed. COP1 climate conference, Berlin.

1996   Research into carbon capture and storage starts.

1997   Toyota Prius is first mass-produced electric-hybrid car.

1998   Antarctic core data on atmospheric CO_2 over 420,000 years confirms predictions.

2000   Britain's first offshore demonstration wind farm.

2003   Scientists warn of coral destruction from acidification of shallow ocean waters, caused by rising atmospheric CO_2. Britain's first commercial wind farm.

2004   Antarctic core data on atmospheric CO_2 over 800,000 years is as predicted. Scientists link 10,000 excess deaths in Europe in 2003 to extreme weather caused by climate change.

2007   The planet's polar regions are warming faster than the rest of the planet. Melting permafrost is found to release methane in a 'positive feedback' mechanism.

2008   The UK is first to legislate for carbon reduction with the Climate Change Act, pledging an 80% drop in CO_2 emissions by 2050 compared with 1990.

2015   COP21 Paris Agreement: 196 countries agree to limit climate change to substantially less than 2 °C (later 1.5 °C) above pre-industrial levels by 2050.

2019   Ice cap collapse is irreversible, making a ten-metre sea level rise possible. With a 1.5 °C temperature rise this may take 10,000 years, but 2 °C reduces this to under 1,000 years. The UN biodiversity report warns of an unprecedented speed and scale of species loss. The UK legislates for net zero by 2050.

2020   New solar cells reach 30% efficiency.

2021   Trends suggest we will reach global warming of 1.5 °C by 2040, significantly earlier than projected, generating more extreme weather. (We reached it in 2024.)

2023   Amid concerns that the COP has become behoven to oil interests, COP28 (Dubai) launches a 'loss and damage' fund to compensate small states for the impact of climate change (promised at COP23).

2023–4 'Hottest-ever June' followed by 'hottest-ever July' etc. for many consecutive months; 2023 is hottest year ever.

2024   After courts rule that the UK government has failed to plan its carbon-
          reduction programme adequately so far, at COP29 (Baku) new PM Starmer
          pledges an ambitious 81% reduction on 1991 levels by 2035. The last ten
          years contain six of the hottest-ever years, including the new hottest, 2024
          (says Europe's climate monitor, Copernicus).

Today   It is increasingly clear that serious, predictable climate change caused by
          excess CO_2 from anthropogenic sources is a real and immediate threat. The
          1.5 °C chaos threshold has been breached: we are in uncharted territory.

Of those seventeen UN Sustainable Development Goals, one (goal 17) is
about partnerships, the 'how' of reaching our goals.[24] The other sixteen concern existential issues that could each make or break the environment, society
or both. They have a common theme: all sixteen challenges can be – are being
– made worse, more serious, more threatening by climate change. Their reso-
lution absolutely depends upon climate change being tackled.

Sixty percent of methane emissions are anthropogenic, the biggest man-
made sources being the growing of rice (a staple food for millions), the burping
of cows and landfill decay. The beef industry does not just remove our trees,
it belches poison into the air too; hence beef has the largest climate footprint
of any food – three times that of lamb or pork. Low-methane strains of rice –
and cattle – are in development, but this is too little, too late.

The burning of carbon-based fuel accounts for three quarters of all greenhouse gas emissions, including 90% of all excess CO_2 emissions. The five
biggest sources of anthropogenic CO_2 are electricity generation, the transport
industry, manufacturing, commercial or residential use of buildings, and the
food industry. Do not let any business say that tackling climate change is not
its responsibility.

More to the point: if business is to profit from solving the world's problems
rather than creating them in the first place, climate change is where it must
start.

PART II

THE ROMANCES

There follows a summary of each story in the *Romance of Great Businesses*, arranged in order of company origin and supplemented with more comprehensive sources than Beable enjoyed 100 years ago. Each chapter then briefly describes the history of the company or, in a few cases, its industry since 1925.

Wedgwood

(1759, Pottery)

Josiah Wedgwood aimed to be 'Vase-maker General to the Universe', believing that business could both promote artistic expression at scale and encourage social change. His assets grew from £20 to £500,000 in his lifetime.[1] Wedgwood designs ranged from excessively dainty and beautiful to skilfully utilitarian; should a customer demand a thousand-piece bespoke dinner set, as Catherine the Great once did, he could provide it.

The youngest of thirteen children, Josiah (1730–1795) learned from his brother, Thomas, a mediocre fourth-generation potter. Aged 9 when his father died, and with lasting knee damage from smallpox when he was 12, Josiah could make pots. In 1775 he outlined his approach: 'Astonish the whole world at once, for I hate piddling.'

Following Josiah's apprenticeship Thomas advised him to find work elsewhere. In 1759 he created Josiah Wedgwood & Sons, specializing in green-glazed ware, knife handles and candlesticks, eschewing more traditional items. In 1765 Queen Charlotte commissioned a tea set that Wedgwood dubbed 'Charlotte ware', later 'Queen's ware'. He continued to innovate, developing transfers as an alternative to hand painting, and adding creamware and black basaltware to his repertoire.

In 1760, before tea became popular, his small company was one of forty-two potteries in Burslem alone. North Staffordshire's roads were poor and crockery was vulnerable, but the area had coal, clay and, later, canal and rail links. The combined income of the forty-two was £7,000, earning Stoke-on-Trent's five towns the appellation 'The Potteries'. In 1764 Josiah married Sarah (née Wedgwood, a distant cousin), an educated woman with good humour and a substantial dowry, who assisted his experimentation. Following a 1768 riding accident Josiah's deformed leg was amputated without anaesthetic and replaced with a wooden prosthetic.

Josiah was friendly with entrepreneur Thomas Bentley (1731–1780), an educated polyglot, from 1762. Whilst Josiah recovered from amputation Bentley oversaw the company in a highly successful partnership, running their new London office and a showroom in fashionable Greek Street, Soho.[2] Both men were nonconformist protestants, radical dissenters. The Liverpudlian Bentley had witnessed and opposed the slave trade, about which he educated Wedgwood.

In London they marketed high-quality items as 'Wedgwood & Bentley'. Josiah created new specialisms, ceramic tiles, miniature relief figures and jasperware (1774), his self-styled 'greatest achievement'. Beautiful designs involved scenes and motifs in delicate white relief affixed to bespoke 'Wedgwood blue' pottery. Competition from Wedgwood hastened the demise of pottery in Liverpool and elsewhere.

Meanwhile Josiah reinvented his factory. Its Italianate name, Etruria, was no accident; his Latin motto read: 'Etruscan arts are born again.'* He kept product samples for posterity and even briefly ran a workshop near Rome. As his workforce grew he adopted a strict division of labour (as advocated by Adam Smith) and restricted children to working no more hours than his men. The 1780s saw William Greatbach, Wedgwood's mould-maker since 1762, effectively run Etruria upon the founder's semi-retirement.

Josiah was a pioneer of ceramic technology, delivering papers to the Royal Society about the science of high temperatures. At the Lunar Society he sponsored scientists such as Joseph Priestley and Antoine Lavoisier, and he shared his revolutionary thoughts with his sons. Wedgwood and Bentley campaigned in vain for the emancipation of women and working-class people, and after Bentley's death Josiah supported the French Revolution. He approached his long-time ally and fellow Staffordshire man Erasmus Darwin for business advice, and George Stubbs painted Josiah's portrait.

Wedgwood's beliefs as a liberal Whig were inseparable from his work: his 1784 ceramic relief medallion depicted a black slave on his knees below the text: 'Am I not a man and a brother?' The much-copied motif was by William Hackwood, Wedgwood's designer for over sixty years. Thousands of medallions were distributed in support of abolition; the image also appeared on jewellery and snuff boxes. Josiah worked with leading abolitionists Olaudah Equiano and William Wilberforce and sent 400 medallions to his friend Benjamin Franklin, America's founding father. Some accused Wedgwood of hypocrisy: did he not sell luxuries to people who profited from slavery? Wedgwood's suppliers also supplied slavers, whilst some early designs had depicted black servants waiting on white families. And did not Franklin himself employ slaves? (Franklin was a late convert.)

---

*Wedgwood's 'Etruscan' designs were based on a collection of original antiquities acquired by Sir William Hamilton, which were probably Greek in origin. (BBC Radio 4, *In Our Time*, 'Vase-mania'.)

Wedgwood also commemorated Wesleyan Methodism and peace with France. Never formally involved in politics, he nevertheless influenced several trade treaties.

Josiah's nephew Thomas Byerley (1747–1810) and all Josiah's sons joined the company. When the founder finally withdrew, in 1790, Byerley took charge.

Josiah died in 1795, bequeathing not only his artistic heritage but his sales techniques too. These included direct mail, money-back guarantees, free delivery, celebrity endorsement, illustrated catalogues, even 'buy one, get one free'. He had reduced the company's reliance on third-party distributors, and by sponsoring turnpikes he had vastly improved Staffordshire's bumpy roads.

In 1798 Josiah's son Josiah 2 (Joss, 1769–1843) gave Samuel Taylor Coleridge £150 to dedicate himself to poetry. Joss's brother John ('Jack', 1766–1844) established the Royal Horticultural Society (1804), whilst frail, rich Tom (1771–1805) became a pioneer of photography. He discovered, under Humphry Davy, that silver nitrate (which turned black when exposed to light) could 'record shadows'.

Joss and Jack ran Wedgwood after Byerley's death (1810) as the Napoleonic Wars hit sales and profits. They introduced bone china – briefly. In 1815 Joss bought Jack's share of the company, condemning his brother's 'gross incompetence', and then immediately had to manage another recession, closing the London showroom. In 1827 Joss's son Frank (1800–1888) became a partner, inheriting the chairmanship in 1843. Frank navigated calmer waters, reopening the London studios, relaunching bone china (which proved a potent export driver) and restoring the founder's approach.

An Anglican, Joss was as committed to abolishing slavery as his Unitarian father. Following the 1832 Reform Act, Stoke-on-Trent chose the 63-year-old as its MP. He retired after one term, persuaded that his Reform ticket (no connection to any party of today) had no future. His parliamentary contribution is officially described as 'silent'.

Frank's son Godfrey (1833–1905) brought a renewed sense of energy from 1859. His pet project was the Wedgwood Institute, combining library, museum and School of Art, for which William Gladstone laid the foundation stone (1863).[3]

In 1884 Godfrey's son Cecil (1863–1916) joined the board, becoming chair when his father died. Cecil initiated the Wedgwood Museum, home to the family archive. The first mayor of Stoke-on-Trent (1910–11), Cecil died on the Somme in 1916. His nephew, Francis Hamilton Wedgwood (1867–1930), succeeded him. Meanwhile Francis's brother Josiah 4 (1872–1943) began a distinguished parliamentary career representing Newcastle-under-Lyme as a Liberal from 1906 and a Labour member from 1919, moving from backbencher, to minister, to peer.[4]

In 1925 Wedgwood's empire was at its height, with 50,000 employees, a royal warrant, £4 million turnover, a global reputation as a luxury brand and a US subsidiary. A steel works replaced the old pottery village, whilst Etruria Hall, once the family home, had become offices.[5]

WEDGWOOD SINCE 1925

Francis was succeeded by his nephew Josiah 5 (1899–1968) in 1930. As company secretary since 1927, Josiah 5 knew the business well, identifying many challenges: poor design, duplication, an old plant, weak directors, economic depression, even subsidence. His modern factory development at Barlaston included 100 homes. Demand fell sharply after World War II despite the opening of Australian and Canadian subsidiaries.

Josiah 5 reopened the museum in 1952 and transferred 2,000 staff from Etruria to Barlaston. The last Wedgwood to chair the company, he retired in 1967, having increased sales sixteenfold to £3.25 million. Insider Arthur Bryan (1923–2011) succeeded him with gusto, floating the company, absorbing seven other potteries (thereby doubling its workforce to 9,000), rebuilding the museum and expanding the company to cover twenty sites. He earned his 1976 knighthood! However, the 1980s recession, from which Stoke-on-Trent never recovered, saw Wedgwood's workforce halved. In 1986 the company was sold to Ireland's Waterford Glass for £360 million. Founded by Quakers in 1783, when the UK taxed glass but Ireland did not, Waterford Crystal had closed in the 1850s, plagued by underinvestment and high costs, before resurrection in 1947. The new holding company, Ireland-based Waterford Wedgwood, had Bryan as president.

After five years of losses Bryan rejected Irish millionaire Tony O'Reilly's attempted buyout (1988) and then resigned. Two years later O'Reilly – who had spent £230 million acquiring a third of the company – became chairman.

Despite the development of more affordable lines, by 1992 a quarter of US trade had been lost, and the unions agreed to job losses and a wage freeze. After acquiring a German porcelain manufacturer in 1997, Wedgwood returned to profit (making $39 million) – but Waterford did not, losing $29 million. Acquisition diversified the product range to include steel tableware, and 2001 brought collaboration with designer Jasper Conran.

In 2005 Wedgwood acquired the assets of rival Royal Doulton and in 2006 moved operations to Eastern Europe and Indonesia, shedding 1,500 jobs. Only some high-end products were still made in Britain. Following the global crash of 2008, the company acknowledged defeat and entered administration, O'Reilly resigned, and the last two Wedgwoods left the board. Waterford Wedgwood Royal Doulton (WWRD), with just 1,800 employees globally,

Table 13. The Wedgwoods. (*Continues on next page.*)

Founder's generation		
Josiah	(1730–1795)	Founder, 1759–90. Nine children (three married Darwins).
Sarah	(1734–1815)	Wife (and distant cousin) of Josiah.
Second generation		
Thomas Byerley	(1747–1810)	Nephew of Josiah, chair 1790–1810.
Susanna	(1765–1817)	Daughter of Josiah. Married Robert Darwin (Erasmus's son). Mother to Charles Darwin.
Ralph	(1766–1837)	Cousin, occasional business partner of Josiah. Funded by Joss, he invented carbon paper.
John (Jack)	(1766–1844)	Son of Josiah, partner 1790–3, joint chair 1810–15. Founded Royal Horticultural Society.
Josiah 2 (Joss)	(1769–1843)	Son of Josiah, partner 1790–1841, joint chair 1810–15, chair 1815–43. MP for Stoke-on-Trent 1832–5.
Tom	(1771–1805)	Son of Josiah, partner 1790–3. Photographic pioneer.
Sarah	(1776–1856)	Daughter of Josiah. Leading female abolitionist, philanthropist.
Third generation		
Josiah 3	(1795–1880)	Son of Joss, partner 1823–42. Married cousin Caroline, sister of Charles Darwin.
Tom	(1797–1860)	Son of Jack. Fought at Waterloo.
Francis (Frank)	(1800–1888)	Son of Joss, partner 1827–43, chair 1843–88.
Emma	(1808–1896)	Daughter of Joss. Married her cousin, Charles Darwin.
Fourth generation		
Godfrey	(1833–1905)	Son of Frank, partner 1859–88, chair 1888–1905.
Clem	(1840–1889)	Son of Frank, partner 1863–89.
Laurence	(1844–1913)	Son of Frank, partner 1868–95.

Table 13. *Continued.*

Fifth generation		
Cecil	(1863–1916)	Son of Godfrey, partner 1884–1905, chair 1905–16.
Francis H.	(1867–1930)	Son of Clem, partner, chair 1916–30.
Josiah 4	(1872–1943)	Son of Clem, MP 1906–42, Baron Wedgwood 1942–3.
Kennard	(1873–1949)	Son of Laurence, partner, ran Wedgwood US 1919–30, chair 1930–46.
(Sir) Ralph	(1874–1956)	Son of Clem, 1st baronet (1917), chair of LNER.
Sixth generation		
Josiah 5	(1899–1968)	Son of Josiah 4, partner 1927–46, managing director 1930–46, chair 1946–67, last Wedgwood-family chairman.
Cecily (a.k.a. Star)	(1905–1995)	Daughter of Francis H., company artist in 1930s.
Seventh generation		
John	(1919–2007)	Son of Josiah 5, esteemed geriatrician, board member 1967–87.

was purchased by American private equity firm KPS Capital Partners. Britain's National Lottery purchased the museum's contents in 2009, selling them to the Victoria and Albert Museum in 2014. The following year Finland's oldest consumer-goods company, Fiskars, bought WWRD, courting controversy by labelling Indonesian-made items with 'Wedgwood, England'.

Conran became Wedgwood's artistic director (2019), and today's brand is unashamedly top range: £280 for a teacup and £1,600 for a teapot, marketed through Fiskars Hong Kong. Fiskars's non-Wedgwood brands include Kitchen Devil and Royal Copenhagen, with just 4% of sales branded 'Wedgwood'. No Wedgwood products are made in Britain.

Survival does not equal success: falling from 50,000 employees in 1925 to a few hundred today, the Wedgwood brand staggers on.[6]

Bass

(1777, Beer)

Beer-making monks exploited Burton's River Trent as early as the eleventh century, but it was 1777 when William Bass (1717–1787) opened his brewery. Home to several established brewers, the Staffordshire town was on the up, buoyed by parliament's recent decision to build the Trent and Mersey Canal nearby.

William's father was John Bass of Hinkley, plumber, smallholder, cidermaker. When John died in 1732 his oldest son, John 2, inherited the plumber's business and William the smallholding. By 1752 the brothers had started a carriage service linking Burton to the equidistant cities of Manchester and London, but John 2 later withdrew. The service's many customers included five Burton brewers.[1]

William bought a well-appointed home, sold his carriage business to Pickfords (the transport company that still exists today) and invested £1,000 in a small brewery. Within seven years he was sending beer to London, Manchester and Russia, via Hull. 'Burton ale' was normally dark, strong and full-bodied, but Bass exploited a taste for something lighter, paler. Most beer was weaker than today's but still safer to drink than water.

A decade on, Michael Thomas Bass (1760–1827), William's son, inherited the company. Do not confuse Michael Thomas with his son, Michael 2 Thomas (1799–1884), nor his son, Michael 3 Arthur (1837–1909).

The brewery was a roaring success. Investor John Ratcliffe joined (1792), and by 1800 Michael had doubled capacity to 2,000 barrels a year. Michael 2 joined in 1817, a challenging year, as the Napoleonic Wars had ravaged the Russian trade. In 1821 the company's first export of India pale ale to the subcontinent was a breakthrough, and soon 5,000 of its 12,000 annual barrels were India-bound. Output was still around that level in 1827, when Michael 2 took over. Michael 2's partners were Richard Ratcliffe (John's son) and John Gretton; the company was Bass, Ratcliffe & Gretton from 1835. The canal's opening boosted trade (1839).

Still the business grew: 1853's output of 140,000 barrels required a second brewery, and a third was added in 1860 as annual production reached 400,000. By 1868 Burton had twenty-six breweries, obliging London's new St Pancras station to incorporate huge cellars. Producing a million barrels in its centenary year, 1877, Bass was the world's largest brewer.

Bass obtained Britain's first three trademarks on 1 January 1876, a burly dray-man securing first place in the queue after sleeping overnight outside the registrar's office. The red, white and blue triangles, which had originally been introduced in 1855, identified which of Bass's breweries produced the beer. Edouard Manet's 1882 painting *A Bar at the Folies-Bergère* features Bass's red triangle.

Back in 1831, against his better judgement, Derbyshire yeoman Michael 2 had helped suppress rioters supporting the Great Reform Bill. He supported working-class emancipation, including the right to organize trade unions. Derby's voters elected Michael 2 as a Radical MP (1848–83), though he aligned with the Liberals from 1859 despite their advocacy of temperance. He was a regular Commons attendee if not a great orator. A strong advocate of and investor in railways, the brewers' champion managed to water down the Liberals' anti-alcohol stance. By 1883 he owned the 2,000-acre Range-more Hall, hailing it as respected landscaper and engineer Sir Joseph Paxton's version of 'paradise'. Michael 2 died just months after leaving parliament; Michael 3 inherited the company.[2]

Michael2 had deemed his younger son Hamar (1842–1898) – horse-breeder, hunt master, cricketer – unfit to serve in Bass due to his gambling habits. So Hamar became an MP, too.

Michael 3 also followed his father's democratic lead, elected first in Staf-ford (1865) and then newly formed Staffordshire Eastern (1868). Knighted in 1882, he saw his seat replaced by a single-member constituency, Burton, in 1885, which Sir Michael 3 held briefly before joining the peerage as Lord Burton in 1886. This 'double elevation' reflects his father's reputation more than his own; Michael 2 had declined several Gladstonian honours. Michael 3 finally split from the Liberals over temperance, joining Joseph Chamberlain's Liberal Unionists (1894).

The family's philanthropy funded libraries, parks and swimming baths in Derby and Burton, though an 1874 critic described Michael 2 Bass's contribu-tion as 'some feathers being given back by the man who had taken the goose'. The Basses built Burton's grand St Paul's Anglican church (grade II* listed) and vicarage (1874), as well as the St Paul's Institute (1878).[3] The institute was extended to include a Liberal Club, also funded by them (1888), which became Burton's town hall in 1892. Fields and a flood-prone river separated the huge brewery estate from Burton town centre. Bass paid for a raised foot-path (the grade II-listed Stapenhill Viaduct, 1899) and a public ferry bridge, enabling brewers to reach their workplace when the fields would otherwise have been impassable. In 1911 councillors erected a statue to Lord Burton. The company donated pale ale and lent buildings to the 1914–18 war effort.

In 1888 Lord Burton overhauled the company. The new legal entity, with limited liability, had share capital of £2.7 million and 2,500 employees.

The Quaker, partner and finance man John Gretton had a son and namesake (1867–1947), known as 'The Colonel'. Involvement in brewing was not unique amongst Quakers, but being an honorary officer in the Staffordshire regiment (1907–22) did rather flout his pacifist heritage. The old Harrovian John 2 Gretton ran Bass's malting department from 1893 before joining the board. He became the Conservative member for Derbyshire South (1895–1906), Rutlandshire (1907–18) and Burton (1918–43). Gretton is credited with bringing down two governments, his back-bench speeches precipitating the departures of both Lloyd George (1922) and Neville Chamberlain (1940). He was variously described as 'kind, generous, self-effacing' but also 'ugly', 'inarticulate', with 'the noble qualities of the mole'. In old age his snores frequently punctuated parliamentary debates, and he remains the only sitting British MP to win two Olympic gold medals (sailing, 1900).

Shortly before Lord Burton's death in 1908, 'The Colonel' assumed the chairmanship, a non-Bass in the office after 131 years. John 2 Gretton believed in brewing but took a narrow, conservative view of business, delivering healthy dividends at first. He regarded marketing as more important than owning pubs, neglecting the company's properties whilst other brewers invested in theirs. He responded to a challenging market by focusing on the quantity of the Bass empire rather than its quality. His strategy was to acquire the assets of other brewers and associated businesses, but he proved a 'one-club golfer'. Gretton's conservatism was evident in both politics and business; his lack of imagination began ringing alarm bells.[4]

Bass had twenty breweries in 1900 but only eight in the 1920s, due to internal reorganization, the 'tied-house effect' and falling post-war demand. Brewers such as Mitchells & Butlers 'tied' their public houses – obliging them to sell only their owner's beers – and invested in them. Weak demand reflected a weak economy, increased taxation (alcohol was a convenient revenue source), and competition from the new media: radio and cinema.

Baroness Nellie Bass (1873–1962), Lord Burton's daughter, who lived in Scotland with her chickens and bulldogs, inherited the Bass peerage due to a 'special remainder' clause. There was still a family member on the Bass board in the 1920s: Nellie's son Brigadier George Baillie (b. 1895).[5] George, son-in-law to the Duke of Devonshire, died fighting in World War II (1941) without succeeding to his mother's title. No subsequent Bass was involved in the company.

In 1925 Bass's Burton site covered 145 acres, including seventeen miles of private railway.

BASS SINCE 1925

Bass acquired and closed down at least seventeen Midlands breweries over twenty years, reflecting Gretton's drive to eliminate rivals, yet by 1930 production was falling. There was a half-hearted, arm's-length merger with Worthington in 1927, though Gretton only ceded the chairmanship to his rival, Arthur Manners, in 1945 – a year after the 77-year-old Gretton entered the Lords. He was succeeded in both the Commons and then, upon his death (1947), in the Lords by his son John 3.

Bass remained a prestigious company, becoming a founding member of the FT 30, the first stock exchange index, in 1935. The FT 30 became the FTSE 100 in 1984.

Bass's profits doubled under Manners but the local legacy faded: the Liberal Club was sold into private hands in 1944 whilst the institute was abandoned in 1947 and demolished in the 1970s.

When C. A. Ball, Manners's former aide, became chairman in 1952 the acquisitions continued.

Sir James Grigg (1890–1964) was a civil servant much admired by Winston Churchill, who manoeuvred him into a parliamentary seat in 1942 and made him secretary for war in the National Government. Upon retiring three years later, Grigg assumed a portfolio of non-executive directorships, including chairmanship of Bass (1959), where he proposed the company's first major merger (after almost 200 years). In 1961 the newly formed Bass, Mitchells & Butlers had M&B's H. Alan Walker as CEO, with Grigg still in place as chairman. Major rationalization, a synonym for job losses, followed.

After the 1962 merger of Charrington with United Breweries the formation of Bass Charrington in 1967 felt inevitable. Bass brought leading beers to the partnership, whilst Charrington brought pubs, Carling lager and soft drinks. In a major change of direction, having ignored property for so long under Gretton, Bass Charrington launched Crest Hotels and reorganized its property assets.

Old habits die hard. In 1970 the company acquired Joules, a West Midlands rival, closing its Stone brewery, sacking both workforce and management, and, four years later, demolishing its premises. Joules described Bass as 'swift, brutal, ruthless'. In 2008 Bass sold the Joules name to a former employee who built a new brewery, resurrected the 'real ale' brand and opened a pub on the former brewery site (2021).

In 1971 the original Bass brewery site was redeveloped. Through the 1970s the brewing arm of Bass Charrington made but a single beer, in both traditional draught (Bass) and pressurized keg (Worthington E) forms. In the 1980s Bass plc owned more pubs than any other brewery, was a leading lager producer (with its Carling line), and had a leisure division of hotels, bingo halls and betting shops. By 1989 it owned 7,000 pubs and the Holiday Inn chain.

The government, a supporter of free markets, deemed 'tied houses' anticompetitive. In 1989 it introduced 'beer orders' to break up the monopoly whereby the 86% of pubs that were 'tied' (to just six breweries) accounted for 75% of beer sales. Supporters of 'traditional' beers welcomed the move, but Bass took its ball home and looked to exit brewing.

Selling many of its Crest Hotels and absorbing the rest into Holiday Inn, it acquired InterContinental Hotels Group, bringing its hotel empire together as Bass Hotels & Resorts. The drinks side of its business (including two breweries) was bought in 2000 by Interbrew, Dutch owner of Boddingtons, Stella and Whitbread, but this aroused the Competition Commission. It obliged Interbrew to sell off Bass Breweries (including the Carling and Worthington brands), though it retained ownership of the Bass name. Operating only pubs and hotels, Bass became Six Continents and acquired Posthouse Hotels. Coors started brewing Bass beer under licence in Burton.

In 2003, having resisted a £5.5 billion hostile bid from Punch Taverns, Six Continents (Bass) split its pubs and restaurants from its hotels. The resulting Mitchells & Butlers pubs included All Bar One, Harvester and Toby Carveries, whilst the residual reverted to the name InterContinental Hotels, with more than 3,000 properties, mostly franchised. In another busy year, 2006, anticipating the UK ban on smoking in enclosed public places, Mitchells & Butlers acquired some Beefeater and Brewers Fayre sites from Whitbread and sold some of its pubs less suited to food sales.

Meanwhile Interbrew, owner of none of the former Bass empire apart from the name, merged with Brazil's AmBev to form InBev, the world's largest brewer. This merged with the American Anheuser-Busch to create the even bigger AB InBev (2008).

Things had become complicated. In 2005 another Burton brewery, Marstons, started to brew Bass on licence from InBev, though Coors retained the brewery franchise. Bottled Bass for export was brewed under licence in Lancashire, Belgium and the US. InterContinental divested its soft drinks to Britvic, whilst Canada's Molson merged with America's Coors to form Molson Coors, which bought the Worthington brand.

Mitchells & Butlers, with 2,000 pubs, blamed the global economic crash for losses of £274 million in 2008 as it fought off another hostile Punch bid. The company issued another profit warning in 2015 as InterContinental Hotels reduced its directly managed properties significantly, though retaining many franchises.

In 2010 Molston Coors reopened Bass's former Burton visitor centre as the National Brewery Centre. That year it brewed 1.6 million litres of Bass, a top-ten canned beer. Today Molston Coors brews Carling on the former Bass Brewery site in Burton, and InterContinental Hotels has more than 4,000 properties under eighteen brands (two thirds are Holiday Inns). Mitchells & Butlers runs 1,700 pubs but brews no beer. Only the name and red triangle connect today's Bass beer with its brewing heritage, an extreme example of a successful company becoming separated from its core brand.

In 2017 the Campaign for Real Ale declared William Bass 'Britain's greatest brewer'. Was this the future he had envisaged?

Horrockses

(1791, Textiles)

The eighteenth century was a revelation for Lancashire cotton as industrial capitalism evolved. As the century opened the fibre was banned from clothing or winding cloths to protect Britain's linen trade, yet cotton would become the most potent driver of technology. What began with power generated by horse and water closed beholden to steam, with the first steam-powered factory opening just sixteen years after Watt and Boulton's 1769 patent. Kay, Hargreaves and Arkwright led the industrial revolution by reinventing textile practices, scaling up, even opening the door to computing. The revolution heralded an era of efficiency, productivity and 'progress'. Changes in the industry presaged many other innovations in a society that began to focus on wealth creation. The 'money-men' intervened in textiles earlier than other industries, prompting resentment of their novel business model.

John 2 Horrocks (1768–1804) was a beneficiary of this changing world in his brief but active career. His Quaker father, John, a Lancashire mason from Edgworth, made millstones and stone tables for textile printing. Young John 2 and his brother Samuel (1766–1842) were the only boys of eighteen siblings to survive childhood. He entered the cotton trade at 14 but returned home when his supportive employer died. Fascinated, he installed two spinning frames inside his father's modest factory. John 2 sold his output to John Watson, owner of the first textile mill in nearby Preston, but, convinced that Watson stood in his way, he vowed to set up his own factory. Bitter political and industrial rivals, the Tory Horrockses and Whig Watsons came to dominate Preston's textile economy.[1]

In 1791 John fulfilled his promise, establishing a hand-spinning, horse-driven carding and loom-weaving business, which quickly expanded. At Turks Head Court he made shirtings, 'long cloth' and yarn. Financiers Richard Newsham and Thomas Greaves became his business partners, building the Yellow Factory, a steam-powered mill on Dale Street. Horrockses won a contract to provide clothing to the British East India Company made from imported Indian cotton. Samuel joined the company, which, by 1802, had seven mills.

Beable tells us that Horrocks was 'a born businessman, of rigid integrity, quick in decision, firm and determined in his judgment'. Such qualities were certainly needed – matters were developing quickly.

John's uncles, Isaac and George Horrocks, replaced Newsham as financiers, whilst John gave the Turks Head Court business to Isaac. Captains of industry often felt the call of public service: Horrocks became a councillor and an alderman, and he fought the two-member Preston parliamentary seat in 1796 as a Tory. Although he lost by fourteen votes, he would win it in 1802. His fellow Preston MP, Whig Edward Smith-Stanley (later thirteenth Earl of Derby and father of a future prime minister), deliberately invested in Horrocks's rival, now Watson, Myers & Co. Watson, who was known for importing child labour from London, died in a debtor's prison in 1807, owing Derby today's equivalent of £1 million.

In 1801 Horrocks built Penwortham Hall. Outside his mills he employed 7,000 home-based hand-loom workers, equal to Preston's entire population a generation earlier! John Whitehead, Horrocks's brother-in-law, joined the company, as did Thomas Miller (d. 1840), a Bolton cotton manufacturer, in 1802.[2]

Horrocks's burgeoning career ended precipitately. Visiting London in 1804 he collapsed and died, aged 36, which doctors attributed to 'brain fever' from working too hard. He left £150,000 to his son Peter and his share of what was now Horrockses, Miller & Co. to his other son, John 3, who sold his shares to his uncle Samuel in 1815, moving with his wife to Scotland after losing their first child. Neither son remained with the company, but Samuel did, inheriting both John 2's role and his parliamentary seat. He remained a Preston MP until 1812, and Peter would sell Penwortham in 1829.

By 1818, fourteen factories across Manchester were using 2,000 efficient steam-driven power looms. Despite Luddite resistance, Britain had a quarter of a million of these by 1850, two thirds of which were in Lancashire.

Horrockses, Miller & Co. traded internationally, sending finished goods to Portugal from 1823, and to India – over and above the company's East India Company contract – from 1830.

The royal commission developing the 1835 Factories Act praised Horrockses as 'a model employer', but twenty years later it might have judged differently. The company argued against reducing child labour as children were amongst its 'most skilful' workers ... and the cheapest. Sometimes children would work informally and without pay for months, to 'earn' the right to be considered for a job vacancy. (In 1816 almost half of mill employees in the North West were under 18; over half were female.)

The year 1840 was destabilizing: Miller, Samuel and Samuel's son all died. Thomas 2 Miller (1811–1865) inherited his father's estate and position; married Henrietta, John 2 Horrocks's niece (1841); became lead partner (1847); and gradually acquired majority, then sole, ownership of the company by 1860. In 1850 he built a mansion at 5 Winckley Square, Preston, where he gathered a fine collection of British art.[3] He had a holiday home in Lytham, and in 1853 he developed Grange Farm, Singleton Hall and the nearby village, becoming one of Fylde's largest landowners, with 100 carriage horses. In 1854 he bequeathed Miller Park to Preston. Under Miller the Horrockses company became known for low wages and intolerance of indiscipline, belying any philanthropic credentials.

By 1850 four in every five Prestonians worked in a cotton mill. Thomas 2 Miller led the united Preston employers in resisting improved pay for their workers, leading to the Preston Lock-Out of October 1853, one of the longest, biggest and most damaging industrial disputes ever (see 'Employees' in the 'Social' chapter).

Charles Dickens visited Preston in January 1854, expressing sympathy for the workers. His observations informed both the 'Cokeville' union leader and the intransigent boss of *Hard Times* (1854). Alexander Challenger, a contemporary supporter of Chartism, said: 'The Cotton Lords of Preston are the greatest tyrants in the country. It is well known that they grind their workmen down more than any other persons, getting their work done cheaper, and therefore they can undersell their neighbours.'[4]

Miller was the most powerful of the Preston cotton giants, with ten mills, 3,000 looms and twelve steam engines, manufacturing 227 miles of yarn each week and employing 3,000. His death in 1865 saw his son, Thomas 3 Horrocks Miller (an army officer), inherit the bulk of the family fortune on his twenty-first birthday (1867), whilst his two daughters each received about £30,000 (about £3 million today).* Edward Hermon, with the company since 1860, became sole proprietor and was Preston's Conservative MP from 1868 to 1881.

Hollins, Bros & Co. of Cromford, Derbyshire, owned a mill adjoining the Horrockses site and had a superior distribution system for finished products. Whereas Horrockses distributed goods only via warehouses in Manchester, London and Glasgow, Hollins delivered to many locations. Following their 1885 merger, creating a limited company, share ownership was largely restricted to members of the two families. Negotiations immediately began for

---

*One daughter, Minnie, pioneered women's right to retain their wealth after divorce on the grounds of abuse (www.winckleysquarepreston.org/heritage/henrietta-miller/).

a further merger, with Crewdson, Crosses & Co.; Horrockses, Crewdson & Co. (1887) would last a generation.

There was a rapid turnover of directors as Horrockses, Crewdson's sales went global. In 1891 it built Centenary Mill, boasting Preston's tallest chimney in commemoration of John 2 Horrocks. The new Manchester Ship Canal (1894) boosted trade, and on the eve of World War I cotton was still Britain's largest manufacturing industry.[5]

London's money-men, the Amalgamated Cotton Mills Trust (ACMT), imposed raw capitalism on Preston's textile industry in 1918 (see 'Case study: cotton' in the 'Governance' chapter). At the time, Horrockses, Crewdson was headed by Sir Frank Hollins, grandfather of his cricketing namesake. W. Galloway of the ACMT replaced him in 1924 and would remain for the next thirteen years.

The ACMT celebrated its contribution to the textiles industry over 130 years in a beautifully produced book, *Concerning Cotton, 1791–1920*. In reality, whilst its constituent companies dated back to the eighteenth century, the Trust itself had been active for closer to 130 weeks.

In 1925 Horrocks had 6,000 employees, 330,000 spindles and 8,300 looms and produced 600 miles of 'long cloth' weekly, enough to encircle the globe each year. Yet it had lost its soul, become detached from history and community, a mere pawn on a financial chessboard.

HORROCKSES SINCE 1925

When it was revealed that Horrockses, Crewdson held an excessive £1.7 million worth of stock, the company was devalued from £5 million to £3.1 million. According to the confident *Financial News*, January 1927:

> Thus once more we see the folly of recapitalising companies on replacement values at a time of abnormal boom. These disagreeable reorganisations have been proceeding throughout industry for the past three years, and the last of them has not yet been seen; but unpleasant as they are, they will leave many of our great industries in a healthier condition.

In 1928 the company invested in artificial silk but was again devalued, to £2.8 million. The 1930s were no better, with further revaluations to £1 million in 1935, £154,000 in 1936 and £97,000 in 1937, when net losses hit £96,000. A new chairman in 1938, E. V. Haigh, saw profit return – but only to £11,000. Was the worst over? Under Donald Beith, chairman from 1940, profits rose, and by 1946 Horrockses Fashions was creating popular dresses by top designers. The company's most successful period involved television costumes, ready-to-wear summer dresses and modes sported by stylish members of the royal family such as Princess Elizabeth (supplying her 1952 royal tour).

But over the next sixty chaotic years Horrockses was constantly renamed and reincarnated as the brand was bought and sold with breathtaking frequency. Its pseudonyms include Hollins, Viyella, Dawson, Dorma, Brookman, Bluewell, Carrington and ACM, a roll-call designed to gratify imaginative accountants more than tasteful customers – a family tree consisting mostly of distant cousins with the odd illegitimate offspring. The Horrockses brand was applied to clothing and homeware, latterly bed linen, but in 1983, when a recently reincarnated Horrockses Fashions ceased trading, the brand died.

Much of the Horrockses site in Preston was demolished in 1965, and in 2003 the Miller family line went extinct, their fortune passing to the Singleton village trust.[6] After a short period as a private school, Thomas 2's mansion is today luxury flats.

Christine Boydell published *Horrockses: Off the Peg Fashions* in 2010, and Joanie Clothing (a B Corp focusing on 'vintage' dresses) credits Horrockses as its inspiration. In 2016 a reconstituted Bluewell relaunched the Horrockses brand as an international fashion label, featuring patterns based on its 1940s 'hits'. Marketed through Asos since 2022, this may not be the success it appears: by 2025 the Asos website had been reporting the Horrockses brand as 'out of stock' for at least two years.

John Horrocks's twenty-first-century memorial is a blue plaque on Fylde Road, Preston, a section of the local bypass having adopted his name.

WHSmith

(1792, Newsagents and Bookshops)

The 'HW Smith' business of Henry Walton Smith (1738–1792) was a simple newspaper stand served by a network of delivery boys around Little Grosvenor Street, now Broadbent Street, Mayfair.[1] In 1792 his son, the first William Henry Smith (1792–1865), was born, but H. W. promptly died. For twenty years his widow, Anna, alongside Zaccheus Coates, kept the company ticking over. W. H. and his older brother Henry Edward got more involved when Coates died in 1812, though H. E.'s heart was never in it. When Anna died in 1816 the sons inherited what was then 'H&W Smith'.[2]

The company moved into nearby Duke Street, acquiring a bookbinding business, a bookshop, a shop in the Strand (1820), including a newspaper reading room, and a publisher in Cirencester. In 1828 H. E. Smith, accused by his brother of 'indolence', left, so W. H. took charge of 'WH Smith'.

William Henry 2 Smith (1825–1891), W. H.'s only son out of seven children, joined the board in 1846. The Methodist workaholic, known for both patience and irritability, was a competent business leader with a lifelong distrust of Catholics. It frustrated young Smith that readers of *The Times* outside London received two-day-old news, despite the efforts of his company's coaches, which had pounded England's roads since the 1830s. The railways now connecting London to every point of the compass presented a huge opportunity, a captive market: passengers. His motto became 'First with the news'![3]

The company installed kiosks at every major railway station, starting at Euston (1848), then St Pancras, eventually opening 400 outlets. W. H. 2 gradually took more control, often without his father's full backing, as W. H. stepped back before retiring in 1857.

By then hundreds of Smith's horses and nine sparkling new trains were dispatching newspapers faster than the Post Office, the only feasible alternative. The company established distribution centres in Dublin, Birmingham, Manchester and Liverpool, a logistics operation that would serve for generations.[4] In 1854 the government repealed newspaper stamp duty, and Smith won a monopoly distributing *The Times* outside London.

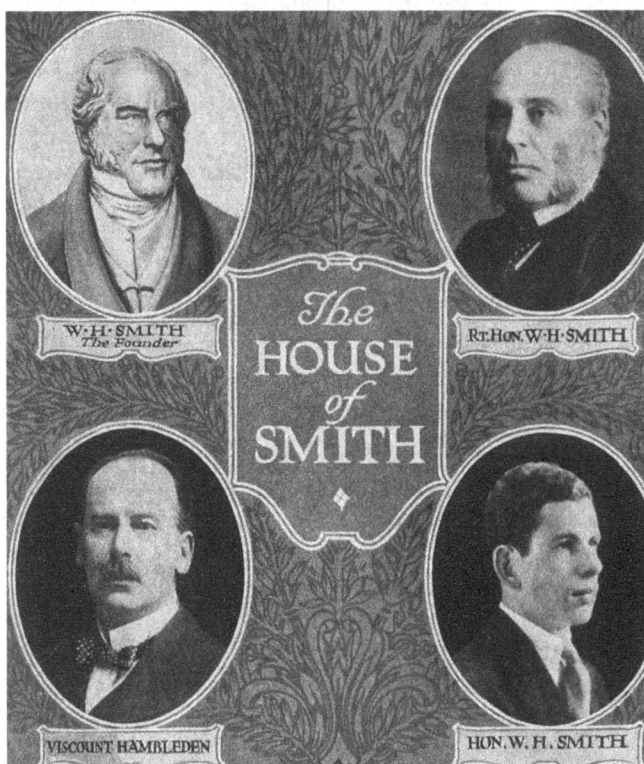

Figure 8. The first four leaders of WHSmith – W. H. 2 is on the top right. (*Source: Romance of Great Businesses.*)

Once a subscription library service was added in 1861 (which lasted 100 years), the model was complete. Learning that the former would-be Methodist minister decided personally on the wholesomeness of reading materials sold or lent, *Punch* dubbed W. H. 2 'Old Morality'.

The tradesman was refused Reform Club membership in 1862, dampening his Liberal passions. In 1865 W. H. 2 fought the two-seat Westminster constituency as a pro-Palmerston Liberal-Conservative, finishing behind two victorious Liberals: Wellington's nephew and the philosopher John Stuart Mill. In an 1868 re-run, with an enlarged electorate and now flying the Conservative banner, Smith beat Mill for the second seat. His extravagant election expenses prompted a bribery investigation – which cleared him.

In 1871 he purchased Greenlands in Hambleden, Henley Management College from 1946.

Smith served Westminster for twenty-three years as a back-bencher, campaigning against poverty and for a London-wide school board. As a junior minister in 1874 he nominally handed the company reins to William Lethbridge until 1885, though Lethbridge was W. H. 2's man.[5] Disraeli appointed Smith financial secretary to the treasury – a junior role befitting his experience in business – and then first lord of the admiralty (1877–80). Having a tradesman in the cabinet, let alone the admiralty, was a novelty! The press had a field day. Gilbert and Sullivan's fictional Sir Joseph Porter, in *HMS Pinafore* (1878), parodied Smith: 'Stick close to your desks and never go to sea / And you all may be the rulers of the Queen's Navee!' After a seven-month spell as secretary for war (1885) Smith became Ireland secretary (January 1886) for just five days before Prime Minister Salisbury lost a confidence vote. Later that year Smith returned to government for five months, again as secretary for war (1886–7).

Constituency boundary changes in 1885 obliged the MP to move on; he represented Strand constituency until his death in 1891. Meanwhile he was simultaneously leader of the House and first lord of the treasury (1897–91), a role normally within the prime minister's portfolio. In cabinet, Smith was regarded as industrious, a stabilizer, whilst having 'no brilliant ability', said Lord Derby. He was competent, if lacking the 'spark' of leadership.

In an unusual recognition of Smith's service, his widow, Emily, was granted the hereditary title Viscountess Hambleden, normally an honour of the male line. Frederick Smith (1868–1928), the youngest of six children but Emily's only surviving son, succeeded his late father as Strand's MP in 1891, unopposed, then survived a blackmail attempt by the serial poisoner Thomas Cream. He served in parliament until 1910 without disturbing the horses, joining the Lords as the second Viscount Hambleden upon his mother's death (1913).

At 23 Freddy had also inherited the business, introducing a superannuation fund (1894), pensions (1895), an overseas branch (Paris, 1903) and more than eighty kiosks across the new London Underground. The 'chain store' had 4,000 employees in 1925. Freddy was active on the boards of King's College and local hospitals, had a distinguished record in World War I, and chaired WHSmith for over thirty years. The viscount's eponymous but posthumous report (1928) boosted hospital building.

When the railway companies put station kiosk contracts out to competitive tender, WHSmith's response was to duck the challenge. It quickly opened 150 shops, often deliberately within yards of railway stations, aimed at keeping travellers happy. The high street model would be at the company's heart for the next century – and beyond.

WHSMITH SINCE 1925

William Smith, third Viscount Hambleden (1903–1948), inherited the chairmanship of WHSmith & Son Ltd in 1928 but was obliged to open the company up to public shareholders in order to fund Freddie's huge death duties.

William built the Art Deco Bridge House (housing bookbinding, stationery and warehousing) on Albert Embankment in 1933 to replace three other sites; it closed in 1967 as the company moved operations to Swindon and was later demolished. A period of serious expansion followed, with the company acquiring small and independent bookshops. In 1948 William's younger brother David inherited what was now WHSmith & Son (Holdings) Ltd, restructuring yet again to pay death duties.

WHSmith developed Standard Book Numbering (1966), later adopted as an international standard (ISBN, 1974). The 1970s saw the first non-family chairman, Charles Troughton (1972–77). A contract with the London Underground lapsed after seventy years, and WHSmith created its own travel agency subsidiary after failing to acquire Thomas Cook (1973).

Between 1978 and 1991 there was a flurry of expansion and diversification through acquisition, leading arguably to a loss of focus; it started with DIY company Do It All and included shares in Yorkshire TV, Lifestyle TV, Our Price, Virgin Music and Paperchase. WHSmith acquired bookstore rival Waterstones (founded by a former WHSmith employee in 1982) in 1989. One hundred and ninety years of distributing *The Times* ended in 1986 as Murdoch's News International moved to Wapping, but WHSmith was soon distributing the *Express, Mail* and *Mirror*.

In the 1990s WHSmith Group plc reversed many of its 1980s eccentricities, closing WHS Travel, selling Do It All and offloading other extraneous shareholdings. The decade also saw a share issue to raise £147 million, allowing expansion and offsetting a £170 million debt. The last Smith family member left the board and the company pioneered online selling (1995). By the end of the decade Waterstones was again independent and – bang on mission – WHSmith acquired its Scottish rival, John Menzies.

The twenty-first century did not start well: substantial restructuring was needed after poor financial performance, and some overseas subsidiaries were sold, although a takeover by European private equity was successfully resisted. In 2006 the company split into its present form, WHSmith plc (retail) and Smiths News plc (distribution). The retail operation expanded into British hospitals and European airports and in 2009 challenged Amazon in the online book market. WHSmith was selling a quarter of Britain's books, records and videos, consolidating this with the acquisition of greeting-card shops.

By 2007 the Post Office was in crisis, closing or relocating 2,500 branches. WHSmith came to the rescue, eventually rehoming more than 200 counters, including dozens of former Crown offices (major branches).

Recent years have brought ever-greater scrutiny of corporate behaviour, and WHSmith was accused of three minor scandals in 2015–17: withholding VAT reductions from airport passengers (paying millions in rebates), overpricing goods in hospital shops (exploiting a captive audience) and under-paying 17,000 minimum wage staff. WHSmith apologized for the last of these, a 'genuine error', and compensated staff as it returned to profit after a lean period. One in six head office jobs disappeared in 2020 when it closed twenty-five stores, but immediately 100 new ones were opened to exploit the withdrawal of Dixons from airports. In the post-Covid travel boom WHSmith Travel (the shops within travel hubs) contributed most to the group in terms of both revenue and profit; its Heathrow branch was the first to house a pharmacy.

Today WHSmith's revenue is restored to pre-Covid health and its market capitalization, of almost £2 billion, is sound. It has more than 1,700 stores, overwhelmingly in the UK, including 100 hospital branches and nine with a revived Toys R Us concession. At 12,000, employment is well below WHSmith's 30,000 peak, and whilst newspapers, magazines and books remain the stores' currency, soft drinks and sandwiches are amongst its 'bread and butter'. It sells 11 million 'meal deals' each year, and 2024 saw its first in-store 'Smith's Kitchen', selling hot food.

In 2024 WHSmith reported its 'strongest ever position', with another 100 stores planned globally. It performs well on environmental sustainability criteria, including a 'Buy back' programme to promote a circular economy in books.[6]

However, 2025 saw a 'back to basics' approach, with the sale of WHSmith's 480 high street stores, henceforth to be known as TGJones, for £76 million. The 150-year-old brand lives on in its many travel hubs, whilst the company retains its superb and time-tested logistics operation.[7]

Schweppes

(1792, Soft Drinks)

Fifty thousand people died on the gallows of Tyburn Hill over the 600 years up to 1783. Near that morbid site in 1925, close by Marble Arch, stood a mansion, the grand UK headquarters of Sch... you know who.

Fizzy drinks are ancient history. The Romans exploited effervescent spring water throughout Europe, inspired by its imaginary health-giving qualities. In Georgian times people revered England's spa towns for bathing and supping, bringing newly middle-class holidaymakers to Bath, Buxton, Harrogate, Leamington and Malvern.

What most impressed Beable back in 1925 was the technology of mass production at Schweppes's new factory in Vauxhall, atop a 150-metre-deep artesian well generating sterile, slightly acid water at 10 °C. Within the concrete palace, automation filled bottles, injected carbonic acid and sealed bottles with corks. Elsewhere workers prepared flavoured syrups, vast vats of lime juice, cordials, 'cyders' and 'fruit wine'. Talented artists worked on advertising, and 100 shire horses were tasked with delivering the product, with similar operations at eleven other UK sites (and Australia). Schweppes had a royal warrant, and the centenary of the Kemp-Welch family stewardship was approaching.

Whoever recreated refreshing fizzy water deserved to make a fortune, and Johann Jacob Schweppe (1740–1821) did both. Schweppe left school at 12, in Witzenhausen, Germany, a tinker and then talented silversmith who took his trade to Geneva, an independent state that would not join Switzerland until 1814. By the 1760s his reputation as a watchmaker and jeweller was blossoming, and his wealth allowed him to indulge in amateur science.[1]

In 1756 Scottish scientist Joseph Black (1728–1799) had first described 'fixed air'. In 1767 Joseph Priestley (1733–1804), Renaissance man, extracted fixed air from alcoholic fermentation and identified it as carbon dioxide, dissolving it by forcing the gas through water using a bladder. Priestley eventually identified a dozen gases, including oxygen, speculated about the inverse square law, contributed to Bentham's utilitarian theories and opened the door to Faraday's taming of electricity. In 1772 he wrote the paper 'Impregnating water with fixed air', mentioning how pleasant the effervescent liquid was to drink.

Another surgeon and chemist, Manchester's Thomas Henry (1734–1816), reproduced German spring water using a pump instead of Priestley's bladder and was perhaps the first to sell aerated water commercially. 'Henry's law' of 1803, which determines how much gas water can absorb, was coined by his son William (1774–1836). Schweppe read Priestley's paper, repeated the experiment and sought to invent an aeration machine, though his 1790 model was fallible. He donated his 'medicated water' to local doctors, claiming that the 'Geneva Principle' combated rheumatism and gout. A colleague, engineer Nicolas Paul, improved the machine, and the two went into business with Paul's father and Henry Gosse. Their soda water, sparkling water or seltzer became the first industrial-scale fizzy drink.

Jacob Schweppe was ambitious but did not entirely trust Paul. In 1792 he agreed to sell the water in London, setting up at 141 Drury Lane, a poor area, in a harsh winter. Britain's duty on 'medicated waters' sold through chemists' shops did not help, though Schweppe was convinced that his purer, more stable, gassier product was superior to that of otherwise competitive local street vendors. After months of slow progress he resisted Paul's call to abandon London, not least as France's war on Britain in 1793 had rendered passage home to Geneva unsafe.

Schweppe judged that the partnership was over and had it legally annulled in 1796, taking the London operation as his share of the business. He set up at 8 King Street, Covent Garden, and then Margaret Street off Cavendish Square. As conventional bottles under pressure did not remain reliably sealed, he designed a glass 'torpedo' with a pointed base: storing it on its side kept the wire-restrained cork moist, preventing shrinkage and thus leakage.[2]

Matthew Boulton, who manufactured James Watt's first steam engine, wrote to Erasmus Darwin (1794): 'Mr J Schweppe, preparer of mineral waters … impregnates it so highly with flexible air to exceed champagne and all other bottled liquors.' Boulton describes three types of Schweppe's 'soda' water: for casual drinking with food, for kidney patients and a highly alkaline laxative version. It sold at 6s6d (33p) per dozen bottles. Darwin, in his reply, joked of the water exhibiting 'Schweppervescence'.

At 59, in 1799, Johann was wealthy enough to retire. He retained an eighth of the company for himself and the same for his daughter, Colette, the only survivor of his nine children, appointing a guardian to oversee their wealth. He sold the other three quarters for £2,250 to three men from Jersey, Henry and Francis Lauzun and Robert George, and retired to Switzerland to take no further part in the enterprise. He died in 1821, wealthy and content, whilst Colette sold her holding in 1824.

The new owners appointed agents to sell the Schweppes product around Britain and by 1803 had regional centres in Bristol, Derby and Newcastle, transporting their waters by canal, coastal vessels and horse-drawn cart. By 1820 they were exporting. Kilner produced the 'Hamilton' glass bottle in 1825, with Schweppe's name embossed upon it.

In 1834 the Jersey men sold Schweppes to a Bath-based partnership of William Evill (1790–1877), a wealthy silversmith, and John Kemp-Welch (1810–1885), a wine merchant.[3]

Progress was rapid. In 1837 the new queen awarded Schweppes a royal warrant. Its largest factory opened at 148 London Road, Liverpool, making fizzy lemonade (1838). It bottled Malvern Water at scale from 1843 and opened factories in Glasgow, Sydney and New York in the 1850s.

The company was the official sponsor of the 1851 Great Exhibition (when its headquarters were at 51 Berners Street), paying £5,500 to associate the Schweppes name with the event. As alcohol was banned from the site, the company had unfettered access to 6 million visitors; it pushed its products hard, boosting nationwide sales by half.

That quinine protects against malaria was known in the seventeenth century; we now know that it kills plasmodium, the microorganism that causes the disease. A product of the Andean cinchona tree, quinine had been prophylactically administered to British troops since the early 1800s. Pitt & Co., not Schweppes, created 'tonic water' in 1858, a still water with a dash of the metallic-tasting drug. The potential for sales to the raj, the governmental system that replaced the East India Company that year, was clear.

By 1868 racegoers routinely drank their refreshing tonic water with gin to mitigate quinine's bitter tang. The combination quickly caught on, so Schweppes added carbonated 'Indian' tonic water to its repertoire in 1871. Today quinine in drinks is restricted to eighty-three parts per million, although side effects from moderate consumption are exceedingly rare. Other than being antimalarial, quinine has no known medical benefit.

In 1870 the company added dry and sweet versions of non-alcoholic ginger ale. Its cinnamon and vanilla 'cola' predated Pemberton's American 'Coca-Cola' by some years.

John Kemp-Welch retired in 1877 and died in 1885, when Schweppes became a limited company worth £432,000. John's son Charles (1845–1916) succeeded him as chairman and managing director. Later, he remained MD when the company separated these roles.

In the 1890s Schweppes was a major victim of the prolific and notorious scammer Ernest Terah Hooley (see 'Fraud' in the 'Governance' chapter). Hooley made £1.25 million from buying the company with borrowed money, selling it to the shareholding public at inflated prices with inflated claims, and then walking off with the profit. The episode shook the company, prompting a rapid succession of chairmen.

In 1893 the headquarters moved to Hendon. Brian Kemp-Welch (1878–1950), already an executive, succeeded his father as MD around 1910 as the marketing budget exceeded £10,000.

Fizzy drinks are often consumed with ice. In 1912 Schweppes supplied the White Star Line's *Titanic* and when 'Women and children first!' was heard James Hawksford, its export manager, was ordered to take the oar of a lifeboat and row, thus ensuring his survival.

In 1925 Brian Kemp-Welch was still MD and the chairman was career soldier Sir Ivor Philipps (1861–1940), a rare 'professional director' whose first board had been that of the Baku Russian Petroleum Co. (1905). Philipps was Liberal MP for Southampton (1906–22) and by 1914 was chairing seven of his fourteen boards. He served in World War I as a brigadier-general, fighting on the Somme and being knighted for war service, and briefly acting as parliamentary secretary to the Ministry of Munitions under Lloyd George in 1915.[4] Philipps joined the Schweppes board in 1914 but stood down to serve in the war. Kemp-Welch asked him to return as chairman, a post he held from 1919 until his death. Despite a steady approach he was no stranger to innovation, building up reserves whilst restricting dividends.

Schweppes had survived a world war and a dedicated con man, developed a simple idea, exploited it, and become a global market leader. Its founder had retired happy. Unusually, the extended family most connected to the company was not that of its founder, yet we use the onomatopoeic 'Schweppes', rather than: 'Care to join me in a gin and Kemp-Welch?'[5]

SCHWEPPES SINCE 1925

'Steady' remained Schweppes's byword. American sales were boosted by prohibition, with 'Sch!' promoting a (dry) nightlife as the advertising budget reached £100,000 by 1930. Fizzy orange was launched in 1931; tonic water production was suspended in 1940 due to military demand for quinine.

Brian Kemp-Welch planned to pass the chairmanship to his son George in 1945. However, the 37-year-old, Stanley Baldwin's son-in-law and a board member since 1936, was killed in the 1944 V1 bombing of Westminster Barracks. The leadership passed out of family hands.[6]

'Schweppervescence' featured in advertising for a decade from 1946. In 1948 Frederic (Eric) Hooper (1892–1963), a former military man who had led John Lewis 1934–42, assumed the chair.[7] He saw profits rise fivefold, and when sugar rationing ended, a four-year price freeze also increased sales. (More on Hooper's philosophy under 'Governance'.)

Commander Edward Whitehead (1908–1978), lately economic adviser to Chancellor Stafford Cripps, joined in 1950 to oversee overseas expansion. The former naval officer, with distinctive facial hair and suave style, fronted advertising campaigns for two decades. After negotiating for Pepsi-Cola to bottle Schweppes in the US, halving the cost of American operations, Whitehead led Schweppes US, making tonic water there for the first time. He received a CBE in 1961.

The company created a 'Schweppes grotto' for the 1951 Festival of Britain.

Mixers constituted most of Schweppes's sales in 1954, its most successful year to date, and in 1956 Sir Eric Hooper was knighted. Sparkling bitter lemon sold 250,000 in its first year (1957), orange 500,000; carbonated drink sales were up 19.7% that year and 15.4% the next; profits exceeded £3 million and six new factories opened.

Sir Eric became Baron Hooper in 1962 but died within months. Former cabinet member Harold Watkinson, sacked in Macmillan's 'Night of the Long Knives', replaced him (becoming Viscount Watkinson in 1964). Benny Hill featured in Schweppes ads from 1961; by 1964 the marketing budget had reached £450,000. The following year aspartame replaced sugar in its 'Slimline' range, and in 1967 divers recovered a preserved crate of Schweppes from a 100-year-old shipwreck, RMS *Rhone* in the British Virgin Islands.

Acquiring Typhoo Tea in 1968 was a change of direction, anticipating another major change under Watkinson: the formation of Cadbury Schweppes (1969; see Cadbury). From a soft drinks perspective, acquisitions were few but significant (such as Canada Dry and Sunkist from Nabisco in 1986, and Dr Pepper and 7 Up for $1.6 billion in 1995), generating a 17% market share in America, including half of the non-cola soft drinks market.

Several iconic advertising campaigns emerged, including William Franklin's 'Sch... you know who' throughout the 1970s and John Cleese's spoof documentary on subliminal advertising, shown in UK cinemas alongside his film *A Fish Called Wanda* (1988).

When things fell apart Cadbury Schweppes was eviscerated. Its non-US soft drinks were sold to Coca-Cola for $700 million (1999), the company failed in a bid for Nabisco in 2000, its US soft drinks were sold in 2008 to Keurig Dr Pepper (later acquired by Mondelez), and the Japanese Asahi then bought Schweppes Australia. Suntory acquired some European rights in 2009, and Coca-Cola closed the Malvern plant in 2010.

Today Coca-Cola owns Schweppes's manufacturing and bottling franchise in twenty-one European countries, including the UK. In twenty-two more it is Suntory, aka Schweppes International. The global soft drinks market is worth $300 billion, with 190 trillion litres consumed each year.

The Schweppes brand is very much alive. The company has long since disappeared.

Pears

(1807, Soap)

Soap is 4,000 years old. Humanity's discovery that fatty acid salts reduce the surface tension of water, emulsify oils and kill microorganisms – and thereby help water clean pretty much everything – was accidental. The late eighteenth century's basic soap was made of animal fats, potash, tallow, lanolin, castor oil, even containing arsenic or lead. A hundred years later some soaps were still not recommended for use on human flesh other than on the coarsest, grimiest, industrial hands. Unfortunately, there was no alternative.

Barber Andrew Pears (1768–1845) left Cornwall in 1789 for Gerrard Street, Soho, to make his fortune. Haircutting and shaving were part of the barber's art, as were hair and wig powdering, rouge and foundation application, and (as the traditional pole reminds us) bloodletting.

Pears soon realized that the tender skin of pampered, high-class gentry, male and female, was rarely exposed to outside air or sunshine. People were even using powders and creams to conceal damage caused by soap itself! Soft, vulnerable white skin, he concluded, needed gentle, pleasant soaps, not poisonous ones. He experimented with glycerine, cedar-wood and thyme oils, perfumed with garden flowers. Many soaps were available, especially from France, but Pears's manufacture was unique: its kind ingredients, soft foam and pleasant smell proved immediately popular. The soap's distinctive transparency, product of a secret thirteen-week drying process, complemented an authentic brand.

Pears started selling his soap in 1807 but could not meet demand. He asked John Watson to help (no relation to Horrocks's rival), but when Watson tried to sell the product as his own, Pears sued him. In 1809 the courts confirmed Pears's right to the intellectual property.

In 1835, three years before his retirement, Pears inducted his grandson Francis (1813–1875) into what was now A&F Pears on Great Russell Street, near the British Museum.[1] They won the soap prize at the 1851 Great Exhibition.

Hygiene, safety and sanitary issues climbed the public agenda as cholera hit in 1853–4; half of Britain's 20,000 dead were Londoners.[2] In 1858 'The Great Stink' prompted debate as parliament's chlorine-soaked curtains disguised the smell. London's biggest-ever construction project, Joseph Bazalgette's £2.5 million dream, involved 82 miles of sewers, 1,100 miles of drains and the canalization of the Thames through London's city centre. John Wesley's words 'Cleanliness is next to godliness!' were used to promote interest in hygiene, rendering Francis Pears's well-informed book *The Skin, Baths, Bathing and Soap* (1859) apposite. In 1862 he opened a purpose-built factory in Isleworth to increase capacity.

The year 1864 was key. Bookkeeper Thomas Barratt (1841–1914) joined and then married Francis's daughter Mary.[3] Francis's son Andrew 2 (1846–1909) ran the Isleworth plant whilst Barratt oversaw sales from Great Russell Street. Andrew 2 was an active Liberal, attentive to the needs of employees and the community. However, Barratt's elevation to partner unleashed a rollercoaster about which Francis was rarely comfortable.

Francis retired around 1875, his confidence in his extroverted partner exhausted. His departure required Barratt and Andrew 2, now co-director, to repay a £4,000 loan. Though challenging, this was achieved: Pears was very profitable.

Hitherto, Pears had spent about £500 over sixty years on advertising. In 1880, his most spendthrift year, Barratt spent £126,000; lifetime publicity budgets passed £3 million in 1925. Barratt was 'the father of modern advertising', claimed Lord Northcliffe, the *Daily Mail*'s founder. Barratt once said: 'Any fool can make soap; it takes a clever man to sell it.'[4] The final quarter of the nineteenth century was an eventful time for the Pears brand.

- Barratt paid John Everett Millais £2,000 for the rights to his painting *Bubbles*. To Millais's annoyance Barratt distributed millions of copies overprinted with the Pears logo.
- He utilized endorsements from celebrities but dumped the first – the ivory-complexioned Lily Langtry – after her lascivious relationship with the Prince of Wales was revealed.
- He laughed at, bought and then reproduced cartoonist Harry Furniss's Langtry parody. A tramp echoes her words: 'I used Pears soap two years ago and have not used any other since.'
- He recruited the brother of Harriet Beecher Stowe, American author of *Uncle Tom's Cabin*, as a celebrity religious endorser, who said, in 1885: 'If cleanliness is next to Godliness, then surely soap is a means of grace.'
- He launched the *Pears Annual*, which ran for more than 100 years, and for the 1897 jubilee a *Cyclopedia*, two years after Lever Bros' equivalent.

- In a parliamentary debate on Irish Home Rule, William Gladstone described the multiplicity of amendments as 'as plentiful as advertisements for Pears' Soap'.

Soap and cleanliness came to embody whiteness, colonialism and imperialism and to reinforce Victorian gender roles. Pears produced an uncontroversial advertisement in 1899 that would surely have been unacceptable today. Beneath a drawing of an elderly, Caucasian, military gentleman washing his hands, the text read: 'The first step toward lightening the white man's burden is through teaching the virtues of cleanliness. Pears' Soap is a potent factor in brightening the dark corners of the earth as civilization advances, while amongst the cultured of all nations it holds the highest place – it is the ideal toilet soap.'[5]

An earlier Pears advertisement, from 1884, contained the phrase 'washing the blackamoor white'. Whilst this phrase clearly had racist overtones (sometimes as 'washing the Ethiopian white'), it comes from Aesop's fables. Its original meaning was 'some things cannot be changed', akin to a leopard never changing its spots, or the tale in which a raven dies of hunger after failing to wash itself as white as a swan.

Meanwhile Pears moved offices to grand premises at 71–5 New Oxford Street. It extended the Isleworth plant, near Andrew 2's enlarged dwelling at Spring Grove House (former home of Kew Gardens' creator, Sir Joseph Banks). The company sold shares from 1897. Pears soap was introduced to India, where it was manufactured from 1902.

Barratt's advertising genius was celebrated by his peers in 1889 with an honorary dinner at New York's Metropole Hotel and again, in 1913, at London's Savoy, shortly before he died.[6] Barratt's home, Bell Moor House in Hampstead, was later occupied by the conductor Sir Thomas Beecham.

When Andrew 2 died (1909) Barratt vetoed the directorial appointment of his son Thomas Pears (b. 1882), then the Isleworth manager. Three years later, Tom was amongst the 1,500 to die on the Titanic. His wife, Edith, survived.

The excitement shuddered to a halt with Barratt's death in 1914. The chair passed to whisky magnate Sir Thomas Dewar, with another of Andrew 2's sons, Robert, as his deputy. Ownership by shareholders now rendered the company vulnerable to takeover; Lever Bros gradually obtained a majority holding in Pears, gaining full ownership in 1920.

By 1925 quiescence had replaced the extrovert Barratt years. Life as a Lever subsidiary was going to be different, and Pears's profile was never so high again. In marketing terms Pears had well and truly washed its hands, changing the face of advertising.

The first step towards lightening

The White Man's Burden

is through teaching the virtues of cleanliness.

Pears' Soap

is a potent factor in brightening the dark corners of the earth as civilization advances, while amongst the cultured of all nations it holds the highest place—it is the ideal toilet soap.

Figure 9. Pears's advertising assumed colonialist attitudes to be normal. (*Source:* Wisconsin Historical Society.)

PEARS SINCE 1925

There is little to report. The Isleworth factory burned down in 1962 and was not replaced, EU rules obliged greater transparency around soaps' contents from 2003, and Pears's *Cyclopedia* was discontinued in 2017. Retaining its distinctive shape and transparent nature, Unilever reformulated the soap into a softer, smaller, less durable form, prompting a backlash from customers (2010), after which the changes were largely reversed. Hindustan Unilever (67% owned by Unilever) relaunched the brand in 2016.[7] Other Pears-branded products are today manufactured in Saudi Arabia.

The golden soap on Britain's supermarket shelves looks as it did a century ago. 'Pears is a skin-care brand,' confirms Hindustan Unilever's website.

Millais's original *Bubbles*, acquired by Unilever with its 1920 purchase, hangs in exalted company in Port Sunlight's Leverhulme Gallery.

Figure 10. The Pears family memorial, including a tribute to Tom, who died on the Titanic, stands in Isleworth churchyard.

Colman's

(1814, Mustard)

Colman's 'iconic and traditional' mustard has always evoked quality, service and values. Its loud yellow tin sports a fiery red bull's head, a pioneering 1876 trademark reminding us of the condiment's association with beef.[1] Its recipe, a blend of brown and white seeds from two different mustard species, is virtually unchanged since 1814, and whilst its distinctive taste and proud Parisian medals may feel continental, it is English through and through.

There was stiff competition for East Anglian mustard as early as the 1720s. Farmers grew the plants, removed the chaff and ground the seeds into powder or paste. Flour miller 'Old' Jeremiah Colman (1777–1851), of Bawburgh, Norfolk, acquired a mill in Stoke Holy Cross in 1804 where he developed the product. Later, the company fed milling waste to the company pigs; in an example of the circular economy, Christmas joints distributed to the workforce came pre-seasoned! Other waste was sold as cattle food or manure. Mustard went to grocers in wooden boxes, or from 1860 in locally made tins, available in twenty-five different sizes by the 1880s.[2] Small portions kept prices affordable.

Old Jeremiah and Ann were childless, but following a family tragedy they adopted several of their eleven nephews and four nieces. In 1823 the oldest, James (1801–1854), became a partner in J&J Colman. Upon James's passing, his own son, Jeremiah James Colman (1830–1898), took the helm. Colman's today is essentially the product of J. J.'s forty-four years in charge.

J. J. Colman cared for his workers instinctively, but as he grew the business he would agonize over the balance between the common good and business success. In 1853 he relocated the factory to Carrow, closer to Norwich (by 1925 the factory would cover thirty-two acres), and built facilities for his workers in the village of Trowse. Under James's wife, Mary, a small school was started for boy employees, with half a day's compulsory weekly attendance, on company time, for a penny a week. In 1857 they constructed a school building, long before state funding, with its own vegetable garden. Colman's bought small houses in the village to rent out cheaply, especially to single female employees. J. J. Colman wrote enthusiastically to his staff: 'That man is sure to be left far behind, who has neglected the cultivation of his intellect[,] while he who strives to improve his mind stands a fair chance of raising himself in the social scale.'[3] He said the school would teach 'Reading, Writing, Spelling, Arithmetic, Grammar, Geography, English History, Drawing, also ... Sacred Scriptures'.

The curriculum also featured traditional crafts, including needlework for girls. J. J. relocated the school to Carrow Hill (1864), and when it finally came under council control, in 1899, it was serving 600 pupils. This building was sold in 1962 but still stands.

In 1855 J. J. Colman adopted today's brand image. Queen Victoria granted a royal warrant in 1866, and further European royal appointments followed – plus those Paris medals (1878).

Although the company produced a range of powders – including flour, laundry blue and starch – mustard was always its core product. (Before bleach, laundry or dolly blue countered the 'natural' discolouration of white fabrics.) J. J.'s wife, Caroline, appointed a company doctor in 1864 and Philippa Flowerday, Britain's first on-site industrial nurse, in 1878. Philippa typically made forty-five home visits each week for ten years before leaving to marry the company gardener. Colman's contributory medical club preceded the NHS by seventy years, and the company paid for employees' coffins until 1949, when they replaced this service with a £10 grant. A canteen provided hot drinks, sold hot lunches at cost price (13,000 in 1868) and sent food parcels home to sick employees. Pay and holidays were the best in the region, the company had a clothes-sharing club, and its sports facilities included Norwich cricket ground.

In 1846 Old Jeremiah had launched *Norfolk News* to campaign for free trade and civil and religious liberty. Twenty-five years later the Liberal J. J. funded the *Eastern Daily Press*, for similar reasons.

Employment at Colman's grew from 50 in the 1830s to 1,100 in 1869. The annual tea party was discontinued after 1880 when numbers became unmanageable (around 6,000 employees and family members). Between 1900 and 1925 it had around 2,000 workers.

The company provided allotments, two pubs and a pioneering profit-sharing scheme. In his will, J. J. Colman left £20,000 per year for twenty years to kick-start a pension fund. The family lived on the Carrow site; after Caroline's death in 1895, they donated land for a children's hospital. How could all this be afforded? J. J. famously said that his profits represented 'the mustard that people leave on the sides of their plate'.

By the 1880s Colman's had operations in Australia, India and South America. Scott took one and a half tons* of Colman's mustard and nine tons of its flour to the South Pole (1901).[4]

Colman's invested in marketing from 1871, painting its railway wagons mustard yellow, whilst Royal Doulton made Colman's-branded ceramic mustard pots. In the 1920s its advertising agency's copywriter was the future novelist Dorothy L. Sayers.

The family's religious and political views guided their conduct. They were nonconformists who believed in 'helping people to help themselves'. J. J. led the Liberal group on Norwich City Council for most of his twelve years there from 1859, campaigning against corruption. Although he became the city's member of parliament (1871–95), the undistinguished orator, William Gladstone's close friend, did not enjoy the role. He was also deputy lieutenant of Norfolk (1880), a magistrate and a co-founder of the Norwich Young Men's Christian Association. His daughter Ethel, another Liberal councillor, served as Britain's first female lord mayor (1923).

J. J.'s 1898 funeral brought Norwich to a standstill. He bequeathed many artefacts to Norwich's museum and library.

After a brief interregnum under J. J.'s cousin, in 1900 Frederick (a.k.a. 'Young Jeremiah', 1859–1942) succeeded his father as chairman; he was already leading a local insurance company, Commercial Union. J. J.'s son-in-law, former Liberal MP James Stuart, joined Colman's as a manager, as did Frederick's son, Lieutenant Colonel Gordon Colman, who sat on the board for the next fifty-five years.† Young Jeremiah introduced a modest programme of acquisitions, including Keen Robinsons in 1903, who made both mustard ('Keen as mustard') and a powder that reconstituted as 'barley water'. From 1908 he chaired a charitable fund to create Cambridge University's School of Biochemistry, later donating his orchid collection to its botanic gardens – his cricket photographs would go to Lord's.[5] After his father had repeatedly refused a baronetcy from Gladstone, Sir Jeremiah Colman was awarded one in 1907. He was still chairman in 1925.

A maximum forty-eight-hour working week, and then a Whitley works council, came in 1918. In 1913 Colman's created a joint venture with Reckitt & Sons of Hull to avoid unnecessary competition in South America, a tangy taste of things to come.

---

*'Tons' refers to imperial tons unless otherwise noted.

†Gordon may have inspired Cluedo's 'Colonel Mustard'. (S. Wright. 2022. Colonel Mustard in the hall, with the lead piping. *Daily Mail*, 4 November, www.pressreader.com/uk/daily-mail/20221105/281784223046308.)

COLMAN'S SINCE 1925

Isaac Reckitt (1792–1862) made laundry blue, grate polish and starch from 1840. The company acquired Robin, an enhanced starch (1899), and Brasso (1905) and then, in 1926, it jointly purchased French's American mustard company with Colman's. Reckitt developed Harpic and the antiseptic Dettol in 1932. From 1938 a formal partnership short of a merger saw both companies retain their stock market identity. Meanwhile, the soap-making Mason family of Chiswick had created Cherry Blossom shoe polishes (1906), in which Reckitt's company invested from 1912. It absorbed Chiswick Products completely in 1948, the year that it finally joined forces with Colman's.

In 1985 Reckitt & Colman acquired Airwick and Carpet Fresh, and Lysol in 1994, doubling the size of its US business. Colman's sponsored Norwich City FC (1997–2001), sharing that distinctive canary yellow with both them and Commercial Union's successor, Aviva.

By the 1990s food had become only a minor part of Reckitt & Colman and was abandoned. Unilever did not buy Colman's as such in 1995 – the company had long since ceased independent existence – merely the right to use the mustard recipe and brand name. Robinson's Barley Water, as the Keen Robinson product was now branded, was sold to Britvic, and the residual firm merged with the Dutch Benckiser (Vanish, Finish, Calgon) as Reckitt Benckiser (1999).

In 2019 Unilever ended mustard production in Norwich, relocating Colman's manufacturing to Burton and Germany and closing the factory in 2020.

Historical Colman paternalism is compatible with Unilever's brand values; the family charity (the Sir Jeremiah Colman Gift Trust) allocates £200,000 each year to Hampshire's good causes. However, in 2024 the Church of England* required the current Colman heirs, Sir Jamie and his wife, Reverend Sue Colman, to step back from public activity when their undeclared knowledge of the activities of an exposed paedophile, the late John Smyth, were revealed.[6]

Unilever announced in 2024 that its first major UK regenerative agriculture project, improving soil quality and yield whilst creating a lower carbon footprint than conventional farming, will grow mustard and mint for its Colman's brand.[7] Today's brand also includes a variety of ready meals, seasonings and recipe mixes, but the mustard itself has not changed.[8]

---

*This was the scandal that led to the archbishop of Canterbury resigning.

Huntley & Palmers

(1822, Biscuits)

Huntley *or* Palmers would be more accurate. Joseph Huntley (1775–1857) set the biscuit barrel rolling when he spent the family savings purchasing a confectioner's shop at 72 London Street, Reading's main thoroughfare, conveniently opposite a coaching inn. Success was modest as there were thirty competing local bakers. Joseph, like his father, was a schoolmaster; his mother used to sell biscuits at the school gate. It was 1822 when J Huntley & Son first produced 'fancies' or 'discretionary' cakes, life's little luxuries. Reading became known for beer, bulbs, bricks … and biscuits.[1]

'Biscuit' means 'cooked twice', a 400-year-old technique generating a dry product with a consequently long shelf life, suited to ocean voyages. The marine theme was reflected in Joseph's product names: Captain, Water, Cabin. He also made cake and seasonal hot cross buns. Joseph realized that hungry travellers' fancies needed protection on long and bumpy journeys, so he sold them in simple but innovative air-tight tins. Fortunately his younger son, Joseph 2 (1807–1895), an ironmonger, worked nearby; his company, Huntley & Boorne, could make 100 tins a day per trained man, protecting the delicate confections.

By 1838 Joseph, aged 63, was unwell and struggling, so his oldest, Thomas, made the biscuits. A cousin, Somerset resident and Quaker George Palmer (1818–1897), having recently completed a miller's apprenticeship, moved to Reading in 1841 to help Thomas, paying £550 for a half share of the business with its eight employees. George's wife was cousin to the Clarks, the Quaker shoemakers.

Thomas did not have his father's entrepreneurial drive; George took sole charge. It is now Palmer all the way, albeit under the Huntley & Palmers (H&P) banner. In 1843 the company acquired a disused canal-side silk factory, with thirty employees and eight agents promoting sales around the country.

George's milling and engineering insight equipped him (with William Exall) to create the world's first fully mechanized, steam-powered biscuit production line (1846). Taking pride in their efficiency, they saw profits surpass

£1,000 in year one, 40% of turnover. Their biscuits included ginger nut, after-noon tea and Bath Oliver. H&P opened a London sales office the following year when George married Elizabeth, with whom he had six sons and four daughters. The Liberal also found time to join Reading Council.

H&P's quality products won a bronze medal at the 1851 Great Exhibition, amongst other international awards over the years.

'This firm', reported Beable, 'has not ceased to progress either in the extension of its business or in the excellence of its manufactures.'

In 1857, as turnover reached £125,000, Joseph died. George's brothers Samuel (1820–1903), who ran the London office, and William (1824–1893) joined the board. When George bought out the interest of Joseph 2, the Palmer takeover was complete (Joseph 2's ironmongery remained independent). H&P received a royal warrant and then similar recognition in France and Belgium.

From 1860 transfer technology allowed rapid, identical decoration of each tin, the previous practice of stencilling having restricted designs to two colours. George then created the brand's unique selling point: as the containers became more ornate, distinctive and elaborate, they took on attractive shapes and features. Between 1868 and 1944 the company sold biscuits in 400 designs of container, some of which have become collectors' pieces. All this was achieved by Joseph 2's ironmongery (known as Huntley, Boorne & Stevens from 1872), although they outsourced some specialist techniques, such as embossing.[2]

By 1865 H&P was the world's biggest biscuit maker, employing 1,000 people (2,500 by 1872), exports accounting for a quarter of output. They introduced employee sickness insurance and a company library.

In 1877 the company bought in a new printing technique, offset litho: direct printing onto each tin's surface with no restriction on design, colours or features. Decoration became ever more bizarre – tins resembled a garden roller, a working clock, a van – whilst maintaining a traditional approach for Victoria's 1887 jubilee and the annual Christmas tin. A particularly striking series was 'Waverley', named after Sir Walter Scott's novel, which mimics a stack of books: 650,000 tins in ten different Waverley designs appeared, 1900–24. Depending on quality they sell for £50–£400 today. Not to detract from the artwork, the company's name appeared only underneath their tins from 1880.

For fifty years George was secretary and fundraiser-in-chief to a Quaker school providing free education. His sons joined the company: George 2 (1851–1913) as early as 1867, later Walter (1858–1910), then two more. Four nephews (Sam's sons) came too. George's older brother William was already on the board; he funded a free library in Reading in 1875 after the council declined to use its new powers to sponsor one. In 1876 William purchased Hoxton Hall, Hackney, a former music hall, transforming it into a Temperance

Mission. William supported many good causes but made many unfulfilled promises: when he died in 1893 his outstanding commitments cost the family more than was left in his will.

Walter became chairman of the new University College in 1885, supported by ongoing family funding. It became Reading University in 1892.

H&P employed 3,000 in 1878. That year George, inspired by Quakers John Bright and Richard Cobden, was elected Liberal MP for Reading at a by-election, standing down in 1885. Never a prolific debater, his maiden speech supported women's suffrage. George lived at Marlston House, Newbury, donating Palmer Park to the Reading public in 1891. Oscar Wilde visited H&P's factory in 1892; his next visit to Reading (1895) was less agreeable ...

George Palmer died in 1897. His sons inherited a turnover of £1.25 million, an annual output of 23,000 tons and 5,000 employees. Still the world's largest biscuit maker, the company boasted 400 different lines. It had a doctor, a school teacher and a 'sick club'. They registered the company as 'limited', and in 1900 a tenth of its output was exported to India, much of the rest going to more than 170 other countries. The protective tins had come into their own.

The Reading factory covered twenty-four acres in 1900. Sixty-two thousand rail trucks visited the firm annually, utilizing twelve miles of on-site track. That year the electors of Salisbury chose Walter Palmer as their Conservative MP; Sir Walter from 1904, he sat until 1906. He died in 1910 (the year of the first iced gem), his baronetcy dying with him.

Reading awarded George 2 Palmer the Freedom of the City in 1902, only the second person to be so honoured. The first was his father, the posthumous patron of a local school (1907). Reading's football team was 'the biscuit men'.

Samuel, George Palmer's last surviving brother, died in 1903. One of his sons, Ernest (1858–1948), was an H&P director. Passionate about opera and serious music, Ernest gained a knighthood in 1916 and was the first Lord Palmer (1933).

Mass production harvested the fruits of that early mechanization. A mythology grew up around the tins and their brilliant designs, much of which was true! Stories include

- natives greeting Sir Francis Younghusband, the first European in Tibet (1904), by proffering a tin of H&P;
- an original H&P tin that is preserved at Scott's Antarctic base camp (1910);
- a 1909 tin design featuring a German soldier, who was tactfully replaced by a Belgian in World War I.

The original shop closed in 1912, and World War I saw production halved. The tin-maker switched to military fabrication, making water bottles, detonators and countless artillery shells from 1915. H&P made biscuits for soldiers, later buying the ironmongers as a wholly owned subsidiary. After the war George V visited the factory on a morale-boosting tour, for which workers were granted an extra week's pay in celebration. Five Palmers appeared in a photograph of 'Directors and senior employees' taken to commemorate the visit.

Other Quaker institutions proudly supported the war effort with non-military contributions, but the appearance here of armaments is interesting. Both the Huntleys and the Palmers were Quakers: where was their pacifist ethos? Howard Palmer, George's nephew and company chairman during World War I, won praise from Kitchener for his efforts recruiting soldiers for the front. Howard's son Reginald (1898–1970) saw active service in World War I, and Reg's son Bill (1925–2020) would serve with distinction both in World War II and, later, in Palestine.

The first takeover threat turned into a mutually beneficial partnership with Peek Freans of Bermondsey, of Garibaldi biscuit fame (1921). (In 1857 James Peek, a Devon-based tea importer, had started this company in collaboration with his son-in-law, miller and ship's biscuit-maker George Frean.) The two companies operated as Associated Biscuit Manufacturers (ABM).

Only in 1922 were pre-war production levels restored, back up to thirty lines. 'Sample tins' were produced, containing only four biscuits, and miniature versions of full-sized tins enclosed tiny copies of popular biscuit styles. A new range of tins doubled as children's toys, such as a doll's pram, pillar boxes and money boxes.

Through the 1920s progress was solid but uneventful. Criticized for exporting jobs, H&P opened a Paris factory in 1923 and then featured at the British Empire Exhibition at Wembley, 1924. The Prince of Wales, the future Edward VIII, awarded another royal warrant (1926).

In addition to previous philanthropies, family members were benefactors of the Royal Berkshire Hospital (there is a Huntley and Palmer Haemodialysis Unit there), the Royal College of Music and Berkshire County Cricket Club. The *Daily Telegraph* called Huntley & Palmers 'the seventh wonder of the commercial world'. They were well placed for the future.

HUNTLEY & PALMERS SINCE 1925

A 1957 story from the Museum of Liverpool reflects H&P tins' legendary status: civil servants drafting the Wolfenden Report, recommending legalization of homosexual acts between consenting men, were concerned that its contents might embarrass female office workers. To avoid blushes the phrase 'homosexuals and prostitutes' was replaced with 'Huntley & Palmers'.[3]

H&P launched the mysteriously named Nice biscuits in 1929, though Dutch and Australian rivals claimed they had created the coconut recipe. George Palmer's statue, possibly the first to include a folded umbrella, was moved from Broad Street to Palmer Park to aid traffic management.

In 1935 ABM, the H&P–Peek Freans partnership, employed more than 7,000 – fewer than the independent H&P had. Many post-war *Windrush* migrants coming to Reading found employment there.

Figure 11. A Huntley & Palmers biscuit tin pays
homage to Wedgwood, 1948.

Tins continued to feature prominently in marketing, though a 1937 one celebrating Edward VIII's (non-)coronation had to be abandoned. A rare new tin mimicked Wedgwood's popular jasperware (1948). The 1953 coronation tin featuring the royal couple was their best-seller, post war, as using photographs became routine. During the 1950s the sample tins were discontinued, and by the mid 1970s most tins had been replaced by paper wrapping. The grade II*-listed Marlston House left the family's ownership, becoming an independent school (1945).

A new manufacturing plant opened at Huyton, Liverpool, under Bill Palmer in 1955.[4] In 1960 ABM absorbed the Jacob's factory there (see Hartleys).

Jacob's, known for cream crackers and Twiglets (1929), started in Ireland, 1885, coming to Britain in 1922. All H&P production was centred on Huyton from 1976, after the Reading site closed (Bermondsey remained open).

The distinctive Lemon Puff came in 1958, when 17% of production was exported. Reg Palmer was the last family chairman (1948–63), and in 1969 H&P and Peek Freans formally merged as Associated Biscuits. In the 1970s the book *Quaker Enterprise in Biscuits: Huntley & Palmers of Reading, 1822–1972* celebrated H&P's history, whilst the company's own 1975 guide on *When to Serve British Biscuits* sensibly advised cocktail party hosts to 'use savoury biscuits'. The company had 18% of the market in 1976.

A tin made headlines in 1979: it was already in shops before lewd images, of rutting dogs and copulating humans, were discovered hidden within its suburban garden design. H&P apologized for a 'silly prank' and withdrew it. Forty years later the artist, Mick Hill, told the BBC that he thought he had had permission for the 'joke', and that two other dodgy tin designs remained out there! Today an original could be worth £200 (magnifying glass required).

By the 1980s, all was not well. In 1982 the American Nabisco (part of Kraft and then owners of Shredded Wheat) paid £83.8 million to acquire Associated Biscuits, with 14,000 employees in the UK and 3,000 abroad. With an 11% market share by 1988, the company was losing money. It ceased manufacturing at Huyton, and in-house tin-making ended in 1985. After Nabisco's takeover by private equity (KKR) in 1989, the French Danone bought Associated Biscuits and the Bermondsey factory closed, shedding 1,000 jobs. Danone acquired the residual Jacob's group in 2004 and then sold its biscuits division back to Kraft (2007). Kraft split into Mondelez (snacks) and Kraft Foods in 2012.

Most H&P lines were rebranded 'Jacob's' by 1990. There was no more H&P branding outside New Zealand, where Griffin Foods still manufactures 'Huntley & Palmers' biscuits under licence. However, 'Huntley & Palmers' was re-registered at Companies House in 2001, and by 2006 the name had been adopted by a startup in Sudbury, Suffolk. Owned by former Jacob's managers who had bought it from Danone, the newcomer focused on 'speciality and fine foods'. Now owned by Freemans, the wholesale food distributors, 'new H&P' aims to sell its products – including biscuits in tins – into mainstream markets. Still small, the company sells the 'ultimate indulgence', Chocolate Olivers, at £8.49 a tube, following the 1930s recipe. John Lennon once requested to be paid in £15 worth of Chocolate Olivers for giving an interview.

Reading Museum's Huntley and Palmers Gallery opened in 2000. A rebuilt George Palmer School became Palmer Academy (2004), and the city celebrated 200 years of 'Biscuit Town' in 2022. Palmer's statue, grade II*-listed, was restored and relocated again, to a pedestrian space. The biscuit company is gone but not forgotten.

Table 14. The Palmers.

Name		Note
George	(1818–1897)	Cousin of Joseph Huntley. Chairman, 1841–97; MP, 1878–85.
Samuel	(1820–1903)	Brother of George. Partner 1857–; chairman, 1897–1903.
William	(1824–1893)	Brother of George. Partner, 1857–93.
George 2	(1851–1913)	Son of George. Director; chairman, 1903–13; MP, 1892–95, 1898–1904. (Made Ronald Poulton heir with company role.)
Sir Walter	(1858–1910)	Son of George. Director; baronet, 1904; MP, 1900–6.
Emily	(1860?–1920?)	Daughter of George, mother of Ronald Poulton.
Howard	(1850?–1919?)	Son of Samuel. Chairman, 1913–19(?). Wokingham has a street and hall in his name.
Sir Ernest	(1858–1948)	Son of Samuel. Baronet, 1916–33; Baron Palmer, 1933–48 (honour unrelated to company). Board member only.
Cecil	(1882–1950)	Son of Ernest. 2nd Baron Palmer, 1948–50.
Ronald Poulton-Palmer	(1889–1915)	Son of Emily. England rugby captain, inherited 1913, died at Ypres. Adding 'Palmer' to his name was a condition of inheritance.
Reginald	(1898–1970)	Son of Howard. Chairman, 1948–63.
Raymond	(1916–1990)	Son of Cecil. Chairman, 1963–?; 3rd Baron Palmer, 1950–90.
William (Bill)	(1925–2020)	Son of Reginald. Director. Last of family to serve on board.
Adrian	(1951–2023)	Nephew of Cecil. 4th Baron Palmer, 1990–2023. Cross-bencher. His only connection with the company was an apprenticeship.
Hugo	(b. 1980)	Son of Adrian. 5th and current Baron Palmer. Not involved.

Cadburys

(1824, Chocolate)

Already known to humans for 5,000 years, chocolate arrived in Europe in the seventeenth century. In the eighteenth, Linnaeus named the cocoa tree *Theobromo cacao*, 'bitter food of the gods', and in the nineteenth Europeans cultivated its South American seeds in tropical Africa. Over more than 100 years, thirteen members of the Quaker Cadbury family led a chocolate concern that demonstrated, legendarily, that doing good and success in business can go together.

Puritan John Cadbury's coat was plain, his hat wide-brimmed. The teetotal pacifist (1801–1889) did not use a cushioned armchair before his seventieth birthday and banned pianos from his home. John campaigned for temperance and against both child chimney-sweeps and cruelty to animals, founding a forerunner of the RSPCA. His sons shared his view that consuming alcohol was an avoidable human failing, aiming to provide an alternative.[1]

John's first wife, Priscilla, died after only two years of marriage. His second, Candia (1805–1855), a Barrow family member and temperance worker, was mother to their seven children, of whom four survived to adulthood. The family charity is, to this day, known as the Barrow Cadbury Trust.

After being apprenticed from 1816 to a Leeds tea maker, John opened a tea and coffee shop in Bull Street, Birmingham (1824), with money from his father, Richard, a rich abolitionist (anti-slavery campaigner). His shop, with a Chinese clerk in traditional dress and the aroma of coffee, stood next to Richard's drapery. John prepared his wares in nearby Crooked Lane from 1831 and later in Bridge Street, where he developed cocoas and chocolate-based drinks for which he claimed medicinal benefits. In 1851, as a member of the precursor to Birmingham Municipal Corporation, John campaigned for an elected council.

By now John and his brother Benjamin owned Cadbury Bros, where they created a chocolate bar, two years after Joseph Fry, and introduced 'half-day Saturdays'. Employees needed time with their families, John believed, reducing the working week when six-, even seven-day working was normal.

Focusing on manufacture from 1849, John passed the shop to his cousin, Richard Cadbury Barrow, who renamed it Barrow's. He obtained permission to use an 1828 Dutch patent for extracting fat from chocolate, which reduced its bitterness and the need for fillers such as starch, producing a nicer-tasting cocoa essence justifiably described as 'pure'. When sugar was added, the so-called van Houten method allowed production of chocolate on a commercial scale.

Figure 12. The first George Cadbury (1839–1922).
(*Source: Romance of Great Businesses.*)

Whilst John's son Richard 2 (1835–1899) joined the company at an early age (in 1851), his brother George (1839–1922), initially an aspiring doctor, spent time apprenticed to the York grocer and fellow Quaker Joseph Rowntree.[2] George believed passionately in education, teaching literacy to hundreds of adults throughout his life.[3]

The 1850s saw a dispiriting downturn, made worse by John's depression after Candia's passing. The company halved its workforce, from twenty to eleven, and was losing money despite a reduction in cocoa bean import duty in 1853 and a royal warrant (1854). When Richard 2 and George assumed the leadership in 1861 they faced immediate problems. They invested in marketing, rationalization and exports, overcoming French competition by introducing candies in 1868. By 1875 the company was making Easter eggs and Valentine's Day items but had dropped tea, coffee and homeopathic infusions.

George sat as a Liberal on Birmingham Council in the 1870s, whilst Richard 2 indulged his artistic side, creating chocolate boxes covered in velvet, lined with silk. After his wife died in her fourth childbirth in 1868 Richard set up a crèche to help single parents, later marrying the daughter of the widow who ran it.

Figure 13. The Cadburys Bournville Factory today.

In 1879 Cadburys built a factory on a greenfield site at Stirchley, renamed Bournville, with eight times Bridge Street's capacity. It had excellent links by canal (for milk) and rail (cocoa and chocolate), and output doubled. Chocolate-covered biscuits joined its range.

George famously reflected on the unsavoury conditions of inner-city Birmingham, echoing his father's sentiment and opining: 'No man ought to be condemned to live in a place where a rose cannot grow.' That year the company started a 120-acre 'garden community' for 230 families at Bournville, which inspired the brand names of both a dark chocolate bar and a malt drink, Bournvita. The company's most famous act of community engagement, the village observed Quaker principles of quality, health and sobriety: by 1900 more than 300 dwellings occupied over 300 acres, with many public facilities, although not, of course, a pub.

Bournville's Arts and Crafts architects acknowledged nature in their designs. The movement's major figures were William Morris (1834–1896) and John Ruskin (1819–1900).

A year after George's wife, Mary, died in 1887, he married friend and fellow Quaker Elizabeth Taylor (1858–1951), who became an enthusiastic campaigner, councillor and magistrate – gaining an OBE in 1918 for her charity work. After George's death in 1922 she led the Bournville Trust, which still manages the community, and also sat on the city's education committee and Birmingham University's governing body. A dame from 1934, she had a local secondary school named after her.

In 1899 Cadburys became 'limited' with shareholders, George remaining as chairman and relatives occupying other board seats. Richard 2 died in Jerusalem, leaving £40,000 to charities including the London Temperance Hospital, having previously given Moseley Hall to the City of Birmingham as a children's convalescent home. When George and Elizabeth 'upsized', their former home became the Woodbrooke Quaker Study Centre (1903).

By the early 1900s Cadbury competed with Rowntree and Terry's, founded by York Quakers, and eclipsed the similarly Quaker-founded Fry's of Bristol. George bought London's *Daily News* (and several local papers) to give voice to liberal and pacifist opinion, specifically opposing the Boer War, and even supplied salesmen with leaflets to explain the family's opposition to the conflict. In 1909, after allegations of slavery in the Portuguese colonies that supplied Cadburys with cocoa, the company withdrew – but too slowly to avoid criticism (see 'Case study: Slavery' in the 'Social' chapter).

In Bournville, Britain's largest carillon, a splendid forty-eight-bell structure (1906), was followed by a church hall (1913) and an Anglican church, St Francis (1925). Although pacifist Quakers did not serve in the armed forces, the company donated chocolate to the front line in World War I and gave buildings for use as hospitals for the war-wounded.

George's son George 2 (1878–1954) introduced Dairy Milk in 1905. By 1914 it was the company's best-selling product, taking mass production to new heights as the world's most successful chocolate bar. Milk Tray followed (1915).

In 1917 Cadburys 'recognized' trade unions and established a works council at Bournville, though it was downgraded in 1926 after some workers joined the General Strike (see 'Employees' in the 'Social' chapter). After World War I, Cadburys redoubled its commercial efforts, creating its first overseas factory

(Tasmania), merging with Fry's and introducing new brands: Flake (1920), Creme Egg (1923), Fruit and Nut (1928) and Crunchie (1929). The company was criticized for the speed with which Fry's former plants were closed.

Cadburys employee numbers tell their own story: from 239 in 1879 to 11,500 in 1925.

CADBURYS SINCE 1925

Progress in the 1930s was solid, with productivity gains offsetting the 2,000 jobs lost during the Depression. Britain's twenty-fourth biggest consumer-goods manufacturer, it launched Whole Nut and Roses, named by Dorothy Cadbury, to compete with Mackintosh's Quality Street. Bournville now exceeded 1,000 acres. Dairy Milk won 60% of its market, and the company canvassed children for new ideas. Thirty years later one child consultee, Roald Dahl, wrote *Charlie and the Chocolate Factory*.

World War II brought the rationing of chocolate and sugar plus the iconic sight of Cadburys vans delivering chocolate drinks to London Blitz victims. By 1962 Cadburys and Rowntree accounted for half of all UK confectionery.

George and Elizabeth's son Laurence (1889–1992) spent fifty years on the board, including as chairman (1944–59). In 1950 the family was shaken by the death of his 24-year-old heir, Julian, in a biking accident. Adrian Cadbury (1929–2015), Laurence's second son, joined the board in 1958, becoming chairman in 1965. Under Adrian a chapel was added to St Francis Church to remember Julian, his sister and her husband (who both died in 1964), and subsequent Cadburys. The career of Cambridge Blue and Olympic rower Adrian, knighted in 1977, included several high-profile business roles; in 1992 he wrote an influential report for the London Stock Exchange, advocating changes to corporate governance regulation.

The first 'Milk Tray Man' TV advert appeared in 1968.

Like Schweppes, Cadburys viewed the upcoming 1970s with trepidation. They identified common barriers to growth, including a subdued domestic market, a narrow capital base and growing American competition. Cadbury Schweppes was formed – technically as a takeover of Cadburys by Schweppes – in 1969, with Sir Adrian as deputy chairman (see Schweppes). The new company quickly acquired Pepsi Cola South Africa and other brands, but its growth strategy enjoyed limited success. After Sir Adrian became chairman in 1974 the approach grew more aggressive, winning franchises for Coca-Cola (in the UK) and Sodastream (in the US). Cadbury Schweppes was the world's third-largest soft drinks company in the 1980s, during which it sold some non-core food brands (including Typhoo) to Premier Foods, acquiring other scalps when Nabisco quit soft drinks in 1986. It sold some US chocolate brands (with associated debts) to Hershey in 1988 and bought Bassetts liquorice products in 1989. Such successes combined with stock market uncertainty to make Cadbury Schweppes itself an attractive target for predators.

Adrian's brother Dominic (b. 1940), who had joined the board in 1975, became chief executive in 1983. On becoming chairman in 1993, he summed up the company's dilemma: 'If you are more than national, but less than global, you are an uncomfortable animal to describe.'

Dominic was knighted in 1997. In 1999 the last Cadbury-family chairman oversaw the sale of the soft drinks business outside the US and Europe to Coca-Cola. The company appointed outsider Derek Bonham to replace Dominic in 2000 but reverted to an insider, Sir John Sutherland, in 2003. Meanwhile several Cadburys TV ads vied for the title 'best of all time'.

Although 2005 saw Cadburys, then the world's biggest chocolate company, acquire chocolatier Green & Black's, with its strong Fairtrade policies, a chaotic decade followed. Seven hundred jobs were lost when the company moved to Uxbridge in 2007, and the 2008 demerger from Schweppes left the residual Cadbury plc under Roger Carr. Trebor Bassett was sold.

Now the world's second-biggest confectioner, it pledged itself to Fairtrade cocoa in 2009, when it rejected a £9.8 billion bid from the American Kraft Mondelez in favour of Hershey's more appropriate offer. But the Hershey deal collapsed, and in 2010 Cadburys shareholders approved a controversial and unpopular £11.5 billion takeover by Kraft Mondelez via private equity. Carr resigned and was not replaced. No longer involved, the Cadbury brothers, Adrian and Dominic, commented in the *Daily Telegraph*: 'A bidder can buy a business. What they cannot acquire is legitimacy over the character, values, experience and traditions on which that business was founded and flourished.'[4]

The Kraft Mondelez fight, depicted as 'traditional family values versus a modern tool of private equity', resulted in defeat. Almost as though it was planned, Kraft Mondelez itself demerged in 2012, splitting into Kraft Foods and Mondelez International (including Cadburys). Mondelez closed several Cadburys factories globally but invested £75 million in Bournville's 'Global Centre for Chocolate Excellence Research'. After 170 years Cadburys lost its royal warrant in 2024. Whilst reasons are never given for decisions on any Royal Warrant, in this case it could be related to Mondelez retaining its operations in Russia during that country's war on Ukraine.

In 2019, almost 100 years after his death, George Cadbury was voted the 'Greatest Ever Brummie' in a poll for Birmingham Civic Society. Beable concludes that Cadburys 'has done more to improve the lot of workers than many acts of legislation', although the 2008 demerger left the company a shadow of its former self. In many cases obscurity would have followed, but the strong 'Cadbury' brand survives.[5]

Prices

(1830, Candles)

In days gone by, had you wanted chunky white candles, night lights, birthday beacons or tea lights, your candle-monger would have reached for Prices. As the twentieth century dawned Edward Price & Co. was the world's biggest candle-maker, serving a seemingly insatiable demand. Pre-Victorian sentiment dictated that 'gentlemen' did not associate with dirt or stink, so the founders hid behind an alias: there was no Mr Price.[1]

Containers of combustible liquid with wicks existed 3,000 years ago, and every major culture evolved such lighting. By the sixteenth century Europeans burnt wicks in rendered animal fat (tallow) to illuminate their homes, and from the seventeenth Britain taxed candle manufacture and sale. Whale fat kept its shape whilst burning slowly, reliably, without tallow's malodourous spitting, but it was expensive. The only other viable candle was made from fragrant beeswax, which, as today, was costly, with limited availability. All this was academic; most families relied on rushes dipped in raw animal fat.

Historically, 'Lanark' evokes textile mills and Robert Owen. But New Lanark was not the only industrial community even in the county of Lanarkshire. In 1779 three Wilson brothers opened Wilsontown Mill, an ironworks. Although English ironworks had long been powered by coke, this was its first use in Scotland, which had hitherto used charcoal. In Lanarkshire all the necessary ingredients – coal, ore, limestone – were found conveniently nearby.[2] The factory pioneered new techniques such as blowing air through molten ore, raising the temperature to burn off impurities, a precursor to Henry Bessemer's manufacture of steel. One Wilson son, William (1772–1860), did not enter the iron business but traded commodities with Russia from London. However, in 1801, international trade having failed to provide him with a living, he joined the family enterprise. His father built a village to house his workforce, possibly at William's suggestion. William reclaimed a peat bog to plant 100,000 pines in a successful forestry enterprise. By 1808 Wilsontown had 450 homes and a shop, modern Britain's first preplanned settlement on this scale.

The Napoleonic Wars brought turmoil to the iron industry. The mill was no longer viable by 1812 and closed in 1815, with 2,000 tons of unsold iron. Forestry and mining could not bankroll the failing enterprise, and as theirs was not the only suffering business, it proved impossible to sell; bankruptcy followed. William returned to London for another go at trading, finding lots of tallow passing through his warehouses.

Some aspects of French science were proceeding at an indecent pace, not least within the laboratory of polymath Michel Chevreul (1786–1889), who, later in his exceptionally long and productive life, would invent margarine (1870). He theorized about the nature of chemical compounds, earning the soubriquet 'the father of organic chemistry'. Chevreul discovered that he could use alkali to split fats such as tallow into fatty acids and glycerine, which was useful for treating burns and skin complaints, preserving food, and manufacturing paint. The solid residue remaining after removing the glycerine, it turned out, also had a use: candles fashioned from it burned clean and odour-free.

Meanwhile, Wilson was relieved that the mill finally sold in 1821 (it would be broken up in 1846). The tallow that he and his business partner, Benjamin Lancaster (1801–1887), were importing in the 1820s contained opportunities. Lancaster's background is obscure, but in 1850 he gave Lancaster Park to the people of Canterbury, New Zealand, his wife's family's home.[3] Benjamin co-opted the name 'E. Price' from a distant female relative. In 1835 Lancaster sold his share of the company to men Beable calls three 'sleeping capitalists'.

Another Frenchman, Adolphe de Milly (1799–1876), patented the stearin candle (1828). Contrasting with de Milly's use of stearin, Wilson bought James Soames's patent technique for extracting fat from coconuts, which he imported from Ceylon (now Sri Lanka). The father of fourteen set up a candle-maker's in Vauxhall with sons David, James and Robert in 1830, a year before Britain fortuitously scrapped its candle tax.[4]

The plaited wick was yet another French patent. Fortunately for William Wilson, in 1836 the only licensed importer of such wicks, Tophams of Ripley, was his supplier. In 1839 came the first paraffin wax candle, made from shale oil.

As the only active owner of Prices, William, like his father, wanted to build a village where his workforce could live in comfort, but the cost of scarce land in London dissuaded him.

William's sixth son joined the board in 1840. George Fergusson Wilson (1822–1902) became a respected scientist, possibly the first to extract palm oil.* His timing was significant: after parliament banned British subjects

---

*A different George Wilson (1818–1859), Britain's first professor of technology (Edinburgh), championed Chevreul's work.

from involvement in slavery in 1833, West African assets were in danger of becoming stranded; something had to replace slavery economically to justify a continued British strategic presence there (see 'Case study: slavery' in the 'Social' chapter).

Palm oil proved ten times more productive than coconut. George perfected the extraction of liquid from palm trees' bright red fruits, separated the oil and made candles from the residue. He was the first to extract candle wax without using poisonous arsenic, and the first to treat it with sulphuric acid to obtain a pure white product, all without breaching de Milly's patent. George was soon trading with plantations in Nigeria, Togo and Ghana; from this would develop the ESG consequences of commercial-scale palm oil 200 years in the future.[5] William Wilson portrayed palm oil as the liberator of the black African: one advertisement showed a white man using a candle to burn through the ropes binding a black slave. And yet, over many years, perhaps 150 million candles – many of them from Prices – had been traded for slaves, whilst conditions for 'freemen' in West Africa's plantations were little better than those of slaves in the New World (as William Lever would discover).

Subjects burned candles to celebrate the royal wedding of 1840, whilst Victoria and Albert themselves enjoyed the new, exotic 'Sherwood' brand of Prices candles at their wedding breakfast. That year the company's eighty-four staff made most of their product from palm oil blended with tallow.

An 1842 patent by Chevreul and another French chemist, Gay Lussac, for the manufacture of stearic acid proved unenforceable. George Wilson registered his own way to make it (using a vacuum pump) and was admitted to the Royal Society and the Chemical Society. For his lilies he gained a place in the Royal Horticultural Society, and his experimental garden would become RHS Wisley.[6]

Price's Patent Candle Company registered as a joint stock company in 1847, with capital of £500,000, its logo illustrating an African presenting Britannia with palm oil. The following year it bought both a patent for the long-lasting night light and a night-light manufacturer, producing 12 million of them in 1852 alone.

Over its next five years the company sold 15,000 tons of candles, acquiring a specialist ecclesiastical candle-maker, Charles Farris, whose brand is still available today. Two years later Francis Tucker & Co. started to trade in oil lamps, so Prices bought them too. It distilled crude oil, initially from Burma, to make benzene (sold as a cleaning agent), kerosene (a future aircraft fuel) and paraffin wax for the robust 'Belmont' candle. Named after its factory's Battersea site on York Road, Wandsworth, the Belmont had a high melting point and good shape retention.[7] It was advertised as 'made expressly for hot climates'.

In 1851 Prices received its first royal warrant and exhibited at the Great Exhibition.

Britain's West African imports arrived in Liverpool, and it was on Merseyside that William's dream became reality with the construction in 1853 of homes for employees adjacent to the new Prices factory at Bromborough Pool, near where Lever Bros would later build Port Sunlight.[8] The Pool's first residents arrived in 1856; its forty-two acres contained 142 homes. The 'garden village' had a strong emphasis on green spaces long before Letchworth's 'garden city'.[9] Bromborough Pool gained a village hall (1858), more homes (1872), a primary school (1898), a pan-denominational church (1890), and then a library and sporting facilities.

Figure 14. Bromborough Pool was an early planned industrial village.

By 1855 Bromborough Pool's nineteen-acre factory had replaced the company's Vauxhall site. Between Bromborough and the eleven-acre factory in Battersea, Prices employed 2,300 people, half of whom were 'boys'. The 1833 Factory Act had banned under-9s from employment – but only in the textile industry. William's evangelical son James gave every boy a Bible, schoolbooks, a slate, breakfast, supper and warm baths. He warned the boys against swearing, smoking and 'disreputable girls'.

Profit-sharing came in 1869, and in 1893 every employee was enrolled in an innovative pension scheme.

Meanwhile George patented his purification of glycerine. When William Wilson died (1860) the company owned 114 patents. Stearin manufacture produced lots of liquid waste, olein, which it successfully marketed as a light lubricating oil (known as cloth oil) for the textile industry, replacing the more expensive olive oil. Many other uses for olein followed.

When the US replaced Burma as its source of crude oil in 1865, costs fell significantly. James 'Paraffin' Young's invention became the main ingredient of Prices candles.

By the turn of the century the world's biggest candle-maker was making 130 types in various colours, hardnesses and shapes, and a luxury Art Deco range would launch in 1920. It dominated the world of lubricating oil for thirty years, not least as official supplier to Rolls Royce.

In 1909 production was taking place in Africa, South America, Asia and New Zealand. With no more Wilsons involved, Prices became a subsidiary of Lever Bros (1919) and was known as Candles Ltd from 1922. In South Africa, the main foreign base for Prices, Lever Bros sold the local operation to a consortium of paraffin-wax-producing giants: Shell, BP and Burmah Oil.

In 1925 there was peace, harmony and contentment in the world of Edward Price. But as Beable turned down the flame of his gas mantle (commercially available from 1892), or switched off his electric light after a day's writing (electric bulbs were just becoming popular), maybe he paused to think: was mass illumination revealing the writing on the candle-makers' wall?

PRICES SINCE 1925

Candles Ltd, the Lever Bros subsidiary, was thriving, with both British factories enjoying solid, if below peak, demand. Candles were made mostly of paraffin, from plentiful oil.

Throughout the 1920s Prices, in its new Lever Bros form, invested in Bromborough Dock on the Mersey's west bank, Britain's largest private dock and the nation's principal site of palm oil import. However, as Unilever (as it was from 1929) rationalized, it closed the Bromborough Pool factory (1936), using the dock to serve its Port Sunlight factory. Wilsontown House was demolished in 1954, and the Scottish mill's remains were designated an ancient monument in 1968.

As demand fell, candle production focused on novelty and ceremonial lines, serving the royal wedding (1947), Elizabeth II's coronation (1953) and Churchill's funeral (1965).

The former South African subsidiary built a life of its own, creating a synthetic liquid wax in 1959. Shell bought out its partners in 1982 to own Price SA outright, developing insecticides and detergents and exporting paraffin wax back to the UK. Price SA was bought by Sasol Chemicals in 1988 and sold in 1995 to Daelite, who closed many locations to focus on domestic candles. Sasol repurchased Price SA in 2007 and sold it to Lion Match in 2015.[10]

Bromborough Dock was converted to a landfill site in 1991.

The 1990s were good for Price's Patent Candles Ltd. Unilever sold it into private hands, where it increased profits fivefold by 1998, employing 300 people (albeit a tenth of its peak). In 1998 its headquarters moved to Bicester, where it was purchased by the Italian candle-maker Sgarbi in 2000. Another Italian firm, SER Wax, acquired Prices in 2002, closing the Bicester site with thirty job losses.[11] Candles, scented candles and diffusers bearing the 'Price's' name are now made in Turin, where SER specializes in high-end products, essential oils and aromatherapy, amongst many other wax applications. Price UK (its current name) was no longer a significant user of palm oil.

Today, Price UK employs eighteen admin staff on a Bedford industrial estate, selling largely decorative Italian candles. Its pension scheme remains within Unilever's.[12] Bromborough Pool contains a mix of privately owned and housing-association-rented tenancies. In its once public buildings, an autism community is being established, partly financed by operating a garden centre (whose car park is the former bowling green). The Bromborough Dock landfill site was deemed complete in 2014 when it reached thirty-seven metres above sea level. It is now a well-kept nature reserve, Port Sunlight River Park, with great views of Liverpool and the Mersey. Methane extracted from the site generates electricity for the national grid.

Waring

(1835, Furniture)

The antique furniture that powers a multimillion-pound industry was once new. Designs by Sheraton, Chippendale, Hepplewhite and Adam are the currency of today's trade; Waring & Gillow made their designs reality.

Richard Gillow practised his trade in Lancaster from 1695, later bringing on board his son Robert (1704–1772) and then formalizing the company in 1731. By 1740 the Catholic Robert was importing mahogany, sugar and rum from the West Indies and exporting fine furniture in the opposite direction. Some of his British expatriate customers were, no doubt, slave owners. His exquisite bespoke cabinets, chairs and other effects were often adorned with fine inlay or upholstery. The company created furniture for the great designers, developing marquetry and helping popularize lacquer work. When Robert's sons took over in 1769 they sought opportunities to export and opened a store in London.

Gillows invented the telescopic dining table, the Davenport desk and the 'trou-madame', a ladies' billiard table. Although others were running the firm by 1821, it retained the Gillows name, its quality furniture gracing many a stately home.[1]

John Waring was a wholesale cabinetmaker, a Belfast Protestant who arrived in Liverpool in 1835. If Gillows represented quality and art then Waring was the master of quantity, scale, broader horizons. This was fortunate, as the emerging Gothic revival (inspired by Barry and Pugin's new parliament) created considerable demand for stylish furniture in classic designs. Under John's son, Samuel, the firm grew through the Arts and Crafts era, acquiring Anderson & Sons in 1885. Samuel tasked his own second son, Samuel 2 (Sam, 1860–1940), one of twelve siblings and a would-be lawyer with an artistic bent, with opening a London branch.

Sam discovered the store of Gillows of Lancaster at 175–81 Oxford Street as competition from mass-produced furniture was growing. Waring & Gillow Ltd was a mutually convenient arrangement begun in 1897, followed by a full merger in 1903 that included Bontors (oriental carpet importers) and cabinetmakers Collinson & Lock. Sam became chairman, and the combined company was soon worth £1 million. It built new premises at 164–88 Oxford Street, 'the world's biggest furniture showroom', opening in 1906. Its external façade is listed for its conservation value.

The company sold public shares whilst marketing its products under both individual and combined names. Austen, Thackeray and W. S. Gilbert all name-drop Waring & Gillow.

Waring created a niche side operation fitting out grand buildings and expensive yachts, including those of royalty. In 1900, working with architect Edwin Lutyens, he installed the Paris Exhibition's British pavilion and furnished the Carlton (1899) and Waldorf (1910) hotels. He created another sideline, construction company Waring-White (1904), building the Ritz Hotel (1906), the Automobile Club (Pall Mall, 1911) and many more. Waring-White employed American techniques, reducing construction time for daunting buildings: when others quoted four years to construct Liverpool Cotton Exchange, Waring built it in sixteen months. He did the same for several majestic post offices and Oceanic House, Trafalgar Square, headquarters of the *Titanic*'s operators, White Star.

Waring felt 'at home' with royalty, winning contracts from several European crowned heads. As he happened to be at Osborne House in 1901, he was invited to oversee Queen Victoria's lying in state there.

Waring sought to promote the beauty and skills of furniture-making, to 'educate the masses in the canon of good taste'. He enticed Harry Gordon Selfridge (1858–1947) to occupy Gillow's former Oxford Street site. Selfridge joined the Waring & Gillow board, and Waring & Selfridge was created to build the American's new store. However, Waring departed that partnership in 1908; his wobbly finances made remaining too risky. Waring-White never paid dividends and built only the first phase of Selfridge's edifice (1909).

From 1907 Waring's extravagance lost him shareholder support, and after Waring-White's insolvency (1910), the courts beckoned. Despite successfully completing Birmingham University's clock tower* and rebuilding the London Palladium, Waring-White was wound up in 1911. Many lost money, but not, somehow, Waring.

He restructured Waring & Gillow in 1912 and in 1914 switched production to war supplies, including wooden aircraft propellers at Lancaster, where Waring-White had built the Ashton Memorial and the town hall. Waring commissioned London's Olympia event space to employ 8,000 tent-makers; at

---

*The world's tallest free-standing clock tower, it is known as 'Old Joe' after University Chancellor Joseph Chamberlain.

his Cambridge Road (now Grove) factory in Hammersmith, they made protective clothing, ammunition belts and horses' nosebags. The service would be repeated in World War II. Journalists accused Waring of profiteering from the war, denying payments to shareholders and enjoying preferential access to government contracts.

Figure 15. Waring's 'Old Joe' is a familiar site on Birmingham's skyline.

In 1918 Waring erected a temporary wooden memorial to Britain's war dead near Marble Arch and pledged £50,000 to build a stone one. When George V wanted design changes, Waring argued instead for Lutyens to create a suitable memorial. After the press raged that Waring's cash properly belonged to his creditors, the government agreed to pay; Lutyens's cenotaph (1920) still stands in Whitehall. The controversy spilled into politics when Sir Samuel was granted a baronetcy in 1919 in recognition of 'public service', and again when he received a peerage in Lloyd George's 'dodgy' 1922 Birthday

Honours list, which was tainted by claims of 'cash for honours'.[2] MPs attacked the peer's disdain of creditors, and his rebuttal, from the Lords' benches, was weak. Beable, who admits that 'I have known Lord Waring for many years', should have resisted the temptation to bowdlerize the story of his friend, who failed to distinguish between company money and his own.

That 1922 elevation cited Waring as 'Pioneer of decorative art in furnishing [and] supporter of charities'. His benevolence was directed towards the Boy Scouts and several other causes, including the Furniture Trades Provident and Benevolent Association.

Through the 1920s Lord Waring continued to chair the company. Waring & Gillow opened a Paris store, led the field in Art Deco design and diversified – into cutlery, furniture for the royal doll's house and equipping the Cuban parliament. Never active in party politics, Waring held annual meetings with representatives of 'capital' and 'labour' at his Kent home. He 'endeavoured to find friendly solutions' to conflicts that might arise between them, but there is no evidence he ever found any.

WARING SINCE 1925

The Lancaster and Liverpool factories remained open, with branches in India and France; Waring & Gillow hosted a modern art exhibition on Oxford Street in 1928. In 1930 Lord Waring was again accused of 'recklessness', owing the company £100,000. He was obliged to stand down as chairman after no dividend was declared, but despite a dramatic fall in the share price, he managed to remain president, temporarily. The company was restructured without him as 'Waring & Gillow (1932)' as he narrowly avoided prosecution. Waring died from a stroke in 1940, his peerage lapsing as his only surviving son had already died.

Inevitable decline followed as the company lost identity and purpose on a corporate playing field. Great Universal Stores purchased Waring & Gillow in 1955, selling the furniture business to John Peters Ltd, who rebranded it Waring & Gillow (Holdings) Ltd. The original Gillows factory closed in 1962 but was immediately reborn as the first home of Lancaster University (1964). The Oxford Street store closed in 1973, and the successor company merged with an old rival to create Maple, Waring & Gillow, forty-eight of whose stores were purchased by Allied Carpets in 1988 to create Allied Maples. The Waring brand was now extinct.

Postscript: in 1995 Allied Maples successfully sued solicitors Simmons & Simmons over the inadequate advice they had been given about that 1988 purchase, now a widely cited 'textbook' legal case. In 2011, Business Dream, John Peters's successor, went into liquidation; John Peters itself was dissolved in 2013.

Kelly's

(1835, Directories)

You won't find 'database', 'GDPR' or 'public domain' in *Romance* in respect of Festus Kelly, but he surely knew of such concepts. He ran a database associated with, but not part of – integral to, but not involved with – the General Post Office (GPO).

Henry VIII appointed a 'Governor of the King's Posts' in 1516; in 1635 Charles I democratized the postal service, and Cromwell later awarded it a monopoly on data transfer. Charles II nationalized the General Letter Office under the postmaster general (1660). One hundred and thirty years later, posties in uniforms and mail coaches raced the length of the land.[1]

John Sparke and Hugh Ferguson, inspectors of post, considered that a central list of traders, merchants and others to whom important letters might be sent would be helpful. In 1799 they established a London business directory, outside the GPO but with its blessing. They compiled their *Post Office London Directory* from data provided by GPO staff and sold copies to interested parties. Benjamin Critchett, another GPO insider, joined them in 1803 and outlived them both, inheriting the database and overseeing it for life.

Meanwhile, James Pigot of Macclesfield (1769–1843) created the *Manchester Directory* (1811), merging it with *Dean's Directory* in 1815. Pigot compiled his *London Directory* in 1823 and separate directories for twenty-eight counties (plus Scotland) between 1828 and 1840.

In 1840 Roland Hill's universal Penny Post introduced stamps, starting with the Penny Black.

Festus Kelly began working for the GPO in 1819 and following Critchett's demise was appointed chief inspector of letter carriers for the London Post Office (1835). The *Directory* constantly proved its usefulness, but it was not, technically, Festus's job to keep it going. However, he followed tradition: he bought the rights to publish the *London Directory* from Critchett's widow, creating Kelly & Co.

By now the *Directory* was a comprehensive listing of tradespeople, businesses, gentry, landowners, charities and others, town by town. Unlike Pigot and other directory-masters, Kelly's massive network of informers knew where the businesses were and, equally important, when they stopped and started trading, enabling him to keep the directory up to date. His informants were uniformed postmen who received tips on top of their Post Office wages but were not employed by him. Other compilers had to find data for themselves or pay for professional researchers. Pigot acknowledged defeat, pulling out of the South East in 1840. Kelly's *Directory* proved lucrative and he bought out other competitors.

Kelly's rivals resented his 'unfair' access to cheap data and accused him of usurping a public role for private gain. Supported by the *Sentinel* newspaper, 'Honest Tom' Duncombe, a playboy Radical MP and rare parliamentary Chartist, raised this inequity in parliament in 1844, but by then Kelly was already paying his informers properly. Without admitting that his previous practice was unethical, Kelly knew that his data was not totally reliable – posties were not skilled at reading.

Using Post Office employees to furnish data to third parties was banned in 1847, but too late. Kelly's directories spread across England from 1845.

When the London Post Office and GPO merged, Kelly's official position ended but his *Directory* continued, including every London postal address. In 1875 he published a *Handbook to the Titled, Landed and Official Classes*, and in 1877 a *Directory of Merchants, Manufacturers and Shippers*. A former apprentice of Pigot, Isaac Slater, inherited his late employer's directories for the north of England.

Both Kelly and Slater died in 1883. The company was taken over by Festus's sons John Richards Kelly (1844–1922), an Eton-educated barrister and Conservative MP for Camberwell, 1886–92, and Festus 2 (1838–1918), vicar of Camberwell and father of artist Gerald Festus Kelly. In 1892 they incorporated Slater's *Directory*, becoming Kelly's Directories Ltd in 1897. From 1912 the *Directory* included some telephone numbers.

In 1921 Kelly's headquarters were 184–6 Strand. The premises were once the offices of Chapman & Hall – publishers of Dickens's *A Christmas Carol* (1843) – and, later, WHSmith.

Beable reflects on how the directory had changed. Early Kelly's directories might have had 15,000 entries, but in 1925 there were hundreds of thousands. There were up to 1,000 pages, bigger and in a smaller font. In the 1849 edition the profession of 'cupper' (coffee taster) was not uncommon, but none were listed in the 1920s. In 1800 there were 8 insurance companies, 150 in 1849 and more than 300 by 1899.

Kelly should have printed his *Directory* on yellow pages.

KELLY'S AND THE POST OFFICE

Today libraries and archives treasure their multiple copies of *Kelly's*, which contain so much information about their historical communities, the Guildhall

Library holding the most complete collection. After a quiet half century, 1980 brought the last published *Kelly's Directory*, then silence. An unrelated online directory, Kellysearch, existed briefly around 2004.

As a state agency the GPO changed little until 1968, when it introduced National Giro, later Girobank, and divided mail into first and second class. In 1969 the postmaster general's role disappeared after 300 years, and the GPO was replaced by a nationalized Post Office. Its growing telecommunications arm (where billing employed Lyons's LEO system) became independent as British Telecom (BT) in 1981, when Britain had 22,000 Post Office branches. The 1987 Data Protection Act regulated the collection, holding and use of personal data in ways that would have alarmed Kelly.

In 1996 ICL (the tech company that had absorbed LEO in 1963) developed a computer system to allow payment of social security benefits through the Post Office. The Benefits Agency rejected the proposal, writing off £750 million of investment, but the government procured it for the Post Office. What was now Post Office Counters introduced the scheme, called Horizon, into 11,500 post offices. Six sub-postmasters were prosecuted in 2000 for alleged shortfalls in their returns, a trickle that would become a torrent of similar prosecutions. ICL became Fujitsu in 2002.

By 2004 Horizon was Europe's largest non-military IT contract. Post Office losses of more than £100 million in 2006, caused by falling demand, led to a proposal to close 2,500 rural branches, as government subsidies across Royal Mail reached £1.7 billion by 2007. Aiming to move into profit by 2011, eighty-five Crown Offices (major branches with more services) were closed, with WHSmith acquiring seventy of them, saving the taxpayer £40 million a year. More closures followed.

In 2010 the government invested a further £1.34 billion to restructure and privatize the service.

Horizon was processing 6 million transactions daily by 2013, though when independent forensic accountants declared it unfit for purpose, the Post Office tried to sack them. As the prosecutions swelled, the Post Office exonerated itself of mismanagement and denied systemic failure. Protesting their innocence, many of those found guilty went bust, got divorced and worse. Two hundred and thirty-six went to prison. Three thousand may have had unsound allegations made against them.

In 2019 the High Court ruled that many of the prosecutions could have resulted from Horizon's defects, whilst the Post Office CEO since 2012, Paula Vennells, was awarded a CBE. The Court of Appeal continued to overturn sub-postmasters' convictions through 2020. The BBC called Horizon 'the UK's most widespread miscarriage of justice'. Today, with many issues outstanding, every wrongly convicted sub-postmaster stands to receive significant compensation, although this may not cover all their direct costs.[2] The incoming government of 2024 pledged to pay compensation in full ... eventually.

ITV received plaudits for its 2024 dramatic reconstruction of the Horizon scandal, *Mr Bates vs the Post Office*. Vennells returned her CBE during the public inquiry, and the Post Office chairman was sacked. The inquiry continued, with witnesses consistently professing profound sorrow but mostly ignorance. Parliament took the unprecedented step of quashing all convictions of sub-postmasters based on the evidence around Horizon, and the police raised the possibility of arrests of the perpetrators of the injustice by 2027. The wronged postmasters' leader, Alan Bates, received a knighthood, whilst the financial lawyer Dan Neidle described the Post Office as 'a huge scandal with a small retail business attached'.[3]

The Four Publishers

The four publishers' 'romances' account for many of the popular periodicals of recent times, and post 1925 they are completely intertwined. Clearly passionate about magazines, Beable dismisses 'here today, gone tomorrow' newspapers as 'not part of the romance'.

CASSELLS (1840)

The short career of John Cassell (1817–1865), was full and frantic. Did growing up in a pub, Ring o'Bells in Hunt's Bank, Manchester, prompt John to champion temperance? Did his limited education, leaving school aged 10, spark his passion for the intellectual liberation of the working classes? Did inheritance by marriage give him space to bring culture to the deprived? Probably.

The bored 13-year-old factory hand chose a carpentry apprenticeship, undertaking at the same time to extend his general knowledge and learn French. At 16 he signed the temperance pledge, frustrated that tea, coffee and milk were expensive, and water unsafe, yet debilitating beer was cheap. What chance did working-class Mancunians have?

The practiced orator, 'young, bony, big and uncultivated', campaigned against the demon drink. Aged 20 he walked to London, preaching along the way, summoning crowds with his rattle and reaching Westminster sixteen days later with just pennies in his pocket. Trained and sponsored by the National Temperance Society, he toured London for six months and then England for two years, promoting the cause.

John and his wife, Mary (née Abbott), settled with his mother in St John's Wood. Mary inherited money that she invested in John's new business, a coffee and tea shop. Their home became a magnet for cultured friends.

After two years on Coleman Street they opened a new venture at nearby 80 Fenchurch Street. John bought a printing press to produce advertising fliers, but within weeks temperance tracts were rolling off it. Mary's brother joined them to run the coffee business, allowing John to concentrate on the *Teetotal Times* from 1846.

Cassell's next, weekly, publication was the *Standard of Freedom* (1848), advocating free trade and religious liberty. An expanded *Teetotal Times and Essayist* followed (1849), and then the *Working Men's Friend and Family Instructor*, thirty-two pages for a penny, a year later. Beable describes the *Friend*'s audience as 'a difficult one to reach on account of [readers'] prevailing ignorance'. The *Friend* celebrated open minds, liberation through reading. Dickens and the Radical Liberal MP Richard Cobden, who became a close acquaintance, praised Cassell.

The political *Quarterly Review* described the *Friend* as 'revolutionary', praising Cassell's sympathetic, unpatronizing manner. The emboldened campaigner took on wider issues: 'Anything short of ... universal suffrage ... will greatly disappoint the majority of non-electors.' Things were moving quickly: Cassell bought a print shop at 335 Strand. Then he focused on the Great Exhibition of 1851, where, with Cobden, he organized cheap accommodation for working-class visitors.[1] His official programme sold 40,000, and afterwards the *Illustrated Exhibitor* reached 100,000.

Twenty-six volumes of *John Cassell's Library* were published from 1851, making history, biography and science accessible, whilst the *London Conductor*, at a shilling, enjoyed 30,000-plus circulation. Cassell always intended the *Standard of Freedom*, soon absorbed into the *Weekly News and Chronicle*, to be 'one of the most talented and vigorous advocates of Liberty, Commercial, Political and Religious'.

From general calls for better education, Cassell's causes became more specific. The *Popular Educator* (1852–5), promoting free education long before the 1870 Education Act, was his proudest achievement; fifty years later, Lloyd George would credit its influence. For Cassell and his contemporary John Ruskin, the power of reading was political. Literacy could open eyes, hearts and opportunities, enhance working people's lives, and reignite the Chartist flame.[2]

The Strand property was too small, so Cassell offered to occupy part of a nearby struggling coaching inn. This was the Belle Sauvage, an Elizabethan playhouse off Ludgate Hill, which had been the London home of both Pocahontas (1616), the Native American princess (perhaps 'La Belle Sauvage' herself?), and Britain's first rhinoceros (1684). Soon the teetotaller owned the whole establishment. It was demolished in 1873 to build a railway viaduct, itself destroyed by a German bomb in 1941.

Cassell launched the *Illustrated Family Paper* in 1853, featuring serialized stories. One, 'The Warp and the Weft', described Lancashire's cotton famine and encouraged donations to support Cassell's former neighbours. On his first American visit, for a temperance convention, he met Harriet Beecher Stowe, author of *Uncle Tom's Cabin*. As an abolitionist Cassell was keen to serialize the novel, which duly appeared in thirteen parts and became Britain's most widely read contemporary book.

In 1852 two struggling printers, Thomas Galpin (1828–1910) and evangelist George Petter (1823–1888), combined their steam-powered businesses in the *Times'* building. Pressured by suppliers, Cassell sought a substantial amount of credit from the pair. They agreed, in return for a controlling interest in his business – so Cassell worked for them, as an editor (1854–8), before repurchasing the company, now Cassell, Petter and Galpin.[3]

During the 1850s Cassells published the *Illustrated Family Bible* in penny parts, followed by the *Illustrated Magazine of Art*. Then came *The Freeholder*, journal of the free land movement, and the religious *Pathway*. He campaigned against advertisement, stamp and paper duties; their abolition ushered in his most profitable period. The company produced illustrated versions of *Robinson Crusoe*, *Gulliver's Travels* and the Bible. Yet another religious publication, *The Quiver*, appeared in 1861.

During his third US visit, in 1859, Cassell set up an office on Broadway. In 1862 he started to sell American lamp oil as Casselline, maybe giving us the word 'gasoline', but his oil-distillation subsidiary did not succeed.[4] The year 1865 brought the weekly *Illustrated History of England*, which sold more than 250,000.

John Cassell died of cancer at home, 25 Avenue Road, Regents Park, on the same day as Cobden. Petter, Galpin and their 500 employees vowed to carry on.

Over the next few years momentum was regained. The *Illustrated Family Paper* became *Cassell's Magazine*, reaching 70,000 in the 1890s and running until 1912. Contributors included Wodehouse, Collins, Stevenson, Barrie, Kipling, Conan Doyle, even, in 1908, Joseph Conrad. *The Echo* (1868–75), a daily paper, was a pet project of Cassell's that was only realized posthumously.

Robert Turner joined the partnership in 1878 (now Cassell, Petter, Galpin & Co. Ltd), but when the partners could not agree a policy on fiction, Petter retired (1883). In 1888 Petter died, Galpin retired and Turner became chairman, heralding a disappointing twenty years. With Thomas Young's 1908 chairmanship things improved, though he took the company private. It was restored to the stock exchange in 1923.

The *City Press* described John Cassell as an 'utter ignoramus' capable of 'indomitable perseverance'. 'Ignoramus' was not, apparently, meant in a negative sense.

But by 1925 there were no new ideas, no founder's energy, no family.

ODHAMS (1870)

William Odhams (b. 1816?), of Sherbourne, Dorset, left home in 1834 to seek his fortune in London, finding work as a *Morning Post* compositor. In 1847 he joined forces with printer William Biggar at Beaufort Buildings, on the site of today's Savoy Hotel, but soon moved to nearby 5 Burleigh Street, where they produced several titles for clients. Publishing was a cottage industry with limited capacity; a publisher's house might have a press in the basement, marketing on the ground floor, composition upstairs. The editor would constantly rove, the family occupying whatever space was left. In 1840, when printing took off, London presses were generating 40,000 newspapers each week.

When the partnership ended in 1870 William Odhams registered a company in Covent Garden's Hart (now Floral) Street. In 1892 he sold it to his sons William 2 (known as WJB) and the sickly John. The boys resented the old man's continuing interference, so in 1894 they set up Odhams Brothers Ltd separately, with twenty employees.

The Odhams 'romance', however, is that of Julius Salter Elias (né Selzer, 1873–1946).[5] Elias was born in Birmingham to a family of Whitby-jet button makers, Jewish migrants from Prussian Poland.[6] They moved to Hammersmith around 1884 to run a newsagents in the Grove, from where Julius delivered a paper round on his way to school. At 13 he became a minion at Carlyle Press in Charterhouse Square. When it closed he approached the Odhams brothers, on his twenty-first birthday, who employed him as an office boy. Within days he was promoted to salesman – at five times the wage – then to junior manager a year later.

When William finally retired, the two firms amalgamated, with a new board of the two brothers, a lawyer and Elias. After restructuring in 1898 WJB was chairman and Elias managing director of Odhams Ltd. The company absorbed *Racing Pigeon*, *Family Doctor* and *Vanity Fair*, amongst others.

Half a century earlier Dickens regularly declaimed at St Martin's Hall, 92 Long Acre. The Queen's Theatre replaced the hall, itself succeeded by Odhams's works in 1905.

Horatio Bottomley, short and round, was Elias's nemesis.[7] Occasional millionaire, racehorse owner, and fraud, Bottomley aspired to be a politician and newspaper magnate. His company founded the *Financial Times* (1888) and briefly published Hansard, parliament's official record (1889–92). That contract ended in debt as he narrowly avoided conviction for fraud, having stepped down as a Liberal candidate due to an 1890 bankruptcy. This did not prevent Bottomley becoming MP for Hackney South in 1906, possibly the last time 'Liberal' was associated with his name. His reputation preceded him: the Commons heard his maiden speech in chilling silence.

The burly, fictitious John Bull is usually depicted with a Union Jack waistcoat and a bulldog, the archetypal British or English nationalist. A publication in Bull's name had loyally supported the Tory cause from 1820 to 1892, and in that spirit editor Bottomley revived the title in 1906.

Initially funded by Ernest Hooley, Bottomley used *John Bull* as a mouthpiece, reviving his earlier column 'The World, the Flesh and the Devil'. His style was populist, hard-hitting, often tasteless, scornful of the pace and nature of democracy. Beable remarks that 'a less far-sighted man than Elias would have feared to touch' the poisonous Bottomley, but Elias did agree to print and distribute the organ. 'I don't take sides,' he argued, but the two men had nothing in common, not background, character or belief.

Within months Julius regretted his decision as Bottomley's flashy, chaotic style generated a pile of unpaid bills. To avoid a large loss on a potentially lucrative contract, Elias took *John Bull* in-house and increased its advertising revenue vastly. Elias's discipline and Bottomley's editorial prowess proved a winning formula, and by 1910 its circulation, equally scandal-driven but now less toxic, was 500,000 and growing.

Although Bottomley's column regularly attacked parliament pre war, that changed in June 1914. After Sarajevo he called for Serbia to be 'wiped from the map', two weeks later demanding the eradication of Germany, too. During World War I Bottomley delivered more than 300 pro-war speeches, many aimed at 'the enemy within' – Britons with German-sounding names. *John Bull* had one of the world's largest circulations (peaking at 1.7 million), and Bottomley used the promise of prize draws to sell government 'Victory Bonds', a precursor of premium bonds. He used £1 million in takings to pay off his debts, not least to his horse trainers and girlfriends.

Odhams's publishing and marketing budgets rose twentyfold between 1908 and 1925. The company's four-storey building was a designated war shelter. When the alarm sounded, late on 28 January 1918, 600 congregated there. A 300-pound bomb penetrated the basement, exploded and demolished the building, killing thirty-eight and injuring eighty-five, yet not a single publication ceased printing as fellow publishers rallied to Elias's aid.

Finding the money to buy himself out of bankruptcy, and still driven by passion and bile, Bottomley returned triumphantly to parliament in 1918 as an Independent in Hackney, attracting 80% of voters to the slogan 'Bottomley, brains and business'. His fellow travellers in the small Commons' Independent Group targeted much of their venom at the proposed League of Nations, their attacks backed by another Bottomley creation, the People's League of Capital and Labour, and by Sir Oswald Mosley.

In 1920 Julius Elias, now running Odhams solo, acted decisively. Recovering from a breakdown he took control of *John Bull*, buying Bottomley out of his lifetime editor's role for £25,000. He created *Ideal Home* and acquired *Hare & Hound*, *Sporting Life* and 12,000 advertising sites – including the Piccadilly Circus illuminations. In 1922 Julius and his wife, Alice, moved to Highgate, where he purchased and demolished neighbouring properties to improve his view.

In 1922 Bottomley was convicted of the Victory Bonds fraud and sentenced to seven years, prompting his second expulsion from the Commons. Inside Maidstone Prison, where Elias visited him, Bottomley renewed Hooley's acquaintance. On his release in 1927, to Elias's annoyance, Bottomley set up *John Blunt* to rival *John Bull*. It failed, and after an unsuccessful 1930 lecture tour he was again bankrupt. He had built a magnificent family home, The Dicker, today Bedes School, Sussex, in a brief millionaire phase around 1900, but when his wife died he was evicted from the house by his son-in-law. He went to live with his lover, actress Peggy Primrose, dying in poverty at 73 to mixed reviews. Elias contributed to his funeral costs.

Bottomley's court case damaged sales of *John Bull*, which fell to 300,000 per week, but Elias was undaunted. The only major publisher ever to be awarded honorary membership of a printers' union (Natsopa) still had a career in newspapers and politics ahead of him.[8]

NEWNES (1881)

The 1870 Elementary Education Act introduced compulsory schooling for children up to 12 years old. In the following years more teachers than ever endowed youngsters with reading skills. The 1890s would thus see the first generation of adults with a literate majority, but what would they read? Books were expensive and there was little demand for leisure reading, whilst accessible reporting of news and opinion was a novelty. George Newnes (1851–1910), purveyor of words to the lower and aspiring middle classes, earned the soubriquet 'the father of modern journalism'.

The son of a Congregationalist minister in picturesque Matlock, George left home at 16 for a Manchester haberdasher's apprenticeship. Initially rewarded only with board and lodging, by the early 1870s George had risen to 'travelling salesman'. On those journeys it amused him to collect 'tit-bits', interesting or witty snippets of information from newspapers, which he pasted into an album. Was this what this new generation needed?

In 1881 *Tit-Bits* issue 1 lacked assured funding, so Newnes asked a printer if he could pay him from its proceeds; he was refused. Newnes sent bundles to wholesale agents on sale or return, including dozens, speculatively, to a London distributor. Meanwhile, Boys' Brigade volunteers roamed Manchester, selling 5,000 copies. After issue 6 the printer returned: could he buy *Tit-Bits* for £16,000? 'No.'

Readers were involved from the start, quizzing experts on law, marriage, medicine – even writing in to an 'agony' column. Competitions were open to all 'irrespective of age, sex, nationality or colour'. The publication was non-political, though an 1890 readers' poll showed 52% opposing Salisbury's Conservative government.

George, his wife Priscilla and Frank, their only surviving child, moved to London in 1884. In 1885 Newnes offered £100 to the family of anyone who died in a railway accident with a copy of *Tit-Bits* about their person, generating thirty-six successful claims over ten years. Alfred Harmsworth (later the *Daily Mail*'s Lord Northcliffe) worked under Newnes.

When the lord mayor of London appealed for donations of a penny a week for hospitals, Newnes promised £10,000, but only once *Tit-Bits* circulation passed 500,000 – which it did in 1890. His credo, 'cooperative philanthropy', cleverly combined both working- and middle-class values.

The 1885 general election returned the Liberal Newnes to parliament for Newmarket, where he sat for ten years. He represented Swansea from 1900 for another decade, during which Frank joined him as Member for Bassetlaw, 1906–10.

Newnes flirted with William Stead, editor of the *Pall Mall Gazette*, in 1890–1. Stead was a Salvationist, a radical, a pacifist, an equal-pay-feminist, a supporter of laws against child abuse – the pioneer of journalistic interviewing techniques was a walking manifesto. They launched the *Review of Reviews* together, a monthly reformist journal, but Stead went too far, thought Newnes, abusing opponents, institutions, celebrities and *The Times*. Stead bought Newnes out for £3,000.*

In 1891 Newnes launched the *Strand Magazine*, the outstanding publication of its genre, which ran for 711 monthly editions. Its cover picture, a sketch of the Strand, evolved with technology, fashion and editors.[9] Issue 6 introduced Sherlock Holmes in Arthur Conan Doyle's 'Scandal in Bohemia'. Holmes appeared in four novels and fifty-six stories; although he died at Moriarty's hands in 1893, he reappeared in *The Hound of the Baskervilles* (1901). After Sidney Paget had given the sleuth a deerstalker, Conan Doyle had the artist illustrate all of his work.

The *Strand*'s circulation peaked at 300,000, plus 100,000 in America. Often running to 200 pages for 6d (2.5p), it introduced H. G. Wells, Wodehouse, Nesbit and Kipling.

The *Pall Mall Gazette* drifted to the right after Stead left. Newnes needed to address this, so he launched the Gladstonian *Westminster Gazette* (1893). The 'pea-green incorruptible' was printed on tinted paper, making it supposedly easier to read in new-fangled artificial light. Readers of his early colour publication *The Million* were, of course, 'millionaires'.[10]

---

*Stead's monument is on London's Embankment. He died on the *Titanic*.

Newnes received a baronetcy in 1895, but struggles with alcohol and money scotched prospects of a peerage. The company moved from Burleigh Street to Southampton Street, where a Lutyens-designed clock, still extant, once bore the twelve letters of Newnes's name in place of its numerals.

Figure 16. George Newnes's clock can still be seen on Southampton Street, London.

He launched the 'Penny Library' series in 1896, and *Country Life* a year later, selling it in 1905 whilst restructuring the company with a million pounds of capital. In 1900 *Tit-Bits* reached a million readers.

Newnes spent much of his wealth in Lynton, Devon, which he knew from his youth, building Hollerday House as a family home. He funded the town's funicular railway (its patent braking system bears his name) and town hall.

Fascinated by technology, he funded two other funiculars (including one in Matlock, 1893–1927) and the Lynton-to-Barnstaple railway line.[11] He funded a British Antarctic expedition (1900), which named a glacier after Frank. When his business struggled, Newnes sold the *Westminster Gazette* to a consortium of Liberal financiers (1908).

George Newnes was diabetic and, approaching 60, unwell. He died in Lynton in 1910, leaving his son – now Sir Frank – the business, home and baronetcy. His shocking debts obliged Sir Frank to sell the home, which, after three years standing empty, mysteriously burned down. Its last remaining stones were redeployed in the cause of flood recovery (1952).

A 1922 edition of the *Strand*, with a full colour cover, introduced Arnold Bennett and Wodehouse's 'Jeeves'. In 1923 the company published an innovative schedule of radio programmes, the *Radio Times*, paying the (private) British Broadcasting Company £1,000 a year for the privilege. (Ethical considerations prevented Odhams from bidding for this contract, as BBC boss John Reith was married to John Odhams's daughter.)

George Newnes's goal, of giving 'wholesome and harmless entertainment to hard-working people craving a little fun and amusement', had been achieved. A planned move – to the purpose-built, impressive Tower House at 10 Southampton Street in 1935 – reflected Sir Frank's confidence.[12]

PEARSONS (1891)

This Sir Arthur Pearson (1866–1921) is not the Pearson publisher associated with Penguin Books, the *Financial Times* or education. That story – from Huddersfield bricklayer to Liberal polo supremo via Mexican oil and a merger with Longmans – is much more romantic!

Pearson, son of a Somerset vicar, won a writing position on Newnes's *Tit-Bits* in an 1884 competition. Six years later, denied a pay rise, he launched *Pearson's Weekly*. It took six issues to find a successful formula, which included a stroke of genius: word puzzles.

A surgeon had claimed that eucalyptus could ward off influenza, so *Pearson's Weekly* was impregnated with it for several weeks – sales rocketed. The *Weekly* and its stablemate, the left-leaning monthly *Pearson's Magazine* (1900–39), introduced promising writers such as George Bernard Shaw, Rudyard Kipling and the American Upton Sinclair.

In 1892 Pearson established a charity to help disadvantaged children. A friend of Robert Baden-Powell, he financed the Boy Scouts' 1908 launch, later publishing their journal (including a Braille edition). Scouts raised funds for Pearson's charity in return.

Alongside Joseph Chamberlain in 1903, Arthur set up the Tariff Reform League, advocating protection of Britain's economy. The following year he bought the struggling *Standard* and *Evening Standard*, changing them from Conservative to Liberal organs. History has not been as kind to Pearson as Beable was: even Chamberlain, Pearson's friend, described his thinking as 'capricious' and 'shallow'.*

In 1898 Pearson launched the *Royal Magazine* (later to feature 'Miss Marple') and then purchased the *Morning Herald*. He merged this with his new creation, the *Daily Express*, to rival the *Daily Mail* on newsagents' stalls, breaking with tradition by carrying news on its front page. He made a failed bid for *The Times* in 1907 and then sold *The Standard* and the *Express* to Sir Max Aitken, later Lord Beaverbrook, in 1910.

Encroaching blindness obliged Pearson to step back from day-to-day management as early as 1899, and surgery in 1908 failed to correct his glaucoma. By 1914, having published a Braille dictionary, he had gone completely blind so invited Newnes to manage the company's publications. Pearson became president of the National Institute for the Blind, raising its annual income from £8,000 to £300,000 in just eight years. He established another charity, later named St Dunstan's, to help soldiers blinded in the Great War. This earned him a baronetcy (1916).

Sir Arthur's 'romance' includes the fight against blindness, his charity work and eight magazine titles. In 1911 the first edition of *Woman's Weekly* contained a cut-out blouse pattern and sold half a million at a penny each.

Pearson died in 1921, drowning after falling in his bath. His son, Sir Neville (1898–1982), deemed too young to inherit the business but not the title, held a senior position at Newnes for life. In 1947 he took over St Dunstan's from his elderly mother, Dame Ethel.

Pearson's Magazine featured Britain's first published crossword puzzle in 1922.

THE FOUR PUBLISHERS SINCE 1925

Both Newnes and Pearson gave readers the best of literature at affordable prices, helping many of the day's greatest writers become household names. Cassell's faith drove his passion for education and temperance. Elias, at Odhams, was not unusual in being a company leader involved in politics, but he was in taking the Labour whip.

---

*See 'Case study: slavery' (in the 'Social' chapter) for the battle between Cadburys and Pearson's *Standard* (1909).

Newnes's company (incorporating Pearsons), which had hit gold in 1922 with its first publication by Richmal Crompton (number one of thirty-eight volumes of 'William'), found similar success in 1926 with the first of six books by Enid Blyton.

With £1.5 million in capital, Elias moved Odhams unequivocally towards newspapers in 1925, acquiring *The People* by writing off its printing debts. With presses at a standstill during the 1926 General Strike, the Conservatives invited Elias to print the *British Gazette*, promulgating the government line, in return for a knighthood (and police protection). After agonizing he declined, unwilling to employ the necessary 'scab labour'. Similarly, John Reith of the BBC also refused to transmit unalloyed government propaganda during the strike, insisting on balance. To counter the *Gazette*, the Trades Union Congress (TUC) published strike news in the *British Worker* (edited by Ernest Bevin of the newly formed Transport and General Workers' Union). Did the unions obtain paper for their publication from Odhams? The suspicion that Elias was involved may have delayed his peerage.[13]

The following year *Cassell's Magazine* was bought by Harmsworth's Amalgamated Press, then the world's biggest publisher and parent of the *Daily Mail*. Amalgamated acquired the remaining assets of Cassells in the 1930s.

By 1929 Pearsons had been fully absorbed into Newnes, retaining the Pearson name only as an imprint (an occasionally used status somewhere below 'brand'). The *Strand* was given a modern cover, featuring a woman's image for the first time, but its American edition closed.

The TUC invited Odhams to buy 51% of the *Daily Herald* (founded during the 1911 printers' strike) if Elias would maintain its pro-Labour line, resolving his problem of excess capacity. Elias accepted and became its chairman, with Bevin his deputy. When three leading Labour MPs joined the national government in 1931, Elias, Bevin and the *Herald* stayed loyal to the party leader, George Lansbury, though the best-selling daily's circulation fell from its peak of 2 million. When WJB retired in 1933 Elias became joint managing director and chairman. Bevin would be the war-time minister of labour, and then foreign secretary from 1945.

In 1932 Newnes launched the *Practical* range of magazines (*Mechanic, Motorist, Wireless* etc.) and *Woman's Own*, one of the most successful women's magazines ever. To balance it, the company launched *Men Only* in 1935 under the Pearson imprint, a 'pocket' magazine with small pages and no pictures.

With sixty newspaper titles, Odhams employed 10,000 in 1935, earning Elias a second nervous breakdown (1937). His recovery was aided by Stanley Baldwin's glowing appreciation of the *Herald*'s coverage of Edward VIII's abdication. Elias went to the Lords as Labour's Baron Southwood in 1937 and launched *Woman*, the first full-colour women's magazine, to counter *Woman's Own*. He published books by Churchill, Dickens and Shakespeare, acquired *Mickey Mouse Weekly* from America, and took on *Tatler* and the esoteric *Debrett's Peerage* – but his bids for Britain's biggest printing plant, Sun Engraving of Watford, were rebuffed. So Elias built his own printers in Watford, with four-colour printing and better-paid staff, poaching key operatives.[14] Issues raised by competition between these printers would haunt the newspaper industry for decades: labour relations, productivity and restrictive practices known as 'feather-bedding'. Elias supported many charities, leading the trustees of Great Ormond Street Hospital and raising £1 million in seven years. He fundraised for the Red Cross during World War II.

Newnes closed the *Royal Magazine*, the last original Pearson publication, in 1939, by which time the *Express* and *Herald* were vying to be the best-selling daily.

The Cassells building was destroyed in the Blitz, and years of nomadic existence ensued. In 1956 Winston Churchill laid the foundation stone for their purpose-built home, Churchill House (35 Red Lion Square, now the Royal College of Anaesthetists); but the stone, originally from Versailles, promptly disappeared. The company commissioned a life-size nude bronze of Pocahontas from artist David McFall to place in the square.[15]

Four years after elevation Lord Southwood made his maiden speech in the Lords (1941), where, aged 81, he became chief whip to a small band of Labour peers. Post war he was again recognized for his charity work, becoming Viscount Southwood, the only civilian elevated in the immediate post-war honours. He died of a heart attack at home on Southwood Lane, Highgate, in 1946, his peerage dying with him. Westminster Abbey hosted an Anglican memorial service; his ashes are in the Southwood Memorial Garden at St James's, Piccadilly. The small, talented but humble proprietor was a salesman, never a journalist.

Newnes's *Strand* ended in 1950, some content transferring to *Men Only*, which featured tasteful 'pin-ups' from 1954 after absorbing *London Opinion* (publisher of World War I's 'Your country needs you!' poster). Newnes purchased *Chambers's Encyclopaedia*, publishing four editions, 1950–6. Sir Frank died in 1955 with no heir.

In 1958 Cassells published Simon Nowell-Smith's history *The House of Cassell, 1848–1958*.

Odhams bought Hulton (publisher of the *Picture Post*, 1935–57) in 1959, and Newnes quit Southampton Street the same year. The *Daily Mirror* acquired the Amalgamated Press (including Cassells), rebranding the group as Fleetway. Newnes, Hulton, Odhams and Newnes's Pearson imprint had been Britain's largest magazine publishers for a decade.

Figure 17. The purpose-built headquarters of Cassells in Red Lion Square were opened by Winston Churchill, 1956.

Odhams moved into books in 1960, buying Newnes but selling *The People* and the *Daily Herald* to Fleetway (1961), and renaming Hulton 'Longacre' (1962). In 1963 Fleetway (the *Mirror*, Cassells) and Odhams (Longacre, Newnes, Pearson) combined as the International Publishing Corporation (IPC), owning provincial papers, 100 consumer magazines, 200 trade and similar magazines, and also books. The newspaper element was named the Mirror Group.

Within the IPC, Odhams launched the comic *Boy's World* to address falling sales at Longacre's *Eagle*. When this failed the comics merged (1964). Odhams produced *Wham!* and *Smash!* and won the UK franchise for Marvel's *Incredible Hulk* and *Fantastic Four*.

The Mirror Group relaunched the *Daily Herald* as *The Sun* in 1964. The Group also owned *The People* and the *Sunday Mirror* (formerly *Sunday Pictorial*). *John Bull* finally closed.

Nova, launched under Newnes's imprint in 1965, was a new breed of feminist magazine, more outspoken on sensitive issues than its antecedents. It was 'politically radical, beautifully designed, intellectual' (said *The Times*). Its edgy content, bold design and quality content made it attractive to both women and (quietly) men. Its first editor was … a man.[16]

Within the IPC Odhams had financial problems and saw its titles cannibalized by stable-mates. It was declared defunct in 1969 when the Mirror Group sold *The Sun* to Rupert Murdoch. The remainder of the IPC was reorganized, with IPC Magazines one of six divisions. *Girl*, *Swift* and *Robin* had already gone, and *Eagle*, the last Hulton comic, died too.

Reed, a paper-maker 30% owned by the IPC's Mirror Group, surprisingly bought the parent company. The resulting Reed International had two divisions, IPC Magazines and Mirror Group Newspapers.

The next decade was spent tidying up. Paul Raymond bought *Men Only* and the last Cassells book series was published (both 1971). The Longacre works were demolished and replaced by an award-winning affordable housing development, Odhams Walk (1973). Although *Nova* closed in 1975 it would publish thirteen more issues in 2000. Newnes's *Tit-Bits* closed in 1984, having latterly featured Isaac Asimov.

The Cassells Pocahontas statue was moved to Greycoat Place in 1981, moved again to Villiers Street and then sold to a private buyer in 1996, when it disappeared from public view; its Red Lion Square plinth remains empty. Cassells was sold to CBS (1982) and then to a management buyout (1986). Macmillan acquired it in 1989, and Cassells then acquired Victor Gollancz in 1992. Orion Publishing Group bought what remained of Cassells (1998) and was itself bought by Hachette in 2003. Cassells came under Octopus Publishing Group (within Hachette) in 2016.

In 1982 Robert Maxwell's Pergamon Press bought Odhams's printing assets from the IPC for £1.5 million and promised to close the printers within nine months; Maxwell kept his word. Four hundred Watford employees transferred to Sun Printers, which also soon closed: new technology is much cheaper to run than labour-intensive traditional printing. In 1994 Maxwell bought Mirror Group Newspapers (later Trinity Mirror, and then Reach), but that is another story.

The rollercoaster continued: in 1992 a Dutch publisher bought Reed International to form Reed Elsevier, and in a 1998 management buyout IPC Magazines became IPC Media. In 2001 this joined the American Time Inc., which metamorphosed into Time Media in 2014. Reed Elsevier became

RELX Group in 2016, and Time Media was bought by Epiris (a private equity firm) in 2018 and renamed TI Media. This was bought by Future plc in 2020. Today, RELX still publishes Newnes-imprinted electrical manuals.

The chaotic fall of the publishing industry was as dramatic as its rise. Just as technology helped newspaper and magazine circulation on its way up (from steam-driven presses to electric lights, offset litho and word-processors), so it undermined the traditional industry with ever-cheaper printing methods, less reliance on labour and the unstoppable force of the internet. All four of Beable's publishers technically exist as 'imprints' today. Even where identifiable, none operate on a scale that might be remotely viable were they stand-alone companies.

Figure 18. Julius Elias is remembered in the Southwood Memorial Gardens in Piccadilly.

Mudies

(1844, Libraries)

The Sumerians kept reference archives 5,000 years ago, yet in early-nineteenth-century Britain access to records of facts, ideas and entertainment was still a novelty. Charles Edward Mudie (1818–1890) did more than anyone to democratize such access. Beable calls him a 'gentle and unaffected man' who 'knew the pulse of the British public'.

Mudie's father was a London bookseller, a modest publisher who ran a small lending library that young Charles helped administer. Only a limited number of books were available, which his father would lend out at a penny (0.4p).

Mudie junior was ambitious. He opened a stationers, bookshop and publishing house in Southampton Row, Bloomsbury, 1840, convenient for the new University of London. He added a circulating (i.e. lending) library in 1844 in the belief that every literate person should have access to the printed word. Accordingly he charged most readers a mere guinea-a-year subscription (£1.05) when other London libraries charged four, even ten guineas. His personal tastes were broad and progressive, including evolutionists Charles Darwin, Thomas Huxley and Alfred Russel Wallace, as well as John Ruskin and William Morris of the Arts and Crafts movement. Mudie even deigned to include some popular fiction on his shelves from the start.

His establishment was forever busy. Servants arrived with their masters' lists; if subscribers could not visit in person he sent their books to them – across the country, if he had to. Crates of books were delivered to captains of liners for passengers' perusal. As few could afford to buy literature, the library was an excellent way to access words.

The Select Library, as it was known, became Mudie's principal trade. In 1852 it moved to a larger property, 30–4 New Oxford Street, at the junction with Museum Street. Branch operations at 132 Kensington High Street and 48 Queen Victoria Street followed, with further branches in Manchester (on Cross Street), Birmingham and elsewhere. He enlarged the New Oxford Street building in 1862, such was customers' demand, its central hall becoming a circular reading room and social centre. Mudie's balance switched overwhelmingly towards fiction; his stock approached a million books, including an eclectic children's section featuring Dickens, Carroll, Homer and Herodotus.

Mudie could make or break publishers and authors. In seeking to promote their work, both groups wondered: 'What would Mudie do?' He recommended works and demanded that contemporary novels were published in three volumes, generating three lending fees. Although this style was not new, his demands altered the way novels were written, in contrast to the serial episodes associated with Dickens. Publishers came to rely on him. When Mudie's libraries stopped ordering 'triple-deckers', in 1894, the model disappeared.

George Eliot (Mary Evans) benefitted from this policy. Mudie would usually request 400 copies of a new book from a publisher, who supplied them at half price; but for Eliot's much-praised third novel, *Silas Marner* (1861), he ordered an unprecedented 3,000. He bought nine tons of Lord Macaulay's five-volume *History of England*; only two publications ever achieved more lends than Macaulay: Disraeli's *Endymion* and Livingston's *Travels in South Africa*. Mudie reserved 500 copies of Darwin's *Origin of Species* from a print run of only 1,250.[1] Surplus books were sold at £5 per 100, recycled to suitcase-makers or pulped for compost.

Authors resented Mudie's rejections. Of the twenty novels written by Lynn Linton, Britain's first female professional journalist, he routinely stocked none, not because they were feminist – they were not – but for reasons Mudie did not have to explain. In general, he said, he avoided 'polluting children's minds'. Perhaps he was thinking of cheap serializations, penny dreadfuls such as *Dick Turpin*? Although it was widely believed that novels encouraged crime and gave women ideas above their station, hence the pressure to censor, writers and other campaigners for personal liberty demanded the freedom to choose what they perused.

When he banned George Moore's *A Modern Lover* the author protested. Mudie replied: 'Your book was considered immoral. Two ladies … object[ed] to that scene where the girl sat for the artist as a model for Venus. After that I naturally refused to circulate your book, unless any customer said he wanted particularly to read [it].' So his bans were not absolute; he would buy a single copy to lend, if requested. This light-touch censorship influenced writers and publishers for fifty years.

In 1860, after Mudie rejected a request from WHSmith to provide lending books for its railway stalls, the newsagents launched its own subscription library, as did Boots and Harrods. By 1870 Mudie had five London competitors, so he focused on quality, service and reputation. His business became a limited company worth £100,000 in 1864; half belonged to Mudie, half to a consortium of publishers.

Mudie won a three-year term on the board of education for Westminster in 1870, alongside W. H. 2 Smith. He supported low-income local families with philanthropic donations and his ongoing, voluntary teaching of literacy. The Library Company of Pall Mall launched a half-guinea service, in which borrowers were also shareholders, but it went bust within two years, paying no dividends.

Early in the nineteenth century Britain had around 200 commercial subscription libraries, plus 100 private ones (including universities). Chetham's in Manchester was the only genuinely 'public' lending library, though its monasterial focus was not for everyone. Many of London's private libraries, with strictly controlled membership, operated like gentlemen's clubs. Outside cities, facilities were rare, though in 1825 the rural Kendal borough in the Lake District (population 10,000) was particularly well served with libraries and literary institutions.[2]

Over fifty years the number of subscription libraries grew: there were 274 in England by 1850, the year the Public Libraries Act allowed nascent local authorities to open facilities. This measure was intended to educate the working classes and occupy idle minds, thus allowing people less time to foment trouble, claimed condescending MPs. A parliamentary report had called for free access to libraries, yet the Act did not oblige anyone to do anything. The Elementary Education Act of 1870 increased literacy goals, raising the demand for reading material. By 1900 there were some 300 free public libraries, a trend boosted by philanthropist Andrew Carnegie, who financed the construction of public libraries from 1883. By 1929 there were 660 'Carnegie Libraries' in Britain (and almost 2,000 in America).

In 1871 Mudie's Library acquired rivals Hookhams of Bond Street and then Booths of Regent Street. Mudie's oldest son, Charles 2 Henry (b.1850), joined the board, preparing to succeed his father.

Mudie's own poetry book, *Stray Leaves* (1872), includes a hymn attributed to the nonconformist: 'I Lift My Heart to Thee, Saviour'.

According to plan, Charles handed over to Charles 2 in 1878, but within a year the son died in pain from acute rheumatism and endocarditis. The tragedy broke the 60-year-old Mudie's spirit. After a brief interregnum his younger son Arthur (1854–1936), a renowned dachshund breeder, took charge alongside his sister Mary.

The library's reputation was solid. Oscar Wilde paid homage in 'Lord Arthur Savile's Crime' (1887): '"Jane writes charming letters," said the Duchess; "... quite as good as the novels Mudie sends us.' *The Importance of Being Earnest* (1895) also features a mention, as does H. G. Wells's *The Invisible Man* (1887): 'We crawled past Mudie's, and there a tall woman with five or six yellow-labelled books hailed my cab.' Virginia Woolf, in *Jacob's Room* (1922), identifies a location precisely as 'Mudie's corner in Oxford Street'. Mudies earns several mentions in Trollope's 'Palliser' series (1864–79) and in the works of W. S. Gilbert.

Charles Mudie died in 1890.

Figure 19. Mudie's competition came from
Carnegie libraries, such as here in Brentford.

At the turn of the century Mudie's libraries had 25,000 subscribers and 7.5 million books. The 100,000 books they bought each year can still be identified by distinctive yellow labels. However, competition was taking its toll and publishers were getting wise: the publisher of *Moby Dick* sold his wares at $1.50 in the US, but in Britain, where they would sell fewer copies because lending was so popular, he charged five times that amount.

Public libraries were the main twentieth-century competitors to Mudies, but how do you compete when your rival is not charging for its service?[3]

MUDIES SINCE 1925

Mudies was becalmed and concerned in 1925. Other subscription libraries had gone, but Mudies, WHSmith and Boots remained. For the other two the library was a small part of and supported by a massive and diverse empire, but Mudies merely serviced readers, as any good library should. Yet it could neither vie with radio and cinema for audiences thirsting for enlightenment or entertainment, nor find a strategy to compete with public libraries. That no one ever sought to acquire Mudies, gain its assets or kill it off suggests that its niche was a cul-de-sac.

The omens were clear. In 1934 Mudies downsized and relocated to Kingsway, close to its origins of a century earlier. In 1936 Arthur Mudie died, and in 1937 a surprise court order wound up the company, probably due to unpaid debts. Mary, Mudie's last surviving offspring, also died.

Harrods bought its stock cheaply and resold the books not quite so cheaply. *The Times* (12 July) devoted an editorial to Mudies, bemoaning the end of an era, the loss of a London landmark, the passing of a cultural icon. During World War II the empty New Oxford Street premises suffered such heavy bomb damage that demolition was inevitable.

Beable wrote positively about Mudie's Library and rightly so: it was a liberator, an informer, more than a trade. In today's parlance it was a 'purpose-led' business. But Mudies was never going to survive competition from public libraries, free at the point of use, funded by the state.

Mudie's highly successful commercial model played a vital role in the development and civilization of British society. Making reading not only accessible but fashionable, when legislation and the maturing public sector were starting to promote education and literacy, Mudies was in the right place at the right time ... before its window closed.

Boots

(1849, Pharmacists)

Jesse Boot, purveyor of herbs and patent medicines, is amongst the best known of Britain's 'rags to riches' retail romances.[1]

The John Wesley volume that most influenced the Methodist Boots was *Primitive Physic: An Easy and Natural Method of Curing Most Diseases*.[2] Wesley (1703–1791) believed that disease was prevented by healthy living supplemented by herbal and similar treatment. And, of course, prayer.

John Boot (1815–1860) opened his 'British and American Botanic Establishment' herbalist store at 6 Goosegate, Nottingham, in 1849. He had inherited the interest from his mother, Mary, who not unreasonably believed that doctors were poisoning people with 'unnatural' remedies such as mercury. 'American' is a nod to Samuel Thomson, an eighteenth-century advocate of botanical self-help, an idea that appealed to the emerging egalitarian nation.

After John died young his only son, 13-year-old Jesse Boot (1850–1931), joined his mother in the shop, now M&J Boot. By 1870 it was open three days each week, selling desiccated plants, roots and flowers with advice on their medicinal use. On other days he roamed the countryside collecting material to be dried and powdered for customers' use. They aimed for a turnover of £20 a week, but by 1870 they exceeded this fivefold.

In 1874 Jesse, in sole charge, held 2,000 items of product yet broadened the customer offer further. After moving to larger premises at 16 Goosegate in 1877, the store expanded to number 18 and then 20. Jesse undercut local competition with his iconic 'health for a shilling' campaign, spread his shop over two floors and installed Nottingham's first electric lift.

Boots & Co. was a limited company from 1880, with £10,000 of capital. Jesse, his family and friends retained share ownership, making them dependent on local banks for investment. Within a year the law changed, allowing shops to dispense prescription medicines and deal in 'poisons'. Jesse recruited a pharmacist, Edwin Waring, who proved as adept at marketing as chemistry. He boosted sales using attractive packaging, low prices and stores in Sheffield and Lincoln.

In 1888 the company became Boots Pure Drug Company Ltd, and Jesse was invigorated by an 1889 trip to America. From 1890 the new company sold non-voting shares to the public to raise funds, whilst consumer demand soon exceeded supply even with a new factory on Island Street. The stress generated by this hungry empire taxed Jesse's health. When friends insisted he take a break he headed for Jersey, where he was perhaps browsing in Rowe's bookshop in St Helier when he noticed the proprietor's beautiful daughter. Within months the couple married – 'indecent haste', declared Florence's mother, boycotting the wedding.

In few of Beable's romances does a woman exert as much influence as Florence Boot (1863–1952), whose flair for commerce was learned at her father's knee. She suggested Boots offer stationery and fancy goods, took an interest in employee welfare, organized social events for staff (with lady chaperones for single females), provided sports facilities and evening classes (1913), and sponsored a school for local children. She employed Eleanor Kelly as Boots's first welfare officer for female employees (1911) and introduced a company doctor (1921). Boots announced that 'the Company has recognized that its responsibility [for employees] does not end with the weekly pay envelope'.

Florence introduced cafés into Boots stores, encouraging customers to tarry, and bought a job lot of second-hand books to launch the 'Book-Lovers' subscription library. By 1898 half of Boots's stores had libraries, normally sited on the first floor and thereby obliging readers to pass displays of other attractive wares before reaching it. Boots even reprinted some classics under the Pelham imprint.

'Pelham' referred to Boots's first department store, at the junction of Pelham Street and High Street, which opened in 1902 when a road-widening scheme created a vacant plot. Described as making a middle-class service available to working-class customers, the store featured electric lighting and sold perfume, stationery, pictures, glass-ware, books, 'portmanteaux' and 'fancy goods', as well as having a large dispensary. Florence and Jesse designed much of the exquisite décor of this stunning grade II*-listed building, now a Zara store.[3]

Severely arthritic, Jesse was recognized for services to the Liberal Party with a knighthood in 1909, the year he endowed the chair of organic chemistry at University College Nottingham. Liberalism was a passion shared with Florence, an advocate of employing women in senior positions in business; Sir Jesse appointed her to the Boots board in 1917, the earliest female in a formal leadership role in any of our stories.[4] In 1920 Florence introduced Boots's Day Continuation School, giving 14- to 16-year-old employees a weekly half day to continue their education. She later donated a further £2 million to University College Nottingham and sponsored a female hall of residence, Florence Boot Hall.

Florence never forgot her roots, donating £50,000 to a Jersey housing scheme for low-income families. Her father's shop became a Boots branch, and she donated land for public enjoyment. (When Jesse died in Jersey, 1931, she had St Matthews in Millbrook refitted in modern style as his memorial: today it is 'the glass church'.)

Boots's annual sales surpassed £2 million in 1911 as the company launched prestigious stores in Princes Street, Edinburgh, and London's Regent Street. By 1914 it had 560 branches, pioneering the chain store concept alongside WHSmith. In 1918, despite the war, annual sales reached £5 million. Its first exports were to India, 1919.

Professional chemists were recruited from Burroughs Wellcome as early as 1895, and the German chemical industry was a significant supplier. World War I obliged Jesse to find new sources of medicines, quickly. He decided to make his own, challenging his scientists to synthesize pure aspirin. Boots was an official supplier to the Ministry of War, not least with a potent water-sterilizing tablet.

In 1920, 70-year-old Jesse sold Boots to an American company rather than pass it to his son, John 2 (1889–1956), but why? Jesse was known to have been disappointed by his oldest child's academic performance at Cambridge, so perhaps he did not trust him. John – 31 years old, married, already in man-agement – had wanted to step up. Jesse was known for being domineering, so maybe he reckoned that two strong personalities at the top was not going to work. Or was it that, just two years after a busy war, John was judged not quite ready? Another theory is that the Americans posed a threat to British pharmacy, poised to out-compete and potentially bankrupt Boots. If you can't beat them ...

Whatever his reasoning, Jesse sold Boots – against John's advice – for £2.28 million to Louis Liggett of United Drug Co. of Boston, a cooperative of franchised drugstores. The sale was conditional on Boots retaining independ-ence and identity, Jesse remaining chairman and his son being guaranteed a job, though Jesse was surprised when Liggett made John a director. Whilst sales rose over thirteen years of American ownership, profits fell.

Boots's first pharma patent was Stabilarsan, a treatment for syphilis (1921). Syphilis was the first disease for which an antibiotic cure existed.

In 1923 the British Medical Research Council licensed Boots's scientists to work with them, and the Prince of Wales visited the company's Island Street factory. Beable visited too; he was impressed that so many aspects of business, from ribbon-making to label printing, were in-house. He beheld mysterious bales and carboys from romantic places: Sudanese gum, Indian senna, opium from Smyrna, Chinese rhubarb. He described Sir Jesse as 'a genius, tired and indomitable'.

John's consolation prize was head of retail, yet within three years he was negotiating with Liggett, successfully persuading the American to float a quarter of his holding on the UK stock exchange. This gave the public access to Boots Pure Drug Co.'s shares, which were bought by John's consortium, reflecting his growing influence and ambition. As the 1920s progressed, Liggett grew increasingly concerned about the American economy, but John's pathway to the future was becoming clearer.[5]

BOOTS SINCE 1925

Jesse retired to Jersey in 1926, leaving John running UK operations. His elevation as the first Lord Trent in 1929 was brief: he died in 1931, when John inherited the title.

In 1927, with manufacturing again at capacity, Boots developed a 200-acre site at Beeston. Starting with 'D1 Soap Factory' (1929), by 1933 ten giants bestrode the site, some grade I listed. The site was so efficient that in 1934 it reduced production to five days a week with no loss of output or pay.

John followed his father in endowing University College Nottingham (1928) – becoming its president (1944) and then the founding chancellor of Nottingham University (1948).[6] In 1954 Boots endowed Nottingham's Lord Trent chair of pharmaceutical chemistry and Lady Trent chair of chemical engineering.

Battered by the Depression and faced with insolvency, Liggett pulled out of the UK in 1932, allowing the new Lord Trent and his British backers to take control of an independent Boots, whose thousandth UK store opened in Galashiels. Boots never forgot its American links.

Jesse Boot Primary School (now part of Nottingham Academy) opened in 1935 as Boots launched its 'No7' range of affordable beauty products. A New Zealand store followed. Lord Trent issued an interesting mission statement: 'Profit is not our main objective. But we are proud of the great health and domestic service that we have built up, and we believe that we can extend that service gradually in the British Empire and make the benefits of our methods and our organisation accessible ... overseas.'

More non-pharma lines followed, including in-house perfumes and Soltan, a non-greasy sun cream. As Boots reached 1,200 stores (1939) Trent pledged to sell on quality, not price.

Boots's war effort included mass-producing antimalarial drugs and penicillin, but after World War II the pace of change slowed, its marketing emphasizing non-pharma lines. Boots fulfilled one in every seven prescriptions from the new National Health Service from 1948 and opened a factory in Mumbai following Indian independence. When it launched a self-service store in

Edgware, the Royal Pharmaceutical Society claimed that 'Americanization' threatened its members' professionalism, but a court rejected this.[7]

In 1953 J. P. Savage, after forty years at Boots, succeeded Lord Trent as chairman, reflecting that with the NHS being such a large customer, opportunities to maximize profit were limited. Was this a change of tack? John 2 died in 1956, leaving four daughters, unable to inherit the peerage.

In 1961 Boots separated the managing director and chairman roles. Arthur Cockfield, with ten years at Boots after the Inland Revenue, was managing director, and the chair was Major Willoughby Rollo Norman (1909–1997), John 2's son-in-law. This restored family involvement – until his 1972 divorce.

The grade II*-listed company headquarters, D90, opened in 1966 at Beeston, but Boot's original Nottingham shop closed, as did the Book-Lovers libraries. Cosmetics under the '17' brand targeted teenage girls, and Boots acquired Timothy White's (1968). White's pharmacies were immediately absorbed, with the last of its general stores closing in 1985. In 1970 Boots Charitable Trust started work, funding medical research and local philanthropy, overseen by Nottinghamshire Community Foundation. The business became Boots Company Ltd in 1971. Beechams, having failed to acquire Glaxo, launched a hostile bid in 1972 but was resisted (and would likely have been blocked by the Monopolies Commission). Boots's own bid for House of Fraser (1973) also failed.

The next decade was dynamic. Ibuprofen (1980), a non-steroidal anti-inflammatory product, sixteen years in development, was its most significant new pharmaceutical product: Britain's top-selling drug earned a Queen's Award (1985).

Boots's focus on expansion was expressed as a dash for acquisitions: it bought Canada's Tamblyn Drugs in 1978, acquired Optrex for £9 million (1983) and opened the first Boots Optician's desk in Nottingham. There were sixty-eight in-store optician desks by 1985, followed by the first stand-alone Boots Optician in Durham. Boots acquired Farley's (baby rusks) in 1986 and went on a spree in 1989, acquiring the chemists Underwoods plus non-core interests such as Children's World and the American Ward-Whites (Halfords cycles, Payless, FADS). The exclusively American elements were soon sold and Payless incorporated into Do It All, which Boots co-owned as a joint venture with WHSmith until 1996.

A new managing director, Sir James Blyth (b. 1940, Baron Blyth from 1995) was in post 1987–98. This vastly experienced director, former sales head at the Ministry of Defence, restructured the company in 1989. At the time, 80% of Boots turnover was in the UK, high street chemists contributing 67% of turnover and half of pre-tax profit.

In a 1993 crisis Boots terminated clinical trials of Manoplax, a congestive heart failure drug linked to premature death; £100 million of investment, fourteen years of development and £20 million of marketing were written off.* Congestive heart failure is incurable, but relieving symptoms is a £2 billion market, of which Boots had wanted 10%. Potential American litigation prompted investor panic, so Boots sold its entire pharmaceuticals division to BASF for £850 million (1994), forfeiting the capacity to develop new drugs.[8] The future was focused on 'well-being'.

Boots introduced sun-cream star ratings for ultraviolet protection, sold Farleys to Heinz (1994) and acquired Croda Cosmetics (1995). In 1996 it introduced its Botanics range, opened its first Irish store and sold Children's World to Mothercare. It launched its 'Reward' loyalty card and opened stores in the Netherlands and Thailand in 1997, selling Halfords to private equity in 2002. New technology allowed the introduction of an online photo service and disposable hearing aids in 2005, when Boots sold its Healthcare International division (Nurofen, Strepsils, Sweetex) to Reckitt Benckiser. It finally merged with another company, Alliance Unichem, in 2006, to become Alliance Boots.[9] We need to know where Alliance came from to understand the rest of Boots's story.

In 1977 Stefano Pessina (b. 1941), a nuclear engineer, inherited his family's Italian wholesale drug company, Alleanza Farmaceutica. In 1991 it merged with two similar French operations to create Alliance Santé. Pessina's wife, Ornella Barra (b. 1953) had her own Italian wholesale pharmacy, Di Pharma, from 1982. She sold it to him, becoming a board member of Alliance Santé, which merged with a formerly cooperatively owned British pharmaceutical wholesaler, Unichem, to form Alliance Unichem in 1997.

Some sources say that what happened next was 'privatization', which sounds respectable. Margaret Thatcher's privatization goal was a share-owning democracy, but what happened here was the opposite. Boots combined with a privately owned body, and the company that emerged was then taken away from shareholders, not given to them. Ownership was concentrated, not decentralized. Transparency and accountability were lost, not gained.

Kohlberg Kravis Roberts (KKR) is an American private equity asset manager with a trillion dollars of assets under management. In 2007, on behalf of one of its clients, it audaciously bought Alliance Boots from its shareholders to create a private company, removing it from the FTSE 100. Not only was this the largest ever transaction of its kind (worth around £12.4 billion), but it was also a leveraged buyout, using debt to finance the purchase. The client was the Italian billionaire Stefano Pessina.

Of that £12.4 billion debt, £9 billion was transferred to the Boots balance sheet, meaning that for years to come profits could be offset against this 'loss' (which was never the company's loss), with a consequent massive reduction in

---

*A full analysis of the failure of Manoplax (flosequinan) was published twenty-four years later.

tax liability. *Ethical Consumer* magazine calculates that Britain's tax revenue was reduced by £100 million per year by this single transaction, and that in total over £1.2 billion of tax was avoided.[10] Pessina owned Boots UK from 2007 to 2014.

In 2009 Boots Opticians merged with Dollond & Aitchison (est. 1750). Boots launched an online GP consultancy and Extracts, a Fairtrade cosmetics brand. Boots's senior pharmacist frankly told parliament that the company sold homeopathic products not because they work but because consumers wanted them. A mutually beneficial (and still ongoing) charity partnership started with Macmillan Cancer Support.[11] Working with Mothercare, Boots introduced clothing and accessories for infants in 2010, and then launched Boots Pharmaceuticals, a self-medication brand.

We pause to consider the American company, Walgreens. In 1901 pharmacist Charles Walgreen Sr bought the Chicago drugstore where he worked, growing it to 600 outlets by 1934. Walgreens pioneered self-service stores and then online pharmacy in 1999, becoming America's second-largest pharmacy chain, with 9,000 stores.[12] Walgreens bought 45% of Alliance Boots for $6.7 billion in 2012, with the option of 100% over three years. Both Boots UK and Boots Opticians featured in the '*Sunday Times* 25 Best Big Companies to Work For' three years running.

Alliance Boots purchased 12% of a Chinese wholesaler in 2014 and made acquisitions in Chile and Mexico as a full merger with Walgreens was achieved. Walgreens Boots Alliance (WBA) has Boots UK and Walgreens as subsidiaries. The value of WBA halved during Pessina's run as its executive chairman.

During Britain's 2015 general election Pessina condemned the 'threat to business' from any incoming Labour government, prompting the response that, as he paid no tax in the UK, he had no right to comment, whilst WBA distanced itself from his 'personal' views. The same year, *Fortune* listed Barra as the fifth most powerful woman in world business, and the Dollond & Aitchison brand disappeared.

The Guardian alleged in 2016 that WBA had overcharged the NHS for patient medicine reviews, and the company's pharmacists complained of undue pressure from managers. In 2017 Boots declined to join other large chains in selling the morning-after contraceptive pill on a lowest-margin basis but came into line after political pressure. Pessina's salary was £13 million; five other directors were paid more than £6 million as Walgreens absorbed 1,900 American Rite Aid drugstores. WBA was the world's thirty-sixth biggest company, with a £136 billion turnover, joining the elite Dow Jones Industrial Average and taking a 40% stake in a Chinese retail pharmacy.

Boots sponsored the UK's four national women's football teams for three years from 2019 but closed 200 underperforming shops as profits fell by almost half, to £167 million. As Boots was voted 'best retail brand' by Brand Index

Women's Choice, Walgreens paid $269 million in fines after ten years of over-charging US Medicare for insulin pens. A new charity partnership, between Macmillan Cancer Support and the No7 brand specifically, was formed.

In 2020, 4,000 jobs were shed and forty-eight Boots Opticians closed. WBA played a key role in America's Covid vaccine rollout, and the 79-year-old Pessina stepped down as executive chairman, replaced by 35-year-old Rosalind Brewer (CEO until 2023).

WBA sold Alliance Healthcare in 2021, but when it looked to sell Boots UK in 2022 it could not find a buyer, despite halving the asking price to as low as £5 billion.[13]

In 2023 there were 2,232 Boots stores in the UK (employing 52,000), as well as in Thailand and Ireland and some franchises in the Middle East. The value for Macmillan from the various partnerships with Boots reached £20 million, winning their relationship the title of 'Most Admired Corporate NGO Partnership' in the respected C&E Advisory poll for the fourth time. More acquisitions followed, some more successful than others. To aid its sale, WBA sold Boots's pension scheme to Legal & General.

Still unable to find a buyer in 2024, WBA considered returning Boots to the UK stock market.[14] The sale was abandoned – but soon reinvigorated following Boots's twelfth successive quarter of growth in sales and market share, justifying an increased selling price of £7 billion. Further streamlining was considered, including the break-up of the entire WBA group.[15]

In retrospect Boots's experience of the acquisition-and-sale rollercoaster raises questions. Its bids for non-core businesses did not make sense, unless driven by the building of empires, acquisition of profit and dilution of purpose. Once the traditional core model had been punctured by a future-threatening failure (the 1993 Manoplax crisis), leading to the offloading of core pharmaceutical manufacture and development, the company was in trouble. Well-being was a rational direction, as was Boots Opticians, even the merger with Alliance Unichem, but after 2007 Alliance Boots became a player in the world of high finance, with retail well-being simply a means to an end. Private equity came in, lacking any prioritized social purpose, offloading billions of pounds in debt and ensuring that a huge retail operation might never pay tax again. This is the antithesis of 'company citizenship'.

Since 2014 Walgreens Boots Alliance has existed to tend its two cash cows. Minor controversies have been ridden out, essential progress towards climate responsibility has been slow. Pessina has realized his ambition: to possess billions of dollars whilst paying as little tax as possible.*

---

*He is worth $6.9 billion as of March 2025, according to *Bloomberg's* Billionaires Index, making him the world's 458th richest person.

Bryant & May

(1850, Matches)

B eable revels in feats of mechanization and automation. In 1925 London's biggest factory was producing 56,000 matchsticks each minute and had a global supply chain, a forestry enterprise and a dynamic image. Five massive steam engines, powered by the anaerobic digestion of waste wood, added yet more romance. Forty years earlier the owner of that factory, Bryant & May, underwent a month of discord that could have destroyed the company, resulting from serious failures of judgement – which Beable completely overlooked.

Before the match was the fuse, a slow-burning rope used to fire cannons, transfer flames between candles and light smokers' pipes. Flints generated sparks to ignite pistols, muskets and, later, gas for lighting or heating, but the portable convenience of the match eluded science. Phosphorus's ability to self-ignite was known from 1669, but controlling it was challenging.

In Stockton-on-Tees, 1826, ammunition-maker John Walker coated splints with sulphur and antimony but sold just 168 boxes in two years; France and Germany banned his product.[1] Simultaneously, Samuel Jones of Reading patented the 'Promethean', a small glass tube that, when broken, released a chemical flare. (Wall-mounted cigar lighters, commonplace in posh establishments of 1925, worked in a similar manner.) A Scottish contemporary, Sir Isaac Holden, improved Walker's model but did not patent his invention. Jones next produced a commercial friction match, the 'Lucifer', a reference to Venus reflecting the morning sun: 'While you've a Lucifer to light your fag', sang World War I's Tommies.

William Ashgard substituted Walker's sulphur with beeswax, improving the smell if nothing else (1843). Swede Gustaf Pash patented a dedicated striking surface with embedded red phosphorus, an invention key to the modern safety match. Charles Suria replaced Walker's antimony with white phosphorus, finally controlling its combustibility. More reliable and cheaper than its predecessors, this novelty would ignite when struck on any hard, rough surface, changing the world of matches.

From 1819 William Bryant (1804–1874) was an excise officer in Plymouth, converting from Methodist to Quaker upon his 1832 marriage. In 1833 Bryant & James, purveyors of soap, grate blacking, grease and other goods, started trading. An Essex Quaker, Francis May (1803–1885), dealer in tea and groceries in Bishopsgate, became Bryant's London agent in 1839. By 1841 Bryant had an office in Tooley Street, and from 1843 May worked for him full time.

White phosphorus is a known poison, originally extracted from bone ash. Direct contact with nasal membranes, eyes, lips and gums causes mutilation, necrosis, even death. Its fumes mimic these effects, over time. In 1850 Austrian chemist Anton Schrötter von Kristelli converted white phosphorus to its red form by heating it in a closed container, reducing its toxicity but not its inflammatory powers. However, the process was not cheap.

In Sweden, 1847, Johan Lundström opened a match factory. At London's Great Exhibition of 1851 he saw Quaker Arthur Albright (of Birmingham's Albright & Wilson) argue the moral case for a safer match made from red phosphorus. Lundström, already in discussions with Bryant & May, was now telling them that he would only produce red-tipped matches. The Quakers accepted the ethical argument and in 1855 invested in Lundström's business; the Swede was promising such quantities that the extra costs would be bearable.

The British market was 250 million matches a day. Bryant & May initially imported ten cases of 720,000 matches each, then fifty, then five hundred on a regular basis, selling 231,000 boxes of 'hygienic' matches in year one. Soon Lundström could not produce the quantities needed, so the company bought production rights from him, for £100, and in 1855 May registered Lundström's patent in Britain. The company made almost 11 million boxes that year, 30 million in 1860. In 1861 Bryant leased Fairfield Works in Bow, the former British Sperm Candles factory, a three-acre site that would double in size as the company replaced the old works with an elegant, Venetian-style, steam-driven factory.[2]

William Bryant took a step back in 1862 to leave his oldest son, Wilberforce (1837–1906), responsible for the new factory, later joined by his three brothers.

Francis May lived at West View on Reigate Hill, where he hosted the annual works party. By 1868 the gentle Quaker, aged 65, was disillusioned, troubled both by Wilberforce and the competitive nature of business generally. When the Bryants 'actively encouraged' May to leave, he appealed to Quaker arbitration to resolve the impasse. Although a tribunal found in May's favour, the dogmatic Wilberforce stood firm. Elders advised May to withdraw, which he did in 1875, dedicating himself to Quakerism.[3] Wilberforce married into money in 1876.

William Gladstone's chancellor, Robert Lowe, proposed a ha'penny tax on each box of matches (1871). With management and workforce united in protest, 10,000 marched from Bow to parliament, demanding the tax's withdrawal. The following day, as newspapers remarked on the absence of 'the usual agitators', MPs alleged police brutality, Queen Victoria chastised Gladstone and Lowe withdrew.

William Bryant's death in 1874 left the brothers in charge. They made changes to the company of 5,000 employees, building a lumber mill on Bow Common to produce their own matchsticks and abandoning the general merchandising business.[4]

Most of Britain's twenty-five match factories used poisonous white phosphorus, with only a minority, including Bryant & May, opting out. 'Phossy jaw' was known to medicine, although few measures were in place to prevent contamination of skin, food or factory air. After an initial toothache and then headache the jaw would 'die' and shed teeth. A single box of Lucifers, ingested, could kill a man. Finland banned white phosphorus (1872), and Denmark, France, Switzerland and the Netherlands followed.

In 1880 Wilberforce and his surviving brother, Frederick, made a big mistake: market forces, they concluded, demanded that they manufacture cheaper, Lucifer-type matches, made with white phosphorus. Their first Lucifer was the 'Flaming Fugee, Vesuvian matches for cigar and pipe'.

Exports grew, to the empire and beyond, though American import tariffs prevented western expansion. In 1884–5 the company acquired factories around Britain by taking over rivals Pace & Sons, Hunt & Co. and Bell & Black. Wilberforce's tactics worked: the company paid dividends of over 20% for three years after its 1884 flotation. Financial observers were not impressed, however, with one describing Bryant & May's annual report as one of 'the most cynically meagre and imperfect documents published by any board in the country', adding accusations of insider dealing.[5]

The typical Bryant & May employee was female, under 20 and Irish. Under 14s worked for 4s (20p) a week; others were paid piece rate. Foremen imposed fines – 3d (1p) for an untidy workspace, 5d for being late, a shilling (12d, or 5p) for possessing a burnt match. Homeworkers, protected by no law, had to buy glue to make matchboxes, whilst those filling the boxes had to pay the boys to bring the trays from the drying ovens. Worst of all, employees who reported toothache were given a choice: get the tooth removed (without a dentist) or face the sack. No Quaker idyll, this! Later, the Bryants claimed ignorance of working conditions, though they certainly knew of strikes in 1881, 1885 and 1886.

In 1888 Bryant & May stepped into history. Falling demand forced workers onto short hours with loss of pay, leading to protests. On 23 June, Annie
Besant, the socialist writer, and Herbert Burrows wrote about the Bow factory
in respect of pay, conditions ... and phossy jaw. Wilberforce Bryant denied
the reports, wrongly blaming the workers for framing him. Challenged to dissociate themselves from Besant's claims by signing a statement, the workers,
led by Sarah Chapman, refused. By now the tinder was dry, and on 2 July an
employee was sacked for refusing to sign; within twenty-four hours 1,400 had
walked out. Four days later the strike was total, and the Bryants railed against
Besant for causing it, when in fact she had had no advance knowledge. Besant,
George Bernard Shaw and other Fabians set up a strike fund.[6]

On 11 July Charles Bradlaugh MP (1833–1891), the Liberal atheist, raised
the strike in parliament. Wilberforce Bryant, a 'conservative Liberal', realized that the dispute was politically and economically damaging and that the
'Match Girls' commanded public sympathy. On 16 July, following meetings
between workers, Besant and management, Bryant settled. The strikers'
successful demands included ending the fine system, a 5% pay rise, reduced
working hours, improved ventilation and sanitation, recognition of the Union
of Women Matchworkers, and reinstatement of the sacked worker.

The UWM was the first women's trade union, a forerunner of today's
GMB. However, in 1903 another strike split the Bow workforce, crippling
the union.

In 1890 the company launched two brands of red phosphorus matches,
'Brymay' and 'Pearl'. Under its 'Darkest England' (1891) campaign the Salvation Army had operated a competing, ethical match factory near Bow, using
safe red phosphorus from the start and paying workers better. Even though
people expressed solidarity by purchasing the alternative (at three times the
price of Bryant & May's!), the new venture was never viable; it ceased trading
in 1894. His sins to some extent purged, Bryant paid a fair price for his local
competitor's assets, but only in 1901 did he cease using white phosphorus.[7]

By 1895 Bryant & May was reduced to 2,000 employees but still solvent. In
1898 French scientists found that adding phosphorus sesquisulphide to white
phosphorus mitigated its harmful effects cheaply. Bryant & May bought the patent and released it for anyone to use, as did Diamond Match in the US, ten years
later. Albright & Wilson were Britain's main producers of sesquisulphide.

Following a misunderstanding with Bryant over tariffs, Diamond bought
a factory in Liverpool in 1901, producing 600,000 'Captain Webb' and 'Puck'
matches per hour. Diamond owned the patent to the matchbook, cardboard
safety matches stapled into a fold of card with a dedicated striking strip.

In 1905 came more change. Bryant & May purchased the 'good will' and
UK assets of Diamond, whilst Diamond bought 54% of Bryant & May's

shares (which the Bryants had mostly repossessed by 1910). 'Swan Vesta' was
the newly merged company's first new match. Wilberforce, chairman in name
only and the last remaining Bryant, died in 1906.

The Berne Convention of that year called for a global ban on white phosphorus. The UK legislated in 1908, banning it from 1911.

From 1909 Bryant & May rebuilt its factories, still with 2,000 largely
female employees, still a giant. In 1913 it bought a major rival, SJ Moreland &
Sons (makers of 'England's Glory') and in 1922 began a forestry venture and
launched a new factory in Liverpool.

The stage was set for Beable to witness state-of-the-art match-making.

BRYANT & MAY SINCE 1925

The twentieth century was far less eventful for Bryant & May. Matches went
out of fashion thanks to cigarette lighters (Zippo launched in 1933), falling
smoking rates, electric cookers, electric ignition for gas cookers, and fewer
open fires and oil lamps.

Bryant & May combined with Abbey Match in 1927, bought some Swedish Match assets worldwide and became the British Match Company (BMC).
A joint venture with Albright & Wilson operated the sesquisulphide plant
from 1929, but little else happened until the 1970s.

A surprising merger with Wilkinson Sword, producer of razors and shaving supplies, created Wilkinson Match in 1973, the year of the first disposable
lighter. From 1978 Allegheny International, a massive American former steel
company now in 'consumer products', started to buy shares in the company,
achieving ownership in 1980. The Bow factory's closure in 1979 (for conversion to flats) saw 275 jobs move to Liverpool; BMC factories in Gloucester,
Glasgow and Melbourne were next to close.

Ominously, Allegheny entered into a revolving credit agreement with
twenty-six US banks in 1986, filing for bankruptcy two years later under
Chapter 11, an American idiosyncrasy that allows companies to avoid paying
debts. After a supposedly respectful period in the wilderness such companies invariably bounce back, magically debt-free, as Allegheny did, a recovery
highlighted on the curriculum of Columbia Business School. In the sale of
nineteen Allegheny subsidiaries, Swedish Match AB acquired Wilkinson
Match but swiftly sold off the Wilkinson Sword element.[8]

By 1994 the Liverpool plant had closed and matches were no longer made
in Britain. The BMC, as Swedish Match UK, was sold to Republic Technologies International (RTI), a French manufacturer of cigarette papers, filters and
vapes (2008). Today a 'Bryant & May UK' website sells only Swedish Match
Industries 'extra-long' household matches.[9] The website's 'Potted history'

page omits the Match Girls, but in 2022 *EastEnders* TV actor Anita Dobson, great-granddaughter of Sarah Chapman, unveiled a plaque commemorating one of Britain's most famous strikes.

Figure 20. English Heritage recognize the Match Girls at the former Fairfield Works in Bow.

Hartleys

(1862, Jam)

Sir William Pickles Hartley (1846–1922), archetypal 'good business-man', merits praise for his commitment to his product, concern for his workforce, involvement in public life and passion for his faith. Beable describes a well-rounded, responsible person of humble disposition, overlooking the mental health problems that plagued Hartley throughout life.

Hartley's mother ran a grocery store in Colne, Lancashire, where his father was a tinsmith. The family of grocers had built Wycoller Hall, Haworth, in the sixteenth century, but it was demolished in 1818. An organist at Colne Primitive Methodist church from age 12, William left grammar school at 14 to work for his mother and at 16 set up his own wholesale grocery despite an ambition to be a chemist.

When, in 1871, a jam supplier failed to meet his obligations to Hartley's esteemed customers, William sued him and won damages. To avoid further disappointment he made his own jam – initially of gooseberry, damson or a gooseberry–raspberry mix; strawberries were only available for three weeks each year. Richer folk, rightly suspicious of adulteration, had the time to make their own jam, so only poorer people actually bought it. When the government abolished sugar duty in 1874, low grain prices lured many farmers to turn land over to soft fruit, and Hartley sold the grocery business. Refusing to use additives or bulk out his jams, within a year Hartley had sold 100 tons of jams and jellies to markets in Lancashire and Yorkshire, thanks to a dozen employees. His product was naturally 'organic'.

In 1883 Hartley's output was 1,500 tons, in six different flavours. In some years his profits were less than the cost of borrowing the capital he had needed to build his Bootle factory.

Primitives were the most working class of the Methodist streams that would merge in the 1930s, a founding force in the trade union movement and supporters of women's emancipation. In 1877 William and his wife, Martha, pledged a tenth of their lifetime income to good causes, as advocated by Reverend John Ross in his pamphlet *Uncle Ben's Bag*. ('Ten-percent-Ross' was a Gaelic-speaking nonconformist Scottish minister and missionary.[1]) They exceeded their goal, giving away a million pounds, a third of their wealth, though the law did not distinguish between owners' personal and company income. Much of their generosity supported the Church itself; in 1885 Hartley cofounded a charity, still functioning, to preserve the fabric of chapels.

Hartley committed to sharing the company's profits with his workforce, using a model he had discovered in France, and announced the scheme at an annual party. Although he describes profit-sharing as 'co-partnership', it was a one-way street: workers were not involved in business decisions, because, Hartley explained, he knew more about business than they did. Beable reports him as saying: 'I am firmly convinced that the spirit of [profit-sharing] would put an end to the conflicts between capital and labour.'

In 1892 Hartley described his faith in these words: 'Our actual creed is what we put into practice, and no more ... we want to be careful to see that our practice is equal to our creed.' He described profit-sharing as a Christian duty, stating his philosophy in 1894: 'It has been my aim from the first to do to [my employees] as I would wish to be done by.'

Whilst other companies professed condescending and patronizing concern for 'the weaker sex', Hartley was practical. Paying men much more than women for the same job was standard elsewhere, but not for the jam-maker, 80% of whose staff were female.

Nevertheless, in 1898 Hartley was accused of under-paying women, obliging some to turn to 'immorality' to make a living. (This was no idle accusation: prostitution supplemented the incomes of many women, single and married, in Lancashire's cotton communities.) He replied fulsomely, if with exasperation:

1. I pay from 20 to 40 percent more for female labour than the general payment by my competitors or others in Liverpool and neighbourhood.

2. In July 1903 I voluntarily increased the wages of all my workpeople both male and female. I had not a single complaint ... this cost me ... £2,000 a year. This is the third time that I have made a voluntary increase in the past ten or twelve years.

3. I have practised profit-sharing for seventeen years. The total amount distributed from the beginning up to last January was over £37,000, and all my people get a share of the profits, both men and women.

4. I provide a fully qualified medical man ... to attend upon all my workpeople free. There is no club and no charge is made. I pay the doctor an annual fee ...

5. I have a large number of superior houses in the village with exceedingly low rents, [most] of them being 3s6d [18p] and 4s6d [23p] per week, which includes rates, taxes and water.

There is no collective bargaining, no *annual* pay rise and no guarantee of equal pay between the sexes, nor are there unions. On the other hand, there are no laws protecting pay or working conditions and no NHS – by nineteenth-century standards his approach was progressive.

Hartley spent over £300,000 training chemists to ensure his product's safety.

The Bootle factory needed investment, but cash came with strings. Martha firmly opposed letting a financier join the board, but when Hartley told him no the man attached crippling conditions to their loan. The company went into debt, partly relieved in 1884 by selling (non-voting) shares to the public. By 1890 Hartleys was back in profit.

As the Bootle operation outgrew capacity, William identified a forty-acre site in Aintree with railway connections. William Sugden of Leek won a competition to design Hartley's Village in 1886. His initial community featured forty-nine Arts and Crafts homes by 1890, rising to seventy-one; its residential streets, laid out in an Arts and Crafts motif, had names like Sugar Street and Strawberry Row. The village had a bowling green at its heart, with sports fields and a lake on the perimeter. Its reputation was such that Hartley was invited to advise Joseph Chamberlain on housing policy.[2] The factory's 750-seat dining hall could feed the entire workforce in two sittings, and Hartley had an on-site villa.

He was active in Liverpool's community and a generous sponsor of Everton Football Club, which played at Anfield. When, in 1891, the pro-temperance Liberal element of the club's board fell out with the landowner and his neighbour, both brewers, the club relocated to nearby Goodison Park. Goodison was the first purpose-built professional football ground, partly funded by the teetotal Hartley. The club retained the name 'Everton', obliging Anfield's new tenants to adopt 'Liverpool'.[3]

Hartley was a justice of the peace from 1893 and a Liberal city councillor from 1895 to 1898. His company's benevolent fund assisted sick and disabled employees and their families from 1894, and he donated £20,000 to create the Aintree Institute in 1897, supporting community education. (The Beatles performed there many times in their formative years.)

Figure 21. The dining hall of the Hartley plant
at Bootle remains proud but derelict.

The Aintree plant was highly successful, producing 100 tons of jam each summer's day, marmalade and candied peel at other times. Six hundred to 2,000 people worked there, depending on the season, but demand overwhelmed Aintree too, and in 1901 Hartley opened a second plant, in Bermondsey. London's largest factory adopted extensive fire precautions because, at 1.5 million cubic feet, it was far larger than otherwise allowed. Bermondsey could store 6 million stoneware jars and produce 400 tons of jam each week, in addition to Aintree's 600.[4]

Chemical preservation was a controversial field. Unlike other jam-makers Hartley never added the natural preservative salicylic acid to his wares, arguing that it should be either banned (as in the US) or highlighted on labels; there were no rules about labelling or safe dosage as there are now.[5] Salicylic acid, found in many fruits, is related to aspirin.

The company sponsored an annual Methodist Lecture from 1897 until 1915. In 1905 Hartley built Southport's 'Jam Chapel', match funding a public subscription. Unusually for a Primitive chapel, its stained glass windows commemorate the family, whose funerals were held there. Today it is a medical centre.[6] A 1906 bequest prompted a Manchester training college for Methodist preachers to be renamed the Hartley (later Hartley Victoria) College. In 1907 Hartley gifted £5,000 to the YMCA, and in 1908 the newly knighted Sir William bought Holborn's former town hall, in London, for £31,000.[7] He enlarged it and sold it to the Primitive Methodist Church as its headquarters, at no profit. Hartley was the first lay president of the Methodist Conference, in 1909.

Figure 22. The Hartley Jam Factory in Bermondsey
is now a housing development.

That year Hartley created a non-contributory employees' pension fund, donating £30,000 over a decade. In 1910 he built ten almshouses in Colne, at his Damside birthplace, and as freeman of the town he sponsored a new hospital there a decade later. Hartley invested in local cotton mills after World War I, not to make money but to help keep them afloat.

By 1912 Hartleys was the world's biggest jam-maker, sourcing British fruit wherever possible and becoming 'Ltd' in 1919. In 1920 it imported a quarter of Spain's Seville oranges for marmalade. Although Hartleys owned several farms by then, most fruit came from other suppliers. Fruit-growers trusted him as he paid good rates, even when sales were depressed. Hartley boasted that a strawberry in a Bedfordshire field at 4 a.m. could be boiling in Liverpool by 2 p.m. and on the table by supper time.

William and Martha had eight children, and their values inspired their third daughter, Christiana (1872–1948). Carer for her now elderly parents, the Liberal member of Southport Council (1920–32) was its first female mayor (1921) and 'married to politics'. Her priorities earned her the title 'the Children's Mayor'; she donated generously to good causes, often working on a cross-party basis. After living for a week as a pauper, Christiana donated £500 to a Labour Party anti-poverty initiative and persuaded her father to match the sum.

Christiana has been described as having 'masculine vigour', 'a woman in a man's world'. She not only served as a director of the company but was chairman (*sic*) briefly when her father died, maybe without precedent in Britain. Others described her as possessing 'clear and concise speech, patience and courage, a love of humanity', never afraid to speak out. As a female magistrate and Poor Relief Guardian she was often in a gender minority of one.[8]

Approaching 80, William must have felt satisfied despite a life of unexplained mood swings. He died in 1922, when the family commissioned Arthur Peake to write a hagiography.[9]

The man who would succeed Hartley, John Higham (1857–1932), started his professional life in his family's cotton business in Accrington, marrying Pollie, the Hartleys' second daughter, in 1899 and inheriting the Higham company's chairmanship. The Liberal Higham served as a councillor for twelve years, winning the parliamentary seat of Sowerby in a 1904 by-election. Upon losing that seat in 1918 he worked for Hartleys.

HARTLEYS SINCE 1925

As the new chairman of Hartleys, Higham, supported by William's grandsons, oversaw 'business as usual' for a generation, despite challenges that included the global Depression. He introduced canned fruit and vegetables.

Prior to World War I, William had considered creating a maternity hospital for Southport, but the conflict delayed the realization of his good intentions. Christiana re-energized the proposal in 1928, laying the foundation stone in 1932; today the Christiana Hartley Medical Practice is still a primary care facility. She used her inheritance to endow annual scholarships for local women to study at Liverpool University and Girton College, Cambridge. Shortly before she died in 1948, Christiana was awarded a CBE and an honorary master's degree.

Hartleys became a £1 million public listed company in 1936. Employment varied with the season, as ever, rising steadily to peak at 6,000 in 1956.

For many years Chivers of Histon, Cambridgeshire, was a significant provider of fruit to jam-makers. It produced its own jam from 1873, a rival to the Hartleys line, and grew blackcurrants to supplement Britain's vitamin C during World War II. In 1959 Schweppes acquired the loss-making Chivers, and then the similar Moorhouse, before paying £2 million for the profitable Hartleys. The Aintree factory was closed as production moved to Histon, Hartley's Village passing to neighbours Jacob's Crackers (see Huntley & Palmers). It upgraded the one-up, one-down homes, whilst Schweppes retained the Victorian factory to make soft drinks until 1984, when it sold the premises to Liverpool Council.

Chivers and Hartleys merged within Schweppes, jointly now bigger than the previous jam-market leader, Robertsons. In 1963 Hartleys launched boiled-in-a-vacuum 'New Jam'.

The 1969 merger of Cadburys and Schweppes was not focused on jam. Narrow margins were squeezed, and the Hartley-Chivers partnership never really worked, its quality range selling only half the amount of the Robertsons 'value' product, which had a third of the market. Two years later Robertsons was down to 26% with Hartley-Chivers steady at 16%, as a new factor, supermarket own brands, made an impact. The Bermondsey plant closed in 1975 and is now flats.

Following a management buyout in 1981, Hartley-Chivers was bought by Premier Brands and fortunes improved. By 1985 it produced 30% of the jam market (75 million jars) and 90 million cans of fruit and vegetables, plus half of all supermarket own-label preserves.

That same year Hillsdown Holdings bought Lockwood Foods, a cannery, out of receivership and subsequently acquired some Beechams food brands.[10] In 1990 it acquired Premier Brands, renaming it Premier Foods. It also purchased the Histon site, recently modernized following another management buyout.

Over the next twelve years the Hartley-Chivers name was bought and sold, with new companies forming and dying regularly. By 1999 Premier Foods was owned by private equity. Following Premier's flotation in 2004 the Chivers products were rebranded 'Hartleys', and sales overtook the (cheaper) Robertson brand, which had dropped its 90-year-old but now controversial 'golly' marketing in 2001. Premier went on a spending spree, gaining Ambrosia, Oxo, Fray Bentos, Batchelors, Homepride and Quorn, and then Birds Custard and Angel Delight from Kraft, whilst selling Typhoo to an Indian company for £80 million.

In 2007 Premier Foods acquired Rank Hovis MacDougall (see Hovis), which included Robertsons, whose jams were discontinued in 2009. In 2012 Premier sold Hartleys to Hain Daniels, a 'natural food' subsidiary created in 2005 by Hain Celestial, itself a former subsidiary of Heinz dating to 1999. Hartleys joined a line-up that included Sun Pat peanut butter, Tilda rice, Covent Garden soups, the Linda McCartney vegan range and some skincare brands. Today Hain Daniels Group includes Histon Sweet Spreads of Leeds, who make Hartleys jellies and jams. Hain Daniels's 1,300 employees produce fourteen different food brands.

The 1981 move to Premier was a desperate act, after which the prestigious Hartleys brand became a mere football. The anonymous Hillsdown Holdings owned around 200 companies in the 1980s, at one point buying one, on average, every six days. Company names flashed across desks, brands became separated from other assets and the nature of the product changed: preservatives and plastic packaging were introduced as jam-making came to resemble playing with a chemistry set. Something had been lost.

Hartley's Village Conservation Area retains much of its former identity, though Hartley's villa is gone and the factory's splendid offices, turreted gatehouse and dining room are derelict, home to scrap merchants, behind a daunting fence.[11]

Whiteleys

(1864, Retail)

The iconic Whiteleys department store in London's West End ranked alongside Selfridges, though it was closer to Paddington Station than to fashionable Bond Street. Beable tells us that William Whiteley (1831–1907) was 'a short, stocky man with enormous energy and a substantial ego'. There was plenty of evidence of both traits.

The oldest son of a West Yorkshire corn merchant, the infant William was fostered to a farming uncle at a time when Wakefield's dominant wool industry was under threat from Australian imports. Leaving school at 14, he nurtured veterinary ambitions but his family had other ideas, so in 1848 he began a seven-year apprenticeship with Harnew & Glover, Wakefield's largest draper. His first holiday was to London, 1851, to witness the spectacular Great Exhibition. One day, he dreamed, he would own a department store as grand as the Crystal Palace.

Whiteley returned permanently to London in 1855, with £7, finding employment with Willey's general store on Ludgate Hill. Other roles followed, including Leat & Sons' ribbon department, befitting his qualifications, and after eight years of frugality he had saved £700. This was enough to go into business, but where? Advisers told him to avoid Westbourne Grove: 'too expensive, you'll need more experience'. Undaunted, in 1863 he rented a shop on the street, at number 31, with twenty-four feet of frontage. He vowed always to pay cash, never to accrue debt or allow credit, to pay on time and keep prices low – even in this newly gentrified area. Unusually, he banned haggling: ticket prices were inviolate.

Whiteleys was initially a draper's store, with two female assistants and an errand boy. William married one of these assistants, Harriet Hill, in 1867, shortly before their son Walter was born; the child died two months later, but four more children followed.

With an ear to customer requests, he added furniture, hardware and grocery, pledging to avoid hard selling and tasteless advertising, and putting no limit on what he could provide if requested. And the customer was always right. By 1864 he had fifteen staff. By 1867 Whiteleys had seventeen departments at 31–53 Westbourne Grove, with the new Bayswater Station enhancing trade. He added dressmaking, an estate agency and a cafeteria (1872), and a massive food hall (1876), which undercut local traders. Adding a decorating service was sound, whilst dressmaking, deliveries and removals also proved popular. Whiteley became a familiar figure in the courts, pursuing shoplifters and defending his reputation through libel cases.

Figure 23. William Whiteley (1831–1907).
(*Source: Romance of Great Businesses.*)

The expansion continued. Although Whiteley boasted that he could provide everything 'from a pin to an elephant', neighbouring shopkeepers did not appreciate the competition and they regularly demonstrated in the street, ceremonially burning Whiteley's effigy. In the 1880s the store suffered three suspected arson attacks and William received death threats.

William and Harriet separated disharmoniously in 1881, though she always spoke well of him thereafter and received a generous settlement. Whiteley rented a small house in nearby Kilburn.

The year 1887 was tumultuous: trade at Whiteleys peaked, with shoppers travelling miles to visit this 'immense symposium of the arts and industries of the nation and of the world'. In August, Whiteley was on holiday in Ostend with his teenage sons when the British Consul brought him news that his shop had burned down. E. H. Shephard, illustrator of *The Wind in the Willows*, had watched the blaze in its cruel glory from Highgate Hill, five miles away. As William later surveyed the scene of absolute destruction, his only thought was to start again. He offered £3,000 for information leading to an arrest, a reward that was never claimed.

The new shop was better than ever, open 7 a.m. to 11 p.m., six days a week. He provided dormitory accommodation for hundreds of staff, subject to 176 rules of 'proper' behaviour backed by a system of fines. Peremptory dismissal was not unknown. Whiteley purchased farmland at Hanworth, Ealing and Hillingdon to grow food and flowers. At its peak his empire employed 6,000 and covered twenty-one adjacent retail premises and twenty-eight residential buildings, plus stables, workshops, offices and farms.

Queen Victoria's family patronized the new store, and its 1896 royal warrant was, unusually, unsolicited. The store's reputation was 'democratic', welcoming all through its doors, and not least into its several restaurants. In 1899 annual turnover reached £1 million. The company was registered as limited by shares – Whiteley held 99% – and he introduced profit-sharing. However, newly required professional auditing revealed significant financial discrepancies, and on 7 June 1899 the *Financial Times* said: 'There is a tendency nowadays among promoters of Industrial Companies to keep the plums of the financial pudding to themselves, and offer the dough to the public, and if there be any plums in this company Mr Whiteley has kept them to himself.'

At lunchtime on 24 January 1907 everything changed. The 76-year-old was in his office at 43 Westbourne Grove when 28-year-old Horace Rayner called by. After employees heard raised voices Whiteley emerged from his office, asked a boy to fetch a policeman and made to return to his desk. Before the boy could oblige, Rayner emerged, shot the old man twice in the head and attempted suicide by shooting himself in the right eye. William Whiteley was dead. Within minutes a constable arrested Rayner – who initially identified himself as Cecil Whiteley – and the assailant was charged with murder. (Beable omits any mention of the manner of Whiteley's demise.[1])

Horace Rayner pleaded not guilty due to temporary insanity, though expert witnesses declared him sane. He was accused of committing blackmail by falsely claiming to be Whiteley's illegitimate son, with notes Rayner wrote in Whiteley's office presented in evidence. When Whiteley refused to pay, it was further alleged, Horace shot him. Whiteley's family was adamant that this upright gentleman could never be Rayner's secret father. Ominously, the family solicitor revealed, without elucidation, that Harriet's 1881 divorce had been granted on the grounds of Whiteley's 'misconduct'.

The witness testimonies fascinated the jury. Whilst there is no evidence that George Rayner – insurance agent, small-time financier and ostensible father of Horace – knew Whiteley prior to 1882, Horace claimed that the two men had 'known' two sisters, Emily and Louie (Louise) Turner of New Cross, in the late 1870s.

Horace was born to Emily in 1879, with George recorded as his father on the registration certificate. George had raised Horace (and two others) with Emily for a few years and continued to see the boy occasionally thereafter. Horace claimed that George told him, several times, that he, George, was *not* his father – although George was usually drunk when he said such things – and the alcoholic Emily once claimed that Whiteley *might* have been. Emily later married another and died in 1898. By 1907 Horace had an unhappy pregnant wife and significant debt. An occasional salesman travelling in Russia, he was neither content nor successful.

Louie Turner's testimony shocked the court: she swore that it was she, not her sister, who had borne William's illegitimate child, and that Cecil Whiteley was alive, well and serving in the navy.* Again, the court saw a birth certificate.

Louie had worked in Whiteley's shop from November 1882. In January 1883 Whiteley had provided her with the 'protection' of a small Georgian house, 13 Greville Road, Kilburn. The house was registered to George Rayner, although Whiteley paid the rent and Rayner and Emily only occasionally visited. Two years after moving in, Louie fell pregnant by her employer; Cecil was born in September 1885. Her sister had first met Whiteley, Louie testified, after Horace's birth. Louie had left William's 'care' in 1888, implying that Whiteley had not seen his son since then.

The jury deliberated. They quickly decided that, whether Horace's suspicion about his paternity was genuine or contrived, and his claim to money legitimate or otherwise, he had committed premeditated murder. Horace was sentenced to death, although a public outcry, including a million-name petition, saw the sentence commuted to life imprisonment. The exemplary if occasionally suicidal prisoner was released on licence in 1919. The revelation

---

*Herbert Cecil Whiteley Turner (1885–1964) rose to paymaster lieutenant commander in the navy. (Imperial War Museum, 'Lives of the First World War': https://livesofthe-firstworldwar.iwm.org.uk/lifestory/6898189.)

that Whiteley had a secret son shocked family and staff, but the business carried on.

The founder's two legitimate sons, William 2 (1871–1937) and Frank (1872–1929), both board members, continued their father's mission. In 1909 the company went fully public, selling shares, just as a competitor, Selfridges, opened on Oxford Street (see Waring). The Hanworth farm was sold for housing. A site at 400 Queensway became vacant through demolition in 1910, so when the Westbourne Grove leases expired, the company took advantage of the opportunity, building 'the biggest shop in the world'. When complete, the new Whiteleys included a theatre, a magnificent 'Scala' staircase, even minigolf on its roof.

Figure 24. Whiteley's emporium, Bayswater, was built in 1910.

Whiteley left £1 million (£100 million today) to provide housing for less fortunate, elderly retail employees. After his sons went to court to enforce a literal interpretation of their father's will in 1911, the family purchased the land for this development: a 225-acre, £40,000 site near Walton-on-Thames. The will stipulated that the site should be 'in as bright, cheerful and healthy [a] spot as possible', and the buildings had to be of 'good and substantial character and of a plain and useful design ... well lighted, ventilated and drained ... protected as far as possible from the North and East winds'. Seven Arts and Crafts architects created the idyllic Whiteley Village, with an octagonal layout. The building of Britain's first retirement village commenced in 1914, and in 1917 the first resident, Eliza Palmer, moved in. A splendid memorial to William Whiteley has graced the centre of the green, spacious, well-served community since 1921.

Figure 25. Whiteley Village, Walton-on-Thames, today.

In 1913 George Bernard Shaw's *Pygmalion* premiered. Henry Higgins, pondering how to turn a flower girl into a duchess, muses: 'Where can I buy a gown?' She replies: 'Whiteleys, of course!'

In the 1920s the Whiteleys staff physician, based in nearby Notting Hill, was a Dr A. J. Cronin. He wrote *The Citadel* (1937), a novel about a Scottish medic practising in South Wales, the homeland of Nye Bevan. The book prepared the ground for both Bevan's National Health Service (1948) and the 1960s BBC TV drama *Dr Finlay's Casebook*.

Beable's story is informed by a talk given to a 1924 convention by John Lawrie, then managing director of Whiteleys, who claimed that the company was the world's first 'Universal Provider'. When a friend had visited America in 1909, Lawrie said, Mark Twain had enquired after William's health. Hearing of William's death then prompted Twain to reminisce about a visit the writer once made to Whiteleys.

The coast was clear in 1925 for the company's next chapter. There had been no acquisition, no merger, no insoluble crisis, no war-time disruption.

WHITELEYS SINCE 1925

William 2 and Frank adopted a distinctly lower profile than their father. William 2 suffered life-changing injuries in a 1925 riding accident and retired, ceding the chairmanship to Lawrie, who oversaw continued growth. Frank died in 1929, William 2 in 1937, a crippled and alcoholic recluse.

The building was extended (1925), and in 1926 James White ('adviser' in the Horrockses and Dunlop stories; see 'Fraud' in the 'Governance' chapter) recommended that Harry Gordon Selfridge acquire Whiteleys to complement his own store. The sale was transacted in 1927, although White's 25% annual dividend 'guarantee' (bribe?) to Whiteleys' shareholders, agreed by Selfridge, proved completely unworkable.

World War II bomb damage decimated the Whiteleys archives. Many properties, but not the main emporium, were sold to keep Selfridges viable. In 1941 those crippling dividends were renegotiated – too late for Harry, who, in personal debt to his store, was sacked by his board. The playboy gambler died in poverty in 1947.

In the 1950s the upper floors of 400 Queensway were converted to offices, where tenants included LEO computers (see Lyons), ICL (later Fujitsu; see Kelly's) and Esso. Selfridges sold the palatial building to America's United Drapery Stores for £1.75 million in 1961. The store's mention in *Pygmalion* was reprised in the 1964 film version, *My Fair Lady*.

Renamed Hartree House in 1970, the Whiteleys building was listed for its conservation value but closed in 1981. It stood empty until 1989, when, after extensive rebuilding by the newly formed Whiteley Partnership, it reopened as a shopping centre – which never really worked.

The building's magnificent Scala staircase featured in the film *Love, Actually* (2003) as further up-market development materialized. The ground floor was redeveloped as a retail food hall in 2008. A developer purchased the site in 2013 but closed it in 2018 after the building featured as 'Whiteley's Folly' in the BBC TV drama *Mr Selfridge*.[2]

Laing O'Rourke won the latest redevelopment contract in 2019 thanks to Norman Foster's majestic redesign, which includes an up-market retail space, 139 apartments and the UK's first Six Senses hotel, retaining the fairytale staircase. Now known as The Whiteley, London, the spectacular venue was formally opened in February, 2025.

The Whiteleys emporium epitomized pre-war Britain. Also included in William's legacy is a pleasant retirement community, untouched by a century of change, nestling between two golf courses in rural Surrey. A care home named after Eliza Palmer opened there in 2019.

Did Whiteley's trading model set service standards so high that its long-term survival could never be assured? He served the middle-class shoppers of Bayswater, where, although customer numbers held up, the socio-economic status of the area went down, reducing his base.

Up-market shopping and leisure apart, the magnificent building alone is well worth a visit.[3]

Swift

(1869, Bicycles and Cars)

Rowley Turner (1841–1917) enjoyed his new French toy, cycling ninety miles from London to Coventry to show it to his uncle. It had two iron-rimmed hickory wheels, minimal steering, no gears or chain and a precarious seat atop a long, horizontal spring. Months later he raced it 123 kilometres between Paris and Rouen, finishing thirtieth of thirty-four taking the flag.[1] This velocipede was the Michaux brothers' 1863 invention, successor to the 'bone-shaker' or 'hobby-horse'. Young Parisian gentlemen considered velocipedes all the rage.

But this is not Rowley's story. It was the name of James Starley (1830–1881) that would resonate around the world of two wheels.

Starley left his parents' Sussex farm, aged 25, for London, initially gardening and repairing watches; he enjoyed inventing things. In 1857 his employer, Greenwich engineer John Penn, asked him to examine a malfunctioning sewing machine, in which Starley identified design flaws and saw the potential for operating improvements. Penn was impressed and introduced James to Rowley's uncle, Josiah Turner of Newton, Wilson & Co. in Holborn, the machine's makers. Cutting a long story short, Starley and Turner – financed by a rich American, Silas Salisbury (1811–1887)* – set up a business in Coventry, a city known for its manufacturing prowess.[2] This was Coventry Sewing-Machine Co. (1859), the European Sewing-Machine Co. from 1863. Starley also dabbled in modifying penny-farthings. When Rowley, the company's Paris agent, turned up in 1869, he found them ready to diversify, prompted by a wave of cheap, imported sewing machines. They undertook to produce 400 velocipedes, 'Turners', to sell back to the French.[3]

Within months the Franco-Prussian War rendered export to France impossible, so even beyond the fall of Paris in 1871 this was not a good time

---

*Salisbury co-sponsored several Starley patents but returned to America, bankrupt, in 1862. (Grace's Guide, 'Silas Covell Salisbury': www.gracesguide.co.uk/Silas_Covell_Salisbury.)

to sell bicycles. Coventry Machinists Ltd (as it was now known) had to find an alternative market.[4]

James suggested improvements, increasing the product's value by making it more comfortable and reliable. His modifications included

- three bicycle gear patents, first used commercially by the 'Ariel' (1871);
- a more reliable tangent wheel, with lighter, stronger, metal spokes (1874);
- an alternative design to accommodate women's long skirts (1874);
- improvements to the (still brakeless) 'Roadster' (1876);
- the 'Coventry Lever' tricycle, essentially a penny-farthing with a lowered seat and a third, stabilizing wheel (1876);
- the 'Royal Salvo' tricycle, whose patented steering mechanism made four-wheeled transport feasible (1877).

James Starley's nephew, John Kemp Starley (1856–1901), came from Walthamstow to work for the company in 1872 and led it after James's death from cancer in 1881.[5] This Starley called his cycle operation 'Rover' and introduced the bicycle chain, recently invented in Manchester by the Swiss Hans Renold. Rover led the market throughout the 1880s, becoming JK Starley and Son and switching to shareholder ownership in 1888, when it ceased making sewing machines and experimented with motorcycles. J. K. initially used solid rubber tyres but adopted Dunlop's pneumatic version, manufactured nearby, from 1890. His definitive 'Rover Safety Bicycle' of 1885 was the blueprint for the modern pushbike, with rear-wheel propulsion and equal-sized wheels.[6]

J. K. Starley, a Liberal member of Coventry Council (1890–6), had idiosyncratic religious views. The Congregationalist published *Starley's Bible*, identical to the King James version except that the New Testament came first. This reflected, he maintained, its greater spiritual importance.

Significant employees of Rover included William Hillman (1848–1921), George Singer (1846–1909) and J. K. Starley's son, also a William, who spoke on 'The evolution of the cycle' at the Society of Arts, 1898. Singer developed the efficient curved front fork of the modern cycle frame (1874). Hillman was another Penn apprentice, who had followed his friend James to Coventry, set up his own bicycle company and eventually became a millionaire from ball bearings and roller skates. At one point there were over forty bicycle-makers in Coventry.

The Rover name was transferred to a separate automobile company created by J. K. Starley with William Sutton, a haberdasher, in 1888. They sold it for £150,000 in 1896, when J. K. Starley began producing experimental electric cars and bikes and relocated to Meteor Works, Coventry, renaming the original Rover 'Swift Cycle Co. Ltd'.[7] That year, battling against cheaper models, Starley sold 11,000 bicycles, profiting by £20,000 from a turnover of £160,000.

J. K. Starley died suddenly in 1901, aged 46.

The government had raised the speed limit for motorized vehicles to 14 mph in 1896 and dropped the requirement for cars to follow a man carrying a red flag. A campaigner against speed limits, Daimler's Harry Lawson, founder of the Motor Car Club of Britain, organized an annual London-to-Brighton 'Emancipation Day Rally' (1896). Road racing became popular in France, whilst British motorists of 1903 were still restricted to 20 mph! The Isle of Man abandoned its speed limit, allowing both racing and time trials. Lawson, now running Rover, was distracted by legal suits concerning patents. Convicted of fraud involving shareholders' money (and Siberian gold, a joint venture with Ernest Hooley), he was sentenced to a year's hard labour. He reappeared during World War I with Bleriot's, aircraft makers, but was again found guilty of fraud. Friends said he was kind, clever ... unlucky.

Fully independent of Rover, Swift was now based at Cheylesmore Works, still in Coventry. In 1903 Swift invented reverse gear for cars and in 1906 acquired S&B Gordon's nearby cycle factory, Quinton Works. It launched a 'cycle car' in 1912, merging car and cycle operations. In the difficult post-war economy Swift sold half its assets to Bean Motors, and between 1915 and 1920 it produced 17,000 cars.

There were 182 automotive manufacturers in Britain's highly competitive market of 1922. Swift found itself unable to pay dividends and, despite new management, the company went into decline.

SWIFT SINCE 1925

Suppliers foreclosed on Swift's debts in 1931, making it one of more than a hundred motor enterprises that failed to compete with juggernauts Austin, Morris and the American Ford.[8]

Although Swift no longer existed, some of Starley's legacy lived on through Rover, still a recognizable (if dormant) brand today. For Britain's car industry a confusing, almost unnavigable century was looming.[9]

Few post-Beable journeys are as simple as Swift's disappearance or as complex as the history of the British automobile industry. The Starleys' original purpose for Rover was lost, and although his inheritors continued to innovate, they had stiff competition.

Oxford's William Morris (1877–1963, not the Arts and Crafts man), a future supporter of Mosley's British Union of Fascists, also started with bicycles. His rival Herbert Austin built cars as a hobby before working for a dominant auto brand, the Vickers brothers' Wolseley (1901). Leyland began by making steam-powered vans, and Daimler had set up operations near Swift and Rover in Coventry. Austin started his company at Longbridge, 1905, and Morris's Bullnose and Oxford models were in mass production by 1912.

The eight-horsepower Rover was the most powerful car of 1920. Swallow Sidecars, formed in 1922, did not enter the car market until 1931, when Swift closed. Swallow too relocated to Coventry. By 1929 two thirds of the market had been taken by Austin, Morris and Ford, with the Morris Minor and the MG (Morris Garages) Midget capitalizing on the end of the universal 20 mph limit.

In the 1930s Swallow (as SS Cars) produced its first Jaguar, and a 30 mph limit was introduced in built-up areas. Plagued by industrial disputes, William Morris (now Lord Nuffield) bought Riley and Wolseley. As World War II started, Rover employed 21,000, moving to Solihull after its Coventry site was bombed.

Post war, SS was sensibly renamed 'Jaguar' and Rover launched its biggest success, the Land Rover, producing 500,000 by 1960. Morris and Austin merged in 1952 as the British Motor Corporation, launching its 'Mini' in 1959. The company acquired Jaguar in 1966, as the national 70 mph speed limit arrived. The following year Leyland bought Rover, and in 1968 it joined the British Motor Corporation to form British Leyland (BL).

Automobile production peaked in the 1960s, but by the end of the decade British vehicles were internationally uncompetitive, takeovers were rife and government support was being mooted. The 1970s saw industrial unrest at unprecedented levels (500 walkouts over thirty months across forty-two BL plants), and BL's 1975 failure was significant. The government controversially intervened to nationalize it, imposing cuts and asset sales and introducing Japanese investment. Jaguar was denationalized in 1984, leaving the residual BL subsidiaries Austin and Rover as Rover Group plc. The Austin brand was retired in 1987, when management buyouts 'liberated' both Leyland Buses and Unipart, BL's parts supplier.

The remaining company was sold to British Aerospace (1988). The government defended the £150 million sale as marking the end of the era of direct subsidy, which had cost the taxpayer billions. Rover Group Holdings passed into BMW's German hands in 1994 and saw its loss-making engine plant sold for just £10 in 2000, despite sales of $8 billion a year. Land Rover was separately, controversially, sold to Ford in 2000.

By 2005, with some Rover assets (but not the brand name) sold to China, British Rover production had ceased. Via Ford, the brand became part of Jaguar Land Rover under Tata's Indian ownership, in 2008. Land Rover remains an innovative international brand, made in five countries, including Britain. Global sales are strong; Jaguar Land Rover's biggest market is China.

Today, Starley's Rover brand rests silently in Tata's hands. There are homages to Starley in the names of two new bicycle companies, Swift (2010) and Starley Bikes (2012), with no known direct connection to the original. The Starley Network is a 500-mile web of cycle paths across England's West Midlands.[10] There is a memorial to James Starley on Warwick Row, Coventry, whilst the Cheylesmore factory fascia now fronts a hotel.[11]

Glaxo

(1873, Pharmaceuticals)

The name 'Glaxo', first applied to an infant formula that 'Builds bonnie babies', apparently emerged from a search for a five-letter name ending in 'o'. 'Gála' is milk in Greek, whilst the suffix '-ose' identifies sugars. 'Glaxo' was dried cow's milk with added lactose (milk sugar). For the Nathan family of New Zealand, their 1902 naming quandary was brief.

However, this story has multiple origins.

Eighteenth-century pharmacies were exciting places of experimentation, debate, ideas and discovery, selling medicines and confections to support their adventures. Sylvanus Bevan (1691–1765), a Welsh Quaker and apothecary, opened his pharmaceutical and pastille shop in Plough Court, Lombard Steet, London, in 1715. In 1794 William Allen (1770–1843), of the Hanbury Quakers of Stoke Newington, took over Plough Court from Sylvanus's son, Job.[1] A scientist, philanthropist and prison reformer, Allen campaigned alongside William Wilberforce to ban slavery, boycotting sugar from 1784 to 1834, and co-created the New Lanark model community with Robert Owen and others in 1814. He was also a cofounder of the Royal Pharmaceutical Society (1841). Allen introduced another Quaker to Plough Court, Luke Howard (1772–1864), in 1797. Howard classified clouds, coining the terms 'cirrus', 'stratus' and 'cumulus' and inspiring John Constable and John Ruskin with his cloud sketches. He organized the first global anti-slavery convention (1840) and helped former slaves resettle in Africa. In 1808 Howard's cousin Daniel Hanbury (1794–1882) joined Plough, and by the 1850s three factories were needed to supply their medicines, infant food and malt preparations. In 1856 Plough became Allen & Hanbury, adding 'Ltd' in 1893, an identity it would keep for more than 100 years.

Burroughs Wellcome was founded by Americans in London, 1880, combining with Henry Wellcome's charitable operations to become the Wellcome Foundation in 1924. Some sources credit Wellcome (1853–1936) with the invention of the medical pill, a regulated, reliable dose of medicine mixed with inert chalk, compressed into an easy shape to swallow. Artists' pencils, which mix compressed graphite and clay in their 'lead', may have inspired Wellcome.

Meanwhile, John Smith ran a Philadelphia drugstore from 1830, with Mahlon Kline as his bookkeeper from 1865. They merged names and interests a decade later.

Beechams patent laxative pills were manufactured in Wigan from 1842 and advertised, not least by the dreadful poet William McGonagall, as a cure-all.[2] The patent mixture of aloe, ginger and soap was devised by Thomas Beecham (1820–1907), an Oxfordshire shepherd and herbalist, grandfather of his knighted classical conductor namesake.

Beechams, SmithKline, Burroughs Wellcome and Allen & Hanbury will all enter the Glaxo story after 1925. For now we return to the Nathans.

Londoner Joseph Nathan (1835–1912), an East End Jew, arrived in Australia in 1853 during the gold rush, having worked in his father's tailor shop from age 12. Melbourne people wisely advised that gold was a fool's errand, so his general store made money not from gold but from gold miners. In 1856 he visited family in Wellington, New Zealand, where his sister's husband, the 'difficult' Jacob Joseph, was almost blind. Jacob offered young Nathan a job in his importation business, which Nathan, pausing only to pop back to Melbourne to marry his sweetheart, accepted.[3] Joseph and Diana had thirteen children, of whom eleven survived to adulthood. Six of the seven boys eventually joined the family enterprise.

By 1861 Nathan was a partner in Jacob's business, which he bought in 1873, renaming it Joseph Nathan & Co. Meanwhile he had gathered a portfolio of virgin land, buying the pockets granted to soldiers leaving New Zealand's army for £25 each. As president of Wellington's Hebrew Congregation, Nathan initiated the construction of a synagogue in 1870. He supported New Zealand's first Jewish prime minister, Julius Vogel, in his pro-women, pro-public-services agenda but held back from public life himself through fear of anti-Semitism.

Things did not go well, obliging Joseph to visit London in 1876 to secure capital. Through the 1880s he took on directorships for infrastructure projects in Wellington: the slipway, the gas supply, the harbour and, his crowning glory, the railway, completed in 1886. The following year he returned to London semi-permanently and in 1899 incorporated Joseph Nathan & Co., valued at £127,000. By now he was exporting frozen New Zealand lamb. David, his oldest, took on his New Zealand directorships.

Nathan's youngest, Alec (1872–1954), initially ran a farm rather than join the store. He had an idea: dried milk. New Zealand's lush fields were perfect for cows, the family owned much pasture and there was room in the market. His father, in London, was impressed.

In 1901 Alec bought an American patent milk-drying process whilst the family invested in equipment and contracted to buy milk from local dairy farmers. Alec conceived of a fortified milk powder to feed infants. Their new factory was at rural Bunnythorpe, where Alec and his brother Charlie lived. Quickly erected in 1904, it burned down and then suffered a major equipment failure – sabotage? Teething problems over, Bunnythorpe was fully functional by 1906, processing 1,500 gallons of milk daily.

The baby food was dried cow's milk with added lactose. The Swiss Nestlé had made the first commercial infant food in 1867, whilst another rival was the American Horlicks, 1890.

The company needed a name for marketing purposes, so it registered 'Glaxo' in Wellington and, with admirable foresight, London too. The brothers made a concerted effort to sell their product through face-to-face meetings with doctors, nurses and welfare workers in New Zealand, Australia and Britain, spending nothing on advertising until they had 8,000 customers. In 1908 the Nathans published the *Glaxo Baby Book*, a mother's guide, as Alec Nathan moved to London. His philosophy, according to his *Australian Jewish Herald* obituary, was that '"the most humble employee should have every opportunity in the business" and those who worked for Mr Nathan knew that this philosophy went into practice'.

Joseph Nathan died in London in 1912, when another son, Louis, took over as chairman. World War I was good for Glaxo: Britain's Ministry of Food purchased 4,000 tons, and by 1917 it was a household name in several countries. Nine in every ten British clinics stocked the product, available across the empire by 1925, aided no doubt by New Zealand's reputation for cleanliness, innocence and sunshine.

During World War I Glaxo recruited the English pharmacist Harry Jephcott (1891–1978) to run its laboratories, the natural business acumen of this train driver's son complementing Kiwi Alec's 'softer' instincts. Jephcott was the first qualified scientist employed by the Nathans; two of the first eight were female.

Daily processing capacity reached 14,000 gallons in 1920. Bunnythorpe had four drying machines, and the company had other factories in New Zealand and Australia. By now its diverse product range included Glaxovo, a malt-based 'food drink', and Ostelin, Britain's first commercial vitamin extract (1924) and Glaxo's first pharmaceutical product. Its vitamin D was cod liver oil with 99% of the oil removed, Jephcott having purchased the rights to the product from Columbia University. Ostelin was added to the fortified milk.

However, after a 'good' war, Glaxo's sales were falling in the early 1920s, partly due to recession. In 1922 only 3% of milk was pasteurized, but Britain's government would change this, to the company's disadvantage: for health reasons it aimed to treat 96% of milk by 1936. If milk itself was safer than it once was, what more did Glaxo offer? Infant deaths had more than halved in the last generation, but could Glaxo claim that success for its infant formula? No. Alarmingly, scientists started to question the very wisdom of giving cow's milk to babies at all.[4]

In 1925 Alec Nathan, now London-based, was managing director. Since 1919 the company's shares had technically been available to the public, although the family held every single one. Beable, fascinated as ever by technology, praises the company's commitment to service and quality. He reports a meticulous approach to hygiene, the proud boast that tuberculosis had never infected Glaxo's milk and the high status enjoyed by the company's scientists.

At Glaxo House, London, the search was on for other ways to put the company's resources to good use.[5]

GLAXO SINCE 1925

Harry Jephcott qualified as a patent lawyer in 1925, becoming a director of the Nathans' company four years later. A subsidiary oversaw Glaxo Laboratories at 891–995 Greenford Road, London (now a listed building), where Jephcott became managing director and added pharmaceuticals to the portfolio. In 1937 Glaxo Laboratories assumed responsibility for the New Zealand dairy-related operation, but by the 1940s Jephcott was focusing on the licensed production of penicillin, of which both Allen & Hanbury and Burroughs Wellcome had been early producers.

Alec Nathan retired in 1945, dying of cancer in 1954.[6] As the new CEO, Jephcott was knighted in 1946, the same year that shareholders liquidated Joseph Nathan & Co. and sold non-core assets such as a fence-exporting business. They floated Glaxo Laboratories, with its continued focus on pharma. Ida Townsend, export manager, was the first woman on the Glaxo board, and griseofulvin, an antifungal agent, its first 'homegrown' pharmaceutical.[7]

Merck and Glaxo isolated and marketed vitamin B12 simultaneously in 1948, as a treatment for pernicious anaemia, and Glaxo developed an innovative treatment for hyperthyroidism. Glaxo's commercial production of cortisone came in 1950, followed by work on steroids and some small acquisitions. With much of its work licensed from US patents, the company feared an American takeover.

Over in the US SmithKline became SmithKline French Laboratories in 1929. Henry Wellcome had died in 1936, leaving the Wellcome Foundation business to the Wellcome Trust, his medical research charity.

Sir Harry (by now a respected philanthropist and a governor of the London School of Economics) retired as managing director in 1956, replaced by Sir Alan Wilson, but he remained as non-executive chairman and honorary president. Responding to the perceived takeover threat, Glaxo Laboratories' first major acquisition (1958) was Allen & Hanbury, which had enjoyed 240 years of independence. The 1960s brought new drugs and new structures, including a new parent company, and Glaxo Laboratories acquired Evans Medical in 1961.

In 1955 Beechams acquired Ribena (a blackcurrant drink launched in 1938, credited with supplying war-time vitamin C); in 1965 it added Macleans toothpaste, Lucozade and pharmaceuticals including artificial penicillin, and then Horlicks in 1969. Glaxo resisted a hostile takeover by Beechams in the early 1970s, after discussions with Boots on a mutually beneficial partnership came to nothing.

The 1970s saw Glaxo create a US subsidiary, incorporate Glaxo Holdings and Glaxo Laboratories, and survive an American anti-trust case. In 1973 Austin Bide, a Glaxo lifer (later to chair British Leyland), became chairman. He was succeeded in 1980 by Paul Girolami, another lifer who had to deal with problems around Zantac (rantidine), Glaxo's ulcer treatment drug. Although it became the world's most-used pharmaceutical product (1984), it was withdrawn from some markets due to cancer concerns. By the late 1980s, after tripling sales in a decade, Glaxo was the world's fourth-biggest pharma company.

Back in America, SmithKline French was growing, becoming SmithKline Beckman in 1982 and SmithKline Beecham in 1989 (ceasing production of Beechams pills in 1998). That year Ernest Mario, an American community pharmacist and director of Glaxo Holdings who had previously worked for SmithKline, was appointed Glaxo's CEO and international sales blossomed.[8] Sir Paul Girolami retired in 1994, succeeded by Sir Richard Sykes (b. 1942), the microbiologist who would later chair Britain's Covid Vaccine Taskforce (2021).

The biggest merger between any two UK companies to date produced Glaxo Wellcome in 1995, the world's largest pharma company by capitalization. It restructured its research capacity, shedding 10,000 jobs worldwide but retaining 59,000 (including 13,400 in the UK) across seventy-six operating companies and fifty manufacturing facilities. By 1999 it had seven drugs in the world's fifty best-sellers. As the third-largest pharma company by revenue, after Novartis and Merck, Glaxo Wellcome's key products included drugs for migraine, asthma, cold sores and AIDS.

Another enormous capacity- and scope-enhancing merger, in 2000, brought together Glaxo Wellcome and SmithKline Beecham to form GlaxoSmithKline plc (GSK). Its Brentford headquarters housed 3,000 employees, with Smith-Kline Beecham's Jean-Pierre Garnier as CEO. Acquisitions focused on HIV, flu and nutrition. A succession of chairmen followed.

The smooth run became bumpy in the new millennium as the High Court instructed GSK to withdraw its claims that low-sugar Ribena would not rot teeth. Then the US Food and Drug Administration uncovered irregularities at a GSK subsidiary, SB Pharmco in Puerto Rico, where a product recall was ordered but not implemented. This led to an FDA inspector in Puerto Rico being fired and a whistle-blowing suit, and in 2005 officials seized drugs worth $2 billion, the FDA's biggest ever haul. In 2010 GSK was eventually fined $150 million, plus a settlement cost of $600 million.

In an unrelated case in 2003, GSK lost a US claim that its patent on Paxil, an antidepressant (annual sales £2 billion), had been infringed by a Canadian generic drug company. Pharma companies regularly rail against cheaper 'generic' copies of their drugs, which they claim deprive them of income needed to invest in research and development.[9] In 2006 GSK settled a US tax dispute, coughing up $3 billion, whilst in New Zealand in 2007 the company was fined NZ$217,000 for overstating vitamin C levels in ready-to-drink Ribena.

Andrew Witty, with Glaxo since 1985, became CEO in 2008. He halved some drug prices in fifty of the poorest countries and released intellectual property to encourage production of medicines for developing nations. GSK became the biggest pharma donor to the Gates Foundation. A decade of acquisitions focusing on biotech followed. Under Witty, GSK endorsed the London Declaration on Neglected Tropical Diseases; Sir Andrew was knighted in 2012. That year GSK pleaded guilty in America to promoting three drugs by exaggerating their scope and benefit, failing to report data, and giving bribes or kickbacks. They were fined $3 billion, in the world's largest case of health fraud.

By 2013 GSK was operating in 115 countries and employing 99,000 people. It volunteered to publish historic clinical trial results and to selectively release AIDS drug patents, first for children, then adults. GSK China was convicted of giving HK$4 billion in kickbacks to promote prescription of their drugs, for which it was fined HK$490 million. Four executives were arrested, an episode that Witty described as 'shameful' and 'deeply disappointing'. GSK started a ten-year partnership with Save the Children in which the charity was given influence over investment priorities on issues such as child vaccines in Africa.[10] In 2023 the partnership was extended for at least five more years, targeting 9 million children who had never been vaccinated, largely in Nigeria and Ethiopia. GSK sold non-core brands Lucozade and Ribena to Suntory and later sold Horlicks, too.

GSK trialled a malaria vaccine in 2014 that the World Health Organization adopted for African use in 2018. An LGBTQ+ pressure group recognized GSK's inclusive employment policies, awarding them its first ever 100% rating.

In 2016 GSK was fined £37 million for UK market manipulation, using bribes to keep generic drugs off the market. Emma Walmsley, its first female CEO (2017), indicated a move away from Witty's Africa focus. A merger was announced in 2018 between GSK's consumer healthcare division (68%) and Pfizer (32%); the resulting Haleon came about in 2022. GSK was the world's largest pharma company by market capitalization, at £70 billion, and the eighth-largest company on the London Stock Exchange.

During the Covid pandemic GSK made 60 million doses of vaccine with Sanofi in 2020 and a billion in 2021. It had forty new medicines and seventeen new vaccines in development, licensing its tuberculosis vaccine to the Gates Foundation. Revenues exceeded £34 billion a year. In 2024 GSK moved to new London headquarters, close to the Francis Crick Institute and King's College, with 3,000 employees on site.[11]

Despite massive and welcome support for health initiatives in poorer countries, Glaxo's recent corporate behaviour appears cold, calculated, clinical. Huge fines for transgressions are of little consequence to a vast organization that may consider itself too big to fail. This is not deliberate or sanctioned criminality, but it is an organization so big that its head does not know what its tails are doing. Internal controls have been found wanting, and enforcement of standards has been inconsistent. Leadership can distance itself from malfeasance, but parts of GSK lack accountability; in the world of pharmaceuticals, trust should be paramount.

It would be remiss to overlook the extracurricular activity that has seen GSK emerge as a huge sponsor of the Gates Foundation, instigate an active, innovative and lasting partnership with a charity focused on child health in the poorest countries, and selectively waive intellectual property rights to increase the impact of medicine on some of the world's most vulnerable people. This is not 'here today, gone tomorrow' CSR; these are the actions of a company citizen.

It is a long way from adulterated dried cow's milk posing as infant formula.

Lever Bros

(1876, Soap)

While shepherds washed their socks by night, all seated round the tub,
A bar of Sunlight soap came down and they began to scrub

— Children's rhyme, 1940s

There is no better example of a company transforming from the dream of a 15-year-old, sweeping the grocery floor, to one of the world's biggest international conglomerates – in one lifetime.

Neither William Lever's younger brother, James D'Arcy Lever (1854–1916), nor any other family member contributed significantly to the family enterprise prior to 1925, and William's son was the only relative to do so thereafter. Young William Hesketh Lever (1851–1925) was a keen if ordinary scholar who lived with his comfortable, teetotal, devout Congregationalist parents, James and Elizabeth. The aspiring architect joined his father's wholesale grocery in Bolton, Lancashire (1867), at a shilling (5p) a week, a wage that rose as his responsibilities, such as bookkeeping, grew. As a commercial traveller for his father, William studied how businesses were run; if success stories inspired him, watching companies struggle intrigued him more.

He married his neighbour, Elizabeth Hulme (1850–1913), in 1874, although only one of their seven children survived to adulthood.[1]

In 1878 William's father acquired an ailing Wigan grocery for William and his brother James to manage, starting their partnership. When a customer, Ann Radcliffe, told him that 'stinking' soap lathered well despite its smell, William experimented. Alongside Bolton chemist William Watson, he found that vegetable oil, the recently introduced palm oil and glycerine were all cheaper and easier to obtain than soap's traditional staple, tallow. He first called his soap 'Honey' but then patented it as 'Sunlight'.

'Sunlight Self Washer Soap' was high quality, nice-smelling and manufactured in affordable portions, a palpable hit. Its innovative cardboard cartons created marketing opportunities. Lever 'radiated force and energy', says Skip-pers founder Sir Angus Watson, his protégé. 'He had piercing, blue-grey eyes which ... flashed with challenge when he was angry [and] the short neck and closely-set ears of a prize-fighter.'

William had global ambitions from 1884 but lacked the infrastructure to meet demand. He set out his company's mission: 'To make cleanliness commonplace; to lessen work for women; to foster health and contribute to personal attractiveness, that life may be more enjoyable and rewarding for the people who use our products.'

There were teething problems. 'Soapers' generally outsourced soap-boiling, which rendered quality unreliable. When Lever found a struggling Warring-ton soap-boiler unable to maintain a forty-product range, he bought the com-pany, boiling his homemade product there five months later. Twenty tons of output each week rose to 450 by 1887.

That year Lever, now a Freemason, developed a new site on the Wirral. He named the disused cement works and adjacent reclaimed marshland Port Sunlight, planning twenty-four acres of industrial operation and a thirty-two-acre township. Thirty architects created a high-quality settlement, each home having a garden and indoor toilet. Lever chose (and contributed to) the designs himself, possibly inspired by the modest 'garden village' built by Prices forty years earlier, just 500 metres to the east. Many marshland ravines were filled, but some were retained as features, such as a rhododendron-lined park and the school's sunken playground. By 1909 the village contained 700 homes, with rents set at a proportion of income, covering 547 acres by 1925. The factory's weekly output was 7,000 tons and 8,000 employees enjoyed profit-sharing, unemployment insurance and medical care.

Beable describes Port Sunlight as 'houses in which their workpeople would be able to live comfortably in pleasant homes provided with baths and gardens'. Another reviewer claims that Port Sunlight was 'a world in which benevolence and coercion were never far apart'.

Whilst Lever preached democracy, his workforce regarded him as autocratic, his paternalism perceived as oppressive by many. Some workers chose not to live at Port Sunlight, suspecting (correctly) that he sometimes vetoed applications for residence. The village included a 'dry' pub, and when the workers asked for a 'proper' inn, with beer, Lever agreed – as long as 75% of residents endorsed the plan. Lever had long supported votes for women, who were stronger supporters of temperance than men, so he conveniently enfranchised female residents in his poll. His ruse failed: 80% wanted alcohol! He conceded.

Lever purchased nearby Thornton Manor as a grand family home in 1888. He improved the house, gardens and amenities, but had much of the associ-ated village demolished to build yet more homes to rent to his workers. He

built nearby Hesketh Grange for his father (1894) and in 1904 purchased The
Hill at Hampstead, now Inverforth House, his main home from 1919.

Figure 26. Lever's Port Sunlight village
combined aesthetics and practicality.

The company acquired limited liability status in 1890, but when it issued
shares in 1894 the Levers owned all of them. James, only ever a minor partner,
contracted diabetes in 1895 and engaged less, resigning his directorship two
years later. Lever fought three general elections, as a Liberal in Birkenhead,
without success. The company opened a New York office in 1895, buying its
first American soaper in 1898 in Cambridge, Massachusetts. 'Sunlight' did
not thrive there, but the 'Welcome' bar did.[2] By 1900 the repertoire included
Lux soap flakes, Lifebuoy body soap, deliberately created as an 'affordable'
product, and Vim scouring powder.

Elizabeth's art collection was initially of items for use in advertising. The
company pioneered cinema publicity as it grew operations in Europe and
Australia and developed US-style promotion, gaining a reputation for market
intelligence. Adverts described Sunlight as 'liberating' for women, though
many endorsements were fictitious.

There were problems on the horizon. Margarine production (in which Lever
Bros was not involved) had increased global demand for palm oil, intensifying

competition and forcing prices up. In 1906 North West soapers, led by Lever, called a meeting aimed at protecting their interests, which the press inevitably described as a cartel, so when Lever reduced the size of his soap bars the *Daily Mail* spouted outrage. Headlines included 'How 15 ounces make a pound' (not sixteen). Lord Northcliffe, the *Mail*'s proprietor, advocated anti-trust legislation to curb the evil British soapers, describing Lever Bros as a 'sweat-shop'. Lever took offence and sued him. On day one of the trial Lever and his lawyers spoke for five hours, accusing the peer (who was conveniently abroad) of trying to wreck their company. The defence capitulated; Lever donated his award of £141,000 to Liverpool University and gave his workers a day off. Nevertheless, sales fell by 60% that year as Lever's shares lost a quarter of their value, costing the company more than £500,000.

William finally achieved his parliamentary ambition in the Wirral, serving a four-year term from 1906 as a Gladstonian Liberal. His maiden speech championed pensions, advocating his own company model, which Lloyd George delivered on a national scale some years later.

He was awarded a knighthood in 1911, the year of the 'Leverville' controversy.[3] The roots of the issue lay in Lever Bros' purchases of agricultural assets in distant countries, intended to secure palm oil at the best price. The company had a contract with the Belgian government, Congo's colonial power, to source it from five plantations covering 2 million acres. The plan was over-ambitious and naive, as Lever again displayed the paternalism bordering on arrogance that some on the Wirral found disturbing. However well-intentioned, his 'moral capitalism' in distant rural Africa was wholly idealistic. With problems compounded by Lever's view that Africans were inherently less capable than Europeans, delivery seemed impossible. There were insufficient local workers available, and migrants were too suspicious to travel there for work. Leverville, as Lever Bros' Congo base came to be called, was a place of 'indescribable ugliness', said Lever's personal secretary, 'marred by violence, hunger, illnesses and failing profitability'.

Lever's approach was enlightened but only in principle, and only compared with other colonial companies in Africa. The worst atrocities – forced labour, beatings, arbitrary execution, rape and more, carried out by a brutal police force – had taken place between 1885 and 1908 under the direct rule of the Belgian king, Leopold II, before international pressure obliged Leopold to hand control to Belgium's elected government. Nevertheless, those scars were not healed, nor had the brutalities been completely eradicated in Lever's day.[4] To Britain, Congo (not part of the empire) was 'out of sight, out of mind'. Responding to the Black Lives Matter movement in 2013, Unilever funded and published independent research into the company's record in both Congo and the Solomon Islands between 1900 and 1930.[5]

Lever persisted and by 1914 was receiving 2,500 tons of palm oil annually from Congo. In 1923 the country got its first soap factory, which retained more of the value of the raw material locally.

At the height of that controversy, 1912, Lever's personal fortune was £3 million. He purchased Stafford House, near Buckingham Palace, renamed it Lancaster House and allowed the government to use the elegant premises for hospitality and conferences. In 1914 he donated land in Bolton for a public park, the first of several such bequests. In 1917, as the first Baron Leverhulme, he was granted hereditary membership of the House of Lords; incorporating a late wife's surname (Elizabeth had died in 1913) into a peerage title is rare, but not unknown.

Lever Bros acquired Price's Candles, Britain's biggest importer of palm oil, in 1919 (see Prices). In 1920 it bought MacFisheries too, including Wall's sausages, incorporating it by 1922. These moves allowed it to scale up its ice cream manufacture, countering the growing influence of Lyons Maid.

There was one more controversy to come.

At 67, William's thoughts turned to retirement. Recalling an idyllic holiday, he bought Lews Castle in Stornoway, in the Outer Hebrides (1918). Excited by the potential for commercial fishing, he purchased the islands of Lewis and South Harris too, for £200,000. Stornoway's population was 30,000, but Lever envisaged that, with investment in fishing and agriculture, he could employ 200,000.[6] He started with an ice factory, essential for storing and transporting fish, adding similar facilities for unloading trawlers' catches in Fleetwood.

Again, Lever did not properly understand local residents. He was frustrated by the strength of Presbyterian Sabbath observance (reasoning that deep sea fishing can observe no such timetable). He discovered, too, that local crofters resented incomers telling them what to do, not least because of the shoddy way the British government had treated them, they claimed, during World War I. Gaelic-speaking crofters occupied six of Lever's twenty-two farms, and the government was unwilling to antagonize them, declining to support Lever's legal action to evict the crofters from his land. Lever persisted: the plan worked sufficiently to service a quarter of the MacFisheries chain.

Obbe, home to most of the new fishing infrastructure, was allowed to be renamed 'Leverburgh' in 1920. Although Lever promised to return excess land to locals, they were again suspicious, so that same year he began selling islands to absentee landlords, disposing of South Harris for only £900. In 1923 the peer sold Lews Castle, abandoning any idea of a permanent Scottish home; after his death the company discontinued the investment.

In 1922 the king elevated the peer again, to Viscount Leverhulme of the Western Isles. William donated Elizabeth's fabulous art collection to the nation as the Lady Lever Art Gallery.

Leverhulme died of pneumonia in 1925 and is buried next to Elizabeth at Port Sunlight. Thirty thousand witnessed his funeral, and an auction of his possessions took fifteen days to complete. Bequests to the nation included Lancaster House, a park in Ealing, and money for Bolton schools – in addition to a huge second park he had donated to that town in 1919 – and Liverpool University's new School of Tropical Medicine. His legacy includes the Leverhulme Trust, a charity that, to this day, gives £100 million annually to good causes. Beable sums up Lever's achievements: 'Side by side with the progress of the company there has been a progressive and enlightened policy of improvement in industrial conditions and the betterment of the people generally'.

By 1925 the company was selling in 134 countries, employing 85,000 and growing. Britain's biggest company of the era was the world's first genuinely multinational private corporation, yet its biggest chapter was still to come.

LEVER BROS SINCE 1925

Back in 1885 the Dutch Van den Bergh brothers registered a UK trademark for 'butterine', and by the 1890s several margarines were available. Jurgens registered 'Stork' in 1901 and, in 1906, the less popular 'Superbum'. Jurgens and the brothers combined to form Unie (1927), which merged with Lever Bros as Unilever in 1929, with public shareholders in both the Netherlands and the UK.

With margarine spurring a renewed demand for palm oil, Unilever expanded Bromborough Dock, Britain's biggest private port and formerly an important transport link for Prices. By the 1960s fats and oils constituted half of Unilever's raw materials. The dock closed in 1986, when it became a landfill site, now a nature reserve.

Political uncertainty militated against European investment in the 1930s, so Unilever sought British and American acquisitions, including Lipton's tea (1938), Frosted Foods (owner of Bird's Eye) and Batchelor's Peas (both 1943), Pepsodent (1944), Sunsilk (1954), and Dove skincare (1957).

One Port Sunlight claim to fame is that the Hulme community hall hosted Ringo Starr's first appearance as The Beatles' drummer (1962).

When the second Viscount Leverhulme died in 1949, Dutchman Paul Rijkens took the chair. The role alternated between the UK and Holland, including occasional joint chairs, and by 1970 Unilever was the world's second-biggest company.

Acquisitions continued, including Brooke Bond tea (1984), PG Tips and the American face cream giant Cheesbrough Ponds (1987), which brought with it Vaseline and Ragú.[7] Calvin Klein and Fabergé followed (1989), Colman's mustard (1995) and Sara Lee (Radox, Badedas) in 2009.

Figure 27. Bromborough Dock, acquired by
Lever Bros in 1919, is now a nature reserve.

Unilever sold its chemicals operations to Imperial Chemical Industries in
1989 for £4.9 billion, developing new and sustainable approaches to agricultural supplies from 1998.

Hellmann's, Knorr and the campaigning American ice cream maker Ben
& Jerry's were added in 2000. Ben & Jerry's was a pioneer of the B Corp
movement (detailed in the 'Environment' chapter), first accredited for high
standards of ESG operations in 1988.

The third Viscount Leverhulme, Philip, had no role in the company and
died with no heir in 2000, after which Thornton Manor fell into disrepair. In
2005 it was sold, restored and reopened as an attractive wedding venue.

The following decade saw more acquisitions, largely health-and-beauty
related, and an expansion into Asian markets. Under the French 'lifer' Patrick
Cescau, Unilever cofounded the voluntary industry body the Roundtable on
Sustainable Palm Oil. Today palm oil is high on the sustainability agenda:
over a million acres of ancient Indonesian and Malaysian rainforest is felled
each year to grow it, at the expense of a major carbon sink. This exacerbates
climate change and biodiversity loss, whilst impacting both rare species such
as orangutans and indigenous tribes suffering human rights abuses at the

hands of developers. Partnering with the charity Rainforest Alliance from 2007, Unilever committed to sourcing its tea sustainably and ethically.

An outsider, the Dutch Paul Polman of Nestlé, formerly of Procter & Gamble, was recruited as CEO in 2009 to address years of poor results and relative sales decline. Whilst sell-offs and acquisitions continued, he launched a ten-year 'Sustainable Living Plan' the following year. Early successful measures included ending animal testing, except where legally required (2011); ending microplastics in cosmetics (2015); and achieving 100% sustainable palm oil by 2015 whilst encouraging others to set a 2020 target. Industry-wide palm oil targets were not met, as demand for the sustainable product vastly outstripped supply. Ukraine is a major producer of other vegetable oils, and in 2022 Russia's invasion halted those exports, disrupting global markets in all vegetable oils, including palm oil.[8]

On the downside, Unilever was fined for historic price fixing of washing powder, as part of a European cartel (2011), and French personal hygiene products (2016).

Polman was co-author of the United Nations' 17 Sustainable Development Goals, published in 2015 (see 'Sustainability' in the 'Environment' chapter). Unilever's acquisitions, especially in premium beauty, continued to include several certified sustainable businesses, such as Pukka Herbs. PG Tips launched its pioneering plastic-free teabag in 2018, but the brand was sold in 2022.

The company rebuffed a massive 2017 takeover bid by Kraft Heinz worth $143 billion, 18% above market valuation, via private equity intermediaries 3G and Berkshire Hathaway. Unilever justified its defiance on the grounds of 'incompatible values' and lack of strategic fit. It then restructured to protect itself from future such hostile takeovers, though the most radical proposal (quitting London to focus on Amsterdam) was eventually abandoned.

In 2019 Polman retired and insider Alan Jope became CEO, reporting 290% returns for shareholders over ten years through values-led trade. Unilever joined sixty businesses and thirteen European governments pledging to halve non-recyclable plastic packaging by 2025.

Completing its response to the Kraft experience, in 2020 the Dutch Unilever NV and the UK's Unilever plc formally merged under one London-based holding company. To help combat Covid Unilever donated over $100 million in goods. After ten years of its Sustainable Living Plan, Unilever's more overtly eco-friendly brands were amongst its most profitable.

When Ben & Jerry's wanted to remove its ice cream from Palestine in 2022, in protest against Israel's illegal occupation of the territory, Unilever resisted and instead sold the West Bank operation to a local franchisee. Two years later Ben & Jerry's was still engaged in a legal wrangle with the parent company. In 2025 Unilever forbade the outspoken ice cream makers from voicing negative comments about President Trump (as they had during the first Trump presidency). Bosses argued that doing so at such a sensitive time – with ice cream operations about to be sold off – was inappropriate.[9]

Also in 2022 Unilever stopped trade involving Russia following the invasion of Ukraine, although its local Russian presence continued to operate, with Jope arguing that this best protected the company's employees and assets. Criticism of Unilever's Ukraine–Russia stance was acknowledged by Hein Schumacher, the incoming CEO in 2023, saying that as no 'worthy buyer' for the Russian operation had been found, there was 'no good option' for action. Schumacher's sudden and premature departure in 2025 was linked by some to a company 'rethink' on its position on ESG and diversity, equity and inclusion (DEI), both of which are embedded into its operations.[10]

Unilever's 2023 global revenue was €60 billion (its highest ever), its net income €8.2 billion (ditto) and it had 148,000 employees (its maximum was 174,000, in 2013). Just thirteen brands accounted for over half of sales.

Today's operating practices confirm Unilever's status as a global sustainability champion, including early adoption of 'science-based targets' to reach net zero carbon emissions, though its targets are likely to be recalibrated in 2025. Still vibrant, Port Sunlight's magnificent conservation area boasts a museum, heritage tours and the scintillating Lady Lever Art Gallery. *Bubbles* (see Pears) is there, as are pre-Raphaelite masterpieces and many Wedgwood milestones, including his anti-slavery medallion.

Unilever continues to build on Lever's discipline, purpose and values, even his ruthless streak. Despite personal faults (he could be insensitive, arrogant, wily), he laid foundations upon which others built, setting standards of altruism and public interest in business that have informed core company operations for over a century.

Beable would recognize Unilever. It continues to show determination, imagination and respect for the planet. Its registered address remains 'Port Sunlight'.

Gamages

(1878, Retail)

Gamages is a strange 'romance' as the retailer hardly stands out: humble origins are normal, astute marketing commonplace and the courage to take risks par for the course. What attracted Beable to Walter Gamage's haphazard and ultimately failing creation?

Being the seventeenth child of a Herefordshire farmer prompted 19-year-old Walter Gamage (1855–1930) to move on. The draper's apprentice toiled close to St Paul's Cathedral alongside his friend Frank Spain. One day in 1878 he took his watch to a repairer who casually mentioned that the area could do with somewhere to buy socks. Spain and Gamage decided to address this, so they invested £88 and rented a shop, at 128 Holborn, for £220 a year.

Their hosiery store, with one and a half metres of frontage, consumed all of the young men's savings, whilst wholesalers denied the newcomers credit. They sold hairbrushes at 1s9d (9p) compared with their rivals' 2s6d (12.5p), struggling to raise £2,000 of income in year one. A sign above their door said: 'Tall oaks from little acorns grow.' Another Gamage adage was: 'Always be satisfied with small profits.' Their ambition was to be the 'People's Popular Emporium', but Gamage had to go it alone as, in 1881, when Spain needed money to marry he sold his share to Gamage for £425.

The shop was extended in 1882 as the 'showplace of London', featuring toys, novelties, and cricket and bicycling supplies, challenging Lillywhite's, its rival, head-on. Gamage's target audience was young, male and athletic, and during the 1880s and 1890s sales of bicycles, sporting requisites and cycling clothing all boomed. There developed a strong market for second hand bikes, for which Gamage required a further extension: his site soon stretched to Leather Lane and Hatton Garden.

Gamage believed in quality products, materials and service. By 1887 the shop was a 'general outfitter', by 1893 a 'cycling and athletic outfitter', making the most of a new phenomenon, leisure-focused spending. In 1896 it started sending lists of products to customers as Gamage developed mail order.

There was further consolidation and expansion in 1897 as turnover approached £120,000, supported by the sale of 25,000 preference (non-voting) shares in Gamage Ltd.

The 1901 census says that Holborn was home to twenty-two bicycle shops, so how could Gamages stand out? Its sheer size helped: a visit became a day out, with more than four acres of browsing over two floors. Its wares included exotic pets, gardening tools, motor parts, fashion, furniture and carpets. Bicycles had become utilitarian, but the motorized French quadricycle (1900), a car in all but name, was a novelty. Automata provided additional visitor attractions, and 100 metres of model railway pulled in the 1902 crowds. Such models became marketing features, as did the venue itself, combining several incongruent buildings in a higgledy-piggledy arrangement of rooms and passageways. In 1903 it even had its own brand of car.[1]

A 1904 expansion took in the demolished site of the Black Bull, where Dickens's fictional Mrs Gamp first met Martin Chuzzlewit. The extension's opening blessed the entire front page of the *Daily Mail* in the first such advert. 'The world's largest sport and athletic outfitter' now included a licensed restaurant, a tobacco counter, and bespoke boots and shoes, whilst parts of the shop had a twelve-metre ceiling and electric lighting. Everything was available on mail order except guns and ammunition. The *Daily Mail*'s opinion was that 'when [Gamage's] projected palatial building proudly raises its head above the neighbouring structures over the dust of the old, the mighty gulf which separated the business methods of the nineteenth and twentieth centuries will be obvious'.

Gamages acquired Benetfink & Co. in 1908, a modest department store specializing in motorcycles and household fittings, utilizing its Cheapside site as a depot. Gamages catalogues alerted middle-class families to every conceivable Christmas gift, with the 1911 publication running to 900 pages, including 49 of bicycles alone. The purchase of WW Harrison of Sheffield, cutlery-maker, led to a mass market for electroplated tableware from 1913.

During World War I Gamages manufactured the Leach Trench Catapult, used by Tommies on the western front to rain mortars on the enemy. Gamage's sons, Eric, Leslie and Cyril, all saw action. The year 1915 was the company's best to date, as though the war was not happening – perhaps its style, range and marketing provided relief from the vicissitudes of life. Another record-breaker came with 1919, as Walter ceded the leadership to Eric (1888–1964). In 1925 the store, now 116–28 Holborn, reached its maximum footprint.

It added glass, ceramics and stainless steel cutlery. When Lillywhite's relocated to prestigious Piccadilly, in 1923, Eric thought hard about whether his mammoth Holborn store was in the right place. Was it time for a very big decision?[2]

GAMAGES SINCE 1925

Gamages was nothing if not ambitious. In 1928 Eric committed to a ninety-nine-year lease of 489–97 Oxford Street at £20,000 a year for four years, £30,000 a year thereafter. His brand new store had forty-one flats above and a façade by Sir Edwin Lutyens, a consultant to the project. Eric went public, but the 500,000 new £1 shares only covered half the cost of the development. He borrowed £450,000 from the Grosvenor estate, calling down only £300,000.

The new store opened in 1930 with 100 metres of frontage, 100,000 visitors on day one and a focus on women's fashion. There were telephones in the hairdressing department, a 400-seater restaurant and rooftop miniature golf. The flats sold well, and when Walter Gamage died that year he reputedly 'lay in state' in the motorcycle department. But in the global Depression the store struggled, closing after only eight months, described as 'one of the biggest retail failures ever'.[3] From early 1931 its stock was offered at huge discounts, but in April the receivers moved in. To recoup losses the building was offered for sale with a £600,000 reserve but withdrawn when offers did not exceed £330,000. It reverted to the Duke of Westminster, as landowner and mortgagee. C&A took it over, modifying it in 1938. It was partially rebuilt in the 1960s and became Allders from 2001, as many C&A stores did, but that also failed.[4] Today the site is occupied by Primark.

The second and last Gamage to lead the company, Eric, died in 1964. After a placid period, in 1968 Gamages surprised many by opening a second store in Romford, Essex, selling the site to British Home Stores just three years later.

The Gamages Holborn store remained open throughout the Oxford Street debacle but closed in 1972. It was an emotional period, with parties and staff reunions; the company collection of historic cricket bats was donated to the Marylebone Cricket Club. There was a brief phoenix moment in 1972 when Gamages reopened, in the former Waring & Gillow store, 164–82 Oxford Street, for a few months only. Gamages followed an old-fashioned approach in what had become a more specialized and 'democratic' environment, says a 2014 academic study.[5]

Today Gamages is no more. There is no trace in Holborn of that disjointed building, deemed void of architectural merit – the site is occupied by Hatton Garden jewellers.[6] Holborn was not a bad place to set up shop, with room to expand, and the company was innovative in both the breadth of what it sold and the manner in which it sold it. Yet the site's characterful labyrinth (read 'disorganized chaos'?) was crying out for rationalization. Taking pressure off Holborn with the Oxford Street 'clean sheet' was sensible, but the investment inadequate and untimely. This had then coincided with both the Great Depression and Walter Gamage's death, both of which were simply bad luck.

Gamages proved disappointing. Although it never charged extortionate prices, its Oxford Street neighbour, Simon Marks (of '& Spencer') was even cheaper – and survived.

Martins

(1885, Tobacco)

Walter Martin (1868–1940), cigar entrepreneur, is a difficult man to track. His greatest achievement boosted the morale of British troops in World War I, albeit almost anonymously.

As a boy, not satisfied with an apprentice draper's prospects, he hawked ginger beer and ink around Guernsey, renting a warehouse for 10s (50p) a year, and later adding hosiery and tobacco to his products. Within two years the 17-year-old and his older brother, Arthur, had generated £3,000, which enabled them to set up a tobacconist shop that Arthur ran for life.

Tobacco became Walter's lifeblood. Unscrupulous competitors adulterated their products with rhubarb, moss and dye. Makers accused rivals of enhancing taste, whilst over in America in the 1880s, tobacco duty accounted for a third of federal income.

Britain's tobacco tax never applied to the quasi-independent Channel Islands, so its cigar trade thrived: Walter Martin sold Cuban cigars to customers on the British mainland by mail order, effectively duty-free. As the duty was higher than the cost of production he could offer mainland smokers huge discounts whilst making substantial profits. His advertisements in *Tit-Bits* claimed he made 'Every smoker his own importer', but offloading the legal responsibility for collecting duty onto postmen proved ineffective, to say the least.

Martin's operation threatened the profits of tax-paying mainland tobacco merchants. In 1896, MPs demanded ministers act, but the government declined. Martin smuggled a stenographer into a furious meeting of the London Chamber of Commerce to hear members denounce him and then shared quotes with his customers to illustrate the threat to their cheap cigars. Martins Ltd took an office at 5 Mark Lane, in the City.

Martin touted for custom, sending packs of cigars to prospective customers, requesting that they recompense him by sending a shilling in postage stamps. When he had accumulated a vast £400 worth he tried to cash the stamps. His local postmaster agreed to take them subject to commission, which Martin found unacceptable. He could pay them into a new account for free, but only

£40 worth per year. Martin offered to open ten accounts, but the rules only allowed one each day. The GPO relented, on a 'never-do-that-again' basis.

Circumstances led to Martin agreeing to pay duty on tobacco sent to Britain, but he continued to operate his growing duty-free trade with other countries. With 100,000 happy customers and 600 staff – the world's biggest mail-order operation – his offices moved to 15 Cheapside (now eclipsed by One New Change) and, later, 210–11 Piccadilly.[1]

World War I was the making of Walter Martin. Working with the *Weekly Dispatch* in 1914, he planned to support servicemen by sending free fags and baccy to the front line. The campaign was funded by public sixpenny (2.5p) contributions collected by the newspaper, as though it were a charity. From November 1914 Martin sold cigarettes to the fund from his bonded warehouses, and as subscribers flocked from Britain and the colonies, even America, the campaign raised a quarter of a million pounds. For every 'tanner' a packet of thirty cigarettes or pipe tobacco was distributed by the military along with a postcard. One side of the card bore a now-iconic cartoon, the other was addressed to a named donor with space for the Tommy to write a 'thank you' message. The card required no stamp and the soldiers sent countless notes of gratitude to strangers.[2]

Martin asked Bert Thomas, cartoonist for *Punch* and the *Strand*, to draw a uniformed soldier, pausing, a rifle slung over his shoulder. He is filling his pipe, intent on a relaxing smoke, above the caption: 'Arf a mo', Kaiser!'[3] The Imperial War Museum ranks this artwork – which the volunteer soldier completed in ten minutes – as the second-best-known of World War I, behind only Kitchener's 'Your country needs you!' The image appeared in reprints and variations, with and without a behelmeted Hun, as well as on merchandise sold to support the fund. The catchphrase re-emerged in 1916, depicting a Russian Cossack jumping out of a coffin to challenge a German, and again as 'Arf a mo', Hitler' over twenty years later.

The *Dispatch* explained: 'Our Soldiers are giving their lives; you are asked to give them something to smoke. It isn't much to you, but it's a great deal to Tommy Atkins.' This collective act of national compassion made Walter Martin very rich. Others came on board: Princess Mary's 1914 Christmas Box to the troops included a pack of cigarettes. By August 1915 Black Cat had distributed 3 million fags to the front, and at the lord mayor of London's 1916 procession 30,000 Greys were given to marching soldiers.

Walter Martin crossed swords with the authorities again: with the onset of war Britain declared all Prussians enemies, so Prince Blucher von Wahlstatt, tenant of the Channel Island of Herm, was ordered to leave – putting twenty-five jobs at risk and affecting every family on the island. The prince left in 1915 and died in 1916, so there was no question of a return. Martin applied for the tenancy, hoping to build a hotel and golf course. Writing to both Roland

Wilkins of HM Treasury and Victor Carey, Guernsey's equivalent, he offered to pay 'the necessary' and enclosed a few cigars. Both clerks perceived this to be attempted bribery so Martin was prosecuted. When the case was heard, in 1918, Walter's friend Harry Gordon Selfridge testified that it was normal for merchants to send samples with correspondence. The court rejected this explanation and imposed a £60 fine plus costs; Martin's employees clubbed together to recompense their boss.[4]

Martins Ltd went public in 1919, issuing 101,000 £1 shares.

Following the war the government doubled tobacco duty from 7s per pound (weight) to 15s6d (78p), and postal charges went up too. Martin's clientele, typically retired and middle class, saw their disposable income fall as Britain struggled. Nevertheless, Martin's 1925 database included 150,000 customers.

We know little of what happened next. Martin had obtained the Royal Hotel at St Peter Port, Guernsey, from his brother's wife's family in 1918, selling it in 1920 to a consortium in which he was the major shareholder.[5] Over the years he returned to the island and remodelled the Royal, spending £20,000 at auction in 1935 to decorate it with fixtures from the prestigious *Mauretania*, once the world's biggest vessel.[6] A lifelong gambler, Martin once 'broke the bank' at Monte Carlo, though his riches rarely lasted.

That same year, separated, Walter Martin published an advertisement inviting Brits to move to Guernsey. He described life there as 'free from cares, free from domestic troubles, free from Income Tax'. In the early days of World War II, Britain encouraged tourists to holiday in the Channel Islands, which were neither 'abroad' nor, lacking conscription, involved directly in the war. In June 1940, however, Churchill secretly decided that if Germany invaded the islands, so close to France, they would not be defended. Days later they were conquered. Major Albrecht Lanz announced the occupation from the same Royal Hotel on 30 June. Twenty-nine days later Martin, still managing director, died, aged 72. The Royal was the occupying forces' headquarters until May 1945.

By 1966 the hotel was part of the Royal Terrace of shops, but it closed in 1992 after a series of fires. An insurance company paid out over £4 million, but when fraud was alleged it tried to reclaim the cash. In 2000 a court found in favour of the hotel, even though it was previously known to have submitted false invoices and exaggerated visitor numbers.

The Royal's remains were demolished in 1999.

THE TOBACCO INDUSTRY

Tobacco duty was first introduced in 1604 at an implausible £1 per three pounds weight because King James hated the 'vile weed'.[7] London's first major tobacco retailer was the House of Carreras (1788), selling cigars, pipes, snuff, cigarettes and loose tobacco. In 1904 it pioneered gift coupons (banned since 2014), and in 1908 Britain banned the sale of tobacco to children. Walter Martin's 'free fags' promoted a big increase in smoking during World War I.

WD & HO Wills of Bristol had automated mass cigarette production in 1883, leading to a rapid rise in consumption, overtaking cigars. Wills contributed more than half of the capital of Imperial Tobacco, a 1901 partnership of thirteen companies. Although this alliance was intended to ward off American competition, a year later it formed a joint venture with the Americans called British American Tobacco. BAT alone sold 10 billion cigarettes globally in 1910, rising fiftyfold by 1976. In 1973 Imperial Tobacco became Imperial Group, with the Imperial Tobacco name now used for a subsidiary. It was Hanson Trust's biggest acquisition, at £2.5 billion (1986); the trust floated it in 1996.

'Peak smoking' was 1948, capturing 84% of adult Britons. In 1955 it was 55% (70% of men, 40% of women), falling steadily to 14% in 2018. Between 2013 and 2023 the prevalence of smoking fell in all groups except younger, better-off women.[8]

Health charities designated an annual No Smoking Day in 1984, and in 2006 the law banned smoking in almost all enclosed public spaces. Over the last thirty years tobacco duty has risen faster than inflation, and the legal age to buy tobacco is now 18. There are bans on general tobacco advertising and restrictions on packaging and point-of-sale promotion. Cigarettes are no longer made industrially in Britain.

Smoking is responsible for 86% of lung cancers as well as perilous heart and circulatory system conditions. Killing 76,000 each year in the UK, it is our leading cause of preventable death and disease, robbing the typical smoker of ten years of life. However, Britain's lung cancer deaths in 2000 were half those of 1965, the world's steepest fall.

Recently technology has found a safer option – or has it? Vaping boomed from the early 2010s, and tobacco companies now hedge their bets. By 2017 half of vapers were ex-smokers, with the number of new vapers falling. Today it is feared that e-cigarettes, especially those featuring nicotine, act as an entry into smoking. Explicit marketing to children is theoretically banned, whilst 'disposable' vapes create their own environmental problems. Imperial Brands (the current incarnation of Imperial Group), the London Stock Exchange's twenty-eighth-largest company, sold 221 billion cigarettes in 2022 and is investing in both vapes and a heated tobacco product purportedly less harmful than cigarettes.

'Big Tobacco' remains highly profitable. The revenue of Philip Morris International, best known for Marlboro since 1904, peaked in 2013–14 at

$80 billion and, despite smoking trends, has remained close to that level ($73 billion to $79 billion) since. In 2017 its $1 billion, twelve-year investment to create a 'Foundation for a Smoke-Free World' was greeted sceptically, with PMI accused of 'riding two horses'. In 2020 it halved its projected spending on the foundation and then terminated it in 2023.[9] PMI's £1 billion purchase of leading asthma inhaler company Vectura (2021) led to the respected pharmacist being ostracized by its peers, to the extent that it sold the company (for a knock-down £150 million) just three years later.[10] PMI acknowledged that the sale released Vectura 'from the unreasonable burden of ... criticism related to our ownership'.

BAT is pledged to 'reduce the health impact of our business'. Its current model (a diverse portfolio with many non-tobacco subsidiaries) delivers a gross profit of over £20 billion a year, a difficult habit to break. Beable makes no reference to the ethics of tobacco in 1925; today's companies, widely regarded as 'sin stocks', are not doing too badly.

His Majesty's Government's income from tobacco duty is around £8.8 billion per year (2024), which is under 1% of revenue, and it has been falling in cash terms since 2011 (apart from a Covid peak of £10 billion).[11] Britain enjoys political consensus on reducing tobacco usage still further.

Hovis

(1886, Bread)

Every true seed contains an embryo, a food store and an enclosing case, and grasses are no exception. In wheat the tiny embryo is known as the germ (an ancient word, only associated with disease in the nineteenth century); the food store is the 'wheatberry' or kernel, from which flour is made; and the less digestible outer case is the bran or husk. The growing embryo causes fermentation, turning flour rancid; if it is not removed this limits the life of bread flour. The miller's job is to separate these constituent parts.

Much of this was known since time immemorial, but it took Richard 'Stoney' Smith (1836–1900) to realize that the germ contained concentrated nutrients. The miller surmised that bread with excess germ could be marketed as having additional health-bringing properties compared with 'ordinary' white loaves. The name 'Stoney' came not from the quality of his flour, however, but from his birthplace: Stone, Staffordshire.

In 1886 Stoney approached Thomas Fitton, a Macclesfield miller, proposing his enhanced flour product; Fitton was interested. Smith patented his recipe in 1887, joining Fitton's board. He steamed the grain to release the germ, lightly toasted it to seal in the nutrients and added the germ back into the flour at treble the concentration that nature had intended. Fitton produced flour to Smith's recipe, salted it and sold it to independent bakers as Smith's Patent Germ Flour, for making Smith's Patent Germ Bread. Later, the bakers would be given baking tins that moulded the product name onto the sides of the loaf. Thus, initially, the company that created Hovis did not bake its own bread.[1]

In 1889 John Figgis Morton (1872–1958) joined Fittons as a £1-per-week clerk but soon demonstrated marketing prowess.[2] He grew to be the creative soul of Hovis, his sales department employing thirty by 1905. Herbert Grimes won £25 for naming the company's new product in one of Morton's competitions: he abbreviated *hominis vis*, 'the strength of man', to 'Hovis' (1895).

A five-floor building on Macclesfield's Union Street dominates the townscape.[3] The canal trans-shipment shed, built in 1831, became Hovis's mill and office from the early 1890s. Adding to this Fitton's second mill at

27 Millbank, London (1898, now Millbank Tower), the company employed 5,000. Hovis Bread Flour Co. Ltd, with £225,000 capital, produced a million loaves per week.

Figure 28. An existing Macclesfield mill
was taken over by Hovis in the 1890s.

Morton continued his work: in 1899 he launched a cycling atlas, highlighting where Hovis was available, and in 1900 a competition to find the best Hovis made by an independent baker. Stoney Smith died that year: his Hovis-themed headstone is in Highgate Cemetery close to that of Karl Marx.[4]

The company was operating at full stretch. Not far from Macclesfield, in a bend of the new Manchester Ship Canal, was Ernest Hooley's Trafford Park. Bread production moved there in 1904, Union Mill henceforward producing only bags, wrappers and baking tins.

Morton became a director in 1905 and his advertising flair was unbounded. More atlases followed, plus treatises on the best sandwiches. The company's 1920s advertising featured Britain's strongest man, Thomas Ince, and work by well-known artists: Mabel Lucy Atwell's sentimentally chubby children and W. Heath Robinson's frantic images could not have contrasted more! Hovis borrowed American advertising techniques, making processed (albeit marginally healthier) bread as attractive as the freshly baked conventional variety.

In 1906 Hovis opened factories in Cape Town and Sydney. London Council's decision to extend the Thames's southern Embankment, compulsorily purchasing Hovis's Millbank site, proved fortuitous. The nearby Grosvenor Road mill that replaced it, adjacent to Vauxhall Bridge in Pimlico, was 'state of the art' in 1914. However, the government took control of the mill to feed the war-time and post-war population. Normal service resumed in 1921.

In the 1920s scientists confirmed Stoney's hunch that wheatgerm was a source of micronutrients, namely phosphorus, zinc, magnesium and vitamins B and E.

Life at Hovis was hectic but productive. In the early 1920s it purchased Marriage Neave, one of London's oldest millers, and then Harrisons of Lincoln. It organized fleets of vans, two company sports grounds and a second Vauxhall bakery.

Did Beable spot a tilde (õ) in a 1921 Hõvis advert? The 1926 spelling, Hõvis, featuring a macron (a flat tilde), hung around for years. Its relevance remains unclear, but the stylistic feature got noticed – as Morton planned.

But as Hovis was getting underway, so was another future flour giant. The only unusual thing about Joseph Rank (1854–1943) was his family's relative wealth. Beginning work at 14 and inheriting £500 aged 21, he rented a mill on Holderness Road, Hull, where he replaced traditional millstones with steel rollers (1885). The steel generated productivity, outperforming a conventional mill twentyfold by 1888 and eventually by forty times. This was a golden opportunity.

Rank's late conversion to Methodism (1883), to which he donated £3.5 million over his lifetime, may have been prompted by self-interest. He declared at an evangelical mission: 'I can have it if I believe. Why shouldn't I believe now?' Joseph Rank Ltd existed from 1889, and by 1902 the Yorkshireman's mills straddled Britain. Rank later told his younger son, J. Arthur (1888–1972), that he was a dunce who would never succeed in business (as his own father had said of Joseph himself). Nevertheless, he bought Peterkin Mill in South London for J. Arthur to make blancmange, cornflour, self-raising flour and custard powder in 1919 – he ran it for just two years.[5]

Joseph opened the huge Ocean Mills in Birkenhead in 1913 to serve the Irish flour market, later moving his headquarters from Yorkshire to London.

The Rank story thus mirrors that of Hovis … for now.[6]

HOVIS SINCE 1925

The Hovis brand has been associated with some bizarre products: volcanic-ash-based cleaning powder, sanitary towels, underwear, antirheumatic devices, lightning conductors, gramophone motor springs, shoe liners, cigarettes, birdcages, spittoons – to name a few.[7]

Twenty thousand independent bakers made Hovis loaves in 1930, creating an audience for Morton's *Book of Sandwich Delights*, which featured such delicacies as a Bovril and nasturtium filling.[8] During World War II, Hovis sponsored an RAF Spitfire called *Hominis Vis*. Wrapped, sliced Hovis was launched in 1950, and after ITV's birth (1955) an early television advert advised: 'Don't say brown, say Hovis!' – used in print thirty years earlier.

Hovis merged with MacDougall Bros, as Hovis MacDougall, in 1957. Alexander MacDougall had been a Scottish Methodist, chemist, canal engineer and teacher whose five sons worked in the family chemical business. In 1846 its Manchester factory had developed sheep dip and lanolin soap from sheep's wool. By 1864 the boys' own company, in London's East End, was making patented 'phosphatic yeast substitute', or self-raising flour.

Meanwhile Joseph Rank's flour was conquering Britain and Ireland. J. Arthur Rank purchased the *Methodist Times* in 1925 and in 1933 convened a group of Methodists worried that American movies were having an 'unwholesome' impact on British society.[9] He founded the Rank Organisation to make commercial films, then Pinewood Studios, and then factories making electrical goods, televisions and photocopiers. By 1946 the Rank Organisation had a £45 million turnover, five studios, 650 cinemas and 31,000 employees, dwarfing Rank flour's 3,000 workers. Rank films were introduced by 'gong men' in their opening sequences from 1936. Famous productions include *The Red Shoes* and *Oliver Twist* (both 1948) and the *Carry On* series, starting in 1958. In the 1980s it made four James Bond films.

To counter the success of British Bakeries' 'Sunblest', Rank launched 'Mother's Pride' bread in northern England in 1937, going nationwide in 1955. 'Nimble', a low-calorie slimmers' bread, followed in 1956.[10]

Joseph Rank died in 1943, when James, J. Arthur's older brother, took on the flour business. When James died unexpectedly in 1952 J. Arthur stepped back from the Rank Organisation to chair the millers. He became a peer in 1957 and finally relinquished the Rank Organisation in 1962, by which time Rank Xerox (a separate company making printers) was more profitable than film production. J. Arthur was treasurer of Methodist Central Hall from 1967 until his death (1972).

With shared concerns about continued competition from Sunblest, another merger (1962) created the giant Rank Hovis MacDougall (RHM). Joseph Rank Jr (1918–1999), J. Arthur's nephew, succeeded him as chairman in 1969.

RHM deployed some legendary TV adverts. In 1968, promoting Nimble ('Real bread – but lighter'), a girl dangled from a hot-air balloon to the tune of 'I Can't Let Maggie Go'. Joanna Lumley ran across a field in 1969 before diving into a lake: 'Nimble is for girls like this: at their best in bikinis. Fit and slim, nimble and neat.' 'The Boy on the Bike' was a 1973 Hovis advert directed in colour by Ridley Scott, filmed in Shaftesbury and set to Dvořák's ninth symphony, later voted the best TV advert ever. Scott remade it in 2006 to celebrate Hovis's 120th anniversary, followed by 'Go on Lad', which was voted 'advert of the decade'.

RHM bought Cerebos, a South African purveyor of salt, for its global networks (1968), and Sir Peter Reynolds became the first non-Rank chairman in 1981. In 1984 a joint venture between RHM and Imperial Chemical Industries produced Quorn, an early plant-based alternative to meat.

Damaged by fire in 1970, the listed Macclesfield mill was converted into flats (1990s); Jacob's made Hovis biscuits from 1980, and Rank's 1913 Ocean Mills was demolished in 1991.

The ailing Rank Organisation ceased trading in 1997, selling Pinewood in 2000. However, the Joseph Rank Trust, an amalgamation of Rank-family charities created 1918–42, still gives £2 million each year to Christian organizations.[11]

Hold tight: in 1992 private equity's Tomkins bought RHM, removing it from the London Stock Exchange. Doughty Hanson (another private equity firm) bought RHM in 2000 and refloated it in 2005. Premier Foods paid £1.2 billion for RHM in 2007. Under the RHM–Premier Foods umbrella, 'Hovis Nimble' became an operating group in 2009, but when Premier Foods ran into trouble, Hovis (including Nimble and wheatgerm flour) was relaunched as a joint venture between Premier Foods (49%) and private equity's Gores Group (51%) in 2014.[12] In 2020 the Leeds-based private equity firm Endless LLP ('More empathy, more energy, more impact') bought the joint venture. In 2021 Hovis reported a £6.1 million loss after incurring costs associated with the Endless purchase of around £8 million.[13] After a good 2022 it reported a £25 million loss in 2023 and a small profit in 2024.[14]

In 2020 Hovis launched a pioneering plastic-bag recycling programme with TerraCycle, donated 250,000 loaves to FareShare during Covid and supported Marcus Rashford's Child Food Poverty Taskforce. Today, 11 million loaves and packs of bread are made every day in the UK. Of all UK bread, 85% is made in large plants such as that of Hovis, wrapped and sliced; 12% by in-store supermarket bakeries; and 3% by independent bakers.[15] Hovis bakes 1.3 million loaves of its various sub-brands each week, across eleven UK sites.

For half a century after 1925 Hovis's distinctive colour, texture and design thrived, boosted by imaginative advertising, especially in the early television years. The RHM merger focused on consolidation, but by 1992 RHM had lost momentum and Hovis its business identity. After its brief period under Premier Foods, Hovis has slipped back into private equity ownership, where despite taking 10% of the market it appears to have had value sucked out of it.[16]

Lyons

(1887, Catering)

My mother took me to a Lyons Tea House on a rare visit to London in the mid 1960s. My memory tells me that the large, light-filled room had massive windows and round tables heaving with scones, petits fours and tiny sandwiches on tiered cake stands. The waitresses wore black with white frilly aprons and dainty headgear. Despite many imitations, the Lyons Tea House experience was the 'real thing'. There were more than 250, mostly in the capital.

The first of two Lyons Corner Houses – larger, prestigious cafés – was a 1909 art nouveau creation in London's Coventry Street. Open around the clock, it seated 5,000, employed 400 and had an area informally designated for gay pickups. The other was in the Strand, immediately west of Charing Cross station, providing a simple menu to light musical accompaniment, again on a grand scale. Different floors housed different-themed restaurants, sold cakes and flowers, had theatre booking stalls, hairdressers and telephone booths. Hotels, a theatre, and several office and factory sites across London completed the Lyons set. At its height, in Beable's time, Lyons employed 30,000 and served 10 million meals each week.

But that is not how it started.

Salmon & Gluckstein had 140 tobacconist shops across Britain when Samuel Gluckstein (1821–1873) sold the business to Imperial Tobacco (1902).[1] Post 1851 there was a nationwide fashion to stage exhibitions and trade shows celebrating jubilees, empires and other commercial opportunities. Often based in temporary facilities, quality catering was rare. Samuel's son, Montague, declared: 'It was my experience at Exhibitions that first brought home to me the dreary ... catering methods of that time.'

The Glucksteins were teetotal and temperance was popular, yet thirsty exhibition visitors were offered beer or wine, not tea, whilst hungry customers had three dismal choices: 'extortionate and unsatisfactory' exhibition catering, a public house or a coffee shop outside the venue, or a 'good pull-up for car-men'. Car-men drove river traffic around Rotherhithe, whilst 'pull-ups' were

Victorian greasy spoons, providers of tuppenny dinners or rice with gravy for a penny. Such mundane establishments were not for metropolitan exhibition clientele! This was an opportunity.

Figure 29. Sir Joseph Lyons (1847–1917).
(*Source: Romance of Great Businesses.*)

Lyons's 1887 founding partners were Samuel's sons (Isidore and the afore-mentioned Montague), Barnett Salmon and Joseph Lyons, a distant relative of Isidore's fiancée. The elderly Salmon – Samuel's business partner and brother-in-law – was soon replaced on the board by his son, Alfred. The likeable if innumerate Joseph Lyons, unencumbered by a foreign name, brought Anglo-Saxon respectability to the company – although all the partners were Jewish. Maybe Samuel regarded catering as 'beneath him' and did not want the family name associated with such tawdry ventures? Cigars, yes, not scones. Lyons joined the group as a relative stranger.

Nor was the extrovert Joseph even a caterer. Once an optician's apprentice, still a decent water colourist, his familiarity with the 'circuit' came from selling gadgets. He would be the frontman: money matters would remain the family's concern.

Lyons's catering for Newcastle's 1887 Jubilee Exhibition included tea at 3d (1p) a pot, compared with the previous 8d. Its tea-shop was the exhibition's stand-out stand, outrageously decorated with Asian themes and equipped with a Hungarian orchestra to serenade imbibers. Its second outing (Glasgow, 1888) introduced the archetypal waitresses' uniforms. A permanent establishment abroad, in Paris, came in 1889, plus a residency at Barnum & Bailey's circus at Olympia; events at Crystal Palace and White City followed. Contracts were handled by Lena (Barnett's wife and Samuel's daughter), a sometime member of the board.

Joseph Lyons had never left Britain, let alone seen Venice, yet suggested to impresario Harold Hartley that they create 'Venice in London' at Olympia. The spectacular was a great success, lasting two years (1891–3), with water-filled canals, 100 imported gondolas and almost 5 million visitors. Joseph, who lived opposite Olympia in Palace Mansions, was made chairman for life.[2]

As the economy thrived the first London teahouse opened in 1894 at 213 Piccadilly; there were more than a dozen by the end of 1895. Lyons purchased Cadby Hall, a former piano factory adjacent to Olympia, its headquarters for the next ninety years.[3]

The company went public, selling non-voting shares. This was much-needed income, as work on the near-derelict Trocadero Music Hall at Piccadilly Circus, recently purchased for £125,000, cost five times the estimate. (It was previously the Argyll Rooms, famed for prostitutes.) This was 1896; the company paid no dividends for several years after. The lavish Trocadero restaurant inspired copycats and namesakes globally until the 1940s, with many Glucksteins and Salmons beginning their careers with menial jobs there.

Through the 1890s Lyons continued to cater for events, such as Lord Northcliffe's Olympia gathering with 8,000 guests, plus royal parties at Windsor and Buckingham Palace.

Initially, Lyons's waitresses survived on commissions plus tips, but when management halved the commission the 'nippies' went on strike. With the Match Girls' dispute still in popular memory (see Bryant & May), the press backed the all-female workforce. Lyons responded by banning tipping and paying a regular wage; employees welcomed the slightly reduced but now more reliable pay.

In 1873, long before the company started, Montague had persuaded five of his brothers and brothers-in-law to form a 'Family Fund' into which all their individual earnings were deposited. Each received an identical wage from the fund, which was only open to males and could never be discussed outside weekly family meetings. All involved would work for the company and have all their housing, medical and living costs met, including servants and chauffeur-driven cars. Daughters who married received a dowry, and women could earn modest amounts outside the fund. With every death assets accumulated; the rules were reviewed every twenty years.

Lyons opened hotels: Strand Palace (1909), Regent Palace (Europe's largest, 1915) and the Cumberland (1933). In 1918 it acquired Horniman's tea and a fifty-acre site in Greenford adjacent to the Grand Union Canal, with access to the Thames via Brentford. Construction included stores (coffee, cocoa, custard powder, confectionery), a bonded warehouse for tea and manufacturing facilities (bread and boiled sweets). The site, including welfare and medical services, opened in 1921. The factory's innovative roof maximized daylight, and production was highly automated, processing 450 tons of tea alone each week. A rail link connected it to the main line at Old Oak Common.

Figure 30. Lyons's Strand Palace Hotel.

Joseph Lyons was knighted for 'public services' in 1911.

Over the British Empire Exhibition's six months at Wembley in 1924, Lyons's 7,000 staff delivered 8 million meals. In 1925 Lyons opened a college of waitressing. The company was valued at £6 million and employed more than 30,000, baking 10,000 loaves every working hour and selling a million packets of tea each day.[4]

Table 15. Lyons's Gluckstein family members.

Name		Note
Samuel	(1821–1873)	Patriarch. Married Ann, twelve children.
Barnett Salmon	(1829–1927)	Co-founder. Business partner of Samuel, married Lena. Nine of their fifteen children lived to adulthood, seven married cousins.
Sir Joseph Lyons	(1847–1917)	Founding chairman, 1894–1917. Distant relative of Isidore.
Isidore	(1851–1920)	Cofounder. Son of Samuel.
Montague	(1854–1922)	Cofounder. Son of Samuel. Chairman, 1917–22.
Lena	(1846–1907)	Daughter of Samuel, Barnett's wife. Sometime board member.
Joseph	(1856–1930)	Son of Samuel, father of Gluck and Louis.
Samuel Montague	(1884–1928)	('SMG'.) Son of Montague.
Major Montague Isidore, OBE	(1886–1958)	Son of Isidore. Chairman, 1950–6. Established Lyons's pension fund.
Isidore Montague	(1890–1975)	('Dore'.) Son of Montague. Chairman, 1956–61.
Hannah	(1895–1978)	('Gluck'.) Niece of Montague. Gender-fluid portrait artist.
Sir Louis	(1897–1979)	Brother of Gluck. Conservative MP, 1931–45; Member, Greater London Council (1950–64); Board of Deputies.

LYONS SINCE 1925

The future opened up with the launch of Lyons Maid ice cream (1925), followed by many retail food brands in the 1930s. Three percent of employees participated in the 1926 General Strike – for a token day.

In 1939 a Lyons teashop became home for Jewish child refugees from Nazi Germany. Lyons management ran several war-time ordnance factories, and its teashops adopted a style known as 'working-class chic'. Lyons made the first square teabags (1944), and in 1947 Princess Elizabeth and Prince Philip accepted a Lyons celebratory cake to mark their wedding.

Lyons was ahead of its time. The Lyons Electronic Office (LEO) was launched at Cadby Hall in 1947, where the system worked in decimal pounds – deemed simpler than asking computers to adopt pounds, shillings and pence! LEO was slow to take off, though by the 1950s external clients were buying into the system; the GPO used it to manage telephone bills until 1981. LEO was overtaken by newer technology in the 1960s, when it was sold to ICL. One Lyons leader described LEO as an 'unhelpful distraction'.

Acquisition and expansion were the post-war order of the day as Lyons Biscuits was rebranded 'Symbol' and the Blackpool Biscuit Company (makers of Bee-Bee biscuits) was acquired. Lyons bought the UK franchise for Wimpy Bars (1953), established an ice cream factory at Greenford to counter Walls (1954) and launched Maryland Cookies (1956). Ready Brek followed (1957), relaunched as an 'instant' oat cereal in 1969. Whilst it is true that Margaret Thatcher worked for Lyons as a research chemist, 1949–51, the story that she invented Mister Softee aerated ice cream is a myth – the Americans did that a decade earlier.

Lyons opened the Steak House chain in 1961, but the 1965 closure of the high-profile but loss-making Trocadero after seventy years was a blow. It stood embarrassingly empty for fifteen years before redevelopment as a gaming- and film-themed 'entertainment centre'.

The 1970s started positively, with the opening of the Tower Hotel, but a decision to prioritize overseas expansion proved disastrous. Brian Lawson Salmon, the incoming chairman, concluded that family dominance of management had been a straitjacket, creating a situation that would not be resolved by buying and selling businesses. Of the sixteen family members then involved, eleven left, some not entirely willingly. Lawson equated the position to 'the flag being brought down on the Empire'.[5]

Most family members had been excited by the prospect of expansion into Europe, with Britain's 1972 entry into the EEC (later the European Union) imminent. In preparation Lyons took on unprecedented debt on advice from Rothschilds, which, thirty years later, was described as the worst the bank ever gave. After the audacious purchase of Tetley's tea, overseas operations rose from 8% of turnover to a massive 43%. When the national economy dived (reaching 26% inflation) and the pound collapsed (1976), the company's foreign assets became liabilities. Prestigious hotels were sold cheaply to reduce the company's debt, the Wimpy franchise was lost, and Corner Houses and tea-shops were closed.* As Lyons sought to raise £10 million, most of its shareholders, previously non-voting, were enfranchised, depriving the family of control. Cadby Hall, later demolished, was sold to Allied Breweries (Tetley beer) as Lyons headquarters moved to 199 Piccadilly.

By 1978 the remaining family leaders were desperate to sell the company; again Allied obliged, creating Allied Lyons for £63 million under the first

---

* Today Brasserie Zedel retains many of the Regent Palace's original ground-floor features.

non-family chairman. In 1983 the Steak House chain closed – though the Dunkin' Donuts franchise was gained. Ready Brek was sold to Weetabix (1990).

The Family Fund, which had nurtured the wealth of the Glucksteins and Salmons for more than a century, was dissolved in 1991, its assets distributed between male members of the family. In 1992 the empire's break-up started in earnest, with Lyons Maid sold to Nestlé and bakery products to Rank Hovis MacDougall (RHM). Allied Lyons bought Pedro Domecq sherry to become Allied Domecq, in turn acquired by Pernod Ricard in 2005, when it ceased trading and Dunkin' Donuts was sold to private equity. In 1995 Lyons's head office closed, and then the Greenford site, now Lyon Way Industrial Estate, in 1997.

The Lyons story has prompted at least two history books: *The First Food Empire* by Peter Bird, a former employee, in 2000, and Thomas Harding's *Legacy* in 2019. Premier Foods, having acquired RHM, still uses Lyons branding on some cakes, including Battenburg and Bakewell Tarts.[6]

Table 16. Lyons's Salmon-family chairmen.

Chairman		Tenure	Note
Alfred	(1868–1928)	1923–8	Barnett's son. Grandfather of Chancellor Nigel Lawson and great-grandfather of Nigella.
Isidore	(1876–1941)	1928–41	Barnett's son. Conservative MP, Harrow, 1924–41.
Harry	(1881–1950)	1941–50	Barnett's son. Great-grandfather of George Monbiot.
Barnett Alfred	(1895–1965)	1961–5	('Barney'.) Alfred's son.
Samuel Isidore	(1900–1980)	1965–8	Isidore's son.
Geoffrey	(1908–1990)	1968–72	Harry's son.
Brian Lawson	(1917–2001)	1972–7	Harry and Isidore's nephew. Forty years in company. Various NHS non-executive roles, 1949–78.
Neil Lawson	(1921–1989)	1977–9	Brian's brother. Managing director from 1969, final family chairman.

Dunlop
(1889, Tyres)

Much of Beable's Dunlop story comes from *Motor Owner*, but the technology, opportunity and guile around the pneumatic rubber tyre is a world of which the magazine misses much. Dunlop himself, a Scot living in Ireland, had recently died, his daughter, Jean McClintock, had not yet published *The History of the Pneumatic Tyre*, nor had Arthur du Cros, the one-time Dunlop chair, written his 1938 tome.[1] One surviving, very rich player, Ernest Hooley ... was in prison.

In the early 1880s John Boyd Dunlop (1840–1921) ran a veterinary surgery in Gloucester Street, Belfast. His son, Johnny, loved his tricycle but was uncomfortable on uneven ground. His inventive father replaced the trike's solid rubber tyres with a folded rubber sheet covered with cloth and sealed with glue to the wheel, a wooden disc, inflating the 'tyre' using a football pump. The rest is history, marked by Dunlop's appearance on a Northern Ireland £10 note (1981) and in Detroit's Automotive Hall of Fame (2005).[2] But a good story has many beginnings.

Aztecs fashioned bouncing balls from latex, discovering qualities that European scientists reported to the Acádemie Royales des Sciences in Paris in 1755. In 1770 the polymath Joseph Priestley discovered that latex could rub out pencil marks, hence 'rubber'. In 1839 American Charles Goodyear used heat to metamorphose rubber into a rigid form; Starley's solid bicycle tyres would be made of this 'vulcanized' rubber. In 1876 Henry Wickham smuggled 70,000 seeds from Brazil to Kew Gardens, London, and from just twenty-five plants a global rubber industry was born. In Malaysia, well into the twentieth century, the rubber trade was tainted by forced labour.

Charles Macintosh of Paisley (1766–1843) got wet in the Scottish rain.* The inventor of a dry bleach was a circular-economy practitioner tasked with finding new uses for the waste products of gasworks, which included naphtha.

---

*This is not designer Charles Rennie Mackintosh: www.britannica.com/biography/Charles-Macintosh.

Naphtha was known to dissolve natural rubber (as discovered in Italy, 1779), which could then be moulded into useful shapes. In 1818 he fused two layers of cotton mesh with a film of rubber in between, creating a product almost as flexible as the cloth itself. Macintosh had invented the mackintosh (with a 'k'), which Birleys of Manchester manufactured from 1824 (Dunlop acquired Birleys in 1925). Today Mackintosh is a 200-year-old luxury brand. Bonded cloth and rubber would be the basis of Dunlop's inner tubes until the tubeless tyre of 1950.

The third root: forty years before Dunlop's Eureka moment, another Scot, Robert Thomson (1822–1873), patented a similar tyre in both France (1846) and the US (1847).

Young Johnny Dunlop enjoyed cycle racing and frequently won, attracting the attention of serious competitors. Professional cyclist Willie Hume adopted Dunlop's tyre, winning seven of his next eight races. This excited those keen to exploit the new tyre for gain, amongst them (William) Harvey du Cros (1846–1918). Dunlop Sr was never an entrepreneur, but Harvey was.[3] This Dublin-based paper-bag manufacturer had seen several of his sons lose to Hume, and he was also a sportsman himself: once Ireland's light- and middle-weight boxing champion, he had won amateur fencing awards and captained the winners of the Irish rugby championship. One of his six penny-farthing-racing sons, Arthur (1871–1955), would represent Ireland at cycling. Harvey himself would be a major shareholder in Swift Motors and briefly chairman of Austin Motors.

Dunlop did not know du Cros, but financiers William Bowden and J. M. Gillies knew both men, and they proposed setting up a business in Dublin to make inflatable bicycle tyres. Harvey graciously agreed to lead the new company, insisting that he 'assume complete control, appoint the directors, write the prospectus and make the issue to the public'. Dunlop deferred to Bowden and Gillies, from whom du Cros secured £25,000. They purchased a dormant company in 1889, renaming it Pneumatic Tyre and Booth's Cycle Agency (later Byrne Bros India Rubber Co.). Dunlop was given £300 plus 3,000 shares and put in charge of product development.

Du Cros set out his ambitions, appointing six directors with global responsibilities. Conveniently, six of his seven sons, some still teenagers, were available. Arthur covered England as, in effect, general manager.

The idea was a hit, though in 1890 Dunlop's 1888 patent was declared invalid due to the Thomson precedent. Fortunately, he had modified the product, enabling tyres to be deflated and removed, and secured further patents (e.g. for tyre valves), so production continued. When Dublin Council threatened to act against the smell associated with rubber production, du Cros moved the enterprise to Coventry.

Growth came easily. Du Cros's youngest son, George, the 16-year-old Canada representative, produced bicycle tyres in Chicago from 1892, the new Australia office received an order for automobile tyres, and production commenced in Germany. In 1894 they started to manufacture bike tyres in Birmingham, at what would become Fort Dunlop.

In 1892 John Dunlop moved from Belfast to Dublin. By 1895 he had had enough and resigned from the company for reasons that are not entirely clear. Was he genuinely awestruck by the sheer potential, realizing it was not for him? Or did he smell a rat? Consoling himself as a director of a large drapery company, he took no further part in the enterprise bearing his name, nor would he become rich, though others would. Harvey du Cros bought Dunlop's shares in what was now the Dunlop Pneumatic Tyre Company and floated a new concern, the Dunlop Rubber Company.

In 1896 du Cros sold the company, now the Rubber Manufacturing Co., to Ernest Terah Hooley for £3 million on condition that both Harvey and Arthur remain in post. Hooley agreed, floated the company to public shareholders for £5 million, repaid those who had lent him the £3 million and pocketed the balance. Du Cros had only valued the company at £2.5 million; he ought to have suspected dodginess (see 'Fraud' in the 'Governance' chapter).

Within five years Dunlop was one of the world's biggest companies. By 1899 bicycle tyre demand was peaking, but the automobile tyre market was looking promising, reflecting the trajectory of Starley, Swift and Rover. Fort Dunlop started to make car tyres in 1900, a few months behind France's Michelin.

The ambitious Harvey du Cros became Conservative MP for Hastings (1906). At the same election Arthur failed to win Bow and Bromley, though Alfred, his brother, won it in 1910. However, Harvey's ill health obliged him to stand down after two years, so Arthur filled the vacancy until 1918, before representing Clapham for the Unionist coalition until 1922.

The Dunlop Pneumatic Tyre Company technically failed in 1912 due to Arthur's alleged mismanagement (Harvey remained chairman). It was resurrected as the Patent Tyre Company, which bought Dunlop Rubber Company shares and vice versa.

In 1913 Arthur's former home in St Leonards was burned down by suffragettes outraged at his opposition to women voting. The gullible Arthur appointed James White (see 'Fraud') as financial adviser, not least to boost US trade; this was not a success.

Dunlop opened a Japanese factory in 1913 as its Birmingham employees totalled 4,000. A major investment in Fort Dunlop followed, covering 120 acres of Erdington by 1917. War-time work focused on solid rubber tyres for military vehicles, with a separate unit for aircraft tyres.

In 1916 the scandalous adultery of the late king, Edward VII, risked expo-sure.[4] As Prince of Wales he had had a ten-year on–off affair with Frances Daisy Greville, Countess of Warwick (1861–1938), a serial flirt, socialist, suf-fragist, cyclist and philanthropist, almost certainly 'Daisy' of 'a bicycle made for two' (1892). The blue-blooded aristocrat would stand as the Labour Party candidate against future prime minister Anthony Eden in his first election (1924). In financial trouble, Daisy was threatening to sell Edward's love let-ters to the press, and when Buckingham Palace restrained her with a court order she looked to the American media. Daisy happened to owe Arthur du Cros £16,000. Possibly in return for writing off the debt, Arthur acquired the incriminating documents from the safekeeping of Clarence Hatry (see 'Fraud') and destroyed them.* Arthur was rewarded with a baronetcy, nomi-nally for his war-time work on ambulances and military airships, for which he was also made an honorary colonel.[5]

Harvey du Cros retired to Ireland in 1918, where he died, leaving his eldest son in charge. In 1921 the hypochondriac Dunlop died from a chill, and Sir Arthur independently set up a meat-packing company that fell into receiv-ership within months. His inability to keep personal and company finances separate had become an embarrassment, so in 1922 the newly divorced mem-ber stood down from parliament. In 1924 he and his brother George took leave from the Dunlop board and in 1928 ended the family's involvement by resigning.[6]

Fort Dunlop continued to grow. In the 1920s the company was worth sev-eral million pounds, with 80% of the site devoted to manufacturing, consum-ing as much energy as Edinburgh. In 1923 Dunlop first produced synthetic rubber from oil, aiding recovery from damage caused by White's 'advice'.

Beable, witnessing an upbeat moment in Dunlop's history, celebrates the quality, purity and reliability of its rubber and its painstaking production efforts: 'a recipe like that of a cake'. With the century of the automobile estab-lished, the company faced only opportunity. 'But for the pneumatic tyre', he writes, 'the bicycle would have enjoyed the vogue of only a passing craze.' Instead it is 'one of the greatest conveniences, the greatest savers of time and labour, the greatest instruments of exercise and good health that the engineer [God] has put in the hands of humankind.'

The bicycle led to the car, then the aeroplane, he mused. Why was it not invented 100 years earlier?

---

*Wikipedia says Daisy received £64,000. See also Swinson, *Share Trading* (see note 34 to 'Governance'); S. Anand, 2010, *Daisy: The Life and Loves of the Countess of Warwick*, Piatkus.

DUNLOP SINCE 1925

Dunlop was without its eponymous founder and all but rid of the du Cros clan. No big character took the reins, but the company was poised to profit hugely from the automobile trade.

Fort Dunlop was the world's biggest single-site employer in 1925, with 3,800 employees. Within two years it had 12,000, producing 95% of the UK's tyres. Although by 1954 (with 10,000) its record still stood, a US firm overtook it in 1970. The highly mechanized factory diversified into golf balls, rubber sheeting, sports gear, floor tiles and bicycle brake pads, whilst the company's 76,000-acre Malaysian rubber plantation was the British Empire's biggest private estate (until it was bombed in World War II).[7]

The du Croses were not quite gone: George V's convalescence at Arthur's Bognor home won the town the suffix 'Regis' in 1929. Sir Arthur's own investment company, Parent Trust & Finance, was wound up after suffering a £3 million loss to a Hatry fraud involving a forged telegram. In 1938 Sir Arthur wrote the gushing *Wheels of Fortune* about the pneumatic tyre, and during World War II his Mayfair home became The Shamrock Club, a guest house for Irish nationals serving in the British forces.[8]

The Dunlop Guide to Great Britain was published occasionally, 1920–53, and in 1932 a Dunlop scientist using a food mixer and an oven invented 'Dunlopillo' for making cushions, mattresses, and seats for cinemas, cars and the newly refurbished House of Commons chamber (1952). In 1936 Fred Perry won the Wimbledon tennis championship wearing Dunlop rubber-soled training shoes.*

Dunlop countered Michelin's revolutionary radial tyre (1946) with the tubeless tyre (1950), which became standard; the company was the global leader in tyre technology. In 1950 the world produced 1.6 million tons of natural rubber and 700,000 of oil-based synthetic product. By 1970 use of natural rubber had doubled, whilst synthetic rubber use had increased eightfold.

By 1970 Dunlop had fourteen operational divisions but was downplaying innovation in favour of consolidating profit.[9] Dunlop Rubber Company became Dunlop UK in 1967 and opened merger discussions with Pirelli, whose operations were complementary in a highly competitive global market. They agreed a 'Union' short of a merger in 1971, but incompatibilities soon emerged between the pyramidal, institutionally owned Dunlop and the decentralized, family-owned Italian company.

As British motor manufacturing declined in the 1970s Dunlop and Pirelli developed mutual suspicions, disagreeing especially on investment policy. The

*Some places call trainers 'daps': Dunlop athletic plimsolls.

final year of profit for Dunlop was 1977; large-scale production ended in 1980 as annual losses reached £14 million. In 1981 the Pirelli Dunlop Union was dissolved, Dunlop sold its plantations and Dunlop UK became Dunlop Holdings, selling much of its European operation to Sumitomo, its former Japanese subsidiary (1982). The losses continued.

The British Tyre and Rubber Company was not what it seemed. Known as BTR by the 1980s, it had not made tyres for thirty years and was not British. It was a finance company known for asset stripping, a subsidiary of the American Goodrich. In 1985 Dunlop UK was obliged by its banks to sell; BTR became its new owner, whilst Sumitomo acquired rights to manufacture road tyres in Britain. By a twist of fate the competing Dunlop and Slazenger sportswear brands now shared the same owner! Within ten years BTR had broken up Dunlop and sold its assets, whilst Sumitomo UK was renamed Dunlop Tyres Ltd. By 1999 the new Dunlop (i.e. Sumitomo) had a joint venture with Goodyear to manufacture tyres for Japan, and Goodyear had its teeth well into the European tyre market.

The Dunlopillo subsidiary (Dunlop Latex Foam from 2002) downsized, and British mass tyre production ended with the closure of Dunlop's Tyneside plant in 2006. Fort Dunlop still houses 'Dunlop UK', distributing Goodyear tyres made in Germany, Slovenia and Poland. It is also home to Dunlop Aircraft Tyres, an operationally independent global company. Another specialist Dunlop plant, making 300,000 tyres a year for racing and vintage cars and motorbikes, closed in 2014.

Dunlop remains a global brand, but in the US, Europe, Australia and New Zealand it is a front for Goodyear; elsewhere Sumitomo owns the name.

One of the world's biggest manufacturers in Beable's day was no longer producing tyres just thirty-five years later. Dunlop's decline was staggering, leaving in its wake only sportswear emblazoned with the identity-free brand.

In 2023 *Nature* magazine showed that deforestation for rubber planting – 4 million hectares since 1993 – was at least double the previous estimate, as was its associated impact on climate change.[10]

Fort Dunlop was sold for redevelopment in 1999. Today this impressive grade II*-listed building, supplemented by a Travelodge and visible from the M6 motorway and beyond, is publicly accessible. Its steel infrastructure has moved less than two millimetres in 100 years, a tribute to sound construction. It has Britain's largest 'green roof' (with lift access and life-sized model cows), a stunning eight-floor-high day-lit atrium and a massive, award-winning LED display sign. It is not marketed as a tourist venue, though there is a café in the foyer.

Amateur industrial archaeologists will find it well worth half an hour.

Figure 31. Looking up: the Fort Dunlop atrium.

Mackintosh

(1890, Toffee)

The phrase 'Darling, let's set up a business … instead of taking a honeymoon' would not launch many successful marriages, but newly-wed Violet Mackintosh (1865–1932) was keen. Back in 1890 she could not have known that she was initiating as rapid a rise from obscurity to global dominance as can be found in any of the 'romances'.[1]

Her husband, John (1868–1920), was a Cheshire-born cotton spinner whose Methodist father and brothers had moved to Halifax to work in a mill. He joined them, aged 10, and at 22 he fell in love. Violet had recently left a different mill to become a confectioner's assistant, hoping to have her own shop one day.

Their £100 in savings was well spent. Violet's rented shop, 53 King Cross Lane, was strategically situated on a bus route where Saturdays were busy, as local workers clocked off at lunchtime. She saw a niche, a confection that would last all week to be topped up the following weekend. British butterscotch was too tough, the newly imported American caramel too soft: what if she combined them? 'Mackintosh's Celebrated Toffee' was an instant, chocolate-free success.

That the word 'toffee' today evokes that slightly soft Mackintosh blend indicates how big a success it was. Violet experimented with different flavours, assigning each a coloured wrapping: malt (blue), mint (green), cream (orange), coconut (pink) and original (red). The yellow-clad 'Harrogate' countered the bitter taste of local spa water. The company's flagship product still uses colour coding.

Soon after John had quit work to help Violet, and Harold (1891–1964) had been born, disaster struck. Not only did John's father, Joseph, die, leaving the son responsible for his sisters and mother, but the bus company changed its routes. Saturdays were no longer as busy.

The Mackintoshes increased production and John took a stall at Halifax market. Sales of the novelty sweet grew, and within a year he was supplying several local stores. Another year later they had expanded beyond Halifax, with dedicated manufacturing and storage capacity. By 1895 Violet's team could not match demand, now measured in tons, so they acquired a site on Hope Street. Greystones, the family's Arts and Crafts mansion, was built in 1900.

In 1896 they added 'Yorkshire Dairy' and aniseed flavours and then started exporting to Spain, Italy and China, sending 'toffee missionaries' to France and Holland. In 1900 their advertising went big-time. John's portrait, sporting a grand moustache, adorns a striking tin of that year above the text 'I am John Mackintosh the Toffee King', with the product described as a 'famous old English sweetmeat'. That is fine if 'famous' means 'in Halifax', 'under ten years' is 'old' and 'English' includes 'half-American'.

Some of their marketing practices, such as giving free sweets to children, would be frowned upon today. Other initiatives were safer, more innovative: competitions, coupon collections and tin pencil cases bearing Mackintosh images.

Again, a bigger factory was needed. They raised £12,000 from public subscription for a site on Queens Road, £3,000 less than they needed. Their bank manager initially described the venture as 'foolhardy', refusing to lend the balance, but relented. They opened factories in New Jersey (1904) and Germany (1906). In 1905 (and again in 1924) every MP received a tin of toffees at parliament's state opening.

Disaster struck again in 1909 with a serious fire at Queens Road. Declining a university place, young Harold went to run their Frankfurt operation in 1910. He settled in well enough to join the German international hockey squad, but World War I frustrated his sporting career; he returned home to serve as a submariner.

Mackintosh reached Australia and Canada during World War I. Their first full-page newspaper advert depicted the kaiser bestriding Europe, confronting a toffee tin hovering over Britain. 'So this is what makes them fight so well,' says the German leader.

With the Frankfurt factory lost and the thousand-strong workforce depleted by conscription, the company struggled. John campaigned on behalf of prisoners of war, raising money for food parcels and supporting employees' families who had lost breadwinners in combat. Fortunately, the workforce soon returned to pre-war levels. When John threw a party for 1,200 staff and their families in 1919, he announced a bonus of £1 for every year of service for all, plus £2 for each household member lost in the war. The bonus was repeated the following year to mark John's death from a heart attack – he had never taken that honeymoon holiday. Violet received many messages of appreciation and condolence, not least from employees.

Harold assumed the mantle, immediately opening the company to shareholders (in principle) and restructuring as John Mackintosh and Sons Ltd. He pledged to continue his father's Methodist values, and the company grew.

Sir Harold, who had become one of Britain's youngest knights aged 31 (1922), was as good as his word. Within two years he introduced profit-sharing, an employee welfare department and social events. From the Halifax plant came a dance band and a light operatic society.

In 1925 the company was worth £750,000, employed 2,000 people and produced ten tons of toffee each hour. Nine out of every ten shares were owned by family members, who received consistently high dividends. Local MP and now Speaker of the Commons John Whitley declared 'open' twelve almshouses commissioned by Violet, dedicated to John.[2] The company built a public hall for Halifax.

It had taken only thirty-five years to reach this point. How much further could Mackintosh go? How well had it prepared for the storms ahead?[3]

MACKINTOSH SINCE 1925

Harold introduced further benefits: a week's annual holiday after six months employment, subsidized medical care, a savings scheme, pensions and generous personalized retirement gifts. The company created a subsidiary, Anglo-American Chewing Gum Ltd, and an Irish joint venture with Rowntree (in 1939 the joint venture became an independent chewing gum company). Quaker Henry Rowntree had established his chocolate business in York in 1862, following a similar path to Cadburys.

Eton-educated Albert Caley (1829–1895) had moved to Norwich in 1857 to make confectionery, including 'Marcho', World War I's military-issue chocolate bar.[4] Acquired by Lever Bros in 1919, Caley's chocolate business was loss-making and preparing to close, but it was rescued by Mackintosh's £120,000 purchase (1930). Under manager Eric Mackintosh, Harold's brother, most Caley lines were replaced by Mackintosh's own, now largely chocolate-covered, products. The Caley factory was inoperative for fourteen years after bomb damage in 1942.

Also in 1930 Mackintosh and Rowntree discussed, but did not pursue, a merger.

In a defining moment Mackintosh launched the eighteen-flavour Quality Street mix (1936), splashing the *Daily Mail*'s entire front page. For over sixty years the tin featured characters inspired by J. M. Barrie's Peter Pan, their costumes reflecting different times and differing global markets. Mackintosh warned shopkeepers that selling cheaper brands would be 'short-sighted', destroying customer confidence.

Back in 1928 Sir Harold had been involved in forming the Halifax Building Society. The knight became a baronet in 1935 and from 1943 led the government's National Savings Committee, the body that launched premium bonds in 1956. His rewards were concomitant, becoming Baron Mackintosh of Halifax (1948) and then Viscount Mackintosh (1957).

More popular brands followed: Rolo (1937), Munchies (1957), Caramac (1959) and Toffee Crisp (1963). The Merry Mack showband launched in 1958.

Family leadership ended when Harold died in 1964. The new management looked to grow by acquisition: Bellamy's liquorice (1964), John Hill biscuits (1965), Gainsborough Craftsmen Ltd (1966, food processing machines) and Fox's Glacier Mints (1969). A company pensioners' home opened in Halifax in 1968.

The year 1969 was busy. Rowntree, makers of Kit-Kat, Aero and After Eight, fended off a takeover from America's General Foods and negotiated with Hershey to make its products in America. Then the long-anticipated merger made Rowntree Mackintosh Britain's biggest confectioner; more than a dozen further international acquisitions made it a truly global enterprise.[5] From 1982 it had headquarters in York, but a 1987 rebrand, back to just 'Rowntree', saw the Mackintosh name lost.

The approaching EU single market of 1992 was a time of both reckoning and opportunity, so in 1988 Nestlé strategically bought Rowntree for £2.5 billion, the UK's biggest ever takeover by a foreign firm. The Caley site closed in 1994; it is now Norwich's Chapelfield shopping centre.

Quality Street, Mackintosh's most abiding legacy, is still made in Halifax and still reflects Violet's original flavours, though nowadays it lacks its distinctive tin. Seven million quality sweets are exported to seventy countries, whilst Nestlé's twenty-two chocolate factories employ 28,000 across the world.

Beable was justified in calling Mackintosh's story a 'romance': the company flirted with Rowntree for decades before consummation. But barely two decades after their union as Britain's biggest confectioner, the company had disappeared.

British Petroleum

(1901, Oil)

Whoever coined 'romance' to describe tales of business success must have had BP in mind. Beable's account sends the imagination soaring over Persian deserts, camels, oil pioneers in pith helmets, oodles of private wealth.* The tale evokes the Gulf's briny waters, Atlantean-scale cities of nodding donkeys and gushing geysers, miles of Heath Robinson pipelines, flirtatious music, rough nomads.

But why did Beable call his tale 'BP'? British Petroleum Ltd came into existence in 1954, thirty years after his book. Yet BP was already familiar to the British public of 1925: before World War I a German company had been selling oil in Britain under the British Petroleum brand. When war started in 1914 the government confiscated the alien's UK assets, selling them in 1917 to the Anglo-Persian Oil Company (APOC) – where the marketing people jumped on the delicious initials.[1]

In 1866 the indebted Irish family of young William Knox D'Arcy (1849–1917), the one-time owner of what would become APOC's oil assets, emigrated to Queensland, where he followed his father into law and financial speculation. One day in 1882 three brothers by the name of Morgan showed William a rock of gold quartz, noting that their property was full of the stuff. D'Arcy and seven friends bought the land for £100,000, with William's legal training helping fend off competitors. D'Arcy arranged that of a million £1 shares in the venture 125,000 belonged directly to him and 233,000 were his in trust; his holding grew to be worth more than £6 million. In Blighty, he claimed, £6 million made you 'someone', so he returned to Britain and bought a law practice (1886).[2]

By 1889 D'Arcy owned a townhouse in Grosvenor Square and a country home at Stanmore Hall, where hung paintings and tapestries by William Morris and Edward Burne-Jones. (Morris described Stanmore as 'a sham'.) His stand at Epsom racecourse rivalled that of royalty, yet such ostentatious

---

*Persia became Iran in 1935.

wealth brought only unhappiness to Elena D'Arcy; the couple separated in 1895, and in 1899 William married an Australian newspaper heiress.

Figure 32. William Knox D'Arcy (1849–1917), founder of BP.
(*Source: Romance of Great Businesses.*)

D'Arcy was not satisfied. He lost money when the Queensland Bank failed, and through the 1890s his shares depreciated, reaching rock bottom in 1905. Beable summarizes: 'Most men would have been satisfied with such a gift of fortune and been content to take their ease and enjoy the riches thus poured out for them ... D'Arcy was of the true pioneer type. He had the energy and imagination which demanded other frontiers to explore.' He was desperate! New wealth was essential to maintain his lavish lifestyle. Within a page we find Beable contemplating the Persian desert: 'D'Arcy secured from the shah in 1901 an exclusive concession for the exploitation of natural gas, petroleum, asphalt and ozokerite [paraffin] throughout the Persian Empire ... The concession was for sixty years and covered 500,000 square miles.'

The technologies to extract oil from the ground, transfer it over distance and process it to create a saleable commodity were known in the US, where black gold was profitable. Following America's first oil strike (Pennsylvania, 1859), the Rockefellers' Standard Oil had become the world's biggest company. Esso/ExxonMobil is its direct descendant.

Persia had all D'Arcy needed to make a second fortune, lacking only roads, railways, pipelines, workers ...

Beable relates that D'Arcy met a young Persian, Kitabji, who described oil seeping out of the ground. Some sources say that D'Arcy's informant was an elderly civil servant named Kitabgi, whilst others claim that it was the British ambassador. Whichever, the lawyer sent geologist H. T. Burls to investigate. The most promising zone was beyond Tembi, hundreds of miles from the coast, requiring a massive investment to make extraction reality. The 'D'Arcy Concession' cost him £20,000 (£2.3 million today), though he had to pledge Persia one sixth of his profits. Throughout the adventure D'Arcy never visited the country, though for a time he owned the entire oil field.

He invested £300,000. His men, led by the robust engineer George Reynolds, faced harsh conditions, but by 1905 two wells were active. Although money was haemorrhaging, this attracted an offer from Imperial Germany to buy the concession: D'Arcy shunned it, resolving to keep the oil British. His investment was speculative as the market for car fuel was still immature (Amoco had been struggling for years) and Persian oil's malodorous sulphur content rendered it unsuitable for domestic heating. D'Arcy had faith in the automobile.

To operate the concession commercially D'Arcy partnered with Burmah Oil. Its former chairman Lord Strathcona (1820–1914), a Scottish-born Canadian, was known to Edward VII as 'Uncle Donald'.[3] The ageing businessman and philanthropist was, at that time, Canada's high commissioner to Britain, having previously served in both the British and Canadian parliaments. Burmah Oil was formed in Glasgow, 1866, to extract oil from the Indian subcontinent in the British interest. The founder's son, John Cargill (1867–1954), began a forty-year term as chairman in 1904. Advised by Strathcona, Cargill backed D'Arcy, but progress on finding reserves was slow, and by 1908 D'Arcy wanted out – but Reynolds would not stop looking. On 26 May, he tapped the first monster source, at Masjid-i-Suliman, blowing oil twenty-five metres into the air.

In 1909 Burmah took 97% of £2 million in shares in the new APOC, naming 89-year-old Strathcona chairman. Its massive stake contrasted with the now parlous state of D'Arcy's finances. D'Arcy remained on the board, accepted 170,000 shares, had his expenses to date refunded but now took a back seat.

When George Reynolds's relationship with his employers deteriorated he was 'let go' (1911). One hundred and forty-five miles of pipeline, two years in the making, connected Tembi to the coast at Abadan. A refinery, roads, railways and power supplies were built as the company commissioned rolling stock, made waterways usable, laid hundreds of miles of pipelines. It added workshops, housing, offices, community facilities and communications. By 1912 the share capital was worth £5 million.

Production from the Abadan refinery started on schedule in 1913, and Burmah's Charles Greenway (1857–1934) succeeded Strathcona as the APOC chairman (1914).

Figure 33. Lord Strathcona's grave is amongst the most opulent in Highgate Cemetery.

In Westminster the first lord of the admiralty, Winston Churchill, was considering switching the Royal Navy's fuel source from coal to oil, but he needed security of supply. Oil was more energy-efficient than coal – ships travelled further on the same volume of fuel. One of Churchill's advisers, Sir Thomas Redwood, had been monitoring D'Arcy's progress: here was the opportunity to secure a reliable 'British' oil supply. Redwood advised Churchill to work with the APOC. Also advising was geologist John Cadman (1877–1941), who would later lead the company.[4]

The government purchased over half of the APOC's shares from Burmah for £2 million, signing the contract just six weeks before World War I, in which Persia was neutral. Britain's first modern nationalized industry secured supplies for the foreseeable future; for a generation Britain's oil supply was wholly dependent on the APOC, which expanded into Turkey and British-controlled Iraq in the early 1920s.

D'Arcy died of pneumonia in 1917, leaving around £50 million.

Persia's monarch, the fourth shah of the Qajar dynasty, had been assassinated in 1896. His son, Mozaffar ad-Din, struggled with the country's constitution and died in 1907. Mozaffar's son, Ali, divided the country into Russian and British zones of influence separated by a neutral zone. In 1908 Ali seized parliament, which was controlled by constitutionalists critical of Persia's failure to control its oil resources. Britain switched allegiance from parliament to the shah, but the upheavals continued; the deposed monarch fled.

The seventh Qajar shah, Ahmad, introduced another constitution (1909), but when parliament was still not satisfied he used Russian troops to eject them in 1911. This constitution remained nominally in force until the Islamic Revolution of 1979.

The local population of 1925, conscious that Persians were not getting rich from their oil, were not happy. Only $1 in every $6 of profit stayed in the country, and few local jobs had arisen. Persia regarded the APOC as secretive, arrogant – 'We're doing you a favour, show some gratitude' – and, they claimed, untrustworthy, failing to deliver on its promises.

Britain, concerned about the potential influence of revolutionary Russia on Persia, backed a 1921 coup to put Reza Pahlavi (1878–1944) in power. A 1925 constitutional amendment replaced the Qajar dynasty with Reza's family, making him shah.

Britain had 6,000 'BP' petrol pumps in 1925, 100 times the number of just four years earlier. The APOC, wholly owned by British interests, was swimming in a complex lake of Persian politics.

BRITISH PETROLEUM SINCE 1925

Although the interests of the British state and the British-owned Persian oil industry were aligned, they were not those of the host nation. Attitudes towards 'foreigners taking our oil' pervaded local politics as successive Persian governments appeared incapable of ruling effectively.

Cadman replaced Greenway, who went to the Lords (1927), and oil output quadrupled. Although oil was found at Kirkuk in Iraq, the APOC's stake in that country was halved upon the demise of the Ottoman Empire (1928). Persia insisted on renegotiating D'Arcy's concession, seeking to retain more of the profit and to allow others access.

Reza's government believed that the APOC's complex structure hid massive profits, so Persia imposed a 4% oil tax (1930). The global Depression forced recalculation in 1931, when APOC profits were down 36% but payments to Persia fell 76%. The shah tore up the concession in 1932 and appealed to the Court of International Justice, though somehow the case was never heard.

Suddenly Persia capitulated, with Cadman credited for the breakthrough. A deal reduced the APOC's operating area by three quarters, established royalties of 4s (20p) per ton, paid Persia 20% of profits (above a threshold) with £750,000 upfront, backdated the agreement to 1931 and extended it forward to 1993. However, the forfeited land was neither productive nor promising, so the APOC retained access to all of Persia's known oil reserves. The APOC agreed to improve workers' facilities but, as previously, barely delivered.

When Persia was renamed 'Iran' in 1935 the APOC became the Anglo-Iranian Oil Company (AIOC). Cadman's peerage arrived in 1937.

During World War II Iran again remained neutral as Venezuela provided half of Britain's oil needs. Amongst the allies only the US and USSR had secure oil supplies.

Sir William Fraser (1888–1970) chaired the AIOC from 1941. Reza Shah abdicated, entering exile and allowing his son, Mohammad Reza Pahlavi (1919–1980), to succeed him. Raised in super-rich European circles, the younger Reza was regarded as out of touch by ordinary Iranians, prompting a rise in nationalist sentiments.

In 1949 Britain proposed that its payments should never fall below £4 million a year, that the AIOC's footprint should be further reduced (another meaningless gesture), and that there should be improved jobs and training – but no added transparency. Fraser told Iran: 'Take it or leave it.'

The shah clashed with his prime minister, Mossadegh, and withdrew to Rome. With anti-British sentiment growing, Iran's parliament nationalized oil. Churchill threatened to secure Abadan, pull the AIOC out and arrange an international boycott in retaliation; the concession was suspended. After America funded a counter-coup the shah returned, detained Mossadegh (1953) and advocated a secular state, but he was heavy-handed, oppressive and naive. The nationalization of oil infrastructure, as the National Iranian Oil Company, was completed; although Britain imposed sanctions, parts of the concession were resumed.

The AIOC became the British Petroleum Company Ltd in 1954, with Fraser still chairman. Iran compromised: under a new Consortium Agreement, only half the industry would be owned by the state, with 20% shared between five American companies, 20% owned by BP (previously 100%) and 10% by others.

The shah's newly progressive tendencies were tactical, his secularism controversial. Yet another coup failed (1958), this time by the army against him, souring US–Iranian relations. Reza fell out with Russia, too.

In 1963 Islamic traditionalists led by Ayatollah Khomeini rioted. When the new prime minister, Mansur, confronted Khomeini, the ayatollah refused to apologize. Mansur slapped him, leading to Mansur's assassination and Khomeini's exile.

Meanwhile, with sea-bed exploitation rules relaxed, BP found viable North Sea gas in 1965 and oil in 1970, so it shifted its focus to more local sources.

Arab oil exporters sought to undermine Western support for Israel by raising prices following the 1967 Middle East war. Petrol rationing in Britain and the 'three-day week' followed, exacerbated by the 1974 Miners' Strike. Iran, however, enjoyed above 10% annual growth for over fifteen years. In 1977 the British government started to denationalize BP, selling a third of its 51% shareholding. In Iran anti-shah demonstrations returned.

The toppling of the cancer-ridden Shah in the 1979 revolution ended 2,500 years of Iranian monarchy. Oil fields were seized, the Consortium Agreement torn up, foreign nationals expelled and Islamic law imposed by clerics. Khomeini, returning from exile, was 'Supreme Leader'. In 1980 the exiled shah died in Morocco and Iran mounted an eight-year war on Iraq. The distracted new regime lost influence on the international stage as oil importers broadened and diversified their supplies.

In the 1980s BP acquired large-scale solar capacity, an early adopter. By the end of the decade the government had sold the last third of BP shares to the market and BP had acquired Britoil, owner of North Sea oil concessions.

John Browne (b. 1948), with BP since 1966, was appointed CEO in 1995. An innovator, committed to renewables, he pledged to reduce operational greenhouse gas emissions by 10% by 2010. 'Operational emissions' would today be called scope 1 and scope 2, overlooking the carbon footprint of the oil BP sells into the market to be burned (the massive scope 3).

Browne was knighted in 1998, received a Responsible Capitalism award in 2000 and became a 'people's peer' in 2001. BP spent $200 million rebranding as 'Beyond Petroleum', a positive approach diluted by criticism that renewable energy never exceeded 4% of its investments. In 2003 BP forayed into Russia and Ukraine; after an explosion in Texas killed 15 and injured 170 in 2005, it was fined for safety breaches.

Lord Browne resigned in 2007, failing to quash media stories about his homosexuality and alleged misuse of funds. BP dismissed the financial allegations as 'unfounded and insubstantive'. Today the author of *Connect: How Companies Succeed by Engaging Radically with Society* advises ministers and boardrooms on climate change. Tony Hayward (b. 1957) took over from Browne as CEO, immediately deepening BP's ties to the Russian state oil company Rosneft, a relationship overseen by Bob Dudley (b. 1955).

The bad luck continued. The Deepwater Horizon rig, leased to BP, collapsed in the Gulf of Mexico in 2010, releasing 4.9 million barrels of oil into the ocean, history's biggest oil spill. BP paid out billions of dollars in costs and compensation and, after pleading guilty to fourteen charges in 2012, was fined $4.5 billion plus a further $20 billion after a 2015 civil trial. Hayward's sympathetic attitude to the accident was not appreciated within the company and he resigned, succeeded by the American former Amoco executive responsible for dealing with the spill, Dudley.

Faced with Chinese competition, BP abandoned its solar power programme in 2011 but returned to the cause in 2017, buying 49% of Lightsource.

Dissatisfaction still rife, in 2016 BP's shareholders vetoed Dudley's proposed 20% pay rise. He retired in 2020, at a time of 'global energy transition', to be replaced by Bernard Looney (b. 1970). Dudley later also resigned from Rosneft, protesting Russia's invasion of Ukraine. Looney pledged to dispose of BP's Rosneft stake, linked to oligarchs and the Kremlin. Due to market disruption caused by the Ukraine war, BP's daily production, at more than 1 million barrels, was only half of its average 2015–20 output.

Looney's 2023 pay package of £10 million (double his 2022 pay) was criticized at a time of a rising cost of living. He resigned, not over this but following allegations of inappropriate past relationships with colleagues, forfeiting £32 million in accrued benefits. BP was the world's eighth-largest oil company by revenue, worth $223 billion, half the size of Saudi Aramco.[5]

By 2024 BP claimed to have become 'an integrated energy company', having recently acquired all of Lightsource. In the run-up to COP28 it joined sixty major UK companies in urging governments to accelerate towards carbon neutrality and energy decarbonization, claiming that its investment plans and business model are now focused on this goal.

Murray Auchincloss (b. 1971) became CEO in 2023 as BP planned to reduce oil output more than any other producer. Activist investors including Bluebell (which ousted Danone's CEO in 2021 for being 'woke') and Elliot (BP's fourth-largest shareholder) demanded that BP *reduce* its investment in alternative energy and *boost* oil output to raise its flagging share price and short-term financial returns.[6] Whilst BP no longer operates in Russia, its 20% stake in Rosneft has not been sold (despite trying), yielding 2022–3 profits of more than $500 million.[7] Lord Browne has supported the British government's policy of issuing no new North Sea extraction licences. Meanwhile, Iran has the world's third-largest oil reserves.

Responding to the demands from activist investors, in February 2025 BP performed a stunning volte-face. It reversed its bold plans to cut oil production, bringing it into line with other big oil companies and calling into question the future of its green investments, principally into Lightsource and hydrogen power. Auchincloss claimed that the company's original plans had taken the company 'too far, too fast', but public opinion disagreed.[8]

BP is very different from Beable's other romances. It is not 'rags to riches'; it arose from the investment of a rich risk-taker. Nor is there any family interest, whilst its high strategic value led to the company spending half of the last century in state ownership.

Skippers

(1903, Tinned Fish)

S kippers are canned, herring-like fish of several genres, although the word can also describe fish that leap from the ocean to evade predators.

Angus Watson is anonymous compared with his brand. The Congregationalist (1874–1961) grew up in Newcastle-upon-Tyne, son of a sanitary pipe manufacturer and grandson of a Chartist activist. An ardent prohibitionist and active Liberal, his business was no childhood dream.

The 18-year-old salesman was much in demand. His fortunate employer, Hector Macdonald, a grocery wholesaler, told him, starkly: 'There are 59,000 grocers in this country and only 138 are our customers.' Watson won four new clients on his first day on the job.

One day a customer showed him a tin of Norwegian 'sardines', smaller than the French or Portuguese varieties, full of flavour, free of bones or scales – and cheaper. Within days, wearing a silk top hat and an inappropriate frock coat, Watson was in Stavanger negotiating the purchase of 1,000 cases for £2,500. The contract included exclusive selling rights, though the Norwegians feared they could not deliver his huge order: fish, labour and canning capacity were all in short supply.

It took Macdonald and Watson three months to sell the first batch. The Norwegians invested in automated canning and were soon producing 5,000 cases a year; over three decades, this added up to 100 million cans. Then William Lever asked Angus to work for Lever Bros for a year in New York. After that he had three choices: continue working for Lever, but in San Francisco; return to Macdonald as a partner; or go into business with his friend, Henry Saint.

Watson and Saint started their wholesale trading business, Angus Watson & Co., with Lever's blessing (1907). They amicably acquired Macdonald's Norwegian contract and called their brand 'Skippers'. Four years later Watson had 1,000 employees and a good reputation, having spent £40,000 on advertising across the UK and US. He was also a passionate adopter of profit-sharing.

On Oxford Street one day Watson spotted a photograph of a hoary old salt, narrating tales of marine derring-do to children perched on a harbour wall, bought the image for seven guineas and used it in marketing. Two years later Duncan Anderson (1838–1916), artists' model and temperance worker, arrived on his doorstep; the Crimean War veteran complained that he was now too well known to continue modelling, so Watson put Anderson on his payroll for life. 'Old Salt' became Watson's second brand name.[1]

Watson's advertising annoyed the French, whose offer of £100,000 for Skippers he rejected. They challenged his use of 'sardine'; sardines were, they argued, tinned French pilchards. Initially the courts backed Watson, but after four years of litigation the High Court ruled, in 1915, that he could no longer describe his fish as 'sardines'. The affair cost Watson £50,000, but Norway contributed £20,000 and then bestowed on him the prestigious Order of St Olaf. When George V offered him an equivalent knighthood he turned it down.

The Skippers brand was well established, and all publicity is good publicity. The company replaced its advertising theme, which had confidently and directly compared British (i.e. Norwegian) Skippers with French sardines, with one that simply said: 'Skippers means everything'. He was selling 70% of Norway's brisling and sild, for which there remained no Scandinavian market.

The company added 'Sailor' tinned salmon and 'My Lady' canned fruit in 1912, completing the brand portfolio.

Supplies of both salmon and fruit dipped during World War I but quickly recovered. During the conflict Watson offered his stock to the government at cost price and was asked to oversee some of Britain's war-time procurement operation. Watson agreed, but when he declined remuneration the offer was withdrawn! Nevertheless, he acted as a consultant for the Ministry of Food, overseeing the export of canned Norwegian food to the war-time allies.

In 1920 Watson sponsored Newcastle's new war memorial.[2]

Watson invested £100,000 in a vacuum-jar packing plant and cannery, City Road Preserving Works, 1921, later adding processing machines, cold storage and laboratories. The state-of-the-art facility processed turkey, chicken, salmon and anchovy. His advertising declared that his 'preserved food' (including soups) contained no additives and was thus 'pure'. He offered to pay £10,000 to charity if someone could prove that his wares, in sealed containers, were less safe than the fresh varieties. There were no takers.

Watson's company was worth £2 million in 1925, with 200 UK-based salesmen and more abroad, serving 80,000 retail outlets – a massive manufacturing and wholesale enterprise. Stavanger had two types of canneries: those that sold to Watson and those that did not.

SKIPPERS SINCE 1925

In 1923 Watson had successfully asked Lord Leverhulme, his former employer, to provide financial guarantees to his company. Leverhulme's death in 1925 gave Lever Bros a controlling interest in Angus Watson Ltd, whose pension scheme is still part of Unilever's today.[3] In 1927 a Watson employee, K. L. Mackenzie, a future leader of the company, wrote an entertaining article on 'Canned fish' for the journal of the Royal Sanitary Institute.[4]

In the Vale of Evesham fruit-growers were frustrated; lacking the technology to preserve fruit, they found that supply and demand for products such as plums were not synchronized, leading to high levels of waste. In addition, they had invested in fleets of lorries to beat the threat of the 1926 General Strike – unnecessarily, as it turned out. To the Littleton & Badsey Growers (LBG, the group representing the fruit-growers of Evesham) Watson offered canning facilities and access to 80,000 retailers whilst delivering savings on both capital expenditure and waste. Britain's fruit trade was worth £10 million a year.

But 1928 brought heavy frosts and a low yield. George 2 Cadbury loaned the LBG £800, but this did not cover its shortfall, so a joint venture (Vale of Evesham Fruit Canners Ltd) was proposed between the LBG, Cadburys and Watson to can fruit locally. Watson ordered 500,000 cans in year one and year two but, inexplicably, only 125,000 in year three. Much confusion within the VEFC was blamed on that year-three order. In year two the LBG had had to buy in fruit to meet Watson's orders; in year three it was selling to others the fruit he did not need. In 1932 the VEFC was bought by British Canners, who closed the cannery in 1936 and sold the land back to the LBG.

Watson had 10,000 employees at this point.

Angus Watson left his life's work behind, joining United Canners as chairman, though he was soon disillusioned by his new colleagues' lack of paternalism. He retired in 1930 at just 56, later becoming a magistrate, a Liberal member of Newcastle City Council and an occasional contributor to *The Spectator*. In 1931 he cofounded the religious publishers Ivor Nicholson & Watson, publishing his essays as *The Faith of a Business Man*. In 1937 followed *My Life: An Autobiography*, but Nicholson's death ended Watson's publishing career. He was appointed divisional controller for the Ministry of Food during World War II, for which he was finally knighted in 1945. Sir Angus died in 1961, leaving his home to Newcastle University, which used it for student accommodation.

With Watson's company occupying a second site, in Southall, Unilever encouraged it in 1964 to join a triple merger with established canners RB Green and Pelling Stanley. The latter imported fish from John West in Oregon, a name it had used since 1888, so the merged entity became 'John West', joining Heinz in 1997. In 2006 MW Brands (owned by Lehman Brothers) acquired most of John West for €425 million, including the Skippers brand, still occasionally employing Anderson's image. In 2010 MW Brands itself was bought by Thai Union, a huge complex of Bangkok-based companies that is a major supplier of seafood to the US and Europe.

John West products today claim to be committed to UN principles of sustainable fishing. Indeed, Thai Union has signed up to several sustainability codes, winning praise for progress on human rights (forced and slave labour, trafficking), sustainable fishing (especially of tuna), 'ghost gear' (abandoned fishing nets, a cause of environmental damage) and catch traceability. Progress was certainly needed! The seas around Thailand remain a 'wild east' of unreliable catch traceability, illegal fishing and overfishing, piracy, and environmental and human rights abuses.[5]

In 2021 Stavanger Museum in Norway reopened after a refit. Besides 30,000 canned fish labels, it dedicates a large exhibition to Angus Watson.[6]

Skippers are available today in either sunflower oil or tomato sauce.

Afterword

It is tempting to conclude that over the last 100 years British businesses have lost more than they have gained. They have grown in profit, size, efficiency, influence on the broader economy and society in general, for good or ill – but they have often lost or mangled some important intangibles such as purpose, ethics and values. The pursuit of profit is not wrong, it is not evil, not pointless, but the pursuit of profit alone – the Friedmanite doctrine – is dangerous and has led business to dissociate from society and neglect the environment.

In fact profit oils the wheels of industry, drives its engine and is the oxygen that keeps it alive. But excess oxygen can be toxic, even lethal: the analogy holds. Profit keeps companies alive, helps us measure performance, attracts and funds investment, growth and progress. 'Extractive capitalism', on the other hand, removes profits from systems to fund (excessive) personal or corporate gain, contrary to the interests of most stakeholders. In a nation where top bosses earn the UK's average annual salary by 7 January each year, where trading shares is far more profitable than making things or doing stuff, where business investment and productivity have flatlined, where damage to climate and planet caused by economic activity goes unrepaired and responsibility goes unacknowledged, where private equity rewrites the rules of competition and some of our more egocentric owners contemplate flying to the moon, what today's world needs is to make capital both more productive *and* more responsible.

Organizational size is not itself necessarily a problem. The humanity of an organization depends on how (and how well) it is managed, not how many employees it has or the size of its turnover. A giant company can be managed well, with integrated purpose and values, yet common twenty-first-century narratives – 'too big to fail', 'faceless', 'inhuman' – suggest divorce from values, dysfunction. Such epithets hide complacency, loss of sensitivity to the needs of people and planet, blindness to 'externalities' and alienation of the workforce. Companies that remain human, that 'break bread together', are those that genuinely succeed. Whilst this is easier in more manageably sized institutions, Unilever shows us that mammoth size is not an absolute barrier to effective and positive management.

Most of the companies described by Beable in 1925 were 'bread-breakers'. Outside the few that survive intact, a century on, few brands today represent the conscientious standards to which some of their nineteenth-century predecessors aspired. Cadburys, for example, still dines out on the values of its founding family; how well do the ethics of Mondelez, the brand's current owner, stand up to scrutiny?

Unilever has realized that the future of the company is linked to the future of the planet and has, by and large, and until now, acted accordingly. GSK has found a way of creating public good and substantial profit at the same time, whilst at its fringes its brushes with the law have been too frequent for comfort. WHSmith has discharged its core functions effectively, mostly, with a good grasp on what is expected of them by stakeholders. BP is addicted to oil, not yet succeeding in making the necessary break to align its values with the best that it has occasionally promised.

The most obvious difference between Beable's time and now is in patterns of ownership. There is clearly a limit to the size of organization that one person can manage. Today we recognize that limiting management positions to relatives, the Victorian way, is short-sighted and inefficient, as Lyons latterly admitted. When company success was indistinguishable from, immutably bound to, the financial success of an entire family, such concentration of power was understandable, but the need for both sharing and managing financial risk rendered narrow ownership models ineffective. The railways demonstrated that there were levels of essential investment, and its associated risk, that went unavoidably beyond what was feasible for a single family to take on board, boosting the alternative of decentralized ownership through shares. There is evidence too that through the Victorian era the leading active families of business became both smaller and less focused, seduced by leisure or alternative careers as a result of acquired and inherited affluence. This generated reduced management capacity even by those traditional standards.

From the point of view of investors – individuals with patient capital – changes in risk perception forced changes in how their investments were managed. This had several impacts:

- a growing and understandable demand by investors to influence decisions made by owners that affected their investment;
- regulation of the hitherto disorganized world of shareholding to eliminate the most dangerous, high-risk and antisocial practices;
- the transfer of ownership from individual investors to the impersonal world of institutional investment.

The pendulum swung, and by the 1960s three more factors – the professionalization of business management by business schools; the dominance of Friedmanism in that environment, in the world of high finance in particular; and the growth of private equity – all sent a message that profit was more important than other measures of outcome and impact. Previous ownership models became still further destabilized, allowing takeovers to become a way of life, and leading to management by spreadsheet. The world's adoption of GDP as *the* global measure of national success – against the advice of its creator – further encouraged that trend. Our stories identify a thirty-year period of relative chaos towards the end of the twentieth century, as ownership became more of a tactic than a passion.

Things had to change.

In *The Company Citizen* I argued that business, our principal source of jobs, wealth, self-fulfilment, inequality, climate change and resource depletion, could provide profitable solutions to many of today's problems – if our relationship with it and expectations of it changed.[1] The impact of business is felt way beyond the bottom line; put simply, the economic system that has caused or contributed to so many environmental and social problems needs to address them, sustainably (in every sense of that word).

That realization – that company sustainability has to be measured more widely than in financial terms alone – has finally entered the mainstream; those who break bread together have discovered the advantages of company citizenship. It has been proven that things are not as Friedman would have had us believe, that doing good and making money are not mutually exclusive. In fact, they must go together. Most industry leaders amongst the FTSE 100 today have strategic policies that acknowledge this. Too many do not.

The reader will recall that Howard Bowen advanced three elements of corporate social responsibility in the 1950s. The first was a national role of creating jobs, paying tax, contributing to the common (economic) good, and this is acknowledged even by advocates of Friedmanism. The second was the Victorian concept of 'do as you would be done by', the acceptance that markets, companies, competition – every aspect of business – works best when rules are agreed, observed and applied: the ethical 'G' of ESG. The third was not simply 'be nice (to people and planet)', as CSR has sometimes been presented, but to go further: help to repair and thereby *improve* the planet and human society. This is what has been missing, and as we teeter on or exceed the boundaries of catastrophe in terms of climate, biodiversity, human rights and resource availability, it is clear that this is where more work needs to be done, and that business is the engine that must drive it.

Governments and communities cannot achieve these objectives alone, especially where people feel uninformed or unsupported, still less when they feel business is pulling in the opposite direction. It sometimes feels as though governments create as many barriers as they break down, though even at their best they cannot deliver if the economy (business) is not on board. Enough businesses now adopt the mantra of 'do no harm' that a broader concept of good business has become a fertile soil in which those who are prepared to actively do good can extend their roots.

On another level, perhaps Beable put his finger on it. Perhaps what has been lost from too much of the business world is the romance, the passion that comes with mission, the idea of a purpose greater than either survival or wealth. The reward that comes from a job well done, the pride from being part of a positive change for the better, the thrill of helping the world avoid one existential catastrophe or another – these things mattered to Beable, and to the Wedgwoods, Cadburys and Levers of this world.

Companies need to drive the economy in a positive, sustainable, survivable direction. We, people and business together, must retreat from the several precarious and irreversible environmental and social precipices on which we find ourselves standing, cowering, today.

The alternative is unthinkable.

Bibliography

Anand, S. 2010. *Daisy: The Life and Loves of the Countess of Warwick*. Piatkus.

Baldwin, T., and Stears, M. 2024. *England: Seven Myths That Changed a Country – and How to Set Them Straight*. Bloomsbury.

Beable, W. H. 1926. *Romance of Great Businesses*. Heath Cranton.

Bowen, H. R. 2013 [1953]. *Social Responsibilities of the Businessman*. University of Iowa Press.

Boyce, G., and Ville, S. 2002. *The Development of Modern Business*. Palgrave.

Browne, J., Nuttall, R., and Stadlen, T. 2015. *Connect: How Companies Succeed by Engaging Radically with Society*. WH Allen/Penguin Random House.

Cadbury, D. 2010. *Chocolate Wars: From Cadbury to Kraft*. Harper Press.

Cannadine, D. (ed.). 2024. *Oxford Dictionary of National Biography* (online). Oxford University Press.

Coyle, D. 2014. *GDP: A Brief but Affectionate History*. Princeton University Press.

Cripps, E. C. 1927. *Plough Court: The Story of a Notable Pharmacy*. Allen & Hanbury.

de Geus, A. 1997. *The Living Company: Growth, Learning and Longevity in Business*. Nicholas Brearley Publishing.

Dore, H. 1990. *William Morris*. Octopus.

Grayson, D., Coulter, C., and Lee, M. 2022. *The Sustainable Business Handbook: A Guide to Becoming More Innovative, Resilient and Successful*. Kogan Page.

Halévy, É. 1949. *A History of the English People in the Nineteenth Century*, vol. 1, *England in 1815* (trans. E. I. Watkin and D. A. Barker), 2nd edn. Ernest Benn.

Halévy, É. 1961. *A History of the English People in the Nineteenth Century*, vol. 2, *The Liberal Awakening 1815–1830* (trans. E. I. Watkin), 2nd edn. Ernest Benn.

Harding, T. 2022. *Legacy: The Remarkable History of J Lyons and the Family Behind It*. Penguin Random House.

Higgins, D., Toms, S., and Filatotchev, I. 2015. Ownership, financial strategy and performance: the Lancashire cotton textile industry, 1918–1938. *Business History* 57, 97–121 (https://doi.org/10.1080/00076791.2014.977873).

Hooper, F. 1948. *Management Survey*. Pelican.

Ingram, D. 1982. *Mr Gamage's Great Toy Bazaar 1902–06*. Macmillan.

Jackson, K. 2001. *George Newnes and the New Journalism in Britain, 1880–1910: Culture and Profit*. Ashgate.

Jones, G. 2023. *Deeply Responsible Business: A Global History of Values-Driven Leadership*. Harvard University Press.

Kay, J. 2015. *Other People's Money: Masters of the Universe or Servants of the People?* Profile Books.

Kitchener, M., and Levitt, T. 2021. *Business Schools and the Public Good*. Chartered Association of Business Schools.

Lawrence, P. (ed.). 2017. *Ambition and Anxiety, 1789–1840*. Open University.

Levitt, S. 1986. *The Victorians Unbuttoned*. Harper Collins.

Levitt, T. 2018. *The Company Citizen: Good for Business, Planet, Nation and Community*. Taylor & Francis.

Loftus, D. (ed.). 2017. *Confidence and Crisis, 1840–1880*. Open University.

Macarthur, E. 2019. *The Virtuous Circle*. European Investment Bank.

Mackie, R. (ed.). 2017. *Decline and Renewal, 1880–1914*. Open University.

Mayer, C. 2018. *Prosperity: Better Business Makes the Greater Good*. Oxford University Press.

Mayhew, H. 2008 [1851]. *London Labour and the London Poor* (ed. R. O'Day and D. Englander). Wordsworth.

Mazzucato, M. 2018. *The Value of Everything*. Allen Lane.

Minney, R. J. 1954. *Viscount Southwood*. Odhams.

Newton, D. 2008. *Trademarked: A History of Well-Known Brands*. Sutton.

Peake, A. S. 1926. *The Life of Sir William Hartley*. Hodder & Stoughton.

Polman, P., and Winston, A. 2021. *Net Positive: How Courageous Companies Thrive by Giving More Than They Take*. Harvard Business Press.

Robinson, W. S. 2012. *Muckraker: The Scandalous Life and Times of W. T. Stead*. Robson Press.

Rowarth, K. 2018. *Doughnut Economics: Seven Ways to Think Like a 21st-Century Economist*. Penguin.

Satre, L. 2005. *Chocolate on Trial: Slavery, Politics and the Ethics of Business*. Ohio University Press.

Stratmann, L. 2004. *Whiteley's Folly: The Life and Death of a Salesman*. Sutton.

Susskind, D. 2024. *Growth: A Reckoning*. Allen Lane.

Swinson, C. 2020. *Share Trading, Fraud and the Crash of 1929: A Biography of Clarence Hatry*. Routledge.

Thomson, I., and Bates, D. 2022. *Urgent Business: Five Myths Business Needs to Overcome to Save Itself and the Planet*. Bristol University Press.

Treneman, A. 2013. *Finding the Plot: A Hundred Graves to Visit before You Die*. Robson Press.

Watson, A. 1936. *The Faith of a Businessman*. Ivor Nicholson & Watson.

Watson, A. 1937. *My Life*. Ivor Nicholson & Watson.

Webster, K. 2015. *The Circular Economy: A Wealth of Flows*. Ellen MacArthur Foundation.

Wilson, J. F. 1995. *British Business History, 1720–1994*. Manchester University Press.

Notes

URLs in notes can also be found at http://sector4focus.co.uk/the-business-of-history.

INTRODUCTION

1   The *Gazetteer and Guide* is available at www.google.co.uk/books/edition/Russian_gazetteer_and_guide/ReILAwAAQBAJ.
2   Tosdall's 1919 review was published in the *American Economic Review* 9(3), 560–2 (www.jstor.org/stable/1804683).
3   A. de Geus. 1997. *The Living Company*. Nicholas Brearley Publishing.
4   G. Boyce and S. Ville. 2002. *The Development of Modern Business*. Palgrave.
5   P. Crowhurst, 'The British Empire' website: www.britishempire.me.uk/trade.html.
6   É. Halévy. 1949. *A History of the English People in the Nineteenth Century*, vol. 1, *England in 1815* (trans. E. I. Watkin and D. A. Barker), 2nd edn. Ernest Benn.
7   F. Hooper. 1948. *Management Survey*. Pelican.
8   D. Susskind. 2024. *Growth: A Reckoning*. Allen Lane.
9   J. Ben-David. 1970. The rise and decline of France as a scientific centre. *Minerva* 8(2), 169–79 (www.jstor.org/stable/41822018).
10 É. Halévy. 1961. *A History of the English People in the Nineteenth Century*, vol. 2, *The Liberal Awakening 1815–1830* (trans. E. I. Watkin), 2nd edn. Ernest Benn.
11 H. Mayhew. 2008 [1851]. *London Labour and the London Poor* (ed. R. O'Day and D. Englander). Wordsworth.
12 International Monetary Fund, 'IMF Data' website: https://data.imf.org/?sk=9d6028d4-f14a-464c-a2f2-59b2cd424b85&sid=1514498232936 (accessed January 2025).

GOVERNANCE

1   Corporate Governance Institute, 'Board diversity leads to better profits': www.thecorporategovernanceinstitute.com/insights/news-analysis/board-diversity-leads-to-better-profits/.
2   University of Reading Special Collections, 'W.H. Smith – Hambleden Collection': https://collections.reading.ac.uk/special-collections/collections/w-h-smith-hambleden-collection/.

3 R. Davies, P. Richardson, V. Katinaite and M. Manning. 2010. Evolution of the UK banking system. Bank of England, *Quarterly Bulletin* 50(4), 321–32 (www.bankofengland.co.uk/-/media/boe/files/quarterly-bulletin/2010/evolution-of-the-uk-banking-system.pdf).

4 D. Lamont. 2023. Stop blaming everything on pension funds. Schroders, 28 March (www.schroders.com/en-gb/uk/intermediary/insights/stop-blaming-everything-on-pension-funds/).

5 J. Dyson. 2023. Interview by D. Martin, E. Cumming and S. P. Chan. *Daily Telegraph*, 22 December (www.telegraph.co.uk/news/2023/12/22/james-dyson-brexit-sunak-inflation-inflation-growth-economy/).

6 D. P. Sotiropoulos, J. Rutterford and C. van Lieshout. 2021. The rise of professional asset management: the UK investment trust network before World War I. *Business History* 63(5), 826–49.

7 D. P. Sotiropoulos and J. Rutterford. 2019. Financial diversification strategies before World War I: buy-and-hold versus naïve portfolio selection. *Business History* 61(7), 1175–98.

8 Amundi, 'Pioneer Fund': www.amundi.com/usinvestors/Local-Content/Product-Pages/Pioneer-Fund/Pioneer-Fund.

9 Principles for Responsible Investment, 'Signatory directory': www.unpri.org/signatories/signatory-resources/signatory-directory.

10 Statista, 'Private equity in the UK: statistics and facts': www.statista.com/topics/9613/private-equity-in-the-uk/.

11 R. Wigglesworth. 2024. Is private equity actually worth it? *FT Alphaville*, 5 March (www.ft.com/content/55837df7-876f-42cd-a920-02ff74970098).

12 D. Rowland. 2019. Corporate care home collapse and 'light touch' regulation: a repeating cycle of failure. London School of Economics, 8 May (https://blogs.lse.ac.uk/politicsandpolicy/corporate-care-homes/).

13 D. Campbell. 2019. 84% of care home beds in England owned by private firms. *The Guardian*, 19 September (www.theguardian.com/society/2019/sep/19/84-of-care-home-beds-in-england-owned-by-private-firms).

14 London Economic. 2024. Private equity profits from children's homes: the dark side of Britain's care system. *London Economic*, 16 September (www.thelondoneconomic.com/news/private-equity-profits-from-childrens-homes-the-dark-side-of-britains-care-system-382865/).

15 A. Gara and A. Heal. 2024. Private equity payouts fell 50% short in 2024. *Financial Times*, 25 December (www.ft.com/content/fefc0f14-5b7b-4eca-aa29-6156e3c4b72e).

16 URL: www.insolvencydirect.bis.gov.uk/freedomofinformationtechnical/technicalmanual/ch73-84/chapter%2075/Part%202/Part%202.htm.

17 L. Hannah. 2017. The London Stock Exchange 1869–1929: new bloody statistics for old? Economic History Working Paper 263/2017, London School of Economics (https://core.ac.uk/download/pdf/83954818.pdf).

18 Statista, 'Number of companies listed on the London Stock Exchange (LSE) from 1st quarter 2007 to 3rd quarter 2024': www.statista.com/statistics/324606/number-of-companies-on-the-london-stock-exchange-uk-quarterly/.

19 Hannah, 'The London Stock Exchange 1869–1929'.

20 D. Cannadine (ed.). 2024. *The Oxford Dictionary of National Biography* (online). Oxford University Press.

21 C. Swinson. 2020. *Share Trading, Fraud and the Crash of 1929: A Biography of Clarence Hatry*. Routledge.

22 J. Pawlin. 2022. A very Victorian scam: the story of Ernest Terah Hooley. Insolvency Service, 2022 (https://insolvencyservice.blog.gov.uk/2022/07/21/a-very-victorian-scam-the-story-of-ernest-terah-hooley/).

23 A. Watson. 1937. *My Life*. Ivor Nicholson & Watson.

24 A. Rippon. 2017. Meet Ernest Terah Hooley, the world-renowned fraudster from Derbyshire. *Derbyshire Live*, 24 September (www.derbytelegraph.co.uk/news/nostalgia/meet-ernest-terah-hooley-world-458789).

25 P. Hooley. 2014. The secret crook who owned William and Kate's new home. *Daily Express*, 18 November (www.express.co.uk/news/royal/536537/Anmer-Hall-Prince-William-Duchess-of-Cambridge-Ernest-Hooley).

26 Boyce and Ville, *The Development of Modern Business* (see note 4 to the introduction).

27 J. G. B. Hutchins. 1960. Review of *Higher Education for Business*, by R. A. Gordon and J. E. Howell, and *The Education of American Business Men*, by F. C. Pierson. *Administrative Science Quarterly* 5(2), 279–95 (www.jstor.org/stable/2390781).

28 A. N. Alim *et al.* 2023. Record buyback spree attracts shareholder complaints. *Financial Times*, May 16 (www.ft.com/content/eaa1a31c-580c-405b-b438-a59504198ac8).

29 M. Kitchener and T. Levitt. 2021. *Business Schools and the Public Good*. Chartered Association of Business Schools (https://d1sqxrh4fb2al3.cloudfront.net/reports/chartered-abs-business-schools-and-the-public-good.pdf).

30 Hooper, *Management Survey* (see note 7 to the introduction). Also *The Oxford Dictionary of National Biography*.

31 British Academy, 2021, 'Policy & practice for purposeful business' (www.thebritishacademy.ac.uk/publications/policy-and-practice-for-purposeful-business/). P. Polman and A. Winston, 2021, *Net Positive: How Courageous Companies Thrive by Giving More Than They Take*, Harvard Business Press.

32 ATT, 'The history of income tax and HMRC': www.att.org.uk/history-income-tax-and-hmrc.

33 T. Bell. 2023. A nice cup of tea is always welcome, but centuries ago it truly was a lifesaver. *The Guardian*, December 10 (www.theguardian.com/commentisfree/2023/dec/10/tea-drinking-good-for-body-and-soul).

34 Make it British, 'The decline of the Lancashire cotton mills': https://makeitbritish.co.uk/blog/lancashire-cotton-mills/.

35 D. Higgins, S. Toms and I. Filatotchev. 2015. Ownership, financial strategy and performance: the Lancashire cotton textile industry, 1918–1938. *Business History* 57, 97–121 (https://doi.org/10.1080/00076791.2014.977873).

36 *Manchester Guardian*: https://pm20.zbw.eu/mirador/?manifestId=https://pm20.zbw.eu/iiif/folder/co/059770/manifest.json.

SOCIAL

1   Boyce and Ville, *The Development of Modern Business* (see note 4 to the introduction).

2   Statista, 'Number of trade union members in the United Kingdom from 1892 to 2021': www.statista.com/statistics/287241/uk-trade-union-membership/.

3   Office for National Statistics, 'Labour disputes; working days lost due to strike action; UK (thousands)': www.ons.gov.uk/employmentandlabourmarket/peopleinwork/employmentandemployeetypes/timeseries/bbfw/lms.

4   London Lives, 'The Poor Law and charity: an overview': www.londonlives.org/static/PoorLawOverview.jsp.

5   P. Thane, 'Memorandum submitted to the House of Commons' Health Committee Inquiry': www.historyandpolicy.org/docs/thane_social_care.pdf.

6   R. Neate. 2023. FTSE 100 bosses 'given average pay rise of £500,000 in 2022'. *The Guardian*, 22 August (www.theguardian.com/business/2023/aug/22/ftse-100-bosses-given-average-pay-rise-of-500000-in-2022).

7   Humanists UK. 2024. Highest number of MPs ever take secular affirmation. Humanists UK, 11 July (https://humanists.uk/2024/07/11/highest-number-of-mps-ever-take-secular-affirmation/).

8   R. Davies. 2020. A timeline of modern British philanthropy. SOFII, 20 August (https://sofii.org/article/a-timeline-of-modern-british-philanthropy).

9   A. Watson. 1937. *My Life*. Ivor Nicholson & Watson.

10 A. Watson. 1936. *The Faith of a Businessman*. Ivor Nicholson & Watson.

11 G. Borthwick, D. Ellingworth, C. Bell and D. MacKenzie, 1991, 'The social background of British MPs', *Sociology* 25(4), 713–17 (www.jstor.org/stable/pdf/42854921.pdf). R. Cracknell, E. Uberoi and M. Burton, 2023, 'UK election statistics: 1918–2023, a long century of elections', House of Commons Library, 9 August (https://researchbriefings.files.parliament.uk/documents/CBP-7529/CBP-7529.pdf).

12 D. Pegg and P. Duncan. 2019. Revealed: one in five peers advise private business while serving in parliament. *The Guardian*, 31 May (www.theguardian.com/politics/2019/may/31/revealed-one-in-five-peers-advise-private-business-while-serving-in-parliament).

13 P. Vogler. 2023. Sweet and sour: how slavery, fake science and the love of profit got Britain hooked on sugar. *The Guardian*, 17 November (www.theguardian.com/lifeandstyle/2023/nov/17/sweet-and-sour-how-slavery-fake-science-and-the-love-of-profit-got-britain-hooked-on-sugar).

14 M. Anson and M. D. Bennett. 2022. The collection of slavery compensation, 1835–43. Staff Working Paper 1006, Bank of England (www.bankofengland.co.uk/working-paper/2022/the-collection-of-slavery-compensation-1835-43).

15 L. Satre. 2005. *Chocolate on Trial: Slavery, Politics and the Ethics of Business*. Ohio University Press.

16 Prime Minister's Office, Home Office and T. May. 2016. Defeating modern slavery: article by Theresa May. GOV.UK, 31 July (www.gov.uk/government/speeches/defeating-modern-slavery-theresa-may-article).

17 Hestia. 2024. On our streets: the changing face of modern slavery in London. Hestia, September (www.hestia.org/Handlers/Download. ashx?IDMF=d609982e-3626-4763-9f49-d46fba8a8f8f).

18 Asos, 'Asos and Anti-Slavery International sign new partnership to 2025': www.asosplc.com/news/ asos-and-anti-slavery-international-sign-new-partnership-2025/.

19 M. Ingleby. 2020. Charles Dickens and the push for literacy in Victorian Britain. Queen Mary University of London, 10 June (www.qmul.ac.uk/media/ news/2020/hss/charles-dickens-and-the-push-for-literacy-in-victorian-britain. html).

20 D. McMenemy. 2018. Public libraries in the UK: history and values. University of Strathclyde, 6 June (https://cdn.ymaws.com/www.cilip.org.uk/resource/ resmgr/cilip_new_website/plss/l1_and_l2_ethics.pdf).

ENVIRONMENT

1   M. Wolf. 2024. Britain needs more than fiscal games. *Financial Times,* 6 March (www.ft.com/content/dab5f449-4cfa-4c42-9270-b211f8b5d7fa). Figure 6 is adapted from this article.

2   D. Coyle. 2014. *GDP: A Brief but Affectionate History.* Princeton University Press.

3   E. Dickinson. 2011. GDP: a brief history. *Foreign Policy,* 3 January (https:// foreignpolicy.com/2011/01/03/gdp-a-brief-history/).

4   Social Progress Imperative, '2022 Social Progress Index: executive summary', archived 10 April 2024: https://web.archive.org/web/20240410021720/www. socialprogress.org/static/8a62f3f612c8d40b09b3103a70bdacab/2022%20 Social%20Progress%20Index%20Executive%20Summary_4.pdf.

5   Ellen Macarthur Foundation website: www.ellenmacarthurfoundation.org.

6   Doughnut Economics Action Lab, 'About Doughnut Economics': https:// doughnuteconomics.org/about-doughnut-economics.

7   H. R. Bowen, 2013 [1953], *Social Responsibilities of the Businessman,* University of Iowa Press. See also A. Acquier, J.-P. Gond, and J. Pasquero, 2011, 'Rediscovering Howard R. Bowen's legacy: the unachieved agenda and continuing relevance of *Social Responsibilities of the Businessman*', *Business and Society* 50(4), 607–46 (https://doi.org/10.1177/0007650311419251).

8   Private correspondence.

9   Charities Aid Foundation, 'Corporate giving by the FTSE 100': www.cafonline. org/insights/research/giving-by-the-ftse-100.

10 In E. M. Epstein and D. Votaw (eds). *Rationality, Legitimacy, Responsibility: The Search for New Directions in Business and Society*, pp. 116–130. Goodyear.

11 Private correspondence.

12 WHSmith, 'Annual Sustainability Reports': www.whsmithplc.co.uk/investors/ results-reports-and-presentations/annual-sustainability-reports.

13 Unilever, 'Unilever celebrates 10 years of the Sustainable Living Plan': www.unilever.com/news/press-and-media/press-releases/2020/ unilever-celebrates-10-years-of-the-sustainable-living-plan/.

14 European Commission, 'Corporate sustainability reporting': https://finance.
    ec.europa.eu/capital-markets-union-and-financial-markets/company-reporting-
    and-auditing/company-reporting/corporate-sustainability-reporting_en.
15 GSK, 'Responsibility reports': www.gsk.com/en-gb/responsibility/esg-resources/.
16 BP, 'UN Sustainable Development Goals': www.bp.com/en/global/corporate/
    sustainability/data-and-how-we-report/un-sustainable-development-goals.html.
17 Polman and Winston, *Net Positive* (see note 43 to 'Governance').
18 UK Research and Innovation, 'A brief history of climate change discoveries':
    www.discover.ukri.org/a-brief-history-of-climate-change-discoveries/index.html.
19 Atlasail, 'The impact of the Royal Navy on deforestation': https://atlasail.com/
    en/blog/the-impact-of-the-royal-navy-on-deforestation-uG66XQZN.
20 O. Milman. 2023. Revealed: Exxon made 'breathtakingly' accurate climate
    predictions in 1970s and 80s. *The Guardian*, 12 January (www.theguardian.
    com/business/2023/jan/12/exxon-climate-change-global-warming-research).
21 A. Bamford. 2024. Report: Big Oil 'deceived public for decades' about
    recycling plastic. *Sustainability Beat*, 16 February (www.sustainability-beat.
    co.uk/2024/02/16/big-oil-plastic/).
22 D. Bartels. 1997. George Cove's solar energy device. *Material Culture Review*
    46(1) (https://journals.lib.unb.ca/index.php/MCR/article/view/17744).
23 The report can be read at https://sustainabledevelopment.un.org/content/
    documents/5987our-common-future.pdf.
24 United Nations, 'The 17 goals': https://sdgs.un.org/goals.

WEDGWOOD

1 Encyclopedia.com, 'Wedgwood, Josiah': www.encyclopedia.com/people/
   literature-and-arts/arts-and-crafts-biographies/josiah-wedgwood.
2 Look Up London, 'The Wedgwood Soho Workshop': https://lookup.london/
   josiah-wedgwood-soho-plaque/.
3 W. E. Gladstone. 1863. Wedgwood: an address. Wedgwood Memorial Institute
   (www.thepotteries.org/docs/005.htm#p.35).
4 Encyclopedia.com, 'Wedgwood, Josiah Clement, First Baron': www.
   encyclopedia.com/religion/encyclopedias-almanacs-transcripts-and-maps/
   wedgwood-josiah-clement-first-barondeg.
5 J. Kollewe. 2009. Waterford Wedgwood: 250 years of history. *The Guardian*,
   5 January (www.theguardian.com/business/2009/jan/05/waterford-wedgwood-
   history.
6 Encyclopedia.com, 'Waterford Wedgwood plc': www.encyclopedia.com/social-
   sciences-and-law/economics-business-and-labor/businesses-and-occupations/
   waterford-wedgwood.

BASS

1 I. Webster, 2019, 'The early history of Bass', *The Beertonian*, 17 December
   (https://thebeertonian.com/2019/12/17/the-early-history-of-bass/). Hinckley

Past & Present, 'The three brewers of Hinckley and district': www.
hinckleypastpresent.org/williambass.html.

2   Spartacus Educational, 'Michael Bass': https://spartacus-educational.com/
PRbass.htm.

3   Burton on Trent Local History, 'Saint Paul's Institute and Liberal Club': www.
burton-on-trent.org.uk/category/surviving/townhall/townhall2.

4   Brewery History Society Wiki, 'Bass, Ratcliff & Gretton Ltd': http://
breweryhistory.com/wiki/index.php?title=Bass,_Ratcliff_%26_Gretton_Ltd.

5   D. Lundy, 'The Peerage' website: http://thepeerage.com/p1311.htm#i13108.

HORROCKSES

1   Lancashire Post. 2018. Tycoon who changed Lancashire forever. *Lancashire Post*,
21 March (www.lep.co.uk/retro/tycoon-who-changed-lancashire-forever-
316180).

2   Lancashire Archives, 'Horrockses, Crewdson and Co, cotton manufacturers,
Preston, Lancashire': https://archiveshub.jisc.ac.uk/search/archives/983d0a7f-
3595-3028-b3bc-2b2d15fe9447. J. Ronson, 2017, 'The archives of Horrockses,
cotton manufacturers of Preston', Archives Hub, 3 January (https://blog.
archiveshub.jisc.ac.uk/2017/01/03/the-archives-of-horrockses-cotton-
manufacturers-of-preston/).

3   P. D. Swarbrick. 2014. A step back in time into Preston's Winckley Square
(part 2). *Blog Preston*, 20 June (www.blogpreston.co.uk/2014/06/
a-step-back-in-time-into-prestons-winckley-square-part-2/).

4   Upon the Isles of the Sea, 'Thomas Miller': https://islesofthesea.wordpress.
com/2017/04/05/thomas-miller/.

5   P. D. Swarbrick. 2015. A nostalgic journey around the former Horrocks Yard
Works in Preston. *Blog Preston*, 13 January (www.blogpreston.co.uk/2015/01/a-
nostalgic-journey-around-the-former-horrocks-yard-works-in-preston/).

6   Richard Dumbreck Singleton Trust, 'History of Singleton': www.singletontrust.
co.uk/heritage.php.

WHSMITH

1   S. Draper. 2015. WHSmith, Broadbent Street, W1K. *London's Historic Shops
and Markets*, 25 January (http://londonhistoricshops.blogspot.com/2015/01/
whsmith-broadbent-street-w1k.html).

2   University of Reading Special Collections, 'W.H. Smith business archive':
https://collections.reading.ac.uk/special-collections/collections/
w-h-smith-business-archive/.

3   K. Baker. 2015. 'Old Morality' and the rise of recreational reading. Railway
Museum, 19 August (https://blog.railwaymuseum.org.uk/old-morality-
recreational-reading/).

4   Vauxhall History, 'W. H. Smith': https://vauxhallhistory.org/w-h-smith/.

5   J. Brooking-Rowe (ed.). 1901. William Lethbridge [obituary]. *Trans. Devon. Assoc.* 33, 34–5 (www.genuki.org.uk/big/eng/DEV/Lympstone/ BrookingRowe1901).

6   Encyclopedia.com, 'W H Smith Group PLC': www.encyclopedia.com/books/ politics-and-business-magazines/w-h-smith-group-plc.

7   Wright, G. 2025. WHSmith sells UK high street arm for £76m to Modella Capital. *Retail Gazette*, 28 March (www.retailgazette.co.uk/blog/2025/03/ whsmith-sells-high-street/).

SCHWEPPES

1   Difford's Guide, 'Schhh… you know who; the story of Schweppes': www. diffordsguide.com/encyclopedia/1253/bws/schhh-you-know-who-the-story- of-schweppes.

2   SpiritSchweppes blog: https://spiritschweppes.com/2014/03/03/ storytelling-schweppes-since-1783.

3   London Remembers, 'John Kemp-Welch': www.londonremembers.com/subjects/ john-kemp-welch.

4   D. L. Jones. 2011. Philipps, Sir Ivor (1861–1940), soldier, politician and businessman. In *The Dictionary of Welsh Biography*, online (https://biography. wales/article/s8-PHIL-IVO-1861).

5   Morning Advertiser, 'A history of Scheweppes': http://9b77602b67a411bd3bc2- 9faaadb585f560e5e16f98bb0c787747.r3.cf3.rackcdn.com/Schweppes.pdf.

6   ESPNcricinfo, 'George Kemp-Welch': www.espncricinfo.com/cricketers/ george-kemp-welch-15985.

7   Royal Society of Arts. 1963. Sir Frederic Hooper [obituary]. *Journal of the Royal Society of Arts* 111(5088), 989–91 (www.jstor.org/stable/41367485). Hooper's management approach (see 'Governance') may have been influenced by his time at the innovative John Lewis Partnership.

PEARS

1   S. Murden. The man behind Pears' soap. *All Things Georgian*, 5 July (https:// georgianera.wordpress.com/2018/07/05/the-man-behind-pears-soap/).

2   Rapid Transition Alliance, 'The first flush of transition': https://rapidtransition. org/stories/the-first-flush-of-transition-the-rise-of-british-indoor-plumbing-and- what-it-tells-us-about-rapid-transition/.

3   Wikipedia, 'Thomas J. Barratt': https://en.wikipedia.org/wiki/ Thomas_J._Barratt.

4   B. Davenport. 2015. Thomas James Barratt: 'the father of modern advertising'. *Studied Monuments*, 29 April (https://studiedmonuments.wordpress. com/2015/04/29/thomas-james-barratt-the-father-of-modern-advertising/).

5   Wisconsin Historical Society, 'Pear's soap': www.wisconsinhistory.org/Records/ Image/IM32305.

6 Print. 2014. The father of modern advertising rides again. *Print*, 27 June (www. printmag.com/advertising/the-father-of-modern-advertising-rides-again/).

7 Hindustan Unilever, 'Pears': www.hul.co.in/brands/personal-care/pears/.

COLMAN'S

1 Naked Kitchens, 'Kitchens unpacked: the story of Colman's Mustard': www. nakedkitchens.com/blog/kitchens-unpacked-the-story-of-colman's-mustard.

2 *Colmans of Norwich*. Unilever Information Guide 3.

3 W. Kett. 2013. The mustard revolution: the life of Jeremiah James Colman. *Shine a Light*, 13 December (https://shinealightproject.wordpress. com/2013/12/13/the-mustard-revolution-the-life-of-jeremiah-james-colman/).

4 M. McGhee. 2013. How brands endorsed the race to the south pole: Colman's Mustard. *Norwich HEART*, 12 June (https://norwichheart.wordpress. com/2013/06/12/colmans-at-the-south-pole/).

5 University of Cambridge, Department of Biochemistry, 'Sir Jeremiah Colman': www.bioc.cam.ac.uk/about-us/history/the-colman-library/sir-jeremiah-colman.

6 BBC. 2024. Minister to step back after Church abuse scandal. *BBC*, 14 November (www.bbc.co.uk/news/articles/ced9w0vv57no).

7 Unilever, 'Future-proofing Colman's ingredients with our first UK regenerative agriculture project': www.unilever.com/news/news-search/2024/futureproofing-colmans-ingredients-with-our-first-uk-regenerative-agriculture-project.

8 Encyclopedia.com, 'Reckitt & Colman PLC': www.encyclopedia.com/books/ politics-and-business-magazines/reckitt-colman-plc.

HUNTLEY & PALMERS

1 Reading Museum, 'Huntley & Palmers timeline': www.readingmuseum. org.uk/online-exhibitions/huntley-palmers-history/huntley-palmers-timeline. T. Farrrell, 2014, 'Biscuit empire: Huntley & Palmers (part I)', *Let's Look Again*, 18 December (https://letslookagain.com/2014/12/ taking-the-biscuit-a-history-of-huntley-palmer/).

2 M. Allum. 2009. Antiques Roadshow expert Marc Allum on Huntley & Palmers vintage biscuit tins. *Homes and Antiques*, 17 September (www. homesandantiques.com/antiques/collecting-guides-antiques/collecting-guides/ huntley-palmers-biscuit-tins).

3 National Museums Liverpool, 'Tin, "Huntley & Palmers Biscuits"': www. liverpoolmuseums.org.uk/artifact/tin-huntley-palmers-biscuits.

4 J. Molyneux, 2020, 'What life was like at one former Merseyside biscuit factory', *Liverpool Echo*, 7 June (www.liverpoolecho.co.uk/news/liverpool-news/what-life-like-one-former-18294597). Guards Magazine, 'Captain Bill Palmer CBE DL': http://guardsmagazine.com/obits/2021%20Summer/08%20Palmer-Bill.html.

CADBURYS

1   Quakers in the World, 'John Cadbury': www.quakersintheworld.org/quakers-in-action/16/John-Cadbury.
2   Quakers in the World, 'Richard Cadbury': www.quakersintheworld.org/quakers-in-action/269/Richard-Cadbury.
3   Quakers in the World, 'George Cadbury': www.quakersintheworld.org/quakers-in-action/270/George-Cadbury.
4   A. Cadbury and D. Cadbury. 2010. As Cadburys we will look to Kraft to live up to our high standards. *Daily Telegraph*, 20 January (www.telegraph.co.uk/finance/newsbysector/retailandconsumer/7029959/As-Cadburys-we-will-look-to-Kraft-to-live-up-to-our-high-standards.html).
5   Encyclopedia.com, 'Cadbury Schweppes PLC': www.encyclopedia.com/social-sciences-and-law/economics-business-and-labor/businesses-and-occupations/cadbury-schweppes-plc.

PRICES

1   Price's Candles, 'Heritage': www.prices-candles.co.uk/heritage.
2   Forestry and Land Scotland, 'Wilsontown's history timeline': https://forestryandland.gov.scot/learn/heritage/visit-heritage-sites/wilsontown/wilsontowns-history-timeline. Clydesdale's Heritage, 'The story of Wilsontown': https://clydesdalesheritage.org.uk/article/story-of-wilsontown/. Forth District, 'Wilsontown ironworks and heritage project': www.forthdistrict.co.uk/villages-history/wilsontown/old-wilsontown/ironworks.html.
3   Christchurch City Libraries, 'The origins of Lancaster Park', archived 11 December 2014: https://web.archive.org/web/20141211150900/http://my.christchurchcitylibraries.com/the-origins-of-lancaster-park/.
4   Vauxhall, Oval & Kennington, 'Price's Candles': www.vauxhallandkennington.org.uk/candles.shtml.
5   B. Wilson. 2022. The irreplaceable. *London Review of Books* 44(12) (www.lrb.co.uk/the-paper/v44/n12/bee-wilson/the-irreplaceable).
6   RHS Lindley Library, 'Mr Wilson's Wisley: the story of a garden like no other': www.rhs.org.uk/digital-collections/mr-wilsons-wisley.
7   Fairy Lamp Club. 2006. Price's Patent Candle Company. *Fairy Lamp Club Newsletter* (39) (https://storage.snappages.site/y3h077nvhv/assets/files/Prices-Patent-Candle-Company.pdf).
8   Old Wirral, 'Bromborough Pool': http://oldwirral.net/bromborough_pool.html.
9   Garden Suburb Movement in Merseyside, 'Price's Village and Port Sunlight', archived 3 February 2017: https://web.archive.org/web/20170203000238/http://www.allertonoak.com/GSM/03GSMPortSunlightPrices.html.
10 Price's Candles, 'History': www.pricescandles.co.za/pages/15124/history.
11 Oxford Mail. 2002. Factory site goes on sale. *Oxford Mail*, 24 October (www.oxfordmail.co.uk/news/6586283.factory-site-goes-sale/).
12 Pensions Archive, 'Unilever pensions': https://pensionsarchive.org.uk/our-collections/unilever-pensions/.

WARING

1 British and Irish Furniture Makers Online, 'Gillow & Company (1862–1897)': https://bifmo.furniturehistorysociety.org/entry/gillow-company-1862-1897.

2 A. Saint. 2014. What became of Waring? Fortunes of an entrepreneur in furnishing, shopkeeping and construction. *Construction History* 29(1), 75–97 (www.jstor.org/stable/43856063).

KELLY'S

1 Automatic Access Limited, 'The History of the Post Office': www.automaticaccess.co.uk/blog/history-post-office/.

2 M. Sweeney. 2023. Post Office: Horizon scandal victims to receive £600,000 compensation each. *The Guardian*, 18 September (www.theguardian.com/business/2023/sep/18/post-office-horizon-scandal-victims-compensation).

3 D. Neidle, X.com post, 27 January 2024: https://x.com/DanNeidle/status/1751292892348395682.

THE FOUR PUBLISHERS

1 British Newspaper Archive, '*Standard of Freedom*': www.britishnewspaperarchive.co.uk/titles/standard-of-freedom/.

2 J. C. Selbin. 2016. 'Read with attention': John Cassell, John Ruskin, and the history of close reading. *Victorian Studies* 58(3), 493–521 (www.jstor.org/stable/10.2979/victorianstudies.58.3.04).

3 Curiosmith, 'Cassell Publishing': https://curiosmith.com/pages/cassell-publishing.

4 A. Bullock. Trade marks and the 1860s origin of the word 'gasoline'. LinkedIn, 17 April (www.linkedin.com/pulse/trade-marks-1860s-origin-word-gasoline-andrew-bullock/). Etymology disputed.

5 London Remembers, 'Julius Salter Elias, Viscount Southwood': www.londonremembers.com/subjects/julius-salter-elias-viscount-southwood.

6 R. J. Minney. 1954. *Viscount Southwood*. Odhams.

7 Spartacus Educational, 'Horatio Bottomley': https://spartacus-educational.com/FWWbottomley.htm.

8 Hornsey Historical Society, 'Julius Salter Elias, Viscount Southwood, 1873–1946: from office boy to press baron': https://hornseyhistorical.org.uk/julius-salter-elias-viscount-southwood-1873-1946/.

9 A. Quinn. 2016. The *Strand Magazine* and its iconic cover. *Magforum Blog*, 31 May (https://magforum.wordpress.com/2016/05/31/the-strand-magazine-and-its-iconic-cover/).

10 A. Quinn. 2019. George Newnes and his millionaires. *Magforum Blog*, 25 July (https://magforum.wordpress.com/tag/george-newnes/).

11 Visit Lynton and Lynmouth, 'The rise and fall of George Newnes': https://visitlyntonandlynmouth.com/history-heritage/the-rise-and-fall-of-george-newnes/.

12 The Victorianist. 2013. 'American magazines were supplanting those of native birth'. *The Victorianist*, 4 April (http://thevictorianist.blogspot.com/2013/04/american-magazines-were-supplanting.html).

13 Minney, *Viscount Southwood*.

14 Sun Printers History, 'Why did Watford "lose the print"?': www.sunprintershistory.com/factlose.html.

15 London Remembers, '(Lost) Pocahontas statue': www.londonremembers.com/memorials/pocahontas-statue. Heritage Gateway, 'Historic England research records: statue of Princess Pocahontas': www.heritagegateway.org.uk/Gateway/Results_Single.aspx?uid=1506422&resourceID=19191.

16 A. Beard. 2013. *Nova* magazine 1965–1975: a history. PhD thesis, Goldsmiths College (https://research.gold.ac.uk/id/eprint/12286/1/Redacted_HIS_thesis_BeardA_2015.pdf).

MUDIES

1 Linda Hall Library, 'Scientist of the day: Charles Mudie': www.lindahall.org/about/news/scientist-of-the-day/charles-mudie/.

2 J. Smith, 2023, 'Vino and venison: Kendal's reading associations in the eighteenth century', *Books and Borrowing 1750–1830*, 20 November (https://borrowing.stir.ac.uk/vino-and-venison-kendals-reading-associations-in-the-eighteenth-century/). Population figure from the *Westmorland Gazette*, 9 June 1821.

3 Victorian Web, 'Mudie's Select Library and the form of Victorian fiction': https://victorianweb.org/economics/mudie.html. G. L. Griest, 'A Victorian leviathan: Mudie's Select Library', *Nineteenth-Century Fiction* 20(2), 103–26 (www.jstor.org/stable/2932540).

BOOTS

1 Boots, 'Boots heritage': www.boots-uk.com/about-boots-uk/company-information/boots-heritage/.

2 John Wesley's New Room, '*Primitive Physic*': www.newroombristol.org.uk/primitive-physic/.

3 K. A. Morrison, 2018, 'Zara (originally Boots the Chemist), 2–10 Pelham Street and 2 High Street, Nottingham: research and investigation', Research Report 73-2018, Historic England (https://historicengland.org.uk/research/results/reports/7498/Zara(originallyBootstheChemist)2-10PelhamStreetand2HighStreetNottingham_ResearchandInvestigation). D. Boyd, 'The history of Boots the Chemist and Boots makeup compacts', *Vintage Compact Shop*, 16 June (https://thevintagecompactshop.com/blogs/antique-and-collectible-history/boots).

4 L. Broadbent. 2023. Florence Boot (1863–1952). *Women Who Meant Business*, 3 July (https://womenwhomeantbusiness.com/2023/07/03/florence-boot-1863-1952/).

5   Reference for Business, 'The Boots Company PLC': www.referenceforbusiness.
     com/history2/2/The-Boots-Company-PLC.html. Encyclopedia.com, 'The
     Boots Company PLC': www.encyclopedia.com/social-sciences-and-law/
     economics-business-and-labor/businesses-and-occupations/boots-company-plc.
6   K. Steenson. 2013. Nottingham's new chancellor. University of Nottingham,
     12 March (https://blogs.nottingham.ac.uk/manuscripts/2013/03/12/
     nottinghams-new-chancellor/).
7   E. Copeland. 2019. The nation's chemist: a study of the Americanisation of
     Boots the Chemist c.1948–1966. Dissertation, University of Bristol (www.
     bristol.ac.uk/media-library/sites/history/documents/dissertations/2019_
     Copeland.pdf).
8   P. Hosking. 1993. Manoplax: from heart to heartbreak. *The Independent*, 24 July
     (www.independent.co.uk/news/business/manoplax-from-heart-to-heartbreak-
     with-millions-lost-on-its-wonder-drug-patrick-hosking-asks-whether-boots-
     ignored-too-many-warning-signs-in-its-enthusiasm-1487095.html).
9   Alliance Healthcare, 'Our history': www.alliance-healthcare.co.uk/about-us/
     our-history.
10   R. Harrison. 2019. Boots the Chemist: trusted brand or predatory multinational.
     Ethical Consumer, 24 June (www.ethicalconsumer.org/health-beauty/
     boots-chemist-trusted-brand-or-predatory-multinational).
11   Macmillan Cancer Support, 'Our partnership with Boots': www.macmillan.org.
     uk/about-us/working-with-us/corporate-partners/our-partners/boots.
12   Walgreens Boots Alliance, 'History': www.walgreensbootsalliance.com/about-us/
     history.
13   J. Jolly. 2022. £5bn Boots sale abandoned as potential buyers struggle to
     raise funds. *The Guardian*, 28 June (www.theguardian.com/business/2022/
     jun/28/5bn-boots-sale-abandoned-as-potential-buyers-struggle-to-raise-funds).
14   G. Wright. 2024. Boots owner reignites £7bn sale plan. *Retail Gazette*, 14 May
     (www.retailgazette.co.uk/blog/2024/05/boots-walgreens-sale/).
15   A. Morgan. 2025. Prospective Boots buyer eyes split of group amid sale
     talks. *Retail Gazette*, 28 February (www.retailgazette.co.uk/blog/2025/02/
     boots-takeover-talks/).

BRYANT & MAY

1   University of Bristol, School of Chemistry, 'Friction match', archived 22 April
     2021: https://web.archive.org/web/20210422172406/https://www.chm.bris.
     ac.uk/webprojects2001/osullivan/friction_match.htm.
2   Historic England, 'Bryant and May match factory, Bow, Greater London':
     https://historicengland.org.uk/services-skills/education/educational-images/
     bryant-and-may-match-factory-bow-10984.
3   Science Museum Group, 'Bryant and May Limited 1884–1927':
     https://collection.sciencemuseumgroup.org.uk/people/cp20300/
     bryant-and-may-limited.

4   National Archives, 'Bryant and May, partnership': https://discovery.
    nationalarchives.gov.uk/details/r/a8c0029f-541e-4427-b331-89723f8c940e.
5   *The Oxford Dictionary of National Biography* (see note 32 to 'Governance').
6   M. Oakley, 2023, 'Match Girls Strike at Bryant and May factory: the 1888
    uprising for workers' rights in London', *East London History*, 28 April (www.
    eastlondonhistory.co.uk/bryant-may-strike-bow-east-london/). J. Brain, 2021,
    'The Match Girls Strike', Historic UK, 19 April (www.historic-uk.com/
    HistoryUK/HistoryofBritain/Match-Girls-Strike/).
7   Salvation Army, '"Matches and morals": the Salvation Army and
    consumer activism in the 1890s': www.salvationarmy.org.uk/about-us/
    international-heritage-centre/international-heritage-centre-blog/
    matches-and-morals.
8   UPI, 1988, 'Allegheny International Inc. files for Chapter 11', *UPI*, 22 February
    (www.upi.com/Archives/1988/02/22/Allegheny-International-Inc-files-for-
    Chapter-11/9178572504400/). Associated Press, 'Allegheny International
    head vows comeback', *Washington Post*, 22 February (www.washingtonpost.
    com/archive/business/1988/02/23/allegheny-international-head-vows-
    comeback/3e561993-b3b4-4d82-8d58-b945f1ff6ed7/).
9   Bryant & May, 'About': www.bryantandmay.co.uk/about/.

HARTLEYS

1   Tain & District Museum, 'Reverend John Ross': www.tainmuseum.org.uk/
    article.php?id=131.
2   D. Rigg. 2022. 'Amazing' village where 'everyone waves' is 'going to wrack
    and ruin'. *Liverpool Echo*, 31 December (www.liverpoolecho.co.uk/news/
    liverpool-news/amazing-village-everyone-waves-going-25870373).
3   LocalWiki, 'History of Everton FC': https://localwiki.org/liverpool/
    History_of_Everton_FC.
4   J. Howells. 2020. Jam yesterday: Hartley's in Bermondsey. Bermondsey-
    Street.London, September (https://bermondseystreet.london/wp-content/
    uploads/2020/09/Jam-Yesterday-The-Hartleys-Jam-Factory-Bermondsey-Street-
    Back-Stories-Number-13.pdf).
5   L. E. Sayre. 1904. Food preservatives: how far are they injurious to health?
    Transactions of the Kansas Academy of Science (1903–) 19, 51–5 (www.jstor.org/
    stable/3624171).
6   My Primitive Methodists, 'Southport Church Street Primitive Methodist
    Church': www.myprimitivemethodists.org.uk/content/chapels/
    lancashire/s-lancashire/church_street_primitive_methodist_southport.
7   My Primitive Methodists, 'Holborn Hall': www.myprimitivemethodists.org.uk/
    content/subjects-2/primitive-methodist-history/holborn_hall.
8   MySefton, 'Spotlight on: Christiana Hartley': https://mysefton.
    co.uk/2019/11/28/spotlight-on-christiana-hartley/.
9   A. S. Peake, 1926, *The Life of Sir William Hartley*, Hodder and Stoughton
    (http://gutenberg.net.au/ebooks07/0701091h.html). My Primitive Methodists,
    'Hartley, Sir William Pickles (1846–1922)': www.myprimitivemethodists.

org.uk/content/people-2/lay-people/surnames-beginning-with-h/sir_william_pickles_hartley. T. Farrell, 2015, 'Spread the wealth: a history of Hartley's jam', *Let's Look Again*, 24 February (https://web.archive.org/web/20240806204321/https://letslookagain.com/2015/02/sweet-success-a-history-of-hartleys-jam/).

10 Encyclopedia.com, 'Hillsdown Holdings, PLC': www.encyclopedia.com/books/politics-and-business-magazines/hillsdown-holdings-plc-0.

11 Hartley's, 'About Hartley's': www.hartleysfruit.co.uk/about-us/.

WHITELEYS

1 Murderpedia, 'Horace George Rayner': https://murderpedia.org/male.R/r/rayner-horace.htm. Proceedings of the Old Bailey, 'Horace George Rayner. Killing; murder. 18th March 1907': www.oldbaileyonline.org/record/t19070318-31.

2 L. Stratmann. 2004. *Whiteley's Folly: The Life and Death of a Salesman*. Sutton.

3 The Elmbridge Hundred, 'William Whiteley': https://people.elmbridgehundred.org.uk/biographies/william-whiteley/. The Whiteley London website: www.thewhiteleylondon.com.

SWIFT

1 Cycling Archives, 'Paris – Rouen 1869', archived 30 January 2022: https://web.archive.org/web/20220130191155/www.cyclingarchives.com/ritfiche.php?ritid=121828.

2 Sewalot, 'James Starley: Victorian Pioneer': https://sewalot.com/starley_sewing_machines.htm.

3 Antique Bicycles, 'Coventry Machinists Co.': http://coventry-machinists-co.british-ordinary-bicycles.ordinary-bicycles.antique-bicycles.net. Coventry Transport Museum, 'Pioneers 1868 to 1900': www.transport-museum.com/visiting/cycle-pioneers-1868-to-1900.aspx.

4 Online Bicycle Museum, '1882 Coventry Machinists Co 'Special Club' 50" Ordinary': https://onlinebicyclemuseum.co.uk/1883-coventry-machinists-co-special-club-50-ordinary/.

5 National Cycle Museum, 'John Kemp Starley': www.cyclemuseum.org.uk/Cycling-History-Other.aspx?ID=8.

6 F. Malizia and B. Blocken. 2020. Bicycle aerodynamics: history, state-of-the-art and future perspectives. *Journal of Wind Engineering and Industrial Aerodynamics* 200, Paper 104134 (https://doi.org/10.1016/j.jweia.2020.104134). See especially figure 4.

7 D. Rubinstein. 1977. Cycling in the 1890s. *Victorian Studies* 21(1), 47–71 (www.jstor.org/stable/3825934).

8 AROnline, 'The whole story': www.aronline.co.uk/history/the-whole-story/.

9 Encyclopedia.com, 'Rover Group plc': www.encyclopedia.com/books/politics-and-business-magazines/rover-group-plc.

10 Transport for West Midlands, 'Starley Network': www.tfwm.org.uk/plan-your-journey/ways-to-travel/cycling-and-walking/starley-network/.

11 Cybermotorcycle.com, 'Rover company history': https://cybermotorcycle.com/
marques/rover/rover-company.htm.

GLAXO

1 Quakers in the World, 'William Allen': www.quakersintheworld.org/
quakers-in-action/284/William-Allen.
2 McGonagall Online, 'Beecham's Pills': www.mcgonagall-online.org.uk/gems/
beechams-pills.
3 J. Millen. 1993. Nathan, Joseph Edward. In *The Dictionary of New
Zealand Biography*, online (https://teara.govt.nz/en/biographies/2n3/
nathan-joseph-edward).
4 R. W. Currier and J. A. Widness. 2018. A brief history of milk hygiene and its
impact on infant mortality from 1875 to 1925 and implications for today: a
review. *Journal of Food Protection* 81(10), 1713–22 (https://doi.org/10.4315/0362-
028X.JFP-18-186).
5 A. J. Smith, 2001, review of *The Business of Medicine: A History of Glaxo*, by E.
Jones, *British Journal of Clinical Pharmacology* 52(4), 463 (www.ncbi.nlm.nih.
gov/pmc/articles/PMC2014575/). GSK, 'History and heritage': www.gsk.com/
en-gb/company/history-and-heritage/.
6 Australian Jewish Herald. 1954. Death of Mr. Alec Nathan. *Australian
Jewish Herald*, 56 November (www.nli.org.il/en/newspapers/
austjewisherald/1954/11/05/01/article/74/).
7 D. Cantor. 1996. Review of *Glaxo: A History to 1962*, by R. P. T. Davenport-
Hines and J. Slin. *Bulletin of the History of Medicine* 70(1), 155–6 (https://muse.
jhu.edu/article/3632).
8 Funding Universe, 'Glaxo Holdings PLC History': www.fundinguniverse.com/
company-histories/glaxo-holdings-plc-history/.
9 Reuters. 2003. Glaxo loses U.S. patent case. *CNN*, 4 March, archived
18 November 2004 (https://web.archive.org/web/20041118212829/https://
edition.cnn.com/2003/BUSINESS/03/04/glaxosmithkline/).
10 Save the Children, 'GSK: corporate partner': www.savethechildren.org.uk/
about-us/who-we-work-with/corporate-partners/gsk.
11 GSK. 2022. GSK announces new global headquarters in central London.
Press Release, 12 December (www.gsk.com/en-gb/media/press-releases/
gsk-announces-new-global-headquarters-in-central-london/).

LEVER BROS

1 National Museums of Liverpool, 'Who was Lady Lever?': www.
liverpoolmuseums.org.uk/stories/who-was-lady-lever.
2 Encyclopedia.com, 'Lever Brothers Company': www.encyclopedia.com/books/
politics-and-business-magazines/lever-brothers-company.
3 B. Henriet. 2017. Hubris and colonial capitalism in a 'model' company town:
the case of Leverville, 1911–1940. *Comparing the Copperbelt*, 2 October (https://

copperbelt.history.ox.ac.uk/2017/10/02/hubris-and-colonial-capitalism-in-a-model-company-town-the-case-of-leverville-1911-1940-benoit-henriet/).

4   Port Sunlight Village Trust, 'Racism, the Belgian Congo, and William Lever', archived 4 April 2024: https://web.archive.org/web/20240404080119/www. portsunlightvillage.com/wp-content/uploads/2022/06/PSVT_Booklet_Racism_ the_Belgian_Congo_and_William_Lever_-_V_FINAL_14.06.22.pdf.

5   J. Tierney. 2021. Report of scoping survey of the Lever Brothers' plantations in the Solomon Islands and the Congo, 1900–1930. University of Liverpool (https://royalafricansociety.org/wp-content/uploads/2022/05/University-of-Liverpool-Scoping-Report-Lever-Bros-Plantations-in-the-Congo-and-Solomon-Islands-1900-to-1930.pdf).

6   Undiscovered Scotland, 'William Lever, 1st Viscount Leverhulme': www.undiscoveredscotland.co.uk/usbiography/l/williamlever. html?utm_content=cmp-true.

7   Cosmetics and Skin, 'Chesebrough-Pond's': https://cosmeticsandskin.com/ companies/chesebrough-ponds.php.

8   Private correspondence.

9   J. Stempel. 2022. Ben & Jerry's says parent Unilever mandating silence on Trump. *USA Today*, 14 February (https://eu.usatoday.com/story/money/ business/2025/02/14/ben-jerrys-legal-battle-unilever-trump/78634157007/).

10 Unilever, 'Unilever Board update': www.unilever.com/news/press-and-media/ press-releases/2025/unilever-board-update-25-02-25/.

GAMAGES

1   Britain by Car, 'Gamage': www.britainbycar.co.uk/holborn/412-gamage.

2   Cybermotorcycle.com, 'Gamages department store': https://cybermotorcycle. com/marques/gamages/gamages.htm.

3   V. Keegan. 2022. Gamages: Holborn's pioneer department store. *On London*, 19 February (www.onlondon.co.uk/vic-keegan-gamages-holborns-pioneer-department-store/).

4   F. H. W. Sheppard. 1980. Oxford Street: the rebuilding of Oxford Street. In *Survey of Lonon*, vol. 40, *The Grosvenor Estate in Mayfair*, part 2, 'The buildings'. London County Council (www.british-history.ac.uk/survey-london/vol40/pt2/ pp176-184).

5   G. Biddle-Perry. 2014. The rise of 'the world's largest sport and athletic outfitter': a study of Gamage's of Holborn, 1878–1913. *Sport in History* 34(2), 295–317 (www.researchgate.net/publication/263547786_The_Rise_of_'The_ World's_Largest_Sport_and_Athletic_Outfitter'_A_Study_of_Gamage's_of_ Holborn_1878-1913).

6   Rennie & Co., 'The history of Gamages and its link to Hatton Garden jewellers': www.rennieco.com/rennie-news/the-history-of-gamages-and-its-link-to-hatton-garden-jewellers.

MARTINS

1 M. Veissid & Co., 'Martins Limited, cigar shippers, £1 shares, 1919': https://veissid.com/product/martins-limited-cigar-shippers-1-shares-1919-nice-vignettes-gvf/.

2 L. Gosing. 2013. Arf a mo' Kaiser: smokes for Tommy; cigarettes and soldiers, WW1. *Picturing the Great War*, 27 November (https://blog.maryevans.com/2013/11/smokes-for-tommy-cigarettes-and-the-british-soldier-ww1.html).

3 Word Histories, ''Arf a mo', Kaiser!': https://wordhistories.net/2019/12/20/arf-mo-kaiser/. Imperial War Museum, ''Arf a mo', Kaiser!': www.iwm.org.uk/collections/item/object/26182.

4 On This Day in Guernsey, 'Herm bribery case comes to court': https://history.gg/herm-bribery-case-comes-to-court/.

5 Jerripedia, 'Royal Hotel': www.theislandwiki.org/index.php/Royal_Hotel.

6 Encyclopedia Titanica forum, 'News from 1935: sale of *Mauretania*'s fitting': www.encyclopedia-titanica.org/community/threads/news-from-1935-sale-of-mauretanias-fitting.30440/. Antique Collecting, 2019, 'M for *Mauretania* in sale', *Antique Collecting*, 26 September: https://antique-collecting.co.uk/2019/09/26/m-for-mauretania-in-sale/.

7 A. Rive. 1929. A brief history of the regulation and taxation of tobacco in England. *William and Mary College Quarterly Historical Magazine* 9(1), 1–12 (www.jstor.org/stable/1920374).

8 Smoking in England, 'Top-line findings': https://smokinginengland.info/graphs/top-line-findings.

9 Tobacoo Tactics, 'Foundation for a Smoke-Free World': www.tobaccotactics.org/article/fsfw/.

10 M. Labiak. 2024. Marlboro owner sells UK inhaler firm over backlash. *BBC*, 18 September (www.bbc.co.uk/news/articles/c4gdpzqp15eo).

11 Statista, 'Tobacco duty tax receipts in the United Kingdom from 2000/01 to 2023/24': www.statista.com/statistics/284329/tobacco-duty-united-kingdom-hmrc-tax-receipts/.

HOVIS

1 Foods of England, 'Wheatgerm Breads': www.foodsofengland.co.uk/wheatgermbreads.htm.

2 Mills Archive Trust, 'John Figgis Morton (1872–1958)': https://new.millsarchive.org/2020/11/25/john-figgis-morton-1872-1958-or-mr-hovis-and-the-triumph-of-advertising-brown-bread/.

3 Geograph, 'Hovis Mill, Macclesfield': www.geograph.org.uk/photo/3164936. M. Nevell, 2019, 'Seasonal archaeology: Union Flour Mill, Macclesfield', *Archaeologytea*, 25 October (https://archaeologytea.wordpress.com/2019/10/25/seasonal-archaeology-union-flour-mill-macclesfield/).

4 A. Treneman. 2013. *Finding the Plot: A Hundred Graves to Visit Before You Die*. Robson Press.

5   Ghostsigns, 'The enduring mystery of the Peterkin Custard ghost sign': https://ghostsigns.co.uk/2021/01/the-enduring-mystery-of-the-peterkin-custard-ghost-sign/.

6   Rank Foundation, 'About us': https://rankfoundation.com/who-we-are/history/. P. Beard, 2018, 'Hōvis: your baker bakes it', *Phil Beard*, 28 September (http://buttes-chaumont.blogspot.com/2018/09/hovis-your-baker-bakes-it.html).

7   Blue Arrow, 'Working with Hovis': www.bluearrow.co.uk/great-places-to-work/working-with-hovis/.

8   P. Beard. 2009. Today's recipe. *Phil Beard*, 13 May (https://buttes-chaumont.blogspot.com/2009/05/todays-recipe.html).

9   BFI Screenonline, 'Rank, J. Arthur (1888–1972)': www.screenonline.org.uk/people/id/447127/index.html.

10   Nostalgia Central, 'Nimble': https://nostalgiacentral.com/pop-culture/food-drink/nimble/.

11   Joseph Rank Trust website: www.ranktrust.org.

12   Talking Retail, 2008. Hovis to adopt Nimble into brand. *Talking Retail*, 12 December (www.talkingretail.com/products-news/grocery/hovis-to-adopt-nimble-into-brand-12-12-2008/).

13   A. North. 2021. Exceptional costs force Hovis into the red with £6.3m loss. *British Baker*, 4 October (https://bakeryinfo.co.uk/finance/exceptional-costs-force-hovis-into-the-red-with-63m-loss/660420.article).

14   D. Riley. 2024. Hovis profits and turnover soar under new management team. *British Baker*, 27 March (https://bakeryinfo.co.uk/finance/hovis-profits-and-turnover-soar-under-new-management-team/689749.article).

15   UK Flour Millers, 'Flour and bread consumption': www.ukflourmillers.org/flourbreadconsumption. Federation of Bakers, 'About the bread industry': www.fob.uk.com/about-the-bread-industry/.

16   Museum of English Rural Life, 'Ranks Hovis McDougall Ltd.': https://merl.reading.ac.uk/collections/ranks-hovis-mcdougall-ltd/.

LYONS

1   Encyclopedia.com, 'Gluckstein': www.encyclopedia.com/religion/encyclopedias-almanacs-transcripts-and-maps/gluckstein.

2   English Heritage, 'Lyons, Sir Joseph (1847–1917)': www.english-heritage.org.uk/visit/blue-plaques/joseph-lyons/.

3   London Remembers, 'Cadby Hall': www.londonremembers.com/subjects/cadby-hall.

4   Kzwp.com, 'J. Lyons & Co.: the bakery department': www.kzwp.com/lyons1/bakery.htm. T. Harding, 'Salmon and Gluckstein', archived 29 March 2024: https://web.archive.org/web/20240329045025/https://www.thomasharding.com/salmonandgluckstein.

5   T. Harding. 2022 [2010]. *Legacy: The Remarkable History of J Lyons and the Family Behind It*. Penguin Random House.

6   Kzwp.com, 'J. Lyons & Co.: origins of the company': www.kzwp.com/lyons1/directors.htm.

DUNLOP

1 Morning Bulletin (Rockhampton, Australia). 1936. Invention of the pneumatic tire. *Morning Bulletin*, 9 July (https://trove.nla.gov.au/newspaper/article/54964822).

2 L. Lunney. 2009. Dunlop, John Boyd. In *The Dictionary of Irish Biography*, online (www.dib.ie/biography/dunlop-john-boyd-a2849).

3 L. Lunney. 2009. Du Cros, William Harvey. In *The Dictionary of Irish Biography*, online (www.dib.ie/biography/du-cros-william-harvey-a2790).

4 British Heritage Travel, 'The secrets of King Edward VII': https://britishheritage.com/history/edward-vii-secrets.

5 C. Baker. 2021. The du Cros Motor Ambulance Convoy. The Long, Long Trail, 26 April (www.longlongtrail.co.uk/the-du-cros-motor-ambulance-convoy/).

6 L. Lunney. 2009. Du Cros, Sir Arthur Philip. In *The Dictionary of Irish Biography*, online (www.dib.ie/biography/du-cros-sir-arthur-philip-a2789).

7 Britannica Money, 'Dunlop Holdings PLC': www.britannica.com/money/Dunlop-Holdings-PLC.

8 Du Cros, Arthur. 1938. *Wheels of Fortune: A Salute to Pioneers*. Chapman and Hall (https://archive.org/details/in.ernet.dli.2015.184704).

9 F. Amatori and F. Lavista. 2007. A troubled international merger: Pirelli Dunlop union (1970–1981). Bocconi University (https://ebha.org/ebha2007/pdf/AmatoriLavista.pdf).

10 A. Chandrasekhar. 2023. Rubber drives 'at least twice' as much deforestation as previously thought. *Carbon Brief*, 18 October (www.carbonbrief.org/rubber-drives-at-least-twice-as-much-deforestation-as-previously-thought).

MACKINTOSH

1 Calderdale Museums, 'A Trip to Toffee Town': https://museums.calderdale.gov.uk/whats-on/exhibitions/toffee-town-online.

2 Toffee Town, 'Timeline': www.toffeetown.org.uk/timeline/.

3 Calderdale Museums, 'A Trip to Toffee Town'.

4 T. Farrell. 2016. A. J. Caley of Norwich. *Let's Look Again*, 1 March (https://letslookagain.com/2016/03/caley-of-norwich/).

5 Encyclopedia.com, 'Rowntree Mackintosh': www.encyclopedia.com/books/politics-and-business-magazines/rowntree-mackintosh.

BRITISH PETROLEUM

1 BP, 'Our history': www.bp.com/en/global/corporate/who-we-are/our-history/early-history.html.

2 Stanmore Tourist Board, 'William Knox D'Arcy': www.stanmoretouristboard.org.uk/william_knox_darcy.html.

3 American Aristocracy, 'Donald Smith, Lord Strathcona (1820–1914)': https://americanaristocracy.com/people/donald-smith.

4   Encyclopaedia Iranica, 'Cadman, John': www.iranicaonline.org/articles/
    cadman-john.

5   Statista, 'Oil production of BP from 2015 to 2023, by region': www.statista.com/
    statistics/270013/daily-regional-production-of-bp/. N. Reiff, 2024, '10 biggest
    oil companies', Investopedia, 8 November (www.investopedia.com/articles/
    personal-finance/010715/worlds-top-10-oil-companies.asp).

6   H. Agnew, T. Wilson and M. Moore. 2024. BP shareholders expect it to scale
    back climate target. *Financial Times*, 6 May (www.ft.com/content/
    88c8b435-7bed-4b75-ae0e-0d2673e08305).

7   Global Witness, 'What BP could do with its £580m wartime Russian
    oil profits': www.globalwitness.org/en/campaigns/stop-russian-oil/
    what-bp-could-do-with-its-580m-wartime-russian-oil-profits/.

8   S. Jack and F. Masud. 2025. BP shuns renewables in return to oil and gas. *BBC*,
    26 February (www.bbc.co.uk/news/articles/c3374ekd11po).

WATSON'S SKIPPERS

1   Jayne's Genealogical Gleanings, 'The old salt: William Duncan Anderson,
    1838–1916': https://jaynefamhist.wordpress.com/fireside-stories/
    the-old-salt-william-duncan-anderson-1838-1916/.

2   Imperial War Museum, 'Angus Watson And Co Ltd': www.iwm.org.uk/
    memorials/item/memorial/48356.

3   Pensions Archive, 'Unilever pensions': https://pensionsarchive.org.uk/
    our-collections/unilever-pensions/.

4   K. L. Mackenzie. 1927. Canned fish. *Journal of the Royal Sanitary Institute* 48(6),
    283–9 (https://doi.org/10.1177/146642402704800603).

5   M. Matlach. 2010. Angus Watson and Co. Limited. *COSGB*, 12 September
    (http://cosgb.blogspot.com/2010/09/angus-watson-and-co-limited.html).

6   Norwegian Printing Museum and Norwegian Canning Museum, 'Angus
    Watson: a man and a brand': www.iddis.no/en/events/angus-watson.

AFTERWORD

1   T. Levitt. 2018. *The Company Citizen*. Taylor & Francis.

About the Author

Tom Levitt is an associate lecturer in sustainability at the Claude Littner Business School, University of West London, and a former member of parliament (1997–2010), business consultant and science teacher. As well as cofounding the social enterprise Fair for You, he is also a playwright, a biographer and a novelist.

Other books by Tom Levitt include *Partners for Good: Business, Government and the Third Sector* (Gower, 2012), *Welcome to GoodCo: Using the Tools of Business to Create Public Good* (Gower, 2014), *The Company Citizen: Good for Business, Planet, Nation and Community* (Taylor & Francis, 2018), the biography *The Courage to Meddle: The Belief of Frances Perkins* (KDP, 2020), *Business Schools and the Public Good* with Martin Kitchener (Chartered Association of Business Schools, 2021) and the novel *A Fallen Man* (KDP, 2022).

Index